CW00969427

ounger Brothers bei...
...āi Meh Race of Ka...
v Khyr or Kh...
& Sheh, may be... =
the Caspian or from th ranges
...eat Hazara ranges, Kohi Baba
...Wakhan & even to Chittral &
...te above Kaffir Traditions, there
...lexander' name or the freeks
forms of Oondroo, Koondroo
So as to bear upon any hint...
Present Kaffir Race of Kaffiristan...
...t of Alexander" freeth Legions —
...ugst the Thurkomans along the
...Traditions, & even now they term
the western or opposite Shores of th...
...s Syer & Syer Khush & the legend
...aub (the upper Marghaub River &

www.kashihouse.com

THE TARTAN TURBAN

BY THE SAME AUTHOR

Into India

When Men and Mountains Meet

The Gilgit Game

Eccentric Travellers

Explorers Extraordinary

Highland Drove

*The Royal Geographical Society's History of
World Exploration* (general editor)

India Discovered: The Recovery of a Lost Civilisation

*The Honourable Company: A History of the
English East India Company*

The Collins Encyclopaedia of Scotland
(co-editor with Julia Keay)

Indonesia: From Sabang to Merauke

Last Post: The End of Empire in the Far East

India: A History

*The Great Arc: The Dramatic Tale of How India
was Mapped and Everest was Named*

Sowing the Wind: The Seeds of Conflict in the Middle East

Mad About the Mekong: Exploration and Empire in South-East Asia

The London Encyclopaedia (3ʳᵈ edn) (co-editor with Julia Keay)

China: A History

*Midnight's Descendants: South Asia from
Partition to the Present Day*

THE TARTAN TURBAN
IN SEARCH *of* ALEXANDER GARDNER

JOHN KEAY

KASHI HOUSE

Published by KASHI HOUSE CIC 2017

Copyright © 2017 John Keay

The author asserts the moral right to be identified as the author of this work.

A CIP catalogue record for this book is available from the British Library

ISBN: 978 1 911271 00 0

Cover, typesetting & reprographics by grfik.com

Printed and bound by CPI Group (UK) Ltd, Croydon, CR0 4YY

All rights reserved. No part of this publication may be reproduced, stored or
introduced into a retrieval system, or transmitted, in any shape or form or by any
means, electronic, mechanical, photocopying, recording or otherwise, without
the prior written permission of both the copyright owner and KASHI HOUSE CIC,
except in the case of brief quotations embodied in critical articles or reviews.

KASHI HOUSE CIC
27 Old Gloucester Street, London WC1N 3AX

kashihouse.com
facebook.com/kashihouse
twitter.com/kashihouse

Endpaper illustrations: based on a folio from Alexander Gardner's journal titled 'A
Scetch on Kaffiristan & the Kaffirs', dated Kashmir, 20 October 1869. Courtesy of
the Centre of South Asian Studies, Cambridge (BX 3 B.20).

For Amanda
who's been living with the colonel as long as anyone

'Like all great travellers,' said Essper,
'I have seen more than I remember
and remember more than I have seen.'

Benjamin D'Israeli, *Vivian Grey*

Contents

Illustrations

Courtesy of the Council of the
National Army Museum, London
(acc. no. 1968-07-470-33).

45. Maharaja Sher Singh and Raja
Dhyan Singh converse while Rani
Chand Kaur looks on from a balcony.
Gouache heightened with gold on
paper, from Pandit Raja Ram Kaul
Tota's Persian history of Punjab titled
Gulgasht-i-Punjab, Lahore, 1864.
Punjab Government Archives, Patiala
(acc no M790). Image courtesy of
Panjab Digital Library.

46. Maharaja Sher Singh on the golden
throne. August Schoefft, oil on panel,
Lahore, c 1841–42. Toor Collection
(photographed by grfik.com).

47. Detail from a panoramic view of the
walled city of Lahore. Watercolour
heightened with gold on paper,
Lahore, c 1846–50. Toor Collection
(photographed by grfik.com).

48. Panoramic view of the Hazuri
Bagh and Badshahi Mosque. Felice
Beato (attributed), albumen prints
mounted on thick paper, Lahore,
c October 1859. Toor Collection
(photographed by grfik.com).

49. A model of the walled city of Lahore
made shortly after annexation.
Photograph, late 19th century. Private
Collection.

50. Maharani Jind Kaur. George
Richmond, oil on canvas, London,
1863. Kapany Collection.

51. Maharaja Duleep Singh in
conversation with Ajit Singh and
Lehna Singh Sindhanwalia, the
assassins of Maharaja Sher Singh.
Gouache heightened with gold on
paper, from Pandit Raja Ram Kaul
Tota's Persian history of Punjab titled
Gulgasht-i-Punjab, Lahore, 1864.
Punjab Government Archives, Patiala
(acc no M790). Image courtesy of

Panjab Digital Library.

52. Pandit Jalla and Raja Hira Singh.
Gouache heightened with gold on
paper, from Pandit Raja Ram Kaul
Tota's Persian history of Punjab titled
Gulgasht-i-Punjab, Lahore, 1864.
Punjab Government Archives, Patiala
(acc no M790). Image courtesy of
Panjab Digital Library.

53. Raja Gulab Singh and Raja Jowahir
Singh. Gouache heightened with
gold on paper, from Pandit Raja Ram
Kaul Tota's Persian history of Punjab
titled *Gulgasht-i-Punjab*, Lahore,
1864. Punjab Government Archives,
Patiala (acc no M790). Image
courtesy of Panjab Digital Library.

54. The old Sikh armoury in the Lahore
Fort. Albumen print, Lahore, c 1900.
Toor Collection.

55. Raja Lal Singh, the ex-vizier of
Lahore. Carte de visite, Agra
or Dehra Dun, c 1857–60. Toor
Collection.

56. Sardar Tej Singh with his son
and nephew. William Carpenter,
watercolour on paper, c 1855.
©Victoria and Albert Museum,
London.

57. A heavily armed Akali-Nihang
on horseback. M&N Hanhart,
lithograph, c 1850, after a painting by
a Punjabi artist. Private Collection.

58. 'General Allard's Cavalry, Punjaub'.
Pencil and watercolour, Punjab, c
1838–39. © The British Library Board
(Add. Or. 1382).

59. Young Akali-Nihang warrior with
a bow in his turban. Prince Alexei
Saltykov, pencil and watercolour,
Punjab, March 1842. Courtesy of
State Russian Museum.

60. Sikh regular infantry. Pencil and
watercolour, Punjab, c 1838–39.
© The British Library Board (Add.

Or. 1381).

61. Colonel Mouton's Punjabi sword with his name inscribed in Gurmukhi script as 'Karnail Matoon'. Steel and gold, mid-19th century. Toor Collection (photographed by grfik. com).

62. Men of the No. 1 Battery of the Punjab Irregular Force stand by their cannon. Albumen print, Kohat (?), c 1860. Courtesy of the Council of the National Army Museum, London (acc. no. 7910-76-89).

63. Major George Broadfoot 'as he rode into Karnal, in January 1843, accompanying Lord Ellenborough from the camp at Firozepur'. Sir Henry Yule (attributed), published in *The Career of Major George Broadfoot in Afghanistan and the Punjab* (John Murray, 1888). Private Collection.

64. Dr Johann Martin Honigberger, physician of Maharaja Duleep Singh. Karl Mahlknecht, engraving, c 1835. Private Collection.

65. First Anglo-Sikh War: 'Drawing of the battle between the Sikhs and English'. Sardul Singh Naqqash, coloured lithograph, Punjab, c 1870s. Wellcome Library, London.

66. The Battle of Mudki: 'Capt Codd of the 3rd Dragoons, cut to pieces between the gun and the wheel'. Ensign Bethune Donald Grant, coloured drawing, c 1846. Courtesy of the Council of the National Army Museum, London (acc. no. 8204-391-8).

67. 'Explanation of a view of the Battle of Sobraon, with the defeat of the Sikh Army, now exhibiting at the Panorama, Leicester Square'. Engraving based on a panoramic painting by Robert Burford and H. C. Selous, published in *Description of a*

View of the Battle of Sabraon, with the defeat of the Sikh army of the Punjab (Geo Nicholls, 1846). Courtesy of the Council of the National Army Museum, London (acc. no. NAM BKS 19907).

68. 3rd King's Own Light Dragoons and the Khalsa Army clash in the Battle of Chillianwalla during the Second Anglo-Sikh War. Henry Martens (attributed), oil on canvas, c 1849–50. Courtesy of www. thequeensownhussars.co.uk.

69. Sir Henry Montgomery Lawrence. Detail from watercolour on ivory, c 1847. © National Portrait Gallery, London.

70. Herbert Edwardes, Henry Lawrence and George Lawrence (standing). Postcard published by Emery Walker Photo Studio, after an albumen print by Ahmed Ali Khan (attributed), Lucknow, c 1856–57. Private Collection.

71. John Lawrence 'Bahadur' (The Brave). Gouache on paper, Punjab, c late 1840s. The Samrai Collection, London.

72. 'The Lawrence Testimonial'. John Hunt and Robert Roskell (designed by Arthur Brown), silver sculpture, London, 1855–56. Courtesy of the Council of the National Army Museum, London (acc. no. 1956-02-885-1).

73. Nawab Sheikh Imam-ud-din, governor of Kashmir during Sikh rule. William Carpenter, watercolour on paper, c 1855. ©Victoria and Albert Museum, London.

74. Panel from 'The Lawrence Testimonial' showing Sir Henry Lawrence with Maharaja Duleep Singh and chieftains seated in the Lahore *darbar*, arranging for the

payment of mutinous troops. John
Hunt and Robert Roskell (designed
by Arthur Brown), silver sculpture,
London, 1855–56. Courtesy of the
Council of the National Army
Museum, London (acc. no. 1956-02-
885-6).

75. Maharaja Sir Ranbir Singh of Jammu
and Kashmir in his darbar. John
Burke and William Baker, albumen
print, 1877. Private Collection.

76. Maharaja Ranbir Singh's boat.
Francis Frith Studio, albumen print,
Kashmir, c 1870. Private Collection.

77. A river scene. George Landseer,
pastel and watercolour on paper,
Kashmir, c 1860. ©Victoria and
Albert Museum, London.

78. Camp scene in a rocky gorge in
Kashmir. George Landseer, pastel
and watercolour on paper, Kashmir, c
1860. ©Victoria and Albert Museum,
London.

79. A nautch in the Shalimar Bagh.
Samual Bourne, albumen print,
Kashmir, 1864. ©Victoria and Albert
Museum, London.

80. Nautch girl. Francis Frith Studio,
albumen print, Kashmir, c 1870.
©Victoria and Albert Museum,
London.

81. Sikh bodyguards in the Kashmir
Army. Samuel Bourne (attributed),
albumen print, Kashmir, 1864.
Private Collection.

82. Alexander Gardner inspecting a
sword with Dogra troops. Samuel
Bourne, albumen print, Kashmir,
1864. Courtesy National Park Service,
Longfellow House–Washington's
Headquarters National Historic Site.

83. Alexander Gardner. Albumen print,
Kashmir, c 1870. Collection of
Gursharan S. and Elvira Sidhu.

84. Holy Trinity Church. Rev. E. A.
Storrs-Fox, gelatine silver print,
Sialkot, February 1928. © The British
Library Board (Photo 496/10(39)).

85. Helena Gardner Botha's tombstone,
Deansgrange cemetery. Joyce
Tunstead, 2015.

86. Alexander Gardner in a tartan
turban. George Landseer, pastel on
paper, Kashmir, c 1865–69. Toor
Collection (photographed by grfik.
com).

Maps

← Astrakhan
Aral Sea

Caspian Sea

UZBEKISTAN

Jaxartes (Syr) River

Khiva • Urgench
Kizylkum Desert

Karakum Desert

Oxus (Amu) River

Tashke

TURKMENISTAN

Bukhara •
Samarkand •
Ura-tyub

• Astrabad

• Merv

¤ Andkhui

Hazrat-Imam ¤
Kunduz

PERSIA

Khawak P

Charikar
Bamiyan ¤ • Begra
Kabu
Khairaba
Ghorband P

Herat • •

AFGHANISTAN

Ghazni •

Astrakhan

Katmandu
Benares

¤ Girishk
• Kandahar

TRAVELS OF
ALEXANDER GARDNER

· · · · · First journey 1819-21
– – – Second journey 1823-4
·–·–· Third journey 1826-30

SIND

KAZAKHSTAN

KYRGHYZSTAN

0   100   200   km
0   50   100 150 miles

CHINA

• Kokand
ojend   • Fergana

ALAI MOUNTAINS

ATEGIN

• Kashgar

Little Karakul Lake

XINJIANG

• Yarkand

AJIKISTAN   PAMIRS

□ Shignan

BADAKHSHAN

• Khotan

• Faisabad

rm

HINDU-KUSH

KONGUR SHAN

KUN LUN MOUNTAINS

shir Road

KARAKORAMS

• Gilgit

Shandur Pass

AFIRISTAN   Chitral

BALTISTAN

□ Chilas

Karakoram Pass

• Jalalabad

KASHMIR

LADAKH

TIBET

• Peshawar

Srinagar •

Zoji La Pass

• Leh

Khyber Pass

Pangong Lake

Indus River

JAMMU

GREAT

PUNJAB

Lahore •   • Amritsar

• Simla

HIMALAYA

NEPAL

Delhi •

Ganges River

RAJASTHAN

Jumna River

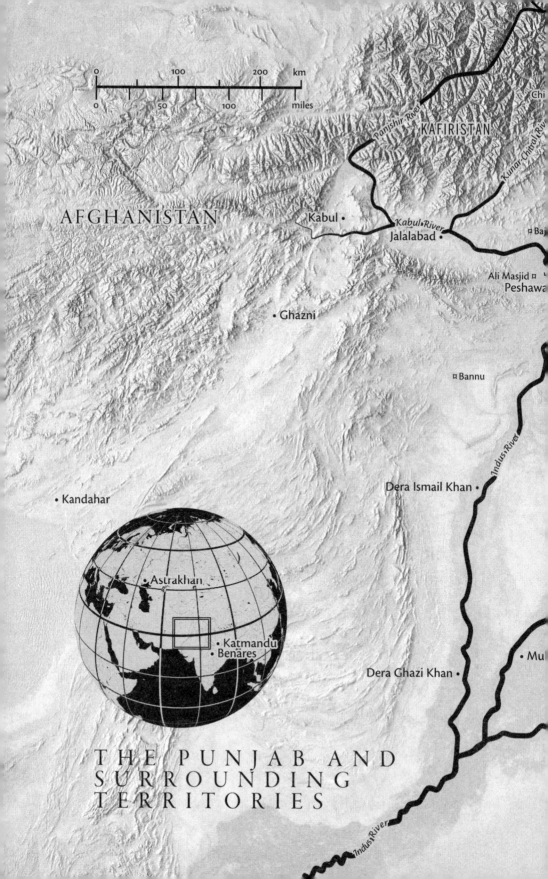

0   100   200   km

0   50   100   miles

Panjshir River

KAFIRISTAN

Chi

Kunar-Chitral River

AFGHANISTAN

Kabul

Kabul River

Jalalabad

¤ Baj

Ali Masjid ¤

Peshawa

• Ghazni

¤ Bannu

Indus River

Dera Ismail Khan •

• Kandahar

• Astrakhan

• Katmandu
• Benāres

Dera Ghazi Khan •

• Mu

THE PUNJAB AND
SURROUNDING
TERRITORIES

Indus River

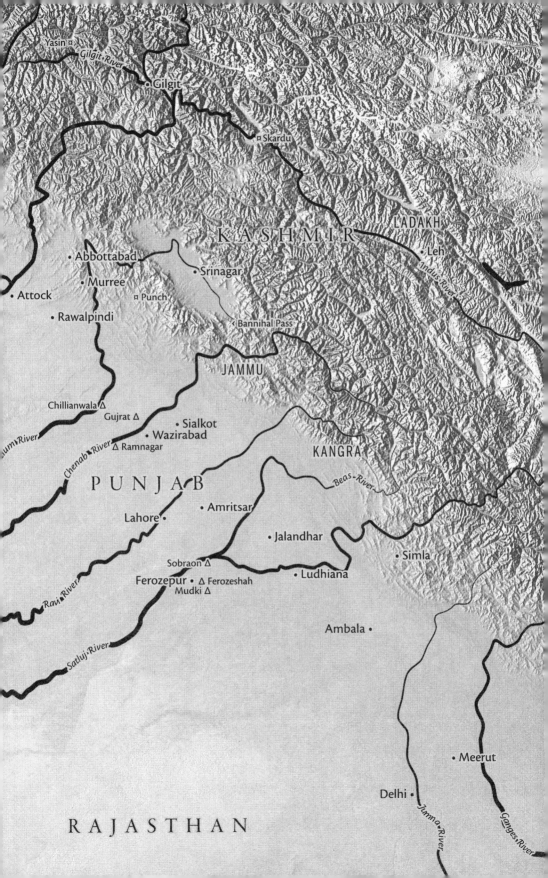

Yasin ⌂

Gilgit River

Gilgit

Skardu

K A S H M I R

L A D A K H

Leh

Indus River

Abbottabad

Murree

Srinagar

Attock

⌂ Punch

Rawalpindi

Bannihal Pass

J A M M U

Chillianwala △

Gujrat △

Sialkot

um River

Wazirabad

Chenab River △ Ramnagar

K A N G R A

P U N J A B

Beas River

Amritsar

Lahore

Jalandhar

Simla

Sobraon △

Ludhiana

Ferozepur △ Ferozeshah

Ravi River

Mudki △

Ambala

Satluj River

Meerut

Delhi

Jumna River

Ganges River

R A J A S T H A N

Acknowledgements

I first encountered Colonel Alexander Gardner's extraordinary story when researching the Western Himalayas in the 1970s. The two books that followed, *When Men and Mountains Meet* (John Murray, 1977) and *The Gilgit Game* (John Murray, 1979), eventually appeared in a single volume as *The Explorers of the Western Himalayas 1820-95* (John Murray, 1998). In each of the original titles a chapter was devoted to Gardner, and various sources and informants were acknowledged, among them Dr Schuyler Jones and Christina Noble. Forty years later, it is no small pleasure to thank both of them for once again taking up the Gardner trail. 'Skye' Jones brought his unrivalled experience of Kafiristan to bear on what has often been supposed the least credible section of the colonel's travels. He also kindly read and commented on the whole typescript. Christina Noble made more suggestions on the text and, as always, shared the fruits of her long affair with the region. It was with her that I first savoured some of Colonel Gardner's old stamping grounds in Afghanistan, Pakistan and Kashmir. Best of all, both Skye and Christina offered unstinting encouragement.

So did, and does, my wife Amanda. She has long eavesdropped on the colonel's odyssey and has made no objection to his seriously outstaying his welcome. This book is dedicated to her with gratitude and love.

To the Royal Literary Fund I am indebted for something just as precious as encouragement, namely income. Cleverly conceived and discreetly managed, the Fund makes the writing of books like this possible by enabling authors to augment their otherwise paltry earnings. I could not have managed without it. My thanks therefore to Steve Cooke, David Swinburne and Bruce Hunter.

But *The Tartan Turban's* greatest debt is unquestionably to Parmjit Singh and his colleagues at Kashi House. It was Parmjit who championed the idea of a book on Gardner, who overcame my reservations with news of unexplored material, and who has never once allowed his enthusiasm for the project to flag. No author could ask for a more congenial and conscientious editor.

Even more unusually, Parmjit and his colleagues at Kashi House volunteered to shoulder the burden of the research. Like the invisible growth-filaments of the edible truffle, the threads of this investigation into Gardner's origins and productions ramified unexpectedly. I only hope I have done justice to the efforts of all those involved. The book is as much theirs as mine, and I am delighted to endorse Kashi House's gratitude to the far-flung scholars who contributed.

Among these, special thanks are due to Dr Bikram Singh Brar who conducted some ground-breaking research throughout the duration of the project, especially on Gardner himself, Helena and their descendants.

Professor Peter Stanley of the University of New South Wales, Canberra and Ms Rose Holley, Special Collections Curator, Australian Defence Force Academy Library, University of New South Wales, Canberra, kindly assisted in sourcing images of the Charles Grey manuscript material.

Joyce Tunstead, archivist and photographer at the Irish Genealogy Project, found the last resting places of Helena and her daughter, Margarita Botha. She also kindly took photographs and provided guidance on pursuing further leads.

Professor Andries Wessels, University of Pretoria, provided significant information regarding Helena's second husband, Christiaan Laurens Botha, and his family. Equally helpful was Professor Kay de Villiers, Botha's son-in-law and the last person alive to have known him, who gave a fascinating insight into the Botha family as he knew them.

The following individuals and institutions are to be thanked for their unstinting assistance with the research effort:

In the UK: Dr Kevin Greenbank (Archivist, Centre for South Asian Studies, Cambridge), Itvinder Singh Hayre, Taranjeet Singh Padam (British Library), Jasdeep Singh Rahal (National Army Museum), Simran Jodha, Verinder Sharma, Dorothy Halfhide (Curator, Thorney Heritage Museum), June and Vernon Bull (Peterborough local historians), Alan Johnson (Archivist, Peterborough and District Family History Society), Sandy Sneddon (Asia Secretary, Church of Scotland World Mission Council), Jacqueline Burrows (Combe Down Heritage Society), Dr Matthew Brown (University of Bristol), Holly Lorraine McKenzie, Frank Bowles (Superintendent, Cambridge University Library) and The National Library of Wales, Aberystwyth, Ceredigion.

In Ireland: Damien Burke (Assistant Archivist, Irish Jesuit Archives), Nigel Curtin (Local Studies Librarian, Dún Laoghaire-Rathdown Libraries Headquarters, County Dublin), Aideen Ireland (Head, Reader Services Division, National Archives, Dublin), John Grenham (Consultant Genealogist, The Irish Times) and the General Records Office, Roscommon.

In France: Dr Christine Moliner (Researcher, École des hautes études en sciences sociales) and Archives Départementales, Département des Alpes-Maritimes, Nice.

In Germany: The Archives of the Bavarian State.

In India: Mingma Pakhrin (independent researcher) and Dr Jean-Marie Lafont.

In Pakistan: Dr Yaqoob Khan Bangash (Information Technology University, Lahore), Qamar Rafiq (Assistant to the Church of Scotland Attorney), Ashaar Rehman (Dawn Newspaper, Lahore) and Abdul Majid Sheikh (journalist and author).

In South Africa: Professor Molly Brown (University of Pretoria), Anne Lehmkuhl (Genealogy Researcher), Derek du Bruyn (Senior Museum Scientist, National Museum, Bloemfontein), Sudré

Havenga (Collections Management Department, National Museum) and the National Archives and Records Service of South Africa.

In USA and Canada: Elizabeth Weigler (Researcher, University of California), Professor Karen Racine (Associate Professor, University of Guelph), and David Daly and Anita Israel (Collection Manager and Archives Specialist respectively of the Longfellow House-Washington's Headquarters National Historic Site, Cambridge, MA).

We were fortunate to receive help with the translation of French, German and Spanish texts from several friends of the project, namely Brigitte Bourdériat, Alec Curry, Ágnes Mészáros, Catalina Recamán Míguez and Signe Olesen.

We are grateful to the public institutions and private collections that allowed us to reproduce their images. In particular, thanks are extended to Davinder Toor (Toor Collection), Anton Bartholomeew, Gursharan S. and Elvira Sidhu, Davinder Pal Singh (Panjab Digital Library) and the Directors of Pushkin Museum and The State Russian Museum.

The editorial effort led by Parmjit Singh was supported by Dr Bikram Brar, Arjan Grewal, Kanwal Madra, Daniel Scott, Harbakhsh Grewal, Amandeep Madra, Iqbal Grewal and Sachna Hanspal.

Special thanks are due to Juga Singh (jugasingh.com/grfik.com), who was the creative spirit behind every aspect of this book's design and layout. An appreciation of his maps, family trees and timeline are vital to fully understand our protagonist's story. Thanks also to Navinder Grover (Teacher Stern) for providing expert legal advice at various stages of the project. Inderjit Kaur and Dilgir Kaur deserve recognition for the wonderful support they gave so freely.

The publication of this book was made possible thanks to the financial assistance extended by the United Kingdom Punjab Heritage Association, Hardeep Singh & Baljinder Kaur Bath and Kanwal Madra.

Introduction

Alexander Gardner might reasonably be claimed as the most extraordinary of all the nineteenth century's great adventurers. Well before more reputable explorers notched up their own 'discoveries' in Inner Asia, this lone Scots-American had roamed the deserts of Turkestan, ridden round the world's most fearsome knot of mountains and fought in Afghanistan for what he called 'the good cause of right against wrong'.

As a hired gun transposed from the American West to the Asian East, for over a decade he had quartered the forbidden lands between what are now Turkmenistan and Chinese Xinjiang. He had survived arrest in Khiva, fled retribution in Samarkand, repeatedly forded the Oxus River (Amu Darya), and wintered in the unknown tundra of the Pamirs. Along the way he had been wounded on numerous occasions, had married an Afghan princess and had quickly been widowed.

At the time, the 1820s, no other outsider had managed anything remotely comparable. 'Single-handed, without any official support and without any geographical training,' he had also explored the Western Himalayas. Twice he penetrated the explorer's Holy Grail of remotest Kafiristan and twice he re-emerged to tell of it. From the Caspian Sea to Tibet and from Kandahar to Kashgar, Gardner had seen it all. And as noted by the first man to retrace his footsteps across the Pamirs, if he hadn't, he couldn't possibly have invented it. When word of his feats filtered out thirty years later, geographers were agog.

Historians would be more intrigued by the aftermath of these travels. Thirteen years as a white-man-gone-native in Central Asia had been followed by fifteen years as a colonel of artillery in the employ of northern India's last great native empire. Here, though the rewards were all he wished for, Gardner met his match in terms of gruesome encounters; the horrors on offer needed no embellishment. His insider's account of the death throes of the Sikh Empire, though somewhat demanding of the reader, would be substantially corroborated and has long since taken its place in the history books. One by one the contenders for the Sikh throne in Lahore were eliminated. Colonel Gardner not only observed the bloodshed but played his part in it. Often he was the only foreign witness to the carnage; throughout he lived in fear for his life.

When war with the British finally extinguished the Sikh Empire, Gardner again reinvented himself, this time as a British informant. Extricating himself from the treachery in Lahore, he survived to tell the tale and did so—repeatedly. In the course of a long and distinguished retirement in the valley of Kashmir the old colonel in the tartan turban became a minor celebrity, sought out by a new generation of explorers and quizzed by passing visitors as the survivor of a brutal, bygone age.

It is from what the colonel divulged to these latter-day disciples, many of them senior public servants, plus some garbled notes in his own hand, that the story of his early life and travels has generally been reconstructed. The nature of this source material leaves much to be desired. The colonel's memory was fading—he was by now in his seventies—while his predilection for enlivening encounters remained unimpaired. Or as one reviewer would put it, his recollections were 'handicapped by adventure'. Like Mr Essper in D'Israeli's *Vivian Grey*, he had seen more than he remembered and remembered more than he had seen. Added to which, his listeners were not themselves infallible. Their different versions of his itineraries were hard to reconcile; the dates didn't match and the places didn't correspond. There were too many obvious exaggerations and far too many doubtful skirmishes.

To a discerning few his story was beginning to look vulnerable.

Come an age when pioneering travellers were assumed to be upstanding and scrupulously honest, Gardner fell woefully short of the norm. The suspicious grew to doubt his nationality and even his identity; the scholarly felt insulted by his blatant fabrications; the virtuous accused him of having stooped to slave-dealing and butchery; and almost everyone found it hard to credit the extent of his travels. On his own admission he had first survived as an outlaw, then prospered as a mercenary. Neither calling deserved respect. Emphatically he was not, as some of his admirers contended, 'one of the finest specimens ever known of the soldier of fortune', nor was he a classic example of 'what men of British race can do under stress of trial and suffering'.

By the 1890s, the greatest traveller of the century was being downgraded to travel's greatest enigma. Reckoned less trustworthy even than Marco Polo's *Travels*, Gardner's exploits were increasingly shelved alongside the medieval marvels rehashed by Sir John Mandeville or the absurdities served up by Baron Munchausen. They belonged to what one authority called 'the apocrypha of travel'. As a result, anthologies of exploration ignored him. So too, as recently as 1991, would *The Royal Geographical Society's History of World Exploration*.

But worse followed. As a result of some original research in the 1920s his character, already badly mauled, had been comprehensively assassinated. He was not, it was now suggested, an American freebooter but an Irish deserter. All his exploits had been lifted from the accounts of others. His itineraries had been composed by perusing an atlas. And his reputation in the Punjab had been as black as those of the parricidal rajas he served. In short 'the man was a prize liar'. His deeds were 'barbaric' and his story 'a myth' concocted from easily verifiable sources.

Yet, nearly a century later, and after making due allowance for the revisionist's perversity, he seemed worth one last look. The old colonel might still be who he said he was, and if his years in Sikh employ were genuine, then so might be his travels. Anyone with even a mildly romantic bent must surely take his side. So intriguing is his story, so naïve his telling of it and so infectious his bravado that the reader feels duty bound to give him some benefit of the doubt.

That, very roughly, was the genesis of this book. In the hope that further research would bring greater rewards than awaited the quest for the colonel's lost fortune, with which this book begins, the net was cast wide—and, as it proved, wisely. Tentative lines of enquiry led to some unexpected documentation. The man was neither as elusive nor as unreliable as supposed. But major mysteries remained.

Then came a breakthrough—the discovery of several reports and lengthy papers written by Gardner himself. Instead of second and third-hand accounts, there existed first-hand testimony from the man himself. A crucial dimension was added to his story. Contentious episodes could now be seen from the colonel's perspective and much of the rest could be reinterpreted in the light of these insights. The challenges faced by those who relayed his story to posterity also became clearer and their editorial compromises more apparent.

What follows does not claim to be a rounded biography. Nor is it a comprehensive vindication. Two hundred years after the tartan-clad colonel first climbed into the saddle, the chances of resurrecting the whole truth, and—more critically—nothing but the truth, are remote. Put-downs like those aired above need to be borne in mind. Some are still valid. The mysteries may be fewer, but the mystique of the world's most endearing enigma lives on.

I

Chasing Shadows

Kashmir, while ever a land to excite expectation, did not normally attract fortune-seekers. Since at least the 1860s, foreigners resident in India, most of them British, had been escaping to this most celebrated of Himalayan valleys in search of diversion. They came in high summer, fleeing the inferno of the north Indian plains to rediscover health, vigour and romance among Kashmir's alpine pastures. Once there, they tramped the hills, fished the rivers, picnicked by the lakes and stalked the scimitar-horned ibex. Afternoons might be spent in the shade, sketching the views. At night they dined beneath the stars on snipe and strawberries. Succumbing to the Kashmiris' combination of fine craftsmanship and outrageous salesmanship, they also stocked up on pashmina shawls, *papier maché* cigarette-boxes and silken carpets. The local economy depended on them. Most visitors expected to come away poorer, not richer.

Rather exceptional, then, was the small party of friends who arrived in Srinagar, the Kashmir capital, in the spring of 1898. The group had reached India from Durban, which was itself unusual. They hailed from the Afrikaner's Orange Free State, with whose government the British were on the brink of war, and their quest was a decidedly delicate one. Christiaan Lourens Botha, a well-groomed young attorney from Johannesburg, had assumed charge of the group; he would later become mayor of Bloemfontein, a member of the Union of South Africa's parliament and judge-president of the Orange Free State. He lent the party an air of respectability and was not to be trifled with.

But it was his fiancée, a petite 32-year old divorcee of more exotic parentage, who was the moving spirit behind this Boer trek into the Himalayas. Helena Haughton Campbell Gardner—the name she had given the registrar of the London borough of Streatham at the time of her earlier marriage to a Bavarian lieutenant—was slightly older than Botha and not conspicuously wealthy. On the other hand she was well connected, she was evidently attractive and she had prospects.

She was also the only member of the party who could lay claim to any first-hand knowledge of Kashmir. Thirty-two years earlier, she had been born there, and somewhere deep in Srinagar's warren of narrow lanes and tall timbered facades she had spent her early childhood. Although not something she advertised, she was herself half-Kashmiri.

Her mother she had known only as 'Bibi Kali'. 'Bibi', denoting 'a native wife', was more a job description than a personal name, while 'Kali' might imply that she was a Hindu by birth. Bibi Kali had been about sixty years younger than Helena's father and was generally recognised as his favourite companion. But they were not together long; she had died when Helena was just two years old. The toddler had then been entrusted to Bibi Chirang, another member of her father's household who laboured under the doubtful designation of 'his second most favourite wife'. Three years later, aged five, Helena had been packed off to Murree, a hill-station with a convent school and now in Pakistan. For the little girl it marked the beginning of a lifetime of uprootings almost as extensive as her father's, though none of them as bizarre.

From Murree, the young Helena had been sent on to England and a second boarding school. In the process she acquired a new home. In 1873, Sir Robert and Lady Davies, he the lieutenant-governor of the Punjab and she, his wife, then resident in England, effectively adopted Helena as a favour to her now dying father. They jointly assumed responsibility for her upbringing and provided a comfortable home for her during the school holidays. Her school was a private one in Combe Down, Somerset, and the Davies' home was near Pe-terborough in the leafy English Midlands. As an inducted member of the local gentry, Helena had flourished.

When in 1877 her father finally died, Helena was left an orphan. She was not, though, without means; for on coming of age ten years later, she found herself heir to an annuity from her father's estate. It paid around £100 a year, the equivalent of nearer £10,000 in today's values and a useful income. Better still, there was the promise of more where that came from. According to Bibi Chirang, who seems to have stayed in touch with the girl she considered her step-daughter, the capital on which the annuity was drawn was substantial; in round figures it amounted to £1million in cash (say £100m today) with as much as ten times more in precious stones and treasure.

Buoyed by such prospects, Helena had embraced society and found no shortage of suitors. In 1886, with Sir Robert Davies on hand to give her away, she had married her Bavarian lieutenant, one Max Jo-sef Gerl, in the parish of St Peter's, Streatham. A baby daughter had followed in 1891, a son in 1892 and a divorce soon after. The pursuit of her patrimony had had to wait. Only after her meeting, three years later, with the plausible Botha and after their relocation to Africa had Helena taken up the challenge of realising that enormous fortune. A will had to be found, a claim registered, a bank vault emptied. It meant going back to India, revisiting the scenes of her earliest child-hood and retracing the trail left by her decidedly mysterious father.

For this father of the soon-to-be Mrs Helena Botha—the shadowy figure behind her disjointed upbringing, the creator of the fortune she coveted and the reason for her 1898 visit to Kashmir—already ranked among the most enigmatic adventurers of the century. A controversial figure in his lifetime, Colonel Alexander Haughton Campbell Gardner had become even more so since his death. The dark deeds in which he had reportedly been involved had sent shud-ders through a generation of upstanding British officials. Likewise his improbable itineraries, in so far as they had been made known, prompted scholarly sniffs of 'disbelief that he had ever visited the regions he professed to describe'. Twenty-one years after the colonel's death, Helena and her Kashmir-bound companions faced a double challenge—to realise his fortune while resurrecting his reputation. For Helena in particular, the quest for treasure went hand in kidskin glove with the quest for truth.

In this connection it can hardly have been a coincidence that 1898, the year of Helena's visit to India, would also see the long-delayed publication of the first authorised biography of her father. *Soldier and Traveller: Memoirs of Alexander Gardner, Colonel of Artillery in the Service of Maharaja Ranjit Singh* had been edited by Major Hugh Wodehouse Pearse and was being issued by the reputable Edinburgh firm of William Blackwood and Sons. Padded out with appendices and a fulsome preface by Sir Richard Temple, formerly governor of Bombay and now a recognised authority on all things Indian in the House of Commons, the book would run to nearly 400 pages. Editor-Major Pearse had never met Gardner and it is not certain that he had met Helena. But he had previously edited the diaries of Lieutenant-General Charles Windham, a hero of the Crimean War and the Indian Mutiny; and though still in uniform (he would win a medal for distinguished service in the Boer War), Major Pearse was a fluent and trusted writer. It was probably on the strength of his reputation as a soldier's memorialist that Helena had sought him out.

More certainly it was she who, four years earlier, had supplied Pearse with the raw materials for her father's *Memoirs*. These materials were problematic. They had defeated more than one would-be editor and were already challenging a galaxy of geographers. In form a jumble of notes in her father's spidery hand, they were interleaved with lengthy transcripts of his life-story as told to others. But the resultant narrative was far from continuous, it was sparsely dated and it was spattered with more outlandish place names and improbable personalities than an extravagant work of fiction. Much of its factual material was difficult to verify; and worse still, it told of travels so extreme and escapades so hair-raising as to tax even the most credulous reader.

Editor-Major Pearse had had his work cut out. But he had persevered, and to considerable effect. Some episodes in Colonel Gardner's long career could indeed be corroborated; there were several respected figures still alive who remembered meeting him; and there were some rather arresting portraits of him. Most of the portraits were photographs but they included a fine study in coloured pastels of the colonel in the late 1860s as exhibited by George Landseer, nephew of the better known Sir Edwin Landseer.

These visual images clinched the case for publication: however unsatisfactory the colonel's narrative, Gardner himself looked every inch what he said he was—a white man turned native who for half a century had lived a life of death-defying adventure in the wilder regions of Asia. The pictures showed a spare figure with abundant whiskers, untrimmed beard and a long straight nose. The brow was furrowed and the staring eyes conveyed a rather startled expression. He looked a hunted man, and about his person he had enough scars to prove it. More obviously, from his egret-plumed turban to the turn-ups of his baggy trews, the pictures showed the colonel dressed from top to toe in nothing but the boldest green and yellow tartan. The cut of the jacket was said to bespeak a native tailor; and though its arrangement corresponded to no known uniform, the material was thought to be identical to that of the kilts worn by the 79th Highland Infantry. Clearly, whatever the colonel's origins, he had been keen to dispel any doubts about his ancestry. Notwithstanding an accent that some thought to be Irish, a mother whom he described as half-Spanish, a childhood supposedly spent criss-crossing north America and a bewildering succession of Asian aliases, Colonel Gardner had chosen to be remembered as a Highland Scot.

Helena was more interested in the circumstances surrounding her father's final domicile in Kashmir. He had apparently fetched up there in the early 1850s when he re-entered the service of a little-loved ruler called Gulab Singh of Jammu. Gulab Singh was one of three brothers who had all been feudatories and counsellors of Maharaja Ranjit Singh, the wily one-eyed ruler of the Punjab and creator of a short-lived empire that stretched from Afghanistan to Tibet. But whereas Maharaja Ranjit Singh had been a Sikh, and so his empire a Sikh empire, Gulab Singh and his two brothers were not Sikhs (and nor were they related to Ranjit Singh). They were Dogras; that is Rajputs by caste and Hindus by religion. They hailed from around Jammu in the foothills of Kashmir and their relationship with the great Ranjit Singh had been subordinate and feudatory, not confessional. Hence, when in the Anglo-Sikh Wars of the 1840s the British had defeated Ranjit Singh's successors and begun annexing his Sikh kingdom, Gulab Singh (his brothers having by then been horribly murdered) had been conspicuous by his absence. Indeed, for withholding his troops during the First Anglo-Sikh War, the British authorities had offered the renegade Gulab Singh a role as their own feudatory. He might rule under British protection as maharaja of his native Jammu and he might incorporate into his state that vast chunk of the former Sikh Empire that comprised Kashmir and its mountain dependencies.

Thus, in 1846, was created the hybrid principality of 'Jammu and Kashmir', the largest of British India's princely states and a bone of contention between India and Pakistan to this day. Gulab Singh and his Dogra successors were confirmed as maharajas of Jammu and Kashmir in perpetuity. The British gave them a free hand in the administration of their state. And 'Gordana Sahib'—as Gardner was known at the time—had at last struck lucky. On the strength of his previous service to the Dogra brothers, he had been appointed colonel-in-chief of the Kashmir state's artillery corps.

Already well past his prime by this time, Colonel Gardner's role in the service of Kashmir's maharaja seems to have been largely ceremonial. He was occasionally spotted taking parades, attending state functions or supervising the casting of new cannon. But in a hill-state with few roads and almost no wheeled-traffic, the artillery was more for show than warfare, as was Gardner. European visitors who encountered the old colonel in the course of his far from onerous duties noted only his striking outfit and his often incomprehensible utterances. This incoherence they attributed variously to his lack of teeth, his liking for alcohol, his considerable age or the sing-song lilt of his rusty English; it could equally have been caused by a physical impediment, namely a gash in his throat which was the most obvious of his many wounds and which obliged him to clamp a pair of forceps to his neck whenever he ate or drank.

Curiosity had tempted some visitors to track the colonel down and enquire further into his history. Yet Gardner himself, though flattered by the attention, had seldom sought out European company. Jealously he had kept his distance and, with it, that air of mystery. He had seemed quite content to serve out his days as an unassuming officer and pensioner in one of South Asia's many native armies.

Helena fancied she knew better. Dim memories of her father's high standing within the maharaja's durbar, plus the hints provided by Bibi Chirang, convinced her of the need to enquire further. Clearly, there was more to her father's story than even the conscientious editing of Major Pearse was unearthing. For one thing there was the fortune. Servants and pensioners of a maharaja were normally maintained by the grant of a *jagir*, this being a right to enjoy part of the annual revenue yielded by a specified village or district. Gardner had evidently been awarded several villages in Kashmir; and given his long service record, Helena assumed that the income from these jagirs had been the main source of his wealth. She also assumed that a jagir was a heritable grant and that its yield must therefore have been quietly accumulating throughout the twenty years since his death. As her father's only known heir, her right to claim these arrears looked worth pursuing.

But in this she was soon disabused. As any British official could have told her, a jagir was not normally heritable; on the death of the holder it reverted to the sovereign unless he specifically bestowed it on the holder's heir. Since no such disposition had been made by Maharaja Ranbir Singh (Gulab Singh's son and successor as of 1857), Helena had no claim on the posthumous income. She did, though, have a good claim on her father's estate as it had stood at the time of his death—and that included the £1million in cash and the £10million in gold, jewels and precious artefacts mentioned by Bibi Chirang. Moreover, such figures were not fanciful. The treasure trove accumulated by the great Sikh maharaja, Ranjit Singh, had included the famous Koh-i-Nur diamond and was worth billions. In 1984 that left by the last maharaja of Kashmir, Gulab Singh's great-great-grandson, was officially valued at some £500 million, though, like the Gardner nest-egg, much of it consisted of jewel-encrusted costumes, saddlery and swords on which it was hard to put a price.

On the evidence of Helena's annuity settlement, the colonel's will had found its way into the safekeeping of a branch of the Agra Bank in Lahore; presumably the cash was there too, even if the whereabouts of the treasure looked less certain. Helena's quest was just beginning.

The Indian itinerary of Helena and her companions remains conjectural—and in truth Helena's entire life-story has to be inferred from the scantiest of references plus rather few official records. But it seems clear that she and her friends, before extending their enquiries to Jammu and Kashmir, first headed for Lahore. As the erstwhile capital of the Sikh Empire in whose army Gardner had once served, as the scene of some of his most high-profile activities, and latterly as the administrative centre of the British province of the Punjab, it was the logical place at which to take up the colonel's trail. There would be people there who remembered him and places he frequented. And there was, of course, the Agra Bank and the precious will.

Arrived in Lahore, the visitors no doubt took a pony-drawn tonga straight to Faletti's Hotel. This was one of a string of colonial-style watering holes that extended north-west along India's Grand Trunk Road to Flashman's in Rawalpindi and Dean's in Peshawar, after which both the road and the hotels petered out in the Khyber Pass. A low white building, generously pillared, with a deep central verandah, dark teakwood floors and well-tended lawns, Faletti's was the tourists' only realistic option as a Lahore base. Without copious accreditation and introductions, the Lahore Club would have been out of the question and there was nowhere else boasting modern facilities. Faletti's was convenient; it was located just off Mall Road, the long boulevard where stood Governor's House and most of the other shade-shuttered temples of British rule, banks included.

Additionally, the hotel must have been familiar to Helena from the reminiscences of her British foster-father. For though projected and run by Andrei Faletti, a Piedmontese chef who had reached India by way of Hammersmith, it had only been built, says the prospectus of its current owners, thanks to 'the fullest possible support' of Sir Robert Davies. As Governor of the Punjab in the 1870s, Helena's guardian had approved Signor Faletti's plans and taken pride in what was Lahore's first purpose-built European hotel.

Excursions from here into the teeming old city of Lahore would have felt like changing continents. The manicured greenery gave way to crumbling masonry and the whitewash to grubby stucco. Stalls selling everything from goat meat to galingal lined the narrow thoroughfares; a colourful throng then blocked them. In a sea of eccentrically tied turbans, the hillman's flat-topped woollen cap hinted at the snowy peaks to the north and the Turkoman's tall black 'flower-pot' hinted at the sandy deserts to the west. The babel of voices that rose above this river of millinery was testimony to both. Business might be conducted in Punjabi, Hindi, Sindi, Urdu, Arabic, Pushtu, Farsi, Kashmiri, Turkestani, Bhoti or any of the hundreds of local dialects. The city being located where the subcontinent merged with the continent, more languages were here spoken than anywhere else in Asia. Temple bells tinkled and the muezzin called the Muslim faithful to prayer; hammering blacksmiths competed with hammering farriers. Dust hung in the air like dirty steam. The noise was deafening, the odours noisome. To the uninitiated it could all seem rather menacing.

Yet it would have held no surprises for any visitor familiar with the works of a young writer called Rudyard Kipling. By 1898, the year of Helena's visit, Kipling was in England, making a name for himself as a poet and writing his inimitable *Kim*; but for much of the previous decade he had stalked the crowded byways of Lahore, rejoicing in the human concourse and exploring oriental lowlife. His father had been appointed curator of the city's museum and young Rudyard had first put pen to paper on the staff of the city's newspaper. After appearing in the columns of this *Civil and Military Gazette*, his early poems and stories had been published under titles like *Departmental Ditties* and *Plain Tales from the Hills*. They were already read and loved.

But above all, it was the saga of *Kim* which would link the names of Kipling and Lahore irrevocably; and just so, it was the plight of Kim himself that would have stirred a pang of recognition in someone as displaced as Helena Gerl née Gardner. Kipling begins his novel by identifying the young Kim in a gang of street-urchins clambering over an enormous cannon mounted (and still mounted) outside the museum near the business end of Mall Road. Quick-witted and fearless, Kim evidently commands the respect of his fellow waifs, whether Hindus, Sikhs or Muslims. Yet like Gardner during his twenty years in this same city of uncertain identities, he doesn't quite belong. As Kipling puts it, 'though he was burned black as any native, though he spoke the vernacular by preference, and his mother tongue in a clipped uncertain sing-song ... Kim was white'.

As much an impostor as the be-turbanned Gardner, Kim was also an orphan, just like Helena. His mother, an English nursemaid who had died during an outbreak of cholera, had been replaced by 'a half-caste woman' who smoked opium and dealt in bric-a-brac. Meanwhile Kim's father, an Irish infantryman who had been on the loose ever since his regiment 'went home without him', had succumbed first to the bottle, then to the woman and her pipe, and so 'died as poor whites die in India'. Kim was alone in the world. About him he had just his wits, his rags and three tightly folded documents crammed into a leather amulet case that he wore round his neck. In just such a neck-pouch Gardner, when travelling in Central Asia, was said to have crammed his route notes lest they get lost or attract unwelcome attention. The papers in Kim's pouch were equally precious; they were the sole evidence of his parentage. One was his birth certificate, another was his father's army clearance certificate and the third was his '*ne varietur*', so called because it bore those Latin words beneath his wiggly signature. Like Helena clutching at the straw that was her father's will, it was not a lot to go on with.

Needless to say, although Kipling may have heard tell of Gardner and seems later to have read his *Memoirs* as edited by Pearse, he can never have actually met him; by the time the young Rudyard arrived in 'that wonderful, dirty, mysterious anthill' that was Lahore, Gardner had been dead five years. But there still roamed in and about the city others of exotic parentage whose fathers, like Gardner himself, had originally been drawn to the Punjab by the generous remuneration on offer from Maharaja Ranjit Singh. Faletti, for instance, the hotelier, is said to have been enticed east by reports concerning the good fortune of General Paolo Avitabile, an Italian who had served under Napoleon before resurfacing in the Sikh army. As sticklers for military drill and as experts in artillery and tactical manoeuvres, perhaps a hundred other foreign mercenaries of French, German, Italian, Spanish, Russian, American and British extraction at one time served alongside him. Most had taken, or been gifted, at least one Indian wife, this being a stipulation of their employment in Ranjit Singh's army. And though by 1898 they and their wives had either died or fled the carnage that had followed the death of the great maharaja, their offspring might still be encountered in the human tide that eddied through Lahore's bazaars. The colonel's trail might not be as cold as Helena feared. By anyone bent on exhuming the past, these people were worth seeking out.

Helena's enquiries may well have started with the most prized of the portly General Avitabile's innumerable progeny. By now in her late sixties, this woman, the daughter of one of the Italian General's doe-eyed Pathan handmaidens, had been such a beauty that, to ensure her virginity, Avitabile had kept her under lock and key from childhood. 'So carefully was she watched,' reported a contributor to the *Calcutta Review*, 'that even her meals were conveyed to her from without by means of a *tour* such as are used at convent gates.' But when in 1843 Avitabile had opted to return to his native Naples taking his hard-won fortune with him, the girl had not formed part of it. Instead the gourmet-general had married her off to the most privileged member of his household, namely his cook, and had made sure that both the bride and groom were handsomely provided for. Indeed, the girl's dowry included such an array of gold jewellery as to incite the interest of the man who succeeded to General Avitabile's command. This was Jodha Ram, an unctuous Brahmin, who though he owed everything to the general's patronage, ill repaid it. By engineering the disgrace of the young couple and the appropriation of the dowry, he 'left both her and her husband in abject poverty'.

Assuming Helena was aware of this hard luck story—and assuming the couple were still in the Punjab—her failure to find them must have been a bitter disappointment; for though her father had had nothing to do with the sequestration of the newly-weds' dowry, it was common knowledge that Alexander Gardner had become all too well acquainted with the machinations of Jodha Ram. He had known the Brahmin well, heartily distrusted him and, in one of those deeds that so horrified his contemporaries, had personally subjected him to a repulsive form of mutilation.

It was so repulsive that it had backfired by discrediting Gardner himself. Major Pearse, taking his tactful editing of the Gardner *Memoirs* to the point of partiality, would see fit to omit all mention of this outrage. Subsequent generations of Gardner critics would be less considerate. One would go so far as to describe Jodha Ram's fate as that of an undoubted scoundrel suffering 'at the hands of a scoundrel as despicable as himself'. The affair was clearly a vital, if bloody, piece in the Gardner jigsaw and it required careful handling. Gardner himself had written a rambling defence of his action; but what Helena would have liked was the reassuring corroboration of someone as closely acquainted with the devious Jodha Ram as had been General Avitabile's hard-done-by daughter.

And there were others, children of mixed parentage born of troubled times and abandoned to obscurity, whose careers had a bearing on Helena's quest. A European calling himself William Campbell had been discharged from Ranjit Singh's service over 'an offence connected with women'. He had then accompanied a claimant to the Afghan throne on that man's return to Afghanistan and had finally achieved distinction in Kabul under another claimant. He had survived until 1866 and his reputation had lasted even longer; it was said that Campbell's progeny were to be found evenly spread right along the 500 miles between Lahore, Kandahar, and Kabul.

Gardner too had served more than one claimant to the Afghan throne, though that was before he enlisted with the Sikhs. More intriguingly in the eyes of his detractors, there was a man known sometimes as Rattray, sometimes as Leslie, whose career bore a much more suspicious resemblance to Gardner's. This Rattray, a mercurial figure possessed of both education and effrontery, had also deserted or been dismissed from Ranjit Singh's service. He too had then 'gone native' in the employ of Emir Dost Mohamed of Kabul and had risen to the command of an Afghan detachment stationed at Ali Masjid in the Khyber Pass. There, in 1837, Rattray/Leslie was discovered by a passing British mission led by Captain Alexander Burnes.

Burnes, a self-appointed authority on Afghanistan, had already been lionised in London for an earlier excursion into Central Asia; more famously, four years later, he would be hacked to pieces when the Afghans got the better of the British in the First Afghan War. But it was John Wood, one of Burnes's British companions and the author of a more sober chronicle, who recorded the impression made by the fickle Rattray.

> We wound up the pass to the Fort of Ali Masjid where we were received by its Commandant, an ill-conditioned, slipshod, turbanned English-man, dissipated looking and robed in a kind of Afghan *deshabille*. His abode was a cave in the mountains from which he and his hungry fol-lowers issued forth to levy blackmail on the passing kafilas [caravans].
>
> ... [This] Lieutenant-Colonel Rattray, for so he styled himself, received us at the head of his column ... but no sooner did the Commandant attempt a manoeuvre than a most ludicrous scene ensued. In utter hopelessness of restoring his scattered legion, [Rattray] disbanded it forthwith and then commenced whacking his men with a cudgel. But he was soon overwhelmed by force of numbers, and forced to desist.

Unfazed by this debacle, Rattray had immediately demanded an advance on the monies owed him for entertaining Burnes and his mission and had then so billeted his mutinous troops that the pro-visions intended for the mission were consumed by his own starv-ing horde. Meanwhile he did the round of the mission's principals, 'quietly proffering, for a consideration, to put us each in possession of the information he had amassed during a long sojourn in those countries'. Rattray's information, which included a personal narrative of his travels that he lent to Burnes, amounted to 'a full and particular account of countries he had never seen, nor heard of, and tribes the very existence of which he was till then unaware of'. For according to Wood, Rattray's revelations had all been concocted from the accounts of others and from his own imagination. In short, he was a fantasist and a con-man, as prone to invention as the infamous author of the exploits of Baron Karl Friedrich Hieronymus von Munchausen.

Munchausen, who had died in 1797, had long since been consigned to ignominy, but the next century had evidently bred its own strain of tall stories. Early in 1898, just as Helena and her companions were beginning their search for Gardner, a certain Louis de Rougemont was hoodwinking both the British geographical establishment and the general public with a sensational account of his three solitary years marooned on a coral reef in the Timor Sea, followed by his three decades living in domestic harmony among the aboriginal inhabitants of Australia's Northern Territories. De Rougemont would soon be exposed; he was recognised as a Swiss valet who had no more survived in the Outback than at the North Pole. But eminent faces had been left with much egg on them and the term 'Rougemontic' had gained a limited currency as the ultimate put-down.

More to the point, it was this scandal that would inform the most damning of all verdicts on Gardner. The revelation would originate with two researchers in Lahore's Punjab Records Office in the 1920s. Reading Wood's account of the meeting in the Khyber Pass, Charles Grey, an ex-army man who dabbled in historical research, and Herbert Leonard Offley Garrett, the Keeper of the Records, lit upon that mention of Rattray giving Burnes his travel notes and were reminded of an almost identical claim in Gardner's narrative. At some point Gardner had also supposedly entrusted part of his narrative to Burnes; and, like Rattray, he too much regretted that it was not subsequently available for inspection, having perished along with Burnes himself. Here, in other words, was the same story and the same excuse. Taken in conjunction with other possible discrepancies and borrowings in Gardner's *Memoirs*, it was a coincidence too many for the sleuthing Grey and Garrett. With much smacking of lips they asserted that 'it was undoubtedly this account [ie of Wood's meeting Rattray] that inspired Gardiner [sic] to concoct his Rougemontic narrative'.

In consequence, Gardner's *Memoirs* as edited by Pearse must, they claimed, be dismissed as derivative nonsense. The colonel was 'a prize liar who passed off other men's adventures as his own'—or worse still, who passed off other men's *fabricated* adventures as his own.

Gardner denunciations like this were nothing new and were common enough even in the 1890s to have discouraged Helena. In rescuing a reputation as dubious as her father's it was clear she could expect little help from a generation which had been either scandalised by his doings or duped by his account of them. But more promisingly from Helena's 1898 perspective, the story of the rakish Rattray had not ended with Wood's exposure. Soon after meeting the Burnes mission in the Khyber Pass, Rattray had reportedly deserted from the Afghan army, converted to Islam and, taking the name of Fida Mohamed Khan, had resurfaced in Bajaur, a Pathan tribal district north of Peshawar.

Then, as now, Bajaur was a hotbed of Islamic orthodoxy in which an eager convert might settle down amicably. From there Rattray/ Leslie/Fida Mohamed Khan occasionally offered his services to the British as an informant, and he also seems to have fathered a child; hence, half a century later (and just three years before Helena's arrival in Lahore) a man said to be the son of Rattray/Leslie/Fida Mohamed Khan had emerged to sudden notoriety as a Pathan leader known as Umra Khan. Marching his well-armed brethren from Bajaur, Umra Khan had led them into the neighbouring valley of Chitral and had there joined other malcontents in laying siege to a British force that had provocatively installed itself in the ancestral fort of the ruler of Chitral.

Occupying a long valley that hugged the still uncertain frontier between Kashmir territory and Afghanistan, Chitral lay 200 miles of snow-flecked mountain from the nearest possible British assistance. A dozen British officers and some 300 men thus found themselves running out of food, short of ammunition and at the mercy of several thousand incensed and much better supplied tribesmen.

The 1895 siege of Chitral had lasted a creditable seven weeks. At
the time it had been headline news throughout the British Empire.
Editor Pearse, then sorting out the Gardner papers as passed to
him by Helena, was well aware that readers of the *Memoirs* would
be interested in whatever the colonel had had to say of Chitral and
the Hindu Kush. Others, like Africa-based Botha, would have been
reminded of the fate, ten years earlier, of General Charles Gordon
at Khartoum.

The British authorities in India were equally mindful of Khartoum. To avoid another such fiasco they responded to the Chitral
crisis with alacrity. Two expeditions, both of them encumbered with
artillery, had been hastily assembled and had fought their way to the
scene. One, following a trail first blazed by Gardner, had mounted
their guns on sledges and hauled them over the mountains from
Gilgit in northern Kashmir; the other trailed up from the Punjab. By
the time they converged at the mid-way point in the Chitral valley,
they had drawn off so many of the fort's assailants that the siege was
over. Umra Khan was among those who had slipped away. He had
presumably withdrawn to Bajaur and it was thought he might still
be there. But so sensitive had the whole area become in the fall-out
from the siege that visiting it was out of the question. Helena had
drawn another blank.

Once again, though, it was not the end of the story. The Chitral
campaign had been wound up, but its aftermath was shedding some
unexpected light on the Gardner puzzle. Given the heavy casualties
and the considerable expense, many observers had started to wonder
what the campaign had been all about. In Westminster the government of the day even asked why there was a British presence in the
Hindu Kush at all. Was it supposed to discourage an improbable
Russian advance on British India by way of some of the highest passes
in the world? Or were the tribesmen themselves to be considered a
threat? Cynics responded by explaining that it was neither; it was
just that there was nowhere else so perfect for a young officer to bag
a sporting trophy one day and a military medal the next.

A more plausible theory was that a British presence in Chitral
would discourage the Afghans from subjugating the people of the

region immediately to the west of Chitral, Then known as Kafiristan, this was a vast and almost inaccessible tract in the high Hindu Kush, and it just happened to be somewhere with which Gardner claimed a close acquaintance. In his *Memoirs* the colonel recalled having visited Kafiristan at least twice; in fact at the time of his death he was still the only European who had returned from Kafiristan to tell the tale.

And quite a tale it was. As an ethnological curiosity, Kafiristan was unique in Asia. Precipitous and road-less, it had long ago slipped into a time-warp. Waves of conquest had eddied round the Kafirs' mountain fastnesses and nibbled into them, but without ever over-running them. In consequence, the Kafirs had retained a novel cul-ture and some distinctive physical traits that were at variance with those of all their neighbours. Pale to ruddy complexions with fair or reddish hair and blue eyes were commonplace among them, as were such un-Asian amenities as chairs to sit on, plentiful supplies of home-made wine and friendly veil-less womenfolk. There were few cereals and there were no mosques. Instead of grain the Kafirs used a flour made from mulberries and instead of Allah, they had their own pantheon of deified ancestors. In defence of these spirits they had been staunchly resisting the proselytising inroads of Islam for at least 500 years.

Some authorities supposed the Kafirs were descended from the Macedonian troops who had accompanied Alexander the Great on his invasion of the Punjab in 326 BC. Gardner himself had aired this idea and had recorded a local tradition that one day a 'white man' would come again to rid the Kafirs of their hostile Mahomedan neighbours. Indeed, according to the colonel, something along these lines had actually happened; for, he reported, 'two Europeans had lived in their country about the year 1770'. He had obtained this information from the Kafirs themselves, although their accounts differed as to whether the two strangers had died in captivity or 'been murdered under the supposition that they were evil spirits'. Editor Pearse thought they could have been Catholic missionaries, the Jesuits having made some pioneering forays into the Himalayan lands in the eighteenth century. They could equally well have been survivors from a wave of freelance adventurers that had swept across

India in the second half of that century and to which Gardner is sometimes seen as a postscript.

But whoever they were and whatever their origin, one thing is certain: Gardner could not have concocted this particular section of his 'Rougemontic' narrative from the accounts of other European visitors for the simple reason that there had been no such accounts. Nor could he have borrowed the idea of a European presence in Kafiristan from reading the only fictional account of Kafiristan. This was in Kipling's *The Man Who Would Be King*, a short and powerful novel about two renegade troopers winning, and then losing, the confidence of the reclusive Kafirs. But the novella had not been published until 1888, some thirty years after Gardner had first put pen to paper on the subject of Kafiristan and some ten years after he had been laid in his grave. If anything, therefore, it must have been the other way round: not Gardner borrowing from Kipling but Kipling borrowing from Gardner.

The Kipling story proved immensely popular. Frequently republished (and in the 1970s filmed by John Huston with Sean Connery and Michael Caine in the leading roles), it fed the fantasies of an age that hankered after proto-imperial romance and relished the idea of a white-skinned individual acquiring personal ascendancy and impromptu rule over some obscure Shangri-la.

Typical of such adventurers was James Brooke, who, far away in Borneo, had realised this dream as the 'White Rajah' of Sarawak in the 1840s; so too, very briefly, had the American Dr Josiah Harlan when in 1839 he claimed to have accepted the loyalty of the Hazara people of central Afghanistan as their 'Prince of Ghor'. In similar fashion, George Thomas, a genial Irish swashbuckler who was otherwise known as 'the Tipperaray Rajah', had carved out a kingdom for himself in what is now the Indian state of Haryana.

Any of these might have provided Kipling with the inspiration for *The Man Who Would Be King*. William Watts MacNair, a cricket-loving surveyor who blackened his face with walnut juice and assumed the part of a Muslim doctor, had actually entered Kafiristan in 1883 and could well have intrigued the *Civil and Military Gazette*'s roving reporter. But MacNair, though possibly the Masonic acquaintance credited with alerting Kipling to the existence of the Kafirs in the first place, says nothing of previous European visitors. Only Gardner provides the three essential ingredients of the Kipling novel—the location (Kafiristan), the legend (of the Kafirs having once admitted white strangers) and the detail (of these strangers being two Europeans of whom the Kafirs were somewhat in awe).

Admittedly, this corroborative trail is a tortuous one. It is ever so with the elusive Alexander Gardner. But in this case the evidence was to hand at the time of Helena's visit. She must have known of the Kipling story and, if she bothered to explore its origins, she might have been reassured about the veracity of one of the most controversial sections of her father's odyssey.

Back in Lahore, while Helena's attempt to rehabilitate the colonel's reputation was getting nowhere, the quest to locate his fortune was faring only marginally better. The Agra Bank did have a branch in Lahore. The bank had survived a mid-century bankruptcy. Better still, it still held a copy of the colonel's will, and this clearly acknowledged Helena as his heir. But that was all. The bank's staff could shed light neither on what the colonel's estate comprised nor where it might be. There was no deposit account waiting to be emptied, no safe crammed with glittering bounty. The treasure hunt was far from over. What Helena needed was to find someone with first-hand knowledge of her father's affairs at the time of his death. That meant following his trail from its controversial high-point in the Punjab to its unsteady conclusion in Kashmir. Having drawn a blank in Lahore, Helena and friends headed for the hills.

From the Grand Trunk Road the only cart-road through the mountains took them past the now hill station of Murree. Though Helena's convent had been joined by other schools and sanatariums, memories of her homesick adolescence there may well have come flooding back. If so, they were soon superseded by earlier and perhaps happier memories when she finally reached Srinagar. The city wishfully known as 'the Venice of the East' had changed little. Rickety bridges cantilevering out from a stack of braced timbers still spanned the meanderings of the Jhelum River. Women dressed in their tent-like *pheron*s bashed the city's laundry on any rock that protruded from the river's muddy banks while buzzard-like kites mewed high above the city's rubbish.

Locating Helena's former home in the maze of narrow alleys was neither easy nor, it seems, very rewarding. The bungalow in which an earlier visitor had reportedly sighted the colonel proved to be not his home but one of several lodges built by the maharaja for visiting Europeans. The colonel's own establishment seems never to have been visited by anyone. If the house still stood, it was impossible to identify and his ménage no longer occupied it. Bibi Chirang had passed away and his other retainers had either followed suit or dispersed.

According to Helena's informants, a much better bet would be Jammu. Because Srinagar was snow-bound for four months of the year, Jammu, the town on the south side of the mountains from which Maharaja Gulab Singh and his successors had originally hailed, still served the state as a winter capital. Assuming Helena's visit was made in April/May, the maharaja and his durbar may still have been in Jammu at the time. Gardner himself had spent as many months there as in Srinagar. In fact he had died there. Anyone familiar with his affairs would be in Jammu rather than Srinagar.

This is not to say that Helena and her companions beat a speedy re-treat from the famous 'vale of Kashmir'. If Srinagar itself had changed little in the three decades since the colonel's death, its environs had been significantly embellished. The several gardens and pavilions laid out around the lakes by visiting Mughal emperors in the seventeenth century had been reclaimed and replanted. Trout from Scotland were being introduced into the Jhelum's side streams; and sporting Europeans were no longer segregated in the riverside lodges erected by the state specifically for them. Instead they lived in regatta style. Back in Gardner's day, the valley's rough-hewn river transports had occasionally been hired out to sportsmen, but as of the 1880s these craft had undergone a transformation. Moored among the willows that fringed the lakes, they were now well-appointed houseboats with sun decks, awnings and projecting verandahs. The patterns of their chintz-covered upholstery competed with elaborate parquetry ceilings and heavily carved walnut furniture. Bevvies of bearers, bare-footed and light-fingered, spread the occasional tables with lace doillies and spread the doilies with floral china. Grateful for a break in such civilised surroundings, the visitors from Africa surely tarried. Perhaps Christiaan Botha tried his hand at fly-fishing; for certain Helena and her friends bought shawls. The Gardner quest could wait. It was hard not to fall in love with Kashmir.

Jammu promised only heat and dust. But as the snows melted and the direct route back to the plains via the Bannihal Pass reopened for pedestrian traffic, Helena and her fiancée dragged themselves away and climbed back over the mountains. Heavy-hearted, they still hoped for some reward; and, somewhat unexpectedly, Jammu was about to provide it. As the air warmed, so finally did the trail.

For in Jammu she found greybeards in the maharaja's employ who remembered her father. Not a few did so with genuine affection. They pointed out his old house; like the incumbent maharaja, who had been a boy at the time, they reminisced about his dexterity with the scissor-like clamp he needed for eating; and they recalled a table in his residence strewn with an assortment of head-cloths, baggy turbans, bear-skin berets, embroidered skull caps and astrakhan head-dresses. These were the colonel's props 'which he would don when telling of his adventures in this or that Central Asian state in which he had served'. According to George MacMunn, the British Inspecting Officer of the Kashmir Imperial Service Artillery (Mountain) at the time of Helena's visit:

> His memory was held in high esteem in Jammoo. There were magnificent gun-parks of fine brass guns that he had cast for the Kashmir Durbar [and] there were many stories current about him.

MacMunn, like Kipling, was too young to have met Gardner. He had been in his thirties when posted to Jammu in 1894 and it was not until 1951, nearly six decades later, that he would be persuaded to dredge up his recollections of what contemporaries had thought of the colonel. By then MacMunn was in his late eighties, twice

knighted and much respected as a lieutenant-general. He would
die the following year. What was in effect his swansong had been
prompted by another debunking of the 'utterly infamous' Colonel
Gardner and his 'worthless' *Memoirs* in a 1951 issue of the *Journal of the
Royal Artillery*. On behalf of all gunners, MacMunn took exception.
This was not how the colonel's comrades-in-arms had remembered
him. Several of MacMunn's informants back in the 1890s had served
under Gardner. Indeed they still performed their gun-drill on the
French words of command Gardner had taught them, presumably
in a hang-over from his days among the ex-Napoleonic officers in
the Sikh army. 'No doubt his adventures as related by himself were
highly coloured at times,' ventured MacMunn, but 'Gordana Sahib'
was 'an interesting relic' and his life 'of great interest'. 'I fancy Colonel
Pearse's story [ie the *Memoirs*] is a fairly correct one,' he concluded.

All of which reminded Macmunn of something else. Back in
1898, a group of strangers had presented themselves at his Jammu
quarters. They were enquiring about Gardner. He could not recall
the woman's name and he was wrong about her husband's nationality,
but unquestionably the visit he remembered was that of Helena.

> While I was at Jammoo a daughter by a Kashmiri mother came and I
> met her. She had, I think, a French husband and had come on a quest
> regarding some inheritance, and was looking for his old bearer.

Sadly MacMunn did not record whether they found this bearer nor
whether they got any further with their quest—probably not if they
then headed off for Bombay and Durban.

But to regain the Grand Trunk Road or the nearest railhead, the
travellers had first to pass through Sialkot, and there they surely visited
the cemetery of the Church of the Holy Trinity. In the shadow cast
by a lofty steeple, this was where the colonel's odyssey had ended.
His death had occurred in Jammu but it had been registered, and his
mortal remains had been laid to rest, at what was then the nearest
place of Christian worship. Following a lifetime of often puzzling
upheavals, this last removal from Jammu to Sialkot was logical enough.
The only thing that was strange about it was the fact that the colonel

had been deemed a candidate for Christian burial.

Quite apart from blemishes of conduct and character that might well have disqualified him from a plot in any cemetery, it was not obvious that Gardner was a Christian, nor that he had ever regarded religious adherence as other than a convenience. He claimed to have been brought up a Catholic but for most of his life he had passed himself off as a Muslim. There is no record of his attending any church service in Kashmir, and of Christian missionaries he had a particular dislike. In 1866, Dr William Jackson Elmslie, a medical missionary in Srinagar, had been called to vaccinate the baby Helena. This the reverend-doctor had done, and he would happily have administered baptism while he was about it. But the father objected. Jackson Elmslie was told that, while the Kashmiris appreciated his medical work, 'they dislike the missionary element'. Three years later, in one of his rambling and typically wordy attacks on various aspects of British policy, Gardner had spelled out the reasons. With official blessing, 'Padree Missioners' were, he claimed in flamboyant language, antagonising the Indian people.

> [They hover] Dick Turpin-like about dark by-ways and corners, where usually they stop the poor unwary traveller, and drawing forth their pocket pistol Bible from their belts, present it and cry 'halt, stand and deliver, your life or your religion'.

It would be better, he went on, if they came armed with some useful craft or agricultural skill to impart to the natives. 'On starving or hungry stomachs... dry tracts and Bibbles [sic] are not always the things that sit best.'

Whether in 1898 the colonel's headstone was still identifiable in the cemetery of the Church of the Holy Trinity is uncertain, but there was definitely an entry of his death in the Sialkot parish registry. It was still there when Grey and Garrett did their sleuthing in the 1920s and, as with all the other glimpses of the colonel, it raised a major problem. In the register someone had altered his stated age at the time of his death. Originally entered as '98 years' (giving a birth date of 1779), this had been struck out and '76' substituted (giving a birth date of 1801). There was no indication of when the alteration had been made, nor whose were the initials that followed it, nor on what authority it had been changed. Why anyone would want to diminish the colonel's lifespan by twenty-two years is as much a mystery as who in India could possibly have testified to his age other than Colonel Gardner himself.

Like everything else connected with Helena's Indian visit, inspection of the registry merely deepened the mystery. It was now unclear when, let alone where, Alexander Haughton Campbell Gardner's extraordinary career had begun. Indeed, some wondered whether he really was Alexander Haughton Campbell Gardner. In a bid to cover their tracks and evade arrest as British deserters, other Europeans in the service of native princes were known to have assumed exotic alibis. Gardner's identity might be equally suspect. On his own admission the colonel had been 'long separated from the world'. The questions now to be answered were: how long, why separated, and from whose world?

Helena and her fiancée returned to Africa none the wiser and none the richer. They were married before the year was out and had a daughter in 1901. But in respect of her father's missing millions Helena would not let the matter rest; such would be her needs that she would eventually make a second bid to realise her Indian patrimony. Meanwhile there was every chance that the colonel's reputation would be imminently vindicated. News had arrived from William Blackwood and Sons of Edinburgh: Major Pearse's edition of the colonel's *Memoirs* was rolling off the presses. The public would at last have a chance to marvel at the exploits and judge the standing of travel's greatest enigma.

2

At Large in Central Asia
1819–26

We left Herat at daybreak, and as the melting of the snow might soon
be confidently expected, the *kafila* took a direct, but little-frequented,
road over the snowy ranges of the Western Hindu Kush. We were, in
all about 100 persons, bound for various parts of Turkestan.

So begins the personal narrative of *Soldier and Traveller*, this being
Pearse's rendering of Gardner's *Memoirs* as released by William
Blackwood and Sons soon after Helena's visit to Kashmir in 1898.
The year in which the *kafila* (caravan) departed from Herat was 1819,
the month January and the narrator Gardner himself. After a long
and thoroughly improbable account of the soldier/traveller's origins
and early career, editor Pearse was finally allowing the colonel to tell
his story in his own words.

Most of us were provided with rough-coated ponies or mules [he
continued]. The region through which we now commenced to travel
was inhabited by the Hazaras, whom we found to be a truly hospitable
race. ... [They] kept us regularly supplied with fresh bread and milk,
and made us welcome to their villages for as long as we liked to stay.

I observed, and it was worth observing, that the farther we journeyed

from the confines of civilisation the more marked and scrupulous was
the punctiliousness with which our wants were met.

Credit where credit was due; however modest the hospitality, Gardner
would always be punctilious in acknowledging it.

Editor Pearse would have preferred fewer compliments and a bit
more in the way of context. In deducing how Gardner had fetched
up in Herat, a dusty city of some antiquity near the Perso-Afghan
border, Major Pearse had already found his geographical knowledge
severely tested. But the Hazaras, the Shi-ite people of central Afghanistan, were comparatively well known and Herat itself was at least on
the map. Though unobliging to travellers, it was evidently a place of
some refinement compared to what lay ahead.

Turkestan, the kafila's destination, was a different matter. Divided
into numerous emirates, khanates and lesser fiefdoms, themselves the
residue of earlier Mongol and Turk incursions, the deserts of Turkestan covered most of Inner Asia and were not for the faint-hearted.
Here life was hard and comforts few. Summer temperatures topped
35 degrees C; winter temperatures bottomed out at minus 35. Water
came mostly from wells and from the seasonal spates of rivers, notably
the Syr (Jaxartes) and Amu (Oxus). Cultivation was the exception
rather than the rule; it was restricted to ribbons of riverine arable and
the terraced plots tucked into upland valleys on the deserts' periphery.

Yet, thanks to the passage of trade, fine brick-built cities of wealth
and distinction thrust their onion domes and minarets above the
hazy horizon. Their names echoed down through the ages—Kashgar,
Bukhara, Samarkand, Khiva. Straddling the trails known collectively
as the Silk Road, Turkestan had grown rich on the east-west transfer
of textiles and teas, ceramics, spices and bloodstock. But the Silk
Road, once the most lucrative exchange in the world, was now in
decline. Maritime sailings were siphoning off the luxury trade, while
emerging empires controlled from Calcutta and St Petersberg were
eyeing up their inland options. Central Asia's khanates, though far
from oblivious, were fair game. Festering with intrigue and bickering
among themselves, their rulers—mostly bearded bigots and paranoid
tyrants—belied the very idea of progress and enjoyed a reputation

for extreme xenophobia. As a result, few European travellers even considered going there. To English-reading audiences in the early nineteenth century, the best known account of the region was still that of the merchant-adventurer Anthony Jenkinson, who had reached Khiva and Bukhara back in the mid-sixteenth century.

Jenkinson, with a caravan of a thousand camels, had been well armed and amply accredited. He was still lucky to have got away alive. For anyone else with a fair-skin and a Christian conscience Turkestan was reckoned a death sentence. 'There is probably no part of the world, not excepting the interior of Africa, which is so dangerous and inaccessible to the European traveller as Afghanistan and the countries of Central Asia,' declared one contemporary authority. William Moorcroft and George Trebeck, Englishmen ostensibly in search of the region's renowned horses, set off from India for Turkestan at almost exactly the same time as Gardner. They would be gone five years and would never be seen again. Nor would Colonel Stoddart and Captain Connolly twenty years later, both of whom suffered torture and death in Bukhara.

Alexander Gardner was well aware of the risks. But, according to Pearse, he was already 34 years old and had grown as cavalier about the dangers he was courting as he was about the itineraries he was following. He 'was about to enter on a career of apparently aimless wandering,' says Pearse, 'which he pursued until his arrival in the Panjab in August 1831, a period of twelve years'. Occasionally he settled down for a few months, never for long. '[S]oon the force of circumstances, or a roving and lawless disposition, compelled him to move on'.

This combination of coercion and mischief-making was, by any standards, an unsatisfactory explanation for the odysseys that followed. Strangers venturing into Tukestan invariably had an agenda. It was what made them so vulnerable. Moorcroft, Burnes, Stoddart and Connolly might masquerade as casual travellers but they were actually acting as emissaries, spies or political trouble-makers. They enjoyed the backing of the British government in India; they made notes and took measurements; they asked a lot of questions; and they often unconsciously offended Islamic sensibilities. Gardner, on the other hand, asked very few questions and appears to have happily conformed to Islamic practice whenever required; he may even have already undergone the formalities of conversion. Nor does he mention a compass or any device for measuring distances; often he himself seems mystified as to his whereabouts. And his notes, when he took them, never outgrew the amulet in which he stuffed them.

Bearded, turbanned, unburdened by the presumption of other travellers and ignorant of exploration as a science, he perhaps stood a better chance of passing unnoticed than most. What rival travellers might have considered a disguise became his normal attire; and what might have been taken for an alias became his identity.

> I have not yet mentioned that my own travelling name was Arb Shah. I passed as a native of Arabia, and met very few in my travels who could speak Arabic. I explained any deficiency of knowledge of my native language [ie Arabic] by telling my interlocutor that I came from the opposite corner of Arabia to that with which he was acquainted, having previously taken care to worm this information out of him.

This none-too-ingenious ruse may have spared him from being instantly unmasked as an impostor. It would, though, be no safeguard against the still commoner fate of being sold into slavery.

Sixteen days' march took the 100-strong caravan from Herat through the western outliers of the Hindu Kush and into the desert. Here, for no apparent reason, Gardner and 'a few companions' left the security of the caravan and struck north. They headed for the Turkoman oasis of Merv (Mary, in Turkmenistan) and were at first reassured by more of that punctilious hospitality. A people Gardner calls the Khalzai, whose 'very comely women' were the most sought after in Afghanistan, passed them on to another hospitable tribe. These were the Therbah, a 'half-savage' people who 'worship the sun and moon, fire and water and resemble in some respects the scattered remnants of the Guebers [or Zoroastrians] of Persia'. With the Therbah chief, Gardner and his companions stayed a month while conducting what he calls, 'expeditions of exploration'. Considering his men were mounted and armed to the teeth, and given that Merv, their desert destination, was a notorious hang-out for slave traders and freebooters, it is reasonable to infer that these 'expeditions of exploration' were in fact raids. Gardner's reticence bears this out. He dismisses them as unworthy of record in the light of 'the far more exciting scenes through which I was destined to pass'.

The first such excitement found the tables turned, with Gardner himself in danger of being classed as booty. A gang of Turki-speaking travellers had attached themselves to the Therbah encampment and, under cover of darkness, secretly opened negotiations for purchasing him as a slave. At six-foot tall and of athletic build, Gardner was evidently rated a prize specimen, fit to grace the bodyguard of any tyrant. The bidding rose to 5 *tillah*s of gold. But the Therbah chief had no intention of betraying his guest and rejected the offer, whereupon 'words grew high and blows were exchanged'. In the scuffle, the slavers came off worse. Disarmed and bound, they were themselves now to be sold into slavery. Then, rather unexpectedly, 'humanity prevailed,' says Gardner. Instead of being enslaved, they were simply robbed of all they possessed.

Merv was now out of the question; in all probability it was the slavers' destination and sanctuary. Turning back on their tracks, therefore, Gardner and his men rode east and south under the protection of a different chief. They headed for Andkhui, the place where, four years later, the irrepressible William Moorcroft would end his days, a victim either of fever or the knife. Here they joined another caravan. It was heading north again, this time for the important khanate of Khiva (or Khwaresm) in what is now western Uzbekistan.

Gardner attached himself to the caravan's leading merchant. He had little choice. By this stage he admits to being penniless and had no prospect of obtaining funds in Khiva. He went along simply because in merchant Urd Khan he had found a true friend and ally. The ability to endear himself to all but the most vicious of adversaries would often serve the colonel well. Companions staunchly stood by him; complete strangers reciprocated his trust. He in turn acknowledged their help with a frankness rare among travellers—and never better demonstrated than during the vicissitudes of the long desert crossing to Khiva.

The trouble began almost as soon as they set off. According to Gardner, 'I fell dangerously ill with a brain-fever'. Through two days he lay unconscious and for weeks thereafter he was too weak to ride. Urd Khan rose to the occasion like a father. He had a bed made up for the invalid in one of the panniers of his private camel-train and there, counter-balanced by Urd Khan's womenfolk on the other side of the shaggy beast, Gardner was borne swaying across the wilderness that was the Karakum Desert. On his own admission he was no more than a semi-conscious passenger when the first heroics were called for.

> During my illness we were one day alarmed by twenty horsemen gal-
> loping up. Urd Khan, as the selected chief of the caravan, was deputed
> to deal with them. His tactics were erroneous. Thinking they were but
> a small party, and calculating on our strength, he told them to be off as
> 'dogs'. Off they went and halted suddenly a mile in front, and seemed
> in a moment to melt away out of sight. We marched on for a few miles
> when suddenly a band of some 400 marauding Turkoman horsemen
> appeared. Urd Khan now changed his tone [sic]. As for me, I was dead
> sick and little cared what became of me.

The Turkoman horsemen proved to be professional robbers rather than slave traders. The lives and freedom of their victims were therefore spared and the caravan was allowed to proceed, but only after being pillaged. Urd Khan had to part with a camel and two panniers full of merchandise, Gardner was relieved of his pony. The others suffered even greater losses. Finally, by way of a head start, they were given till noon the next day to make themselves scarce. They made for the Oxus River (Amu Darya), but had barely crossed it before another body of horse swooped in for the kill. Happily the newcomers were frustrated by the shortage of river boats. With the threats and curses of their pursuers renting the desert air, the caravan limped on towards Khiva. Gardner likened their plight to that of a wounded camel shadowed by circling vultures.

Two marches short of their destination it was dissent within their own ranks that nearly proved his undoing. A Jewish merchant in the caravan complained that Urd Khan had been complicit with the robbers. On the grounds that his own property had been unfairly depleted, this man took his complaint to the Khan of Khiva and, for good measure, added the news that Urd Khan was protecting a white man, in fact a Russian spy. The stern-faced Khan ordered an enquiry; the accused, of course, was Gardner.

Russians of any sort were not welcome in Khiva. The Khanate straddled the corridor through which Tsarist influence and Christian doctrines were being insinuated into Muslim Central Asia. Moreover Khivan justice was not something to be trifled with. In 1863, the Hungarian traveller Arminius Vámbéry here witnessed its usual outcome by attending a public execution.

> [The condemned] looked like lambs in the hands of their executioners [he would write]. While several were led to the gallows or the block, I saw how, at a sign from the executioner, eight aged men placed themselves down on their backs on the earth. They were then bound hand and foot, and the executioner gouged out their eyes in turn, kneeling to do so on the breast of each poor wretch; and after every operation he wiped his knife, dripping with blood, on the white beard of the hoary unfortunate.

Such cruelty, however revolting, struck Vámbéry as neither wanton nor unusual. Shariah law sanctioned the sentences, the Khan was applauded for his severity, and 'no day passes but someone is led away from an audience with the khan, hearing the fatal words pronounced which are his doom, *"Alib barin"* (Away with him)'.

For entering Khiva uninvited, Gardner faced a similar fate. To establish his true identity, three of the Khan's wiser and more widely travelled henchmen were despatched to examine him. Gardner himself was still convalescent. He remembered how Urd Khan 'hovered round my couch during this perilous interview and plied me with incessant gruels while magnifying my deplorable state'. The interrogators were unmoved. Illness could be feigned. The invalid would have to do better—and did so. Throwing caution to the winds, he amazed everyone by blurting out what was the first recorded confession of his real identity. Arb Shah, the Arab who spoke no recognisable

Arabic, was suddenly discarded; and instead Gardner came up with something even more improbable. 'I told them the truth—that I was an American.'

Even Urd Khan was taken by surprise. The inquisitors were simply suspicious.

> One of them, a very enlightened man, thought to pose me [ie trick me] by a conclusive and abstruse geographical question: 'Could I go by land from America to England?' I promptly answered, 'No!', at which, as much delighted by his own superior learning as at my reply, he declared that he was convinced.

For once Gardner had good reason to be grateful to America's founding fathers. 'Americans they consider 'Yaghistanis', or Independents,' he explained, since they too had resisted European rule. Anyone claiming American nationality deserved a fair hearing in Khiva.

But whether this bombshell about his nationality was indeed the truth or just a brilliant piece of improvisation is debateable. Editor Pearse never questioned the colonel's assertion. On the other hand most of his latter-day detractors would find ample evidence to discredit his claim to American citizenship. They dismissed it as a fabrication aimed at covering his tracks. Dredged up on the spur of the moment, it served him well enough in Khiva and, when occasion demanded, it would continue to do so. In the years to come a few childhood memories of American places and dates, plus an exotic family pedigree, would also emerge. But whether these substantiated his claim or merely embellished his fabrication was again contested. In sticking to his story he must have been aware that his credibility was at stake; yet so tantalisingly vague and improbable were the few details of his past which he did let slip that they could be read either way. It was as if the colonel had determined to remain as much an enigma to posterity as he was to contemporaries.

In Khiva, instead of a doom-laden 'Away with him' from the ruler, it was the dependable Urd Khan who whisked him away—to the safety of a friend's home in Khiva's twin city of Urgench. There Gardner continued his convalescence. 'During all this time I had no resources of my own and lived entirely on the munificent hospitality of my Eastern entertainer'. But Urd Khan was eventually called away and the combination of penury and poor health obliged Gardner to look elsewhere. He applied for assistance to someone he calls Monsieur Sturzky, a German who had accompanied him into Asia and who had also fetched up in Uzbekistan. Sturzky offered no encouragement. He too had fallen foul of the Khiva authorities. They had stripped him of everything and he was lucky not to have been murdered. Instead, he had been forcibly castrated. Now, also ill and impoverished, he wanted nothing more than to return to civilisation. Together, therefore, the two men scraped together a travel-chest and headed west. By way of the Aral Sea and the steppe, they reached the east coast of the Caspian, and there, says Gardner, 'I took ship to Astrakhan'.

The great port of Astrakhan stands at the north-western extremity of the Caspian beside the delta of the Volga River. It was a Russian city in Russian territory. Gardner already knew it—and Astrakhan knew Gardner. He was back within 'the confines of civilisation'. The first of his three barely credible forays into the rough and tumble of Turkestan was over.

As always, Gardner's *Memoirs* are desperately short on dates. Useful pointers—like the changing seasons, an occasional mention of Ramadan or the proper name of Khiva's ruling khan—are also omitted. After that snowy departure from Herat in early 1819, there is nothing to indicate how long he was on the loose in Turkestan or when he finally resurfaced in Astrakhan. Probably the escapade lasted no more than a year. He was certainly back in Astrakhan in 1820 and he apparently remained there for the next two years.

Unfinished family business detained him. According to Pearse, who tentatively reconstructed his earlier movements from the often inconsistent accounts left by Gardner himself, he had originally fetched up in Russia because the elder of his two brothers had made good there. This brother, the head of the family since the death of their father, was a senior engineer in the service of the Russian empire.

Gardner had duly tracked him down to Astrakhan and had there acted as his understudy until he had picked up sufficient knowledge of mineralogy to be promised employ on his own account.

Then in 1817 the brother had died after a fall from his horse. Part of his estate, which included that of the surviving brothers, had subsequently been frozen and the promise of employment withdrawn. It was this turn of events that had persuaded Gardner to take off into Turkestan in 1819; and it was the pressing need to realise his full share of the estate that had brought him back to Astrakhan in 1820.

The sum involved was considerable. Gardner claimed it was £6,000; and thanks to the fortuitous intervention of an influential cousin, he did manage to realise it. But he also managed to spend it. Some went on paying off his debts to Urd Khan, some on a mixture of wagers, unwise investments and easy living. By 1822 he was heartily sick of Russia and not much wealthier than when he had arrived there. It was time to move on. Indeed, Pearse supposed this was the turning point that would determine his future.

> He then became restless, and in the month of February [1823] again set out on his Asiatic travels. He could not, he says, rest in civilised countries and, being free from family ties, was persuaded that he would find happiness among wild races and in exploring unknown lands.

> Realising, therefore, the scant remains of his fortune, Gardner embarked for the last time on the Caspian Sea.

Again he headed for Turkestan. On landing on the eastern shore of the Caspian, his Russian servant was dismissed and his Russian furs discarded. He wanted to erase all evidence of his sojourn under Tsarist rule. Instead he adopted an Uzbek outfit described as a peaked fur cap, black sheepskin coat, baggy knee-length drawers, heavily bandaged calves and short black boots. By way of identity he resumed his old alias of Arb Shah; and by the time he regained the Aral Sea he had acquired a few companions. One of these was returning to Khojend (Khujand), a sizeable city in what is now Tajikistan. Gardner agreed to accompany him. Warned away from Khiva by word from Urd Khan, the two travellers took a much more easterly route by following the Jaxartes River (Syr Darya) through the Kizylkum Desert to somewhere in the vicinity of Tashkent, then striking south.

Along the way their numbers swelled. An Afghan lad whom Gardner had taken into his employ on the previous journey got wind of his return and was welcomed back with delight. Gardner always called him 'my faithful Therbah'; he was certainly faithful, and it was as guests of the fire-worshipping Therbah people that they had first met. More impressive was a man with three Bactrian camels in tow and an entourage of hardy Uzbek scouts. He claimed to be Polish and went by the name of Aga Beg. Gardner suspected that he was really an escaped convict from Siberia. They conversed together in French and it was supposedly on this Aga Beg's advice that the party steered well clear of anywhere of consequence. Aga Beg greatly feared detection—and so may Gardner if his movements were again tainted with plunder.

Approaching Khojend, they stuck with this preference for open country and gave a wide berth to the nearby town of Ura-tyube (Urateppe, Istaravshan). It was not wide enough. Night found them sandwiched between an encampment of marauding Kipchaks and the rapacious freebooters despatched from Ura-tyube to engage these Kipchaks. 'There was nothing for it but to make the best of things,' recalled Gardner. Since the Kipchaks looked the stronger party, Gardner favoured making common cause with them. But this time it was his own tactics that were 'erroneous'. 'From the date of this *rencontre* the whole destinies of myself and my party were changed and our horizons were dark with presages of imminent disaster.'

Whether or not they had already been acting outside the law, they now had little choice in the matter. In a vicious triangle of plunder, the Ura-tyube freebooters demanded twenty of their horses, 'five of which were mine,' adds Gardner, 'very fine animals'. He refused. Then it was the Kipchaks's turn. Having invited Gardner and his men to parley, the Kipchaks raided their camp in their absence and made off with not just their horses but Aga Beg's camels as well. Gardner demanded restitution—to no effect. Meanwhile the Ura-tyube men were still insisting he hand over the horses he no longer had. 'We ...

grew desperate. We swore on our drawn swords to recover our horses and property by stratagem or force, or die for it.'

> Aga Beg had two trusty men, as familiar as wild beasts with the intricate ravines about the place, and such ground was homelike to my faithful Therbah. We determined to make a midnight *daur* (raid), recover our horses, plunder as much as we could in reprisal, and escape by the ravines.

Three nights later, when the Kipchaks seemed lulled into a sense of security, they put the plan into effect. 'It was a daring deed,' says Gardner. Yet it worked. With twelve of the best horses and as much saleable booty as they could cram in their saddle-bags, they made off into the night.

> We knew that the pursuit would be close and furious, and the whole country would soon be up. We were at the mercy of Aga Beg's guides, but felt that we could rely on him and them. Our hope was to reach Samarkand, where he had property and a powerful connection.

Now outlaws, with all quarter out of the question, they took no chances. When, at dawn-break, three of the Ura-tyube horsemen overhauled them, the foreign fugitives were ordered to halt and surrender 'in the name of the government'. They refused; and when the Ura-tyube men 'threatened to fire', Gardner notes simply 'we slew them'. He claimed they did so 'in self-defence'; an impartial observer might have thought it 'in cold blood'.

The same treatment awaited some Turkoman riders who overtook them a few days later. One said he had been despatched from Samarkand to arrest a desperate band of robbers.

> We declared that we too were in pursuit of [the robbers]. We might easily have killed him, but agreed that by letting him pass on we might divert suspicion from ourselves.

With Samarkand clearly on the alert, another change of direction was called for. 'Wearily but in good heart,' they turned south. 'Food we obtained by levying contributions from everyone we could master,' says Gardner, adding the usual caveat, 'but we did not slaughter unless in self-defence.'

Two hundred miles ahead, safety of a sort beckoned on the other side of the Oxus. Anciently the river here formed the frontier between an unruly Turkestan and an even more unruly Afghanistan. They fixed on Hazrat Imam, a place of both sanctity and sanctuary on the opposite bank, then rode hard for it. But while hiding among rocks at the river's edge, they received intelligence that here too they were expected. 'Our party were proclaimed "dogs of Mervites" all over the country and no one would dare take us in.'

They crossed the river nevertheless. Now in a hopelessly divided Afghanistan, they had the choice of several warring jurisdictions. To 'Arb Shah', whether as an Arab or an American, it made little difference. But Aga Beg, the Pole, favoured the fortunes of Dost Mohamed Khan, the emir in Kabul who was currently asserting his authority over the east of the country. The plan seems to have been to throw themselves on the emir's mercy and offer him their services as mercenaries in return. First, though, they had to traverse the northern district of Kunduz, whose ruling *beg* was the same cut-throat Uzbek who would waylay William Moorcroft's party a year later. Wisely they avoided the beg and his minions but were again, says Gardner, 'compelled' to kill a party of three armed men.

Gardner is quite candid about these killings. Since no such murderous encounters are recorded during the first foray into Turkestan, they may be read as out of character. By now, though—it must have been late 1823—he was 'finding life under such circumstances a trifle too exciting', as the tongue-in-cheek Pearse puts it. His scruples, such as they were, were being eroded. In the free-for-all of Central Asia, survival was the sole imperative, and if that meant eliminating opponents, then so be it. Those they killed were invariably outnumbered and out-gunned. And the excuse of self-defence carried little conviction; indeed by insisting on it so often, he doth protest too much.

But why, one might ask, make mention of the killings at all? They could only discredit him. Anyone keen to blacken his character would pounce on them as proof of his villainy; and anyone merely doubtful about the reliability of his story would dismiss them as sensation-seeking embroidery. Either way, discretion in such matters would have been much the better part of candour.

Alternatively, perhaps he was just getting into the spirit of things. With a long life to follow, and a long narrative to unfold, he recognised the importance of engaging his audience. Obscure blood-lettings in Central Asia would help prepare the listener for the better-attested and more horrific carnage that awaited him in Lahore.

By then he would be an officer under orders and on the pay-roll of a powerful empire. But in the 1820s he was just an independent adventurer. The trickle of European military experts who were already heading for Lahore to take service with the Sikh Khalsa had learned their trade in the armies of Napoleon or of British India. Gardner had never yet, so far as is known, seen active service under any colours. Claiming close encounters in Turkestan, whether real or imagined, was meant to establish his credentials not just as an engaging raconteur but as a useful man to have on one's side.

Confusingly much the same could be said of another American called Gardner. This was William Linnaeus Gardner whose claimed exploits in the service of various Indian rulers in the 1790s had included leaping down a fifty-foot precipice, being tied to the muzzle of a loaded cannon and marrying an Indian princess. Eventually he was inducted into the British East India Company's army as colonel and commander of the irregular Gardner's Horse.

So far as is known William Linnaeus Gardner was unrelated, and probably unknown, to Alexander Gardner. But Alexander Gardner would certainly have been familiar with the exploits of other turn-of-the-century adventurers in India like James Skinner, who formed the even more illustrious Skinner's Horse, or the legendary George Thomas. Thomas too had laid claim to improbable feats of strength and strategy to secure his first command in another of India's private armies, that of the Begum Samru, the diminutive dancer who carved out a statelet north of Delhi and led her own troops in battle.

As per the wordy title of Thomas's biography, he, 'by extraordinary talents and enterprize, rose, from an obscure situation to the rank of a general, in the service of the native powers in the north west of India'. Indeed it was in the face of the rising Sikh power that 'the Tipperaray Rajah' had projected his own conquest of the Punjab. Had he succeeded—and he nearly did—there would have been no Sikh empire for Alexander Gardner to set his sights on.

In Gardner's case, love of adventure for adventure's sake never obscured his long-term ambition of lucrative employment in a regular army. It was certainly behind the plan to join Dost Mohamed Khan of Kabul after the flight from Turkestan in 1823, although it would be another six years before it could be put into effect. Events, as so often in Gardner's career, derailed intentions. For no sooner had his fugitive party crossed the Hindu Kush en route to Kabul than they were again waylaid.

> At last we came upon an outpost of the Kohistan region of the Kabul country, and were stopped by a mounted guard. We demanded the name of the ruler. The guard declared it to be Amir Habib-ullah Khan of Kabul, Kashmir and Peshawar. We desired to be brought before him. The guard refused. We persisted, and seeing a threatening of an attack, disarmed two of them [ie of the guard], but the third escaped and flew for aid. The crisis was now approaching.

What made it a crisis was that they had blundered into the wrong camp. Instead of the powerful Dost Mohamed, they had announced their presence to his nephew, a young man whom the Dost had just ejected from the throne and whom he was now hounding across the hill country north of Kabul. Gardner and his men, in rough-handling three of this young pretender's troopers, had invited trouble; and sure enough, within an hour, says Gardner, they heard 'the trampling and rushing sound of distant cavalry'.

> We could see them coming on like a desert storm for a mile and I had barely time to order my followers to mount and to place myself at their head when the cavalcade was upon us. I received them with a respectful

military salute…. By this time we were completely surrounded by the chief's party and I knew that we were in their power and that nothing but audacity and tact could save us.

As at Khiva in 1819, the game was up. It was time to put their cards on the table. Ordering his men to be silent on pain of death, Gardner confronted their captor and 'explained myself frankly'. He admitted that he was a stranger, one who hailed from the New World ('Habib-ullah had never heard of it') and a Christian to boot. Presumably he also explained how he came to be in Afghanistan and why he had assaulted the guards. Presumably, too, he spoke in halting Persian, that being the preferred lingua franca in this part of Asia and not a language that Gardner spoke with facility. All this took a while, during which Habib-ulla's rage subsided. Indeed he visibly mellowed. He promised that the secret of Gardner's birth would be respected and, if anything, he seemed amused by the fracas at the outpost. The colonel's uncanny ability to charm a potential adversary had again saved the day. Instead of a gaoler they had found a friend.

> The affair ended by the generous chief sending then and there a distance of three miles for a sumptuous repast and Kabul vintages wherewith to recruit our famished frames. He then took us with him to his fort, where he recounted to me all his history, his hopes and his sufferings.

As the first historically attested figure to feature in Gardner's *Memoirs*, Habib-ulla Khan and his story merit some attention. Possibly aware of this, Gardner listened patiently to the prince's tale of woe and found himself deeply moved by the plight of this 'brave and persecuted man'. Liberal consumption of the Kabul vintages contributed to the occasion and by the time Habib-ulla had finished, Gardner was persuaded that he could do no better than offer to him the services he had intended to offer Dost Mohamed. A deal was quickly struck. Though Aga Beg, the mysterious Pole, preferred to head back north, Gardner was taken on as the commander of 180 of Habib-ulla's picked horse. They were 'to be employed in forays into the enemy's country and in levying contributions on all caravans, especially seizing all property that was intended for Dost Mohamed Khan'.

In this congenial task Gardner would be at Habib-ulla's side for the next two and half years. He got to know him well and had no hesitation in proclaiming him the noblest of princes. Generous to a fault, Habib-ulla proved unsurpassed in action, a stranger to dissimulation, and 'as attractive, and his face as handsome, as his stature was gigantic'. All of which is in striking contrast to received opinion and flatly contradicts every other known mention of ex-Emir Habib-ulla Khan. In short, Gardner's paragon was everyone else's monster. *Ergo*, Gardner must have been hopelessly duped; either that or he was as much a monster as his employer; or he had made the whole thing up.

Stern critics like Grey and Garrett of the Punjab Public Records Office were confident it was the last. Describing Habib-ulla as 'a sordid, bloody-minded, cowardly and drunken ruler' who alienated even his followers, they could only assume that Gardner had never met him. For good measure they cited a French history of Afghanistan by Générale J. P. Ferrier to the effect that eventually the vanquished Habib-ulla 'by way of consolation, plunged into every kind of debauch, and continued to reside at Kabul, where he still lives in a miserable plight, given up to the excesses of the most filthy kind.' But Ferrier, who is better known for his own book of 'wanderings' in the region, was writing twenty years after the event. He never reached Kabul and he certainly never met Habib-ulla. He relied on hearsay, indeed on precisely the calumnies put about by Dost Mohamed Khan against which Gardner had warned.

Gardner was not blind to Habib-ulla's shortcomings. The young chief could be vain and intransigent; moreover the 'liberal opinions and jovial habits' that Gardner found so attractive in him were anathema to most devout Afghans. But the wily Dost Mohamed Khan had wilfully exaggerated these traits to portray him as a veritable Satan. By himself affecting 'great religious austerity' and by promising the zealous mullahs large tracts of Habib-ulla's Kohistan territory, the Dost had given the struggle against his nephew the character of a holy war. In this context Habib-ulla's every move was intentionally misconstrued. He was famously accused, for instance, of killing two of his sisters. He did not deny it, and to his string of crimes—apostasy, drug-addiction, unnatural sexual practices and of course alcohol—the Dost added that of parricide. But, as Gardner understood the matter, the dreadful deed had been performed at the insistence of the two sisters. Disgraced by the forceful attentions of the Dost himself, they had demanded Habib-ulla kill them. They had also entrusted him with the task in which he was now engaged, that of wreaking revenge. Such a scenario was by no means unique in Afghanistan's blood-stained annals and was in fact about to be repeated.

Under his new colours, Gardner led what he called 'a life in the saddle, one of active warfare and continual forays ... for the good cause of right against wrong'. Caravans were raided, skirmishes fought, battles generally avoided. Habib-ulla based himself on the fort of Parwan near Charikar. Some 50 miles north of Kabul, it commanded the main route to the capital from the Oxus plus that from Bamiyan and the west.

One day, about six months into this assignment and so presumably in 1824, word reached Habib-ulla that one of Dost Mohamed's wives would be returning via Bamiyan from a pilgrimage to Hazrat Imam. She had gone there to seek the blessings necessary to conceive a child and it was said that she was returning under heavy guard because she had been entrusted with a consignment of gold.

The temptation was too great to resist. On the Ghorband Pass, the cavalcade was ambushed. 'We attacked them in front and rear, and they were largely outnumbered.'

> Eventually we cut off the camels laden with treasure and those on which the lady and her attendants were carried, and Habib-ulla committed the entire prize to my care, while he covered our retreat.

A running fight ensued in the course of this retreat but Gardner played no part in it. Instead he rode alongside the camel within one of whose panniers the 'princess' reposed. It was, however, the camel's other pannier that held his attention. In it he had glimpsed, he says, 'the beautiful face of a young girl who accompanied the princess'. He fell in step and rode as close as he dared.

The emotional needs of a single man were ill-served by free-booting in Central Asia. Gardner, though a connoisseur of the local beauties, had so far avoided any dalliance. Not until his life became more settled in the Punjab and then Kashmir would women play a part in his story. But there was always room for an exception.

> On the following morning Habib-ulla Khan richly rewarded all his followers, for he was generous to a fault; but I refused my share of the gold and begged for this girl to be given to me in marriage as the only reward I desired. She was of royal birth on the mother's side, being the daughter (as was at once discovered) of one of Habib-ulla Khan's nearest relatives. He, however, freely and willingly gave her to me, and established me as commandant of a fort near his own abode. There I was very happy for about two years, in the course of which time my wife made me the father of a noble boy.

Reading this confession, either in the original or in the first proofs of Pearse's edition of the *Memoirs*, Helena Gardner must have experienced some unease. Was it possible that this girl with the beautiful face had a prior claim to her father's estate? Could this explain the mystery of the estate's whereabouts? And did Helena herself still perhaps have a half-Afghan step-brother living at large in the Kohistan passes? The possibilities were many, none of them reassuring.

But she needn't have worried. Gardner would never reveal the name of his first wife or that of their child. In fact it was as if he could hardly bear to mention them at all. 'I must hurry over this part of my history,' he says.

While blissful enough in their hill-top redoubt, the newly-weds knew little in the way of peace. By 1826 the fortunes of war had turned against Habib-ullla and 'the struggle was nearly over'. His several thousand men had dwindled to a few hundred, they were surrounded on three sides, and every engagement was bloodier and more desperate than the last.

> Well do I remember the occasion of the Dost's last attack. Snow was still lying on the ground in large and deep patches. My troop had been reduced in the previous day's fight from ninety men to thirty-nine.

The enemy had been most pertinacious and ... I felt that we were at our last gasp when an express message reached me from Parwan, which Habib-ulla was defending in person. My heart beat with sad forebodings too awfully to be realised.

The message summoned him to a rendezvous where he learned that Habib-ulla had been defeated and his fort captured. The twelve survivors were now fighting a rear-guard action. Gardner was needed. Though he had just received the sword slash to the throat that would trouble him for the rest of his days, he hastened to join them. 'Cutting my way through the enemy,' he found Habib-ulla with a badly wounded arm and himself now 'received a ball in my knee'. Worse was to follow.

Habib-ulla, on seeing me, drew me aside, and, with a stony countenance in which all outward sign of emotion seemed to have been frozen down, told me that all was over with my unfortunate wife and little baby.

The Dost's men, from their victory at Parwan, had proceeded to his own 'castello'. It too had then fallen and all within had been put to sword. It was unlikely there were any survivors, yet he went to see for himself.

The silence was oppressive when I rode through the gateway of the fort, and my men instinctively fell back, when an old mullah (who had remained faithful to our party) came out to meet me with his left hand and arm bound up. His fingers had been cut off and his arm nearly severed at the wrist by savage blows from a scimitar while striving to protect my little child.... The sole survivor, the aged mullah, at first stood gazing at me in a sort of wild abstraction, and then recounted the tale of the massacre of all I loved.

The garrison had given a good account of themselves. Indeed the fort had been nearly saved when Habib-ulla had come to the rescue. But when he and his men had then been driven off, the assailants had shown no mercy. They entered the fort and 'put all in it to the sword'. The mullah alone had been spared, since killing a cleric was inconsistent with the Dost's pretended orthodoxy. But the child he had attempted to save had been cut to pieces.

> There he lay by the side of his mother. I had left them all thoughtless and happy but five days before. The bodies had been decently covered up ... but the hand of the hapless young mother could be seen, and clenched in it the reeking *katar* [dagger] with which she had stabbed herself to the heart after handing over the child to the mullah for protection...

> I sank on my knees and involuntarily offered up a prayer for vengeance to the Most High God. Seeing my attitude, the mullah, in a low solemn tone, breathed the Muhammadan prayers proper for the presence of the dead.... [Then] rising I forced myself and him away from the room, gave him all the money I had for the interment of the dead, and with fevered brain rode away forever from my once happy mountain home.

In Gardner's rambling and often challenging narrative, this passage stands out as a *tour de force*. Editor-Major Pearse, in a discreet footnote, offered some information gleaned from one of those to whom Gardner had originally dictated his story: 'to the end of his long life Colonel Gardner was unable to tell without tears the sad story of his Afghan wife and child'.

Yet Messrs Grey and Garrett would be unmoved. They dismissed 'the pathetic story of the melancholy deaths of his wife and son' as simply 'a figment of the imagination'. As with the character assigned to Habib-ulla Khan, the narrator had let his fancy run away with him, although they offered no more by way of authoritative contradiction than the presumption that a garrulous scoundrel was incapable of genuine sentiment. If he wept at all, it was not over his loss of a family but over the delusional effect of his inventive powers.

Nor was Gardner's the only family to be consigned to oblivion by the rout. Habib-ulla had earlier sworn that none of his own womenfolk would suffer disgrace at the hand of Dost Mohamed Khan like his sisters. He was now as good as his word. Before himself surrendering he stabbed to death an unknown number of wives and female slaves. Gardner simply mentions that Habib-ulla's 'dreadful intention in regard to his family' was fulfilled; Pearse supposes that his mind had become 'unhinged from his misfortunes'. Either way, Habib-ulla's defiance was over—and so was Gardner's first Afghan interlude.

> The days which immediately followed the departure of Habib-ulla Khan seem a wild and sickening dream. I was wounded in the neck and the leg, and my companions were all more or less disabled. Our party numbered eight souls. The greatest danger attended any appearance on our part on the northern plains. There was nothing before us but to plunder to support life.

Crippled and starving, they headed north-east into the high Hindu Kush.

A worse send-off could scarcely have been contrived for what would turn out to be much the longest and most ambitious of all Gardner's journeys into the unknown. His reputation as an explorer would largely rest on it. But in what was less an escapade than an escape, he advanced with an eye to what was happening behind and little thought for what lay ahead or whether he was breaking new ground. The resultant narrative is perhaps his least credible. It is also his most erratically documented.

3

To the Roof of the World
1826–28

A major problem in assessing the fidelity or otherwise of Gardner's *Memoirs* is that most of the notes and transcripts on which they were based are no longer available. Passed to editor Pearse by Helena in 1894, this material was presumably returned to Helena at the time of publication but is then heard of no more. All subsequent attempts to trace it have failed—and should any reader know of its whereabouts, this author would be keen to hear from them.

In the absence of the original documentation it becomes impossible to judge to what extent even that part of Pearse's narrative that is attributed to the colonel himself is actually in his own words. Probably not much. The few compositions in Gardner's hand that do survive indicate that heavy editorial intervention would have been essential; for though he told a good story and occasionally showed a neat turn of phrase, he often repeated himself and rarely used one word when four or more, all meaning much the same, were available. To anyone compiling a thesaurus the colonel's reports would be a godsend. He also dispensed with the benefits of conventional punctuation, took a random approach to capital letters, showed no respect for consistency of spelling and sometimes allowed ink to clog his nib to illegible effect. The results can be testing and sometimes unintelligible. Nor is this all. His few dates do not always fit, his itineraries obey no obvious

logic and his narrative is decidedly erratic. Quite short marches are
so packed with drama and observations as to fill several pages; whole
months in *terra incognita* then slip past in a couple of sentences.

These failings are most noticeable in the account of his third
and last great journey, that of 1826–30. But in reconstructing parts
of this odyssey, Pearse had the advantage of two monographs, both
based on Gardner's personal testimony and both still extant. One was
compiled by Michael Pakenham Edgeworth, a Bengal civil servant
who had met Gardner in Multan in 1851. It claims to be an abstract
of Gardner's original travel notes yet is so packed with outlandish
names and preposterous claims as be almost unreadable. It did the
colonel's reputation as a credible observer no favours at all and is
chiefly notable for its publication date of 1853. This makes it much
the earliest version of Gardner's wanderings and therefore the least
susceptible to having been edited in the light of later travellers' reports.

The second magazine article dates from 1870 and is from the pen
of Sir Henry Marion Durand, who was lieutenant-governor of the
Punjab immediately before Sir Robert Davies, the man who became
Helena's English foster father. Durand encountered Gardner in Kashmir when on an official visit there and was impressed. He thought
him 'one of the most extraordinary men in India' and, after 'several
hours' of interviews, wrote a brief overview of the colonel's career
entitled 'Life of a Soldier of the Olden Time'.

Finally, as well as these two articles, a report in the colonel's own
hand of which Pearse was unaware has since come to light. It is not
a travelogue and it deals solely with Kafiristan. But since the corresponding section of the colonel's travel notes was that which was
said to have perished in Kabul with Sir Alexander Burnes, it is of
considerable interest.

All of these items, while helping to fill the gaps left by the original materials, afford some insight into editor Pearse's methods. But
Pearse, along with those others whose verbatim transcriptions of
Gardner's story comprised much of the material handed over by
Helena, laboured under a further disadvantage: he was not himself
acquainted with Central Asia. Current maps of the region were far
from comprehensive and notions about the distribution of its in-

habitants were hazy. Even supposing the colonel's memory to have been infallible, which it wasn't, and his imagination to have been deficient, which it wasn't either, incidents could easily be misplaced and observations misattributed.

Gardner himself, of course, carried no maps whatsoever. The place names he recorded in his notes were gleaned from conversations with those he met. Uttered in a variety of languages, they must often have been misheard, then misspelled and eventually misidentified on such maps as he later consulted. Some toponyms may indeed have been invented, others are clearly more in the nature of local descriptions than designations; it is perhaps a wonder that any at all, beyond the obvious, are recognisable. When plotting his route on a modern map, one finds the margin for error as wide as the windswept 'Roof of the World' to which happenstance was now about to conduct the colonel.

Still with the faithful Therbah by his side, still with the five sturdy horses he had claimed back from the Kipchaks, and now accompanied by half a dozen other survivors of the Habib-ulla debacle, Gardner slunk away from the Afghan Kohistan and repaired into the high Hindu Kush. All his followers were wounded, all were exhausted and all were wanted men. Recuperation and sanctuary were their sole concerns. The prospect of a marathon circuit of the greatest knot of mountains on the planet would have appalled them. In the annals of exploration few expeditions can have set off into the great unknown so handicapped and ill-equipped.

For clothing they had what they wore, which in Gardner's case now comprised a tall black Turkoman hat, a black sheepskin coat with a hair-rope girdle, and a pair of 'Turki overall boots'. For food they relied on what fortune brought their way. A passing group of Indian travellers was immediately waylaid but yielded only skins and spices, together with a few tails of Afghanistan's famously fat-tailed sheep and 'a big lump of reddish-black salt'. Rats made off with the sheep tails, though alternative protein came courtesy of an avalanche from which they excavated 'a large hyena-like animal'. 'Disgustingly rotten' and later identified as a wolf, it was smothered in spices, singed over a reluctant fire and provided 'a hearty meal, half raw'. To men obliged, both figuratively and literally, to lick their wounds, the block of salt was the most welcome acquisition. Fragments dissolved in water were rubbed into damaged flesh, then covered with poultices of powdered charcoal and clay 'and so left for twenty-four hours'.

The night cold was intense. They nestled among crags at about 9000 feet, their prospects being as bleak as the view. Some passing holy men were stripped of their robes, and from them they learned that another group of Habib-ulla fugitives had been taken prisoner by Ali Murad, the slave-hungry beg of Kunduz. Once again the obvious line of retreat—that north to Hazrat Imam and back across the Oxus into Turkestan—looked too dangerous. Instead they stuck to the mountains, following a trail that skirted the mysterious land of Kafiristan en route to Badakshan in the north-east corner of Afghanistan.

Their number rose to thirteen with the addition of more Kohistani troopers fleeing Dost Mohamed's vengeance. Three other unfortunates were simply 'taken in the Inderab valley ... one as a guide and the other two as *bona fide* slaves'. Together they all crossed a high ridge, later identified as the 12,600 foot Khawak Pass near the head of the Panjshir valley. From there 'a fatiguing ride through deep defiles and watercourses' brought them onto a plateau ringed by caves. Gardner calls the spot Ghaur-i-Pir Nimchu, 'the place of the Nimchu Pir'. Nimchu, he elsewhere explains, is the name given to those Kafir communities living on the outskirts of Kafiristan who had adopted Islam; and *pir* is the title awarded to Muslim saints. The saint in question proved ancient and partially blind, but much respected and, above all, tremendously hospitable. His disciples washed the travellers' feet, re-dressed their wounds and spread bearskins and fleeces on the ground for them to sleep on. Food was plentiful and 'the best wine of Kafiristan was not wanting,' adds Gardner.

Next morning they all prayed together; then 'we too, feeling a reverence for the holy man, our protector, went through the usual ceremony and became his disciples'.

The good *pir* also presented me, as a special mark of favour, with a fine leopard-skin mantle and cap to match, the latter about three quarters of a yard high. But his highest mark of favour was his presenting me with an old and worn-out Koran, which he ceremoniously hung round my neck in the large cave. I here formally and in his presence assumed command of our small party, each one promising to give strict obedience to my orders.

The pir also provided a guide and 'sixty gold Bokhara *tillahs*' wrapped in a Russian silk handkerchief. 'We each of us bent down and received his parting blessing... then embraced his disciples and took leave of them with regret and affection'.

This had been Gardner's first encounter with the Kafirs, albeit they were Nimchu Kafirs of the Khilti tribe, a people despised by other Kafirs for forsaking the beliefs of their ancestors and despised by other Muslims for their lax adherence to Islam. Kafiristan proper he declares to be 'one huge fortress, well kept by the able hands of its brave inhabitants'. In fact Ghaur-i-Pir Nimchu was said to be the farthest point reached by Timur the Lame (Tamberlane) when he attempted to subdue the Kafirs; an inscribed slab of marble recorded the event and carried a date corresponding to 1398. Gardner was obviously intrigued by this most un-Asiatic of people and his interest was heightened when, by way of an inducement to stay, 'they promised to place 20,000 brave Khilti Kafirs under my command'. A similar pledge would be made to The Man Who Would Be King in Kipling's story. Though acceptance at the time would have brought the wrath of Dost Mohamed down on the pir and his good people, it was not an offer Gardner would forget. He would return to Kafiristan.

Zig-zagging north for the Oxus and then east again to circumvent Kunduz and its slave-seeking raiders, Gardner and his followers were stopped in their tracks by a local curiosity. It was the first of numerous monumental features noticed on the journey and, like the others, it would do much to undermine the credibility of his narrative. So many caves and chasms of prodigious dimensions, so many Cyclopean pinnacles, ruined cities, inscribed megaliths, 'mephitic vapours' and massive gemstones would put his readers in mind of *King Solomon's Mines*. Some of these curiosities were man-made, some natural, and some, as here, supernatural; but however gigantic, all would somehow elude the enquiries of subsequent travellers in the region. The first was no exception.

> It was a colossal figure of a horse, now lying prostrate on its left side, the head turned to the north. It had evidently at one time been erect, as the stumps of the four feet were still in position: they were part of the platform and had evidently never been detached from it, I assured myself that there was no joint or cement, and that the entire figure must have been hewn from the solid rock.

The fact that the horse had not shattered when it fell he ascribed to the hardness of the stone, 'a black flinty porphyrite with beautiful veins of dark red and green running through it. On striking it with my knife it rang like bell-metal. I should say that its height when erect was about 15 feet to the withers.'

The existence of such a figure was not entirely incredible. Two hundred miles to the west the famous Buddhas of Bamiyan were also cut from solid rock. Though of sandstone and not free-standing, they were over ten times taller than the horse—until, that is, they were dynamited by Mullah Omar's Taliban disciples in 2001. But Gardner makes no mention of the Buddhas and seems never to have passed through Bamiyan. Instead, and as if the horse were not in itself far-fetched enough, he relates a local tradition to the effect that the animal once had wings and belonged to a giant. The giant kept it to fly down from his mountain home for assignations with 'a beautiful queen of these parts'. Then one night the giant found the queen dead, whereupon he cut off the horse's wings and buried himself under a mountain.

> The horse waited so long for him that it was turned into stone, but always remained facing north, expecting its master's return. Hence it is that it often calls aloud to him, as has been said.

If this story was meant to authenticate the discovery, it failed. Suspicious readers simply concluded that the horse was as fantastical as the legend and hence the travel writer no more to be trusted than the antiquarian. 'Well-known names now and then occur in the diary', wrote Colonel Sir Henry Yule, a distinguished geographer who struggled with Gardner's notes before they passed to Pearse, 'but amid the phantasmagoria of antres wild and deserts vast, of weird scenery and uncouth nomenclature, which flashes past us in the diary till our heads go round, we alight upon those familiar names as if from the clouds; they link to nothing before nor behind.' It reminded Yule of the yeti, 'that *uncanny* creature which is said to haunt the eternal snows of the Sikkim Himalya, and whose footsteps are found only at intervals of forty or fifty yards'.

The yeti might have been specially created for Gardner, yet he neglects to claim even a sniff of one. On the other hand, in the case of the stone horse, he had chosen to prejudice his questionable discovery by appending an even more fanciful legend. There may, though, be a rather prosaic explanation. Conceivably a natural rock-fall had once upon a time left four vaguely hoof-like stumps *in situ*, while depositing at a distance a much larger chunk of stone which, seen at a certain angle, did indeed resemble an equine torso. This freak of nature would have given rise to the legend, and the legend appealed to Gardner as substantiating the horse. Nowhere does he claim that the horse was actually sculpted, merely 'hewn'. As with the Bamiyan Buddhas, any features—ears, tail, etc—would have resulted from later modelling in clay or stucco, materials on which time and climate would have taken their toll. Without the legend, and without a bit of imaginative license, it might not have been recognisably a horse. Gardner's crime was simply that of making a mount out of a megalith.

'Shortly after leaving the horse', the 13-strong expedition met a herdsman armed with a bow and arrows. Next day this man guided them to a ruined fortress that Gardner calls Takht-i-Suleiman, 'Suleiman's Throne'. It was more an archaeological site than a fort but 'massive and extensive'; each of its cut stones 'weighed several tons'. Then came a village, the first they had seen since parting from Habib-ulla, followed by another Takht-i-Suleiman and, a few pages later, another village that was the first they had seen since parting from Habib-ulla. Clearly either the colonel's notes or Pearse's reading of them had gone awry here.

Likewise, the travellers were warned on at least three occasions

that the region was infested with Kunduz marauders on the look-out
for easy prey to enslave. To avoid this danger, they veered east again,
heading for a pass that led to Jerm (Jorm), a place of some importance in Badakshan. The pass was finally in sight when, heralded by
great peals of thunder, a gang of some fifty heavily armed horsemen
suddenly materialised in their rear.

> It was now raining heavily, with dark heavy clouds all around us. Gal-
> loping for the pass at full speed, we arrived within 600 or 800 yards
> of it, well in advance of our pursuers, when a small party of five men
> emerged from the pass and charged boldly towards us, loudly ordering
> us to halt in the name of the Kunduz chief Mir [ie beg] Ali Murad.

Though now trapped, Gardner ignored the order. Two of their opponents then hoisted their matchlocks to fire. Happily the ever
faithful Therbah charged them just in time—the rain must have
been dousing their tinder—'and quickly unhorsed and slew both
of them'. The other three were also overpowered and killed. But by
then the main body of the pursuit was upon them. Swords slashed
and blood mingled with the mud as Gardner and his men backed
into the mouth of the pass.

> Their overwhelming numbers, however, soon broke our ranks, and they
> unfortunately got mixed up with us; there was no room for orderly
> fighting and it was a mere cut and thrust affair.

> Soon we had only seven men left out of thirteen, and we slowly retreated
> up the pass, keeping them off as well as we could. In the pass we lost
> two more men ... and were now reduced to five, each of us severely
> wounded. I myself received two wounds, one a bad one in the groin
> from an Afghan knife and the other a stab from a dirk in the chest.

In the end they were saved by the elements. With the rain falling
heavier than ever, darkness came early. Their assailants withdrew,
'no doubt the plundering of the dead being their chief inducement'.
Gardner and his four remaining companions rode on through the

night. Soaked to the skin and pelted with hailstones, they relied on the lightning to show them the path. All were again wounded. Their commander was so faint he was barely able to stay in the saddle. It was not just the bloodiest affray in which he had been involved but, given the amount of circumstantial detail, one of the more convincing.

At daybreak they cleared the pass. Loss of blood and sheer exhaustion then compelled them to halt. They fed their horses but were too tired to eat themselves. Gardner slumped to the ground and admits to sleeping the entire day. 'Whilst I slept my Therbah sat watchful by my side, and no expostulation of mine could induce him to lie down and take rest'. Nor would his Therbah accept thanks for his bravery or sympathy for the wounds he had himself incurred.

It was a trait in 'these rude people' that Gardner much admired. In his crusty old age he would like to think that he too had to some extent contracted this *sangfroid*. Woe betide, therefore, anyone who adverted to what he called 'the tokens of my younger and wilder days', in other words his 'fourteen or fifteen wounds'.

> Nothing annoys me more than to be asked how I got this and where I received that. If such a question had been asked me in Turkestan, I should certainly have knocked the man down who questioned me.

Rising to his theme, and encouraged by the recollection of this, his most sanguinary engagement, the colonel then added one of his rare apologias.

> And I may here say, once and for all, that in all the occurrences of my past, misspent life, I was invariably actuated in my inward soul by feelings at once honest and upright, at least so far as my poor senses allow me to judge between right and wrong.

All of which could be an instance of touching naivety or a case of over-icing the cake. It is left to the reader's poor senses to judge between humility and humbug.

✻

As with Gardner's previous journeys, that of 1826–30 is vague as to distances and dates with few clues even as to the season. A reasonable supposition would be that he had left the Afghan Kohistan in late summer, crossed the Hindu Kush a week or so later and spent a couple of autumnal months in that part of Badakshan that is south of the Oxus (or 'the garden of the East' as he calls it). This is consistent with the dated entries in the abstract published by Michael Pakenham Edgeworth and with the suggestion that he then wintered across the upper Oxus in what is now Tajikistan before describing a long northern loop through and round the high Pamirs in the Spring of 1827. The loop was preferred over a straight west-east crossing of the Pamirs because, assuming it was by then Spring, it would have been no season to brave the sub-zero temperatures of the so-called *Bam-i-Dunya* or 'Roof of the World'.

Badakshan might have provided more congenial winter quarters, except that it was still within range of 'the robber *beg* of Kunduz'. To avoid another encounter like the last, Gardner's depleted party was again obliged to shun all human contact. After a week's convalescence following the affray in the pass, they rode in the direction of Jerm but with no intention of passing through it. 'I think, after two or three marches we entered the Kokcha valley and crossed that river eight or nine miles above Jerm,' he says. The Kokcha is a southern tributary of the Oxus; and the unusually candid 'I think' suggests that this was a case of his trying to reconstruct his route with the later benefit of a map. 'Thence,' he continues, 'we struck for a ford on the eastern branch of the same river, north of Yomal and between that place and Khairabad'. He also mentions Faisabad, the capital of Badakshan; the town was said to be in ruins following an attack from Kunduz, and it too they avoided. None of these places featured in the Edgeworth abstract of 1853 but all were shown on maps that may have been available to him in Kashmir in the 1860s, when his travelling days were over.

The few Badakshani hamlets they did enter were inhabited by Tajiks, an Iranian people who were reckoned fair game by the Uzbek slavers of Kunduz. These Tajiks offered further proof of Gardner's dictum that the remoter the place the more hospitable the people.

In fact they made the travellers so welcome that they stayed on 'for a certain time'. Just how long is anyone's guess, but the Tajik settlement in question he calls Zaruth Nao.

As luck would have it, they were here joined by an unlikely three-some, all of whom were destined to fill the gap left by the merchant Urd Khan of the first foray into Turkestan and the Polish fugitive Aga Beg of the second. One of the newcomers was a respectable Syed, or descendant of the Prophet, called Ali Shah; his origins go unrevealed but he was evidently not an Afghan. Another was this man's resourceful but unnamed servant; and the third, 'curiously enough' says Gardner, was a Hindu called Jey (Jai) Ram. All three were well armed and well travelled. They spoke numerous languages and, though apparently roving around for pleasure, passed them-selves off as *hakims* or doctors, 'to which they added astrology and fortune-telling'. Undoubtedly the most interesting company that Gardner had yet encountered, they dressed his latest wounds and those of his companions with such skill 'that my Therbah declared that they had been sent by God for our succour.'

On Syed Ali Shah's advice, Gardner and his men stayed an extra three weeks at Zaruth Nao. They explored the nearby remains of another ancient site, noted its two immense 'cairns' and penetrated deep into a long and lofty cavern on whose polished walls were to be seen 'the mutilated remains of idols which had originally been cut out of the rock in pretty high relief'. The Syed explained that they were Kafir deities and related how Badakshan had once been Kafir country, the cave having been the site of at least two Muslim-Kafir massacres.

A more likely explanation would be that the 'cairns' were in fact crumbling Buddhist *stupas* and that the 'mutilated idols', like those of Bamiyan, were Buddha or Bodhisattva figures. Similar sites in the northern mountains of Afghanistan and Pakistan would soon be identified as evidence of the spread of Buddhist worship to China in the first centuries AD. It was not, though, until the mid-nineteenth century that archaeologists and scholars would reinstate the history of Buddhism in India and then chart its spread beyond the subconti-nent. Since both Buddhists and Kafirs had suffered at the hands of an advancing Islam, the Syed could hardly be blamed for confusing the followers of the Middle Way with the reclusive infidels of Kafiristan.

When Gardner and his party finally left Zaruth Nao and Badakshan, they did so in company with their new friends. The Syed and his followers were heading for winter quarters in Shignan, on the edge of the Pamirs, before proceeding to Yarkand (now Shache) in eastern or Chinese Turkestan (now Xinjiang). Here, in other words, was a plan of sorts, and the company of the Syed would lend to Gardner's party a degree of respectability. With a resolve born of despair over their fugitive existence in Afghanistan plus total ignorance of what lay ahead, Gardner and his men agreed to accompany them.

At the time no one bar a few local graziers and *kafila-bashi*s knew much about the upland wastes and snowy peaks of what are now eastern Tajikistan and southern Kyrghystan. Marco Polo, in describing a Silk Road trail as uncertain and yeti-like as Gardner's, is thought to have passed this way en route to China in the late 1260s. Since then the only non-Asiatic known to have followed in Polo's footsteps was a Jesuit missionary and native of the Azores called Bento de Goes, who had disguised himself as an Armenian merchant to cross from Afghanistan into China in 1603. Gardner is unlikely ever to have heard of de Goes and he was probably ignorant of Polo at the time. But it was to Marco Polo that geographers were indebted for the two names that helped fill this particular void in their maps, and it was these names—'Pamir' and 'Bolor'—that Gardner adopted in his own account.

According to Marco Polo, either Pamir, Bolor or both were 'said to be the highest place in the world'.

> The plain is called PAMIER, and you ride across it for twelve days together [recalled Polo], finding nothing but a desert without habitations or any green thing, so that travellers are obliged to carry with them whatever they have need of. The region is so lofty and cold that you do not see any birds flying. And ... because of this great cold, fire does not burn so brightly, nor give out so much heat as usual, nor does it cook so effectually.

Though unknown to Polo, it was, of course, not the cold but the altitude of 13–16,000 feet that made cooking problematic. For most of the year, icy winds so blasted the scant herbage that horses went hungry and, when later some Russians established an outpost in the Pamirs, their hens refused to lay and the growing season proved too short for carrots.

But Bolor, according to Polo, was worse than 'Pamier'. It was much more mountainous, took forty days to traverse, and was just as bereft of habitations. The only exception was that in the high mountains there dwelled 'savage idolaters, living only by the chase and clothing themselves in the skins of beasts'. 'They are, in truth,' Polo concluded, 'an evil race.' He was probably referring to the Kyrghyz, though it could just as well have been the Kafirs.

In time, convention would award the term 'Pamir' to the succession of shallow east-west valleys which traverse this high altitude tundra in the heart of Asia. Along the valleys flow the feeder rivers of the uppermost Oxus, Shignan being at the junction with the parent stream of one such, the Shakh-dara. It was John Wood, the naval lieutenant who accompanied Alexander Burnes to Afghanistan in 1837, who would write the first detailed account of the Pamirs and record their local epithet of *Bam-in Dunya*, 'Roof of the World'.

'Bolor', on the other hand, became something of a moveable feast. Some geographers awarded it to the great jumble of mountains to the south where the Hindu Kush collides with the Great Himalaya and Karakoram ranges on the Xinjiang-Kashmir border. Others supposed it an alternative name for the Pamirs in general or, more specifically, for the range of lofty peaks that terminates the Pamirs in the northeast. Confused by all this, Pearse consulted Francis Younghusband, whose several forays into the area made him the end-of-century's leading authority. In September 1894, Younghusband wrote back to Pearse from Chitral on 'the Hindu Kush frontier'. He had never heard anyone use the term 'Bolor', nor indeed the term 'Hindu Kush'. 'In these countries ranges of mountains seldom have a name,' he wrote. 'An outside traveller has therefore to invent a name to apply to the mountain-range which he visits.' In Younghusband's opinion, Gardner had probably done just that with Polo's 'Bolor', and he might have been encouraged to do so by mistaking the local word *bala*, meaning simply 'upper' or 'higher up', for the same proper noun.

Blissfully unaware of the controversy that would envelop 'Bolor', Gardner approached Shignan with more pressing matters in mind. First came the problem of how to cross the ice-choked Oxus. The main bridge over the river had been destroyed, leaving only some suspended rope bridges 'which, as we had horses, left us nothing for it but to make a bridge or raft'. They opted for a combination of both but could find nothing to construct them with and no one to help them.

> Finally we managed with incredible difficulty to bind blocks of ice together with straw ropes, which when covered with grass formed a means of crossing for us and our horses.

The horses were still those 'excellent animals ... which I stole in reprisal from the Kipchak chief'—which was not quite the same as his earlier statement about them being his own horses that he had 'reclaimed' from the Kipchak chief.

Once safely across the river, another concern surfaced. As someone with an interest in mineralogy Gardner was particularly intrigued by reports of Shignan's ruby mines. Indeed, these reports may well have influenced his decision to accompany the Syed in the first place. Now, within a week's march of the mines, he was determined on an inspection. The Syed and Therbah were less keen; but after a night 'without food or a light for our pipes, with the keen wind blowing down upon us from the snowy heights of the Bolor Mountains and the Pamir steppes', he again tried to engage their interest.

> The next morning I was still more importunate about the ruby mines, fearing to lose the opportunity of a lifetime, and eventually I prevailed. So ... leaving the remainder of our party with strict orders to lie close, the Syad, the Therbah and myself started off, armed with stout spears.

But, in what was his first experience of the Pamirs, things did not go to plan. They travelled on foot, which was sensible enough, and carried matchlocks as well as the stout spears. Yet they omitted to carry any provisions other than the Syed's supply of opium, which, for an excursion expected to last at least two weeks, was not at all sensible. The hope was that they would meet with kindly graziers, but already the going was proving worse than expected. Halted by the first icy torrent, they waded it after roping themselves together, then toiled uphill to 'at least 13,000 feet'. From the top there was no sign of habitation and so no prospect of food or shelter. 'Night was approaching,' says Gardner, and with it came a less predictable visitation.

> Just then we came upon an exciting wild hunt. A quantity of wild sheep tore past us, hotly followed by wolves. My Therbah promptly shot one of the sheep, but two wolves disputed our right to it. We shot the nearest one but others came and hovered round. Now we were in a fix, for we had no materials for a fire, and jaded as we were, had the prospect of a night's skirmishing with hungry wolves, leopards, hyenas and jackals.

The Syed was better off, having chosen to 'sustain himself by his unfailing resource of opium'. Semi-comatose, he was nevertheless left to keep watch over the dead sheep while Gardner and the Therbah went in search of fuel. In the course of this foraging, they ranged far and became separated. Animal dung and a few bits of shrub were found but they would hardly suffice to roast a sheep. When Gardner spotted a scrubby bush in the distance, he accordingly made for it. This was a mistake. He was promptly set upon, or in his own words 'nearly eaten', by another pack of wolves.

> Just as I hurried up and shot the first depredator, the main body threw themselves alike on his dead body and mine. I tried to force my way through them, but one of them gave me a sharp nip, and the taste of blood made him set up an unearthly screech, which, being taken up by the others, proved my salvation, for my friend the Therbah hurried up, shouting and firing into the midst of them. At this they slowly and sulkily retreated.

That night they dined on mutton, albeit again 'warm, rather than roast', and 'after a long argument', the Syed got his way: the quest for the ruby mines was to be postponed indefinitely. Instead they headed back to their companions—though not without further incident.

At the stream for which they had roped themselves together on the way out, they were hailed by two strangers, one young, one old, and both armed. The Syed introduced himself, and the strangers showed him all due deference. They helped the Syed disrobe for the stream and directed him out into it. Then, when he was half-way across, they scooped up his boots and clothes and made off into the hills. Gardner and the Therbah, being more suspicious, had held back. They now gave hot pursuit. They recovered the clothing—the thieves had dropped it in their haste—and returned to the stream.

> We speedily recrossed the ford, not knowing how many more marauders might be about, when "bang" went a matchlock, and a ball struck the ground at our feet. A second shot went through the Syad's *pirpank* (a high, conical black lambskin cap), and a third took off the top joint of the second finger of my poor Therbah's left hand. The ball struck him while waving his arm to me to fire. Feeling that there was no hope for it, I took steady aim, fired, and rolled over the elder robber, who fell down the *khad* (declivity).

Apart from 'a few dropping shots', they were then unmolested and regained their companions in camp without further mishap.

Next morning Gardner awoke to find the Hindu Jai Ram and the Syed's servant already up and about as they listened to a tale of woe from three passing strangers. The youngest of the three strangers looked decidedly familiar. Gardner alerted his Therbah and together they sprang upon all three and 'overpowered them in an instant'.

The prisoners were bound with ropes, and the justice that ensued was rough. The Therbah demanded instant retaliation for the damage to his finger but was persuaded to defer to Shignan's legal process. At the nearest fort, the matter was taken in hand by the local chief, or *bai*. A confession to a three-year spree of robberies was extracted from one of the prisoners, the mullahs were called, and sentence handed down. It was between death and slavery, the choice being left to the aggrieved. All save one voted for slavery. The three convicted then had their heads shaved, one was knocked down to the bai as his personal property and the other two were 'sent away to meet a slave-dealer who would take possession of them'.

The 'dissentient voice' in all this was of course Gardner's. Presumably his vote was for clemency rather than death, although he doesn't actually say so. At a time when slave-trading had just been outlawed throughout the British Empire and slavery itself was about to be abolished, he should perhaps have made his position clearer. As it was, he appeared, in this case as in others, to have been complicit in enslavement and, whether he was a British subject or an American, he could expect only censure as a result. Those familiar with his later and more heinous actions in the employ of the Sikh Empire would pounce on his travels as little more than slaving raids and present them as damning evidence of an already incorrigibly unprincipled character. Gardner's defence, that of 'When in Rome ...', was the same in both cases.

By the Laws, manners, and Customs of one Country, acts are acknowledged crimes, or discrepancies, which in other climes are, and may be considered, and are extolled as, virtues [punctuation adjusted].

4

The Third Journey
1828–32

Contrary to the timeline already suggested, editor Pearse has Gardner spending the winter of 1826–7 nowhere near the Oxus in Shignan but with 'a noble robber-chieftain… at the fort of Tak, or Kurghan Tak' on the other side of the Pamirs. From there, says Pearse, 'he set forth in the spring of 1827 on his journey to Yarkand' and in the same year crossed the Kun Lun, Karakoram and Great Himalaya ranges to Ladakh and Kashmir.

This is perfectly possible, but unless he then whiled away a completely unchronicled eighteen months somewhere between Kashmir and Chitral, it brings him back to Kafiristan no later than the beginning of 1828, so leaving an unexplained hiatus of two years before the next recorded date. By then, early 1830, he is in southern Afghanistan seriously pursuing the possibility of gainful employment, an objective soon to be realised in the service of Ranjit Singh and his Lahore-based empire.

One way of settling the question of when Gardner actually crossed the great mountain spine of Asia ought to be by consulting the dated diary entries abstracted from the colonel's travel notes by Michael Pakenham Edgeworth in his barely comprehensible article for the *Journal of the Asiatic Society of Bengal* of 1853. According to these entries, Gardner and his companions did indeed speed across the

deserts and over the passes, reaching Yarkand on 24 September, Leh
in Ladakh on 28 October and the 'Cashmeer' valley on 10 November.
There they halted for just six days before pushing on through the
mountains to Gilgit, Chitral and Kafiristan, at which point Edgeworth's abstract peters out with the usual excuse that Gardner's notes
on Kafiristan had been lent to Burnes and lost when the latter was
murdered in Kabul.

Yet the dates as preserved by Edgeworth, while certainly helpful,
would be a lot more so if the year to which they applied were clearly
stated. Sadly it is not, although internal evidence suggests it must
have been 1830 or even '31—in other words three to four years after
that given by Pearse and two to three after that proposed above.

Edgeworth's fast-forward of the Gardner itinerary is explained by
his whole timeline being radically different. According to the note
with which he introduces his abstract, Gardner had originally set
out from Astrakhan not in 1819 (Pearse's date for the first foray into
Turkestan) nor in 1823 (that for the second) but in 1829. As a result,
what Pearse calls the colonel's 'twelve years of apparently aimless
wandering' are condensed into two, with the inevitable reduction
of both miles travelled and excitements encountered.

The beginnings of the first journey from Herat are just about
recognisable in the Edgeworth abstract; but after that the itinerary
follows a different course, leading not to Khiva but segueing straight
into the Badakshan sector of the third journey and thence, as noted,
to Yarkand and 'Cashmeer'. Gone altogether is the second journey
and the Kipchak contretemps at Ura-tyube; gone the mysterious
Pole who called himself Aga Beg and the gallant prince Habib-ulla;
gone, too, the two and a half years of fighting 'for the good cause of
right against wrong' in Kohistan; and gone forever the heart-rending
account of Gardner's young family and the fate that overtook them
in their 'happy mountain home'. In effect, over half of the narrative
offered by Pearse in the *Memoirs* is nowhere to be found in Edgeworth.
The odd discrepancy might be expected, but this is tantamount to
a wholesale refutation.

Given that Edgeworth's account was published in 1853, Gardner
had ample time to correct it or to disavow it altogether. The story of

his life as later outlined to Sir Henry Durand is substantially different and it was on that 1870 account that Pearse relied for the bare bones of the *Memoirs*. But, so far as is known, neither to Durand nor to anyone else did Gardner repudiate the Edgeworth version or offer an explanation for it. Nor, with any conviction, does Pearse, other than to grumble about Edgeworth's shoddy editing.

Sterner scholars naturally took the glaring inconsistency of the two accounts much more seriously. In their view the colonel's unreliability stood exposed, as did Pearse's gullibility; most of the travels, and most of the years they supposedly occupied, could now be dismissed as the product of the colonel's fertile imagination. And it was not the only case of gross fabrication. As will appear, much the same manipulation of movements and dates seems to have happened when the colonel was in his early twenties and living on the other side of the world. Adding a decade or more to his narrative whenever he felt so inclined looked to be one of his weaknesses. It was no doubt some awareness of this that lay behind that posthumously revised estimate of his age to which the Sialkot parish register bore witness.

But the critics would concede that Edgeworth's abstract, even when comprehensible, left much to be desired. Edgeworth, a botanist and administrator, had been even more out of his depths than Pearse. Confronted by what he describes as Gardner's 'several volumes of country paper', each filled with cramped and often illegible notes about a part of the world of which he knew nothing, Edgeworth—or more probably his Indian clerk—had transcribed things he could read (like the dates), guessed at place names he had never heard of, preserved some typically exaggerated accounts of the curiosities that so appealed to Gardner, and skipped much of the rest. His date of '1829' for the departure from Astrakhan could easily have been a typographical slip for '1819'. And the missing travels might well have been in a sheaf of 'country paper' that he never got around to consulting.

As so often, the evidence, whether for or against the colonel, proves inconclusive. All that can be said with any certainty is that both the year and the itinerary of the journey from the Pamirs to Yarkand are conjectural, and that the onward journey to Kashmir, though less conjectural, was hastily executed and sparsely recorded.

Leaving Shignan and heading east into the high Pamirs, Gardner and his friends had found themselves among the semi-nomadic Kyrghyz. 'Small, deep-sunken eyes, depressed forehead and nose, and high cheek bones' declared them 'pure Tartar', thought Gardner. They kept sheep, camels and shaggy-maned ponies and trained 'some splendid Shahbaz hawks'. As so often, the women were 'the more pleasing-featured portion of the community' with their (surprisingly) 'light-brown hair, blue eyes and rosy cheeks'.

This reminded the colonel of the Kafirs. The colonel was often reminded of the Kafirs. The charms of the Kafir women far exceeded those of the Kyrghyz and were proverbial throughout Asia. He waxed quite lyrical on the subject—'hair varying from the deepest auburn to the brightest golden tints, blue eyes, lithe figures, fine white teeth, cherry lips and the loveliest peach blossom on their cheeks'.

As guests of the bai, or local chief, Gardner and friends stayed with the Kyrghyz for 'about two months'. They attended the bai's wedding—the bride absconded, a fearful bloodletting ensued and the 65-year old bridegroom had to be 'consoled by marriage with a lovely girl of fifteen'—and they made an excursion to the south to renew their quest for the ruby mines. This time they found the mines but were disappointed. 'They consisted, somewhat to my surprise, of cave-like burrows about 1000 feet above the river,' says Gardner. None had been worked for centuries and to gain entry they had to wade through deep slush. With so little to report, it was greatly to the colonel's credit that he said no more. Success as a prospector was proving elusive.

> In my wanderings I lost no opportunity of inquiring about the various mines that existed in the regions which I visited, but I never found one which seemed likely to repay attention.

He was, though, privileged to inspect a very remarkable ruby whose discovery dated back to the time of Timur. It belonged to an ancient *fakir*; he kept it in a hole in the middle of his hut and rather generously presented it to the bai. For it was 'very valuable, from 150 to 200 carats in weight—a pure lustrous gem'. It was also engraved with what Gardner took to be a small Zoroastrian altar and an inscription in the 'Scytho-Bactrian' script.

Unlucky as a prospector, Gardner was frankly out of his depths as an archaeologist. Five years later a small and bedraggled traveller calling himself Charles Masson would take up residence in Kabul and begin noticing the abundance of old coins offered for sale in the bazaars. This interest heralded a series of sensational discoveries as Masson combed the country north of Kabul collecting a total of around 80,000 coins plus numerous other relics, seals, images and artefacts. At Begram, on a plain that lies within a day's ride of what had been Gardner's 'happy mountain home' and has since been encased in the concrete of the 'Bagram' Air Base, the finds were so numerous that Masson rightly believed he had come across the site of Alexandria ad Caucasum, one of the cities founded by Alexander the Great. On the evidence of the coins thereabouts and at Jalalabad, northern India's history in the centuries immediately preceding and following the birth of Christ (or the Common Era) would be substantially reconstructed. Similarly the importance of Buddhism in the region would be revealed by the stupas Masson opened and by the statuary and relics he excavated. It was altogether one of the nineteenth century's greatest archaeological hauls. Thanks to the impecunious and much maligned Charles Masson, Eastern Afghanistan would stand revealed as the richest imaginable depository.

Masson and Gardner may never have met, although there is every reason to suppose they knew of one another. The former first passed through Kabul and Kandahar in 1828, when Gardner was adrift in Tajikistan and Xinjiang, and did not return until 1832, by when Gardner had passed over the Khyber Pass and into the Punjab. But Masson submitted several reports on his findings and wrote a three-volume account of his travels. Published in 1842, the account would have been available to Gardner and Edgeworth when the latter produced his abstract in 1853. It may well, therefore, have been from Masson that the term 'Indo-Scythic' as applied to the inscription on the great ruby was borrowed. Masson had used the term for the writing on a series of coins dating from approximately the first century BC and had then applied it to the kings who issued the coins. The colonel, whose education did not extend to such things as epigraphy, seems to have adopted it to add an air of authenticity to his description of the ruby.

It may, too, have been by way of returning a compliment. For as of 1828, and for reasons to be explained, Masson had also been declaring himself an American citizen. He probably got the idea from Josiah Harlan, a doctor who came seeking adventure in Afghanistan and would briefly find it as the sovereign 'Prince of Ghor'. But Harlan, though indeed an American citizen, was both distrusted and detested by Masson. If the archaeologist wanted a more discreet and less controversial role model, Gardner's career was providing it.

Swapping one bai for another as they traversed the Pamirs, Gardner and his companions reached a place he calls Bolor Kash. 'It was about the end of August 1826' says Pearse (or more probably 1827). They stayed there a fortnight, followed by a month in the 'northern Bolor ranges'. Here they put up in 'a cave occasionally used as shooting-lodge'. The travelling was extremely difficult and 'at one time we took seven days to cover forty miles'. Clearly, they were making progress of a sort, although where and how much it is hard to say.

> Our intention now was to go up towards the Ustum valley, south of the Alai ranges, and about mid-way between the Terek Pass and Lake Karakul; but winter approached, and a noble robber-chieftain, Shah Bahadur Beg, to whom we had been introduced, would have detained us hospitably.

The noble robber-chieftain occupied the fort at 'Tak or Kurghan Tak', which was not the better known Tashkurghan to the south-east but 'two and a half days' good marching from the fort of Bolor Kash, and north or north-west of it'. This suggests they were now veering away from the Pamirs, as does mention of the Alai mountains, the Terek Pass and (Little) Lake Karakul. All lay to the north-east, with the Terek Pass being on a recognised route from Samarkand and the Fergana valley to Kashgar and Yarkand in Xinjiang. The route passed round the lofty mountain range sometimes known as the Kongur Shan, which was probably that which Gardner intended by 'Bolor'. And the same range nowadays marks the frontier between Tajikistan and the People's Republic of China. Xinjiang or eastern Turkestan, though the home of the Muslim Uighurs, was then as now under the control of Beijing.

As it happened, Gardner's foray into the Celestial Kingdom would have to wait. Instead, they did spend the winter at 'Tak or Kurgan Tak'. After another week's march, they had found their route already snow-bound and had returned to accept the robber-chief's offer of hospitality. Like Habib-ulla, Shah Bahadur Beg proved a man after Gardner's heart. His generosity could not be faulted, and Gardner's final encomium to him gives a likely indication of how the long winter months in the high Pamirs were spent.

> He considered that, with women, wine, good horses, good guns, good dogs, good falcons, and with a *castello* on the top of a crag in Yagistan [a generic term for anywhere beyond the pale of government], all life could offer was at our feet.

Reluctantly resuming their travels in the Spring, they again rode north and east. The last of Gardner's Kohistani comrades headed back to Afghanistan and were replaced by three new followers, presumably Tajiks or Kyrghyz. Including the Therbah, the Syed, his anonymous servant and the Indian Jai Ram, that made eight in all.

Emerging from the mountains, they found themselves in the Karategin (Qarategin) district of what is now northern Tajikistan. Here they turned east along 'the great Alai valley or plateau'. Pearse, having little else to relate, reminds readers of the *Memoirs* that this region had traditionally been 'considered as the site of the Garden of Eden and the birthplace of the human race'. Gardner obligingly confirmed the opinion. Its wild fruits were the equal of the cultivated fruits of Kashmir, and the adjacent mountains housed aboriginal tribes that he thought must be related to the primordial Kafirs. The tribes were called the Keiaz, the Akas and the Grums (the last being lapsed Akas who had adopted Islam, like the Nimchu Kafirs). Many lived in caves, some were barely acquainted with fire, and a few were said to eat people. They had various divinities—'but also worshipped obscene figures'—and, like the stone horse of Badakshan, they would successfully evade the enquiries of every subsequent visitor to this day.

Finding Gardner's account of the onward journey into Xinjiang particularly 'incomplete and confused', Pearse at this point turned to Pakenham Edgeworth's abstract. The Alai tribes as described by Gardner are included in Edgeworth; so too the sure-footedness of the yak, when this new means of transport was first encountered in the Kongur Shan; and so too the pangs of thirst experienced when crossing the Xinjiang desert to Yarkand.

Yarkand itself, the first city Gardner had entered in five long years, got short shrift. It detained the travellers for just three days and afforded Pearse barely a paragraph, all of it lifted word-for-word from Edgeworth. The city comprised a Muslim city and a Chinese city, each with its own governor; the gates of both were closed at night, the combined population was 80–100,000 of whom 15,000 comprised the garrison, and the principle articles of trade were tea, shawls, wood, porcelain and 'chrysoprase beads'. Compared to the generous treatment awarded the mysterious Akas and their ilk, this was scant fare indeed. For a fabled metropolis which no non-Asiatic had succeeded in reaching within living memory, it was particularly disappointing.

Pearse stuck with Edgeworth's sparse account for most of the rest of Gardner's third journey, but he supplemented it with extracts from Sir Henry Durand's 'Life of a Soldier of the Olden Times'. Needless to say, the two sources were not always in agreement. According to Durand's recollection of Gardner's testimony, the travellers spent not three days in Yarkand but fifteen and were made to camp in the no-man's land between the Muslim and Chinese quarters, presumably because neither chose to claim them as their own. The party also adopted a new guise. It was one in which 'Arb Shah', if he still used that alias, would have been quite at ease.

> Here Gardiner [sic] joined a Pilgrim Caravan for Mecca [says Durand].
> He put on *haji* dress, etc, and reached Leh [in Ladakh], from whence
> he was sent with five or six others to collect the pilgrims coming from
> Khotan and the Eastward; and while on this errand he saw the Pangong
> Lake and village of Chugsul. Having collected the pilgrims he returned

to Ladakh and from thence went on to Srinagar [in Kashmir].

The 'errand' back across the mountains to Khotan (now Hotan, east of Yarkand and also in Xinjiang) represented another first for nineteenth-century exploration. It was also one that featured not at all in Edgeworth. But an odder thing about both accounts was that nowhere does either make mention of the terrain between Xinjiang and Ladakh. Earlier travellers, like the now deceased Moorcroft and his party (who had been prevented from attempting the route in reverse), had never failed to notice its evil reputation; later travellers would write whole books about it. After all, it was probably the most challenging trade route in Asia. With five of the highest frequented passes in the world, including the 19,000-foot Karakoram Pass, it claimed so many lives that the yak caravans could find their way by following the trail of bleached bones left by men and animals who had previously succumbed to its dangers.

Pearse supposes that Gardner's failure even to mention the physical challenges was 'because it was really much easier travelling than many passes which he had already traversed'. Certainly higher passes are not necessarily more difficult passes; yet how anyone could cross the Kun Lun, Karakorams and Great Himalaya without noticing the dangers posed by any of them does rather beggar belief.

It is also curious that Gardner refrained from inserting into his narrative any of the information about the route amassed by subsequent travellers. By the time he was sharing his adventures with Sir Henry Durand in 1870, several Europeans had first-hand experience of the 'Karakoram Calvary'; he himself had been living in Kashmir long enough to be well acquainted with its community of Turkestani traders; and at the time he was personally pursuing a dubious commission to send a consignment of arms over the same trans-Himalayan route. He must at least have known the names of the main passes and have experienced the effects of the extreme altitude.

Likewise, after ten years surrounded by Muslims, he can hardly have failed to notice that the religious landscape had changed. Ladakh, a western extension of the Tibetan plateau, is Buddhist. Maroon-robed monks spill from the flat-roofed monasteries stacked against the hillsides, and the bunting of prayer flags trails from every crag. Yet neither Edgeworth's abstract nor Durand's overview contains any mention of such things.

The only named pass is the 'Zwaga-la' (ie Zoji La) between Ladakh and Kashmir. At little over 11,000 feet, it may well have been child's play compared to those that had preceded it, but it proved noteworthy only for the fact that the descent coincided with a major earthquake. The colonel gives no account of how this catastrophe affected his party, only that it killed 11–12,000 of Kashmir's inhabitants. As a result the Valley was not its usual radiant self.

> The stench from the corpses was frightful, and the survivors were afraid to bury them. In consequence a kind of plague broke out in a few days, people fell to the earth with vertigo and nausea and their bodies turned black. The natives fled in all directions.

The 'plague' was obviously cholera. It probably accounted for more of the dead than did the earthquake; and both disasters being eminently record-worthy, one would expect to find some third-party confirmation of them. In 1827 no such visitations are noticed anywhere in Kashmir. But in 1828 there was indeed a major earthquake followed by a cholera epidemic. Godfrey Thomas Vigne, a British sportsman, artist and intelligence-gatherer, noted their effects during a visit to the Valley seven years later, as did Baron Karl von Hugel, who was there in the same year as Vigne.

This would seem to confirm that the date was now indeed 1828 and that Gardner had passed two winters in and around the Pamirs, not one. But again, the evidence is ambiguous; for according to Vigne, the earthquake struck in June of that year, while Edgeworth's dates give November for the arrival in 'Cashmeer'. Since the cholera can hardly have taken hold in the few days needed to get from the pass to the Valley, it may be that Durand misunderstood Gardner, and that it was not the earthquake itself but news of it that overtook him on the pass. Alternatively the colonel, like many other travellers including Marco Polo, may here have been guilty of tampering with the chronology to dramatise his narrative.

More certainly, at the time—whatever it was precisely—Kashmir was already under Sikh rule. Back in 1819, when Gardner had first launched out from Herat into Turkestan, Maharaja Ranjit Singh, already well established as the ruler of Lahore, had unleashed his Sikh warriors against the then Afghan rulers of Kashmir. Cavalry and two guns had accompanied this expedition over the hills which, after an initial reverse, 'won an almost bloodless victory'; and thus was Kashmir 'added to the Lahore dominions'. Gardner is therefore correct in naming Kirpa Ram, from a Brahmin family in the service of the Sikhs, as the then 'governor of Kashmir for Maharaja Ranjit Singh', although this is hardly proof of his being there.

With the cholera still raging, the travellers were not of a mind to linger in Srinagar. According to Edgeworth they halted three days, and according to Durand, they stayed at the Mehmanghur, or 'guest house', near the city's Dal Gate. There they met some Afghan merchants who let slip an interesting item of news: in Afghanistan the star of the noble Habib-ulla had reappeared and 'was again in the ascendant'. Without hesitation, says Durand, 'the adventurous soldier decided at once on joining his old Chief'.

Still accompanied by the Therbah, the Syed, the latter's unsung servant and the Indian Jai Ram, Gardner passed swiftly down the Kashmir Valley to Baramula and Sopore, then took off north-west back into the mountains. The sudden exit from the Sikh domains may also have been dictated by the need to avoid detention by the regime. Foreign intruders with neither an invitation nor accreditation could expect to be referred to Lahore and closely questioned, which meant indefinite delay. More surely the direction of their exit was prompted by the hope of renewing contact with the Kafirs as well as locating Habib-ulla. As usual Gardner seems to have been blissfully unaware that he was also embarking on what posterity would regard as the most significant achievement of his entire mountain circuit.

As is the case with the previous roughly 1500 miles of unexplored territory, the final stages of Gardner's marathon are not well served by either Edgeworth's abstract or Durand's outline. In the absence of any other material, Pearse nevertheless had to rely on these two sources; and with reservations, several distinguished geographers thought him right to do so. In the opinion of Major-General Sir Henry Rawlinson, president of London's Royal Geographical Society in the 1870s, this sector of Gardner's route was of outstanding importance and could not possibly have been recorded without his actually travelling it. Writing in 1872, so 44 years after the journey, Rawlinson was insistent.

> Gardner actually traversed the Gilgit valley from the Indus to the Snowy Mountains and finally crossed over into Chitral, being in fact the only Englishman up to the present time who has ever performed the journey throughout.

Aside from the obvious quibble that the 'Englishman' in question denied being English, this was powerful testimony and of great relevance in Rawlinson's day. Gardner's route via Chilas on the upper Indus to Gilgit, and then across the 12,000-foot Shandur Pass into Chitral, was clearly a practicable proposition and had subsequently become something of an obsession with late nineteenth-century strategists in British India. In the 1860s, Gardner himself had fanned this concern by writing a paper on the subject. Pearse evidently had a copy of the paper and, in the absence of anything meatier, quoted from it extensively rather than attempt a chronicle of the actual journey based on Edgeworth's garbled extracts.

In this lost document of perhaps 1864 Gardner recalled that in the 1850s an Afghan force had used the Chitral valley and an innocuous pass from there into Badakshan to capture Jerm and then Kunduz from the rear. His point was simply that, by using the same route in reverse, an expedition from what, by the 1850s, was rapidly becoming Russian Central Asia might well take Kabul in the rear.

Twenty years later, it was the possibility of Russian infiltration into British India itself that kept the alarm bells ringing. Rawlinson and his military colleagues in the 'forward' school of British strategic thinking resurrected and authenticated Gardner's untroubled passage from Kashmir to Kafiristan as evidence of the permeability of what was now called 'the northern frontier'. Scrolling forward another couple of decades, it was this same concern, heightened by recent Russian advances as far as the Chinese frontier, which lay behind a series of decidedly 'forward' moves by the British. A military outpost was re-established at Gilgit in 1889, Chitral was repeatedly penetrated by Younghusband and others in the early 1890s, and Chitral's fort was effectively commandeered in 1895. As noticed, when the occupying force in Chitral was immediately besieged, the route taken by one of the columns sent to relieve the siege was precisely that of Gardner in 1828. All of which, in Pearse's partisan words, 'shows that as a student of "the great game in Central Asia", he was in the front rank'.

Back in 1828 the threat to India's borderlands from Tsarist Russia was as yet negligible. Gardner neither foresaw it nor mentioned it. Rather did he identify a resurgent Afghanistan under Dost Mohamed of Kabul, the spade-bearded adversary of Habib-ulla, as the threat to be countered. In particular, he feared for the survival of his old friends, the Kafirs. For centuries their Islamic neighbours had been encroaching on their ancestral territories in Badakshan and the Pamirs. Kafiristan was their last redoubt and, according to Gardner, when that fell, the Kafirs would be finished. In short, he sensed another fight for 'the noble cause of right against wrong'. Moreover, his alarm was justified, if a little premature. For by the time William Blackwood and Sons published Pearse's edition of his *Memoirs*, Kafiristan was no more. In 1896, and partly as a quid pro quo for a permanent British presence in Chitral following the siege, the ruler of Kabul was allowed to overrun the country and incorporate it into the kingdom of Afghanistan. Ever since it has been known as 'Nuristan'; the *kafir*s (ie 'infidels') were converted and the name of their land changed accordingly, *nur* meaning 'light' or, in this case, Islamically 'enlightened'.

There was an inevitability about all this. The features that made these secretive mountaineers so intriguing—their isolated existence, their evident antiquity, their anomalous ethnicity, their implacable hatred of Islam and their complex tribal system—also made them a temptingly vulnerable target for Kabul's zealotry. In espousing their cause against the expansionist designs of Dost Mohamed, Gardner saw himself as rendering a service to the Kafirs themselves as well as to his old chief Habib-ulla.

And perhaps there was more. On hearing the news of 'two Europeans having lived in their country about the year 1770', he may well have formed the idea of reprising the feat. The Khilti Kafirs had supposedly offered him command of 20,000 warriors; and as he now left the Chitral valley to climb back into Kafiristan, he took the unprecedented step of dismissing all his companions. The Syed, the servant, the Hindu and even the faithful Therbah were to wait for him at an agreed spot further down the Chitral valley. Save for a Kafir 'priest' as guide, he went into Kafiristan alone. He was surely up to something.

At which point editor Pearse, with his audience on the edge of their seats, ducks behind his lectern. 'The full diary ... of this most interesting passage in Gardner's adventurous life' he says, was lost. It was of course that lent to Burnes and 'destroyed when [in 1841] that unfortunate officer was murdered at Kabul and his house pillaged'. In fact, Pearse here admits that the whole journey from the Pamirs to Kafiristan had suffered the same fate. 'All that remain [are] some disconnected notes and allusions', some of them 'written on the margin of various printed pages concerning Kafiristan'.

The 'notes and allusions' referred to were those of Edgeworth, who had been the first to mention the loss of the original materials; and the marginal jottings have never been traced. What has to come light, though, is 'A Scetch on Kaffiristan and the Kaffirs' written in a familiar hand and rife with all the usual eccentricities of expression. It runs to 24 sides of foolscap, is dated 'Cashmear 20th Octr/69' and carries the signature of 'A Gardner'. Found among the papers donated to Cambridge University by General Charles Lionel Showers (who seems to have consulted Gardner about the defence of the Hindu Kush in 1869), it was first published with a masterful introduction by Dr Schuyler Jones CBE in a 1977 edition of the *Afghanistan Journal*.

All of which may be considered highly fortuitous. A former director of the Pitt-Rivers Museum and then emeritus professor of ethnology at Oxford, Schuyler ('Skye') Jones has roots in the Amer-

ican mid-west, interests in Africa and an unrivalled knowledge of
Afghanistan. With a presence to match this pedigree, 'Skye' Jones
has sometimes been supposed the inspiration for Indiana Jones. In
Jones, Gardner's 'Scetch' had found its way into safe hands.

Assuming the rediscovered 'Scetch' to be authentic, writes Jones,
'the manuscript is of special interest as it predates the earliest confirmed European penetration of Kafiristan by sixteen years'—or
indeed by nearer sixty years from the date of the actual 'penetration'.
Yet a problem remains.

> Of all the many Europeans who lived and travelled in South and Central
> Asia in the 19th century, none is more mysterious than Alexander Gard-
> ner. Doubts and uncertainties are attached to everything about him.

In this case the doubts stem from the nature of the data provided in
the 'Scetch'. On the one hand, Gardner's detailed descriptions of the
Kafirs' domestic arrangements carry a degree of conviction—despite
their extravagant wording and bizarre capitalisation.

> ... the Kaffirs of the present day, South of the Khaimeh River & Along
> its north Banks[,] reside mostly in well[-]built Stone & timber built
> Houses, usually built on the steep Slope or Side of some high hill or
> mountain[,] the Houses rising in tiers or Terraces one above & in the
> rear of the other, which if they Could be Seen from a distance would
> not doubt make them Appear Picturesque[.] But they Are generally
> So Situated & screened from view by surrounding mountain heights,
> which are usually bare rocky granite Massive walls and inaccessible
> peaks, as to preclude their being Seen untill [sic] by the tortuous and
> difficult path by [which] they can usually be but solely Approached,
> they are Actually Come upon, & as it were burst upon the view all at
> once, as often turning round the sharp Angle of some rocky wall[-]
> like Cliff along the narrow slippery and dangerous merely a single goat
> track verge of some darksome Chasm[,] deep abyss or rocky precipice ...

Similarly, it is hard to fault Gardner's mention of 'the neatness and
Elaborate Carved workmanship of the woodwork such as that of the

Door frames [,] Door Pillars, Poſts etc ...'

> ...low wooden benches alone on which they sleep arranged on one or
> more sides of the room of the house or Cave are Covered with planks
> etc which are also neatly worked & Carved on the edges[.] [B]esides
> this they use low square or Octagonal stools on Chounkees, six to eight
> inches high & 2 to 3 feet in diametre [sic] on which they sit and also
> use as a table...

The detail here is explicit and accurate. It can scarcely have been
dreamed up or purloined from some garrulous informant. This is
not, however, the case with Gardner's long and repetitive exposition
of Kafir beliefs and religious practices (which is frankly unreadable),
nor with his brief excursion into Kafir hiſtory, nor with his vague
notions of Kafiriſtan's geography. Perhaps the beſt recent map of
Kafiriſtan is that prepared by Dr Lennart Edelberg, Schuyler Jones's
Danish colleague; but apart from a few possible similarities in the
hydrography, all attempts to relate Gardner's observations to the
map have failed.

Jones, with a personal knowledge of Kafiristan dating back to the
1950s, studied the 'Scetch' closely in the hope that it would answer
the burning question of 'whether or not Gardner himself ever visited
Kafiristan'.

> Unfortunately it does not [answer the question, he concludes]. The
> information could have been obtained from talking with local people in
> different sectors of the North West Frontier Province. It may even have
> been compiled partly from maps and other documents. But ... several
> leading explorers and geographers of the day believed him.

Much the same could be said of all Gardner's other travels, in fact of
his whole life. Jones, it seems, would like to believe him, and perhaps
he is almoſt persuaded. But in the end scholarly caution prevails. The
'Scetch on Kaffiriſtan and the Kaffirs', he says, is beſt seen simply as
'a curious memorial of a moſt remarkable man'.

✳

According to Edgeworth, it was late April when Gardner disappeared
into Kafiristan. But since Edgeworth's April extracts follow immediately on those of November with no interruption of the itinerary
in between, this could be a mistake for December. The year was presumably 1828 (if December) or 1829 (if April). When he re-emerged
from Kafiristan is anyone's guess. It was probably in mid-to-late 1829.
According to Durand and Pearse, he rejoined his former companions
and proceeded on down the Kunar, or Chitral, River to Jalalabad.

Thereabouts 'a band of Khyberi outlaws attached themselves to
him' in unexplained circumstances. Simultaneously the Syed, the
Syed's servant and Jai Ram detached themselves from him, also
without explanation. Perhaps they felt their peaceable credentials
compromised by the company of the warlike newcomers, Of his
former companions only the faithful Therbah remained.

Approaching Kabul he learned, in Durand's laconic phrasing,
that 'Habib-ullah was nowhere and Dost Muhammad everywhere'.
Générale Ferrier says Habib-ulla was living in poverty in Kabul, Pearse
that he had gone on a pilgrimage to Mecca and died there. His star
had never risen. Gardner was now at a loose end, and with a band of
Khyberi desperadoes in tow, he needed a plan.

He came up with an idea that dated back to his pre-Turkestan
days, that of seeking service under the Shah of Persia. Ghulam Rasul
Khan, the leader of the Khyberis, then seconded the idea. Giving
Kabul a wide berth, they took the well-trodden route through Ghazni
to Kandahar.

It was early Spring 1830 when they entered Afghanistan's southern
city and there they were promptly detained. Kandahar was controlled
by a triumvirate, formerly a quinquumvirate, composed of Dost
Mohamed's brothers. Four more brothers, soon reduced to two, held
Peshawar on the Indian side of the Khyber Pass. There had once been
22 of these Barakzai brothers but incessant fighting and intrigues
were taking their toll; for the Barakzai brotherhood was seldom of
one mind, each and every one having his own eye on Kabul and on
the emirate that Dost Mohamed so coveted.

The Kandahar brothers, instead of betraying Gardner and his men to Dost Mohamed and packing them off to Kabul, preferred to extract a ransom. They relieved Gardner of a crystal hookah given him by Aga Beg, his Polish companion on the second journey, and then demanded 150,000 rupees for the safe passage of his party on to Herat and Persia. Gardner seems to have agreed to these terms, although whether he paid the ransom, and if so, where he got the money, is not revealed. The letter of safe conduct he received in return was presumably in Persian, which neither he nor his Khyber men could read. When he presented it at Girishk, a fort near the Helmand River beyond Kandahar, they were invited to partake of an evening meal and in the middle of it were summarily seized and 'cast into the subterranean dungeons of the castle'. The letter, it transpired, was not a passport but a gaol sentence. In a matter of days the Therbah and Ghulam Rasul Khan and his men secured their release; but Gardner remained a prisoner.

> Now [says Pearse] was shown his remarkable influence over those who from time to time became his followers – for none of the Khyberis would desert him but went round to the priests [*ulema,* pirs and *mullahs*], exciting sympathy on his behalf.

This eventually did the trick. Negotiations got underway and after nine stifling months in detention Gardner too finally emerged from his dungeon. But there was a price to pay. Freedom came on the condition that he abandon the Persian plan and issue an affidavit as to his fair treatment in Kandahar. Ghulam Rasul Khan thought this not good enough. He led his men back into Kandahar to demand 'money to help them on their way'. It was 'flatly refused'.

The Khan then came up with the bright idea of augmenting his leader's appeal by enhancing his status. Having somehow procured the appropriate robes, he formally invested Gardner in the presence of a respected fakir as a *shahzada*, or prince of the blood. This infuriated the Kandahar brothers but appealed to some of their disaffected subjects. When he finally issued forth from his retreat outside Kandahar in late 1830, 'Prince' Gardner rode at the head of a small army of forty troopers, 'several of whom had shown extraordinary fidelity to him'.

An army, however small, needed an income. Somewhere north of Ghazni they met a well-appointed caravan bound for Kandahar and travelling under the protection of its ruling brothers. Back in the business he knew best, Gardner did not hesitate. Revenge was sweet. He befriended the caravan's merchants, offered them an escort and, having allayed any suspicion, 'seized and bound' them—'as they would have treated him and his party in the proper time,' adds Durand.

> He took from them their Kashmir shawls, embroidered kullas, etc— literally 'spoiling' them—and then he made direct for Kabul, to tell the story and throw himself and his party on the generosity of Dost Muhammad.

Pearse calls this unexpected turnaround a case of his 'taking the bull by the horns'. It was certainly risky, not to say suicidal. Whether Dost Mohamed realised that the man now posing as a shahzada was in fact Habib-ulla's former henchman and the head of the young family his own men had massacred is unclear. Gardner presumably hoped not. He was counting on the Dost's short memory, his deep-seated hatred of his Kandahar siblings and his ever-pressing need for loyal and experienced cavalrymen.

To gain Kabul ahead of any pursuers they rode around the clock. On arrival, they made straight for the Bala Hissar (or 'great citadel') and demanded an audience. The situation was ripe for another admission of Gardner's nationality, though Durand is silent on the matter.

> They presented their arms, horses and property to Dost Muhammad, and asked permission to tell their story in private to the warlike Chief. He heard them patiently, agreed that they had been badly treated, said that they had done quite right to take the law into their own hands, and that, for his part, he would not receive anything from them of their property, but that they must leave his country as soon as possible. He gave them two guides and sent them on their way.

Durand here pauses the account given him by Gardner to reflect. It was possibly the colonel's finest hour, he thought. His 'great self-pos-session and confidence' had again paid off, and while applauding this 'cool audacity', Durand could not but note his reticence; 'for do what he might, no one seems to have accused him of too much forwardness'.

Self-promotion, an activity that the British disparaged as whole-heartedly as they practised it, may well have been alien to Gardner. Durand, who had listened to his account over 'several hours', was in a good position to judge. But perhaps in this mention of his self-deprecation there lies, too, a hint of the candour and charm with which the colonel disarmed not only the likes of Durand, Davies and Showers but Dost Mohamed, Habib-ulla and countless others. Those who met him, liked him; and those who knew him best, doubted him least.

Still with his forty-strong following, but minus the Therbah who preferred to return to his Afghan family, in January 1831 Gardner proceeded down the Kabul River and back across the Kunar River to Bajaur. A hilly tract adjoining Chitral and now part of Pakistan's Federally Administered Tribal Areas (FATA), Bajaur was at the time ruled by one Mir Alam Khan, to whom Dost Mohamed had given Gardner an introduction.

The introduction was not without design. Ever a hot-bed of jihadist activity, Mir Alam Khan's territories abutted other tribal territories with an equally uncompromising reputation. Some of these were currently hosting hordes of bearded fanatics loyal to a fiery Indian cleric called Syed Ahmad. Hailing from Bareilly in what is now Uttar Pradesh, Syed Ahmed had imbibed Quranic orthodoxy in Delhi, acquired a massive following among North India's Muslims, and spent as much as two years in Arabia. Returning with a heady mission that combined Wahhabi intolerance, jihadist zeal and messianic (or Mahdist) delusions, Syed Ahmed had, in Gardner's words, 'raised the green standard of the Prophet in the Yusufzai hills between Pe-shawar and Attock and proclaimed a religious war against the Sikhs'. By 1831 he was being hailed as 'Defender of the Faith, the glitter of whose sword was now to scatter destruction among the infidels'. His scimitar-wielding cohorts had already taken Peshawar at least once and were terrorising the adjacent Sikh territories.

In directing Gardner and his men into this maelstrom, Dost Mohamed was practically committing them to fighting alongside Mir Alam Khan and Syed Ahmad's bloodthirsty disciples in a jihad against the might of the Sikh army, the finest in non-British India. Gardner, though, saw it differently. He was relieved to be leaving Afghanistan; in that land of blood-feuds 'there were too many Afghans whose fathers and brothers had met him in battle'. Like George Thomas a generation earlier, he saw a much better chance of steady employment in the heavily militarised Punjab between the Khyber Pass and the advancing frontiers of British India. In a meeting with Syed Ahmad's leading disciple, he passed as a bona fide Muslim and became convinced that jihadists could be as easily recruited as the Khyberis who had followed him to Kandahar and back.

> The enthusiasm which he [the disciple] aroused suggested to me that I might do worse than join the Syad his master, as I saw a good opportunity of getting together such a body of followers as would make my services valuable to any ruler to whom I might subsequently offer them. Therefore, when Mir Alam Khan proposed to me to take command of those of his followers who desired to array themselves under the sacred banner of the Syad or Khalifa as he now styled himself, I fell in readily enough with his wish.

At the head of 'some 250 well-armed and warlike mountaineers, all burning with religious zeal', Gardner rode forth towards the Syed's headquarters at Balakot. But 'owing to the mistake or treachery of the guide', he says, they arrived a fraction too late.

It was too late, that is, to save the Syed. He and his leading disciples had met their match in a troop of the Sikh irregulars known as Akalis. Gardner had not encountered these indigo-clad fanatics before. Later he would become something of an authority on them, recording their lawless disposition, marvelling at their indifference to danger and briefly becoming one of them in the least likely of all his reincarnations.

At Balakot the Syed and his chief disciple had been detached from their forces ('which fought very badly without their leader') and were making a last stand. The Akalis showed no mercy.

> Even as I caught sight of the Syad and the *maulvi* [recalled Gardner], they fell pierced by a hundred weapons. Those around them were slain to a man, and the main body dispersed in every direction... I was literally within a few hundred yards of the Syad when he fell, but I did not see the angel descend and carry him off to Paradise, although many of his followers remembered afterwards that they had seen it distinctly enough.

Though too late to affect the outcome, Gardner had timed his arrival perfectly for the orgy of plunder that followed. 'My Khyberis and Yusufzais were equal to the best in this matter, and cut down several of the Hindustani fanatics [ie the Syed's Indian followers] who had joined them for protection, and whose clothing or equipment seemed to them a desirable acquisition.'

Notwithstanding such treachery, Gardner received a warm welcome when he returned to Bajaur. Mir Alam was not unhappy to learn of the fate of the Syad and was relieved that his own men had not had to fight. Meanwhile, glutted with booty, Gardner's Khyberis trailed back to their homes. Gardner himself took the opportunity to catch up with his paperwork.

> It was while in comparative ease and security, and habited as a Mussalman at Bajaur, that I managed to jot down the rough records of my wanderings. As a devout man I carried the Koran suspended from my neck, and in its leaves I deposited my scraps. After a time the holy book got so bulky that I had to devote my tobacco-pouch as a receptacle for my writings.

It is not clear from this which of his wanderings he is referring to, nor whether the 'scraps' were the raw materials from which he distilled his 'rough records' or the product of this process. Because Pearse's account of his exploits since leaving Kandahar is more colourful than that before Kandahar, it seems there must have been some source available to him other than Edgeworth and Durand. Presumably that source was the 'rough records' Gardner penned at Bajaur, and presumably therefore they covered only the years 1830–31.

Later in the summer of 1831 (the battle of Balakot that put paid to the Syad had been fought on 8 May) his labours were interrupted by a long awaited summons. Word of his audacious reputation had evidently spread; and it must have been supplemented by less reliable reports of his other accomplishments. For the summons took the form of an invitation from the governor of Peshawar to 'enter his service as chief of artillery'. Having fired nothing more lethal than a matchlock for at least ten years, Gardner might have excused himself. He chose not to. He presented himself and was duly awarded 'a liberal salary' plus the privilege of dining each night with the governor. More surprisingly, the governor 'took a great interest in artillery, but I taught him all that he knew on the subject'. Who taught the colonel all that he knew on the subject is not revealed.

The governor in question was Sultan Mohamed Khan, an Afghan and one of the ubiquitous Barakzai brothers. But, more to the point, Sultan Mohamed Khan was already a vassal of the Sikh maharaja, Ranjit Singh, since it was the Sikh ruler's forces that had restored his rule in Peshawar after the last of the Syed Ahmed's raids on the city. Thus Peshawar had effectively passed to the Sikhs, whose territories now extended to the Khyber Pass; and thus Gardner, though serving under an Afghan prince, was already indirectly in Sikh employ.

The arrangement proved just a prelude to direct employ. After six months—so in the Spring of 1832—'a letter was received by Sultan Muhammad Khan from Maharaja Ranjit Singh desiring my services'. Gardner complied. In leisurely fashion he wound up his affairs in Peshawar and travelled across the Punjab to Lahore in company with the maharaja's master of stud.

On the way he made the acquaintance of his first non-Asiatics since the mysterious Pole he had known as Aga Beg. At the town of Gujrat, for instance, he put up with the American Josiah Harlan. It must by now have been May 1832. Harlan, who had withdrawn from Afghanistan for a lucrative interlude in the employ of Ranjit Singh, was only appointed to the governorship of Gujrat province in that month.

Knowing the maharaja's regard for foreign mercenaries, and possibly on Harlan's advice, Gardner here finally cast off his 'Mussulman habit'.

> I should mention that on meeting my countryman Harlan I resumed the character of a *wilayati* or foreigner, and resumed also the name of Gardner, which I had abandoned for so long that it sounded strange in my ears. The Sikhs usually called me 'Gordana'.

From Gujrat he proceeded to Wazirabad, where he again stayed 'four or five days' with the district's foreign governor. This was none other than the portly Paolo Avitable, the Neapolitan general whose reputation as a *bon viveur* and lothario was matched only by that of his blood-lust for extreme forms of punitive justice.

Finally he drew near the crumbling splendours of Lahore, where he met two more ex-Napoleonic officers. General Claude Auguste Court was in charge of the maharaja's artillery and General Jean Baptiste Ventura commanded the infantry regiment raised and drilled on the European model which was known as the *Fauj-i-khas* (literally the 'Royal Brigade' but more commonly the French Brigade). Both these men had been in Sikh employ for some ten years, and it was Ventura, the more senior, who presented Gardner to the Sikh court.

The date of this presentation cannot have been earlier than May/June 1832. Unless Gardner had dreamed up his role at the battle of Balakot, cut short his six months in Peshawar and never met Harlan at Gujrat—all of which could easily have been verified—he could not possibly have reached Lahore any earlier. Yet sleuthing through the Sikh entries in the Punjab Records nearly a century later, Messrs Grey and Garrett would stumble upon a letter—no. 4 in Letter Book no. 137—and be scarcely able to contain their delight. Here at last was official and irrefutable evidence that Gardner was not the traveller he said he was. The letter, written by the news-writer of the Sikh court, must be presumed genuine. As per Grey and Garrett's translation it read as follows:

> 15th December, 1831. Messrs Khora and Gardiner, two Europeans about 35 years of age, light hair and complexion, presented themselves with

a nuzzur [token gift] of five rupees each, and were at once admitted to an audience. The Maharajah asked from what quarter they came, and with what object. They answered that they were formerly serving in a ship of war, but not being satisfied with their position, quitted it, and proceeded from Bombay to Peshawar, where Sultan Mohomed Khan had entertained them on Rs 3 per day. They were with him six months, but having heard of the liberality of His Highness, they had applied for their discharge and come to Lahore.

The Maharajah asked what baggage they had with them. They said, a riding horse each, and five or six servants... They say that they are Americans, and that there were originally three of them; but I hear that one died.

'Here then are solid and unimpeachable facts!' yelped Grey. The man described by Sir Richard Temple in the preface to the *Memoirs* as 'one of the finest specimens ever known of the soldier of fortune' turned out to be 'an ordinary deserter from the British service, Army or Navy'.

Before this prosaic and faded old entry of 97 years ago [continued Grey], which has probably lain almost unnoticed since the day it was written, vanishes like the Genii's palace, that beautiful edifice built around Gardiner's romantic story, peopled by the creatures of his imagination, and buttressed by the testimony of so many credulous and simple-minded gentlemen.

The archives had spoken. Diligent scholarship and dogged research had chipped away at the heavy varnish and laid bare the ugly truth. 'The agreement of the dates is exact,' Grey went on, 'According to Gardiner's own statement, he arrived at Lahore in 1831 from Peshawar, and the only difference is that he does not mention a companion.'

Nor, as a matter of fact, does he anywhere mention arriving in 1831, since he didn't. To put it kindly, Grey's convictions were making him careless. None of which exonerated all those 'credulous and simple-minded gentlemen'—Durand, Rawlinson, Yule, Temple and others but above all Pearse—who had accepted Gardner at his face value. And none of which disqualified the other revelations contained in the news-writer's report.

Yet it did leave room for doubt. And perhaps the biggest doubt of all was, if Gardner wasn't who he said he was, who was he? Grey and Garrett were pretty sure he was no more an American than Masson, the elusive archaeologist. And since it was now established that Masson had assumed both his name and nationality to obscure the fact that he was a deserter from the East India Company's army, they were confident that the same was true of Gardner.

But in contrast to Masson, there was no evidence to substantiate Gardner's being a deserter. Rather the colonel could point to years of previous travel in Inner Asia and, before that, to a long and intriguing upbringing on the other side of the world. Beginning among the American Great Lakes some thirty years before he launched himself into Turkestan, this back-story embraced no less than four continents and was so preposterous as positively to invite the scalpels of Grey and Garrett. They would oblige. Yet, to others more cussed of mind, the sheer improbability of the whole story was what lent it a certain credibility. Since no one in their senses would believe such a tall tale, why bother to invent it? Why not invent something that was at least plausible? In other words, why go out of one's way to invite ridicule? Unless, of course, it was not invented.

As Grey and Garrett extended their dissection of the colonel's life-story to its beginnings on the eighteenth-century frontiers of North America and to what he always called his 'miss-spent youth', such questions seem not to have occurred to them.

5

The Early Years
1785–1819

If there was one thing about which Alexander Gardner was consistent, it was that he was an American. He had declared it to his inquisitors in Khiva, confided it to the noble Habib-ulla and confirmed it to Josiah Harlan. He had confessed it to Maharaja Ranjit Singh as per the Lahore news-writer's report and he would insist on it to all the British officials he subsequently met. These included Michael Pakenham Edgeworth, Sir Henry Marion Durand and such others as recorded their encounters with the colonel in a form that was available to Pearse. As with his travels, the details and dates of his early life would often differ. But the setting was always the same: it was North America.

Pearse never seriously doubted this American dimension. 'Early Life and Travels, 1785–1819', his relevant chapter in the *Memoirs*, must have been approved by Helena; she may even have contributed to it. But because neither Edgeworth nor Durand goes into much detail on this phase of Gardner's life, and because Helena herself seems to have been unable to provide any documentation on her father, Pearse must have relied on some other source.

The likeliest contender for supplying such information is one Frederick Henry Cooper, the author of an incomplete and never published biography of Gardner dating from the 1860s. Editor Pearse admits to using Cooper extensively but, like all the other papers entrusted to him, Cooper's work disappeared after the publication of the *Memoirs*.

Frederick Cooper met Gardner in 1864. A civilian administrator, Cooper had been posted to Kashmir to act as liaison between the maharaja of Kashmir's government and the swarm of British holiday-makers who had begun descending on the Valley during the summer months. It was not a very demanding post and, hearing tell of 'an old European commandant' living as a native in the back streets of Srinagar, Cooper had issued an invitation. The bewhiskered figure that strode into his compound at the appointed hour must have come as a pleasant surprise.

> The old colonel, while on the verge of his eightieth year, had a gait as sturdy and a stride as firm as a man of fifty. Some six feet in height, he usually wore a tartan-plaid suit... [but] the photograph [see image no. 1] gives but a dim idea of the vivacity of expression, the humour of the mouth, and the energy of character portrayed by the whole aspect of the man as he described the arduous and terrible incidents of a long life of romance and vicissitude.

This first meeting led to several others, indeed 'a series of conversations'. The colonel told his story and Cooper, sometimes with the help of a colleague, copied it down. All the transcribed material, which covered events up to the crossing of the Pamirs, was said to have then been verified and approved by Gardner himself; and it was probably this same material that comprised the 'about a hundred pages' which, according to Rawlinson of the Royal Geographical Society, 'Mr Cooper had already printed when death put an end to his [Cooper's] labours in 1871 [actually 1869]'.

In the course of these interviews Cooper got to know the colonel better than any other British official. He may well have commissioned the famous photograph of him and, being already the author of a mawkish account of the 1857 Indian Mutiny (aka Great Rebellion, First War of Independence, etc), he clearly saw Gardner's story as a publishable venture. To this end, even if the narrator himself was innocent of exaggerating, it is quite possible that the scribe was not; for Cooper came with a reputation for suspect judgement and blood-thirsty inclinations.

In the early days of the 1857 Mutiny, as district commissioner of Amritsar, he had been responsible for ordering the disarmament of one of the East India Company's regiments. Stationed at nearby Ajnala, the 26th Native Infantry was duly relieved of its weapons on 30 July. In the panic conditions of the time, it was no doubt a reasonable precaution. But Cooper had then so mismanaged matters as to provoke the now unarmed men into resistance and flight, in the course of which as many as 500 were shot, executed, died in detention or were buried alive. Cooper showed no remorse over the action. In his book he even took an indecent pride in it. He saw it as vengeance for the mutineers' massacre of British personnel elsewhere in India. Several respected British figures concurred by applauding the salutary effect of his prompt action on other wavering regiments.

But none of this could disguise the scale, the treachery or the savagery of the crime. In the House of Commons, Cooper was censured and, though in India his action was hushed up, his career suffered. His later appointment to Kashmir was probably intended to keep him out of harm's way. Gardner, assuming he was aware of all this, may have had reservations about entrusting his story to such a controversial figure. Pearse certainly knew the risk of relying on Cooper's testimony. He acknowledged that Cooper was 'a man well known in his day for a terrible act of severity performed by him in the execution of his duty' and evidently hoped, by doing so, to deflect criticism of himself as having been duped by 'the butcher of Ajnala'.

On meeting the old colonel, Frederick Cooper apparently found Gardner's spoken English 'quaint' and 'graphic'; yet it was 'wonderfully good considering his fifty years of residence among Asiatics'. It was delivered in an accent that occasioned no comment from Cooper and was presumably not American; neither was that of most others born in America of English-speaking parents in the eighteenth century. A few of the colonel's other acquaintances would note a distinctly Irish brogue, but for this too there would be a ready explanation.

Despite the loss of several of his diaries, and 'except as to precise

dates', Cooper thought the colonel's memory 'singularly tenacious'.
The year of his birth as given to Cooper and then adopted by Pearse
was 1785. (This would make him 91 when he died in Jammu, not 96
as per the original entry in the Sialkot parish register nor 76 as per the
amendment.) His father, he claimed, had been a doctor by profession
and a Unitarian by conviction. Unitarians rejected the notion of a
Trinity and were a tolerant, progressive and sometimes clandestine
Protestant sect. Dr Gardner seems to have been typical of them. The
son of a Scottish immigrant, he had fought in the American War
of Independence, corresponded with George Washington and the
Marquis de Lafayette, and had subsequently been employed by the
Mexican government as 'the principal official of a town and district
on the banks of the river Colorado'.

There, Dr Gardner had met and married Miss Haughton. A Ro-
man Catholic lady of good family and more exotic antecedents, Miss
Haughton was either the daughter (according to Durand) or the
grand-daughter (according to Cooper), of 'a major in the English
army well known in his day as a traveller in Africa, in which mysterious continent he [had] eventually lost his life'. Miss Haughton's
mother had been of Spanish descent but with a hint of Aztec blood
and family connections in France and Italy. Although neither the
parents nor the grandparents are given first names, it is tempting to
suggest that Miss Haughton herself may have been called Helen or
Helena. The colonel would always remember her as 'a well-educated
and accomplished woman, of a rare sweetness and strength of character'; and, given this high opinion, it is likely he named his own
daughter after her.

No sooner had they married than Dr Gardner and his bride left
the Colorado River in what was then part of Mexico and headed
north to set up home 'on that portion of the shore of Lake Superior
which is nearest to the source of the Mississippi'. There, presumably
in Wisconsin, Mrs Gardner gave birth to six children, three girls
and three boys, the youngest of whom was christened Alexander
Haughton Campbell Gardner. The girls were brought up as Catholics
like their mother, the boys as Unitarians like their father. But when
the young Alexander was four, the family retraced its steps back to

Mexico and made a new home, this time 'near the mouth of the river Colorado and not far from the town of St Xavier'. Dr Gardner, now employed in the Mexican medical service, here 'acquired considerable property in addition to some inherited by his wife'. Mrs Gardner looks to have won the tug-o-war over the religion of their children; in Mexico, the boys, like the girls, were sent to the Jesuit-run mission school in St Xavier.

There, aged 12, Alexander gave early signs of a rebellious nature and suffered as a consequence. He refused to attend Mass or make his confession and was ostracised by both the Jesuit teachers and his largely Spanish-speaking schoolfellows. 'Isolation in youth is hard to bear,' says Pearse; it was, though, the ideal preparation for the life of a reclusive freebooter among the resolutely Muslim and often hostile peoples of Inner Asia. So too was the close study of a 'book of travels among the American Indians' which became the schoolboy's one great consolation. He had spied the title on the principal's shelves while awaiting chastisement. He asked to borrow it, was refused, and then, in Pearse's words, 'took an opportunity of possessing himself of it'. On his own testimony, the theft, as much as the book itself, whetted his appetite for a life in which scruple would play little part and resourcefulness was everything.

> From this early period [Gardner would recall], the notion of being a traveller and adventurer, and of somehow and somewhere carving out a name for myself, was the maggot of my brain.

In 1806 he completed his schooling at the advanced age of twenty-one. The following year his mother died. His eldest brother had already left America to carve out a career for himself in Russia, and young Alexander was minded to follow in his footsteps. Prior to the opening up of California, the Russia of Tsar Alexander I was considered a land of boundless opportunity. Scots in particular had been heading there in numbers since before the time of Catherine the Great. As admirals and generals, various Gordons, Greigs and Keiths had commanded the Russian forces; in St Petersburg, Baird's iron-works turned out the best ships and mining machinery; and somewhere between the

Caspian and the Aral Seas, Scottish missionaries ran a steppe settlement where they failed to make a single convert.

There was nothing more improbable about seeking adventure in Russia than about the family's peripatetic movements in America. Wanderlust coursed through the veins of both the Gardner and the Haughton families. Yet even supposing that the colonel's shaky memory occasionally allowed his imagination to run riot, these American and Russian connections seemed such elaborate fabrications as to be counterproductive. Instead of inviting credence they positively challenged it. *Ergo* they could, just conceivably, have had some basis in fact.

Admittedly they also left a lot of questions unanswered. Why were his parents not more clearly identified? Why and how did they flit back and forth across the American continent? Why was the topography—'the shore of Lake Superior nearest the source of the Mississippi', 'the mouth of the river Colorado', etc—so excessively vague? Why would anyone forsake 'the land of the free' for the uncertainties of an absolutist regime on the other side of the world? And, above all, where was the telling detail, the one observation, anecdote or encounter, which, by virtue of its unassailable veracity, would authenticate the rest? For anyone already suspicious of the colonel's fidelity to the facts, 'the early life and travels' as sketched by Pearse on the basis of Cooper's information cried out for forensic attention.

Over a century later and buoyed by their findings in the Punjab Records, Messrs Charles Grey and Herbert Garrett duly weighed in. But in doing so they were often rather more cavalier than the evidence merited. By equating 'the banks of the river Colorado', where Dr Gardner met Miss Haughton, with 'the mouth of the river Colorado', where the family later settled near the place called St Xavier, they confounded the geography; and in their eagerness to discredit the whole saga they could be as guilty of fabrication as the colonel. Thus they ridicule Pearse for dwelling on how Gardner 'often sadly lamented with tears in his eyes' the death of his mother; they even refer the reader to the relevant page in Pearse. Yet no such statement is to be found there.

More seriously, they rubbish the few concrete details that Gardner had let slip. After exhaustive research, for instance, they assert that 'the town of St Xavier has faded off the map'. Indeed they doubted if it had ever been on it.

> We have looked up Arrowsmith's atlases of the early nineteenth century [and] we find no trace of it; which is curious, for apparently it contained a Jesuit seminary of considerable importance.

In similar fashion Major Haughton, the explorer who had lost his life in Africa and was either the father or grand-father of Mrs Gardner, was dismissed as another figment of the colonel's imagination. 'Unfortunately, no record or mention of his [Haughton's] travels exists in contemporary works,' they announce.

Yet basic research indicates that they were wrong on both counts. Major Daniel Francis Haughton—or Houghton, the spelling preferred by Grey and Garrett—had indeed been a conspicuous figure in the exploration of Africa, albeit West Africa. Mungo Park's *Travels in the Interior of Africa* (1799), much the most famous of all contemporary works on the region, mentions him on the very first page. Haughton had been the Fort Major at Gorée near the mouth of the Gambia River in 1779–83 and it was his death while trying to reach Timbuktu and the River Niger in 1791 that had prompted Mungo Park's despatch on the same mission. The Haughton/Houghton family was an extensive one and hailed from Ireland. Whether the major had a daughter or grand-daughter who found her way to Mexico has not been established, but it is certainly possible.

As for the town of St Xavier, it could be argued that a location nine miles south of Tucson in what would become Arizona is not exactly 'near' the mouth of the Colorado River; but it is within a couple of hundred miles of it—and nearer still to the Gulf of California into which the river debouches. Here stood, and still stands, the sun-bleached and once Jesuit mission of San Xavier del Bac. Founded in the 1690s to serve converts from among the native American Papago people, it flourished as both a seminary and a school throughout the eighteenth century. It remains the best preserved of all the Spanish missions north of the present Mexican border and attracts numerous pilgrims and sightseers to this day. Because it didn't feature in Arrowsmith's maps, didn't mean it wasn't there.

So credit where credit is due. If the colonel did indeed cook up his American childhood, he must, at the very least, be congratulated on his ingenuity in sourcing the ingredients. More charitably, a township that featured on no known map could be seen as evidence of first-hand experience, and an African explorer who had evaded the notice of many contemporaries could be seen as proof of personal knowledge. Like the maggot lodged in Gardner's young brain, the germ of truth had a way of infecting the most far-fetched of his narrational extravagances.

Reaching the year 1807, and with the 22-year old Gardner poised to cross the Atlantic, editor Pearse takes the occasion to interrupt his story with a virtuoso piece of understatement. 'There is some mystery as to the manner in which he passed the following five years,' he says. In reality, the period in question was more like fifteen years and the mystery more akin to a maze, with many dead-ends and no assured exit.

> He himself states that he was in Ireland during the greater part of the [first five years], preparing partly for a maritime life, to which he was then inclined. It is probable that while in Ireland he acquired a certain knowledge of the science of gunnery, and also assimilated the tenacious accent of 'the distressful country'. In after-years his knowledge of artillery and his strong Irish brogue gave occasion to those unfriendly to him to accuse Gardner of being a deserter from the British artillery. This charge was, however, quite unsubstantiated, and there are no grounds for giving it the slightest credit.

Grey and Garrett, of course, would think there were ample grounds for accepting it as gospel. Brandishing the evidence of Gardner's statement as recorded by the Lahore news-writer, they would insist that he was indeed just that, 'an ordinary deserter from the British

© Surrey History Centre

2

3

The challenge of collating and editing Colonel Gardner's *Memoirs* fell to Major Hugh Pearse [2]. Michael Pakenham Edgeworth [3] had already alerted geographers to the extent of his travels, and Sir Henry Marion Durand [4] was the first to publish a verbatim account of them.

Helena Gardner's 1898 quest for her father's lost fortune led her to Srinagar in Kashmir. Somewhere in the maze of canals [5] and dank alleys radiating from the Jhelum River [6], the colonel had set up home. It was there that Helena was born and from there that the colonel sallied forth on parade.

Previous Colonel Alexander Haughton Campbell Gardner in his famous tartan outfit [1]. This photo of 1864 by Samuel Bourne was reproduced as the frontispiece of Pearse's *Memoirs*. Though the tartan was not certainly that of the 79th Highland Infantry, the turban's egret-plume was indeed a mark of the highest distinction.

4

From boarding school in the hill-station of Murree [10], Helena had been sent to England and the care of Lady and Sir Robert Henry Davies [7], lieutenant-governor of the Punjab. To realise her father's considerable estate, Christiaan Lourens Botha [8], the attorney who would become her second husband, accompanied Helena to India. There, Sir George MacMunn [9] introduced them to some of Gardner's old retainers.

The incentive for military adventurers to seek fame and fortune in the East had been provided by careers like that of George Thomas. While the young Gardner was taxing his Jesuit school-teachers, this 'Tipperaray Rajah' was commanding a private army [11, on horseback top-left] for the redoubtable Begum Samru before carving out his own 'kingdom'.

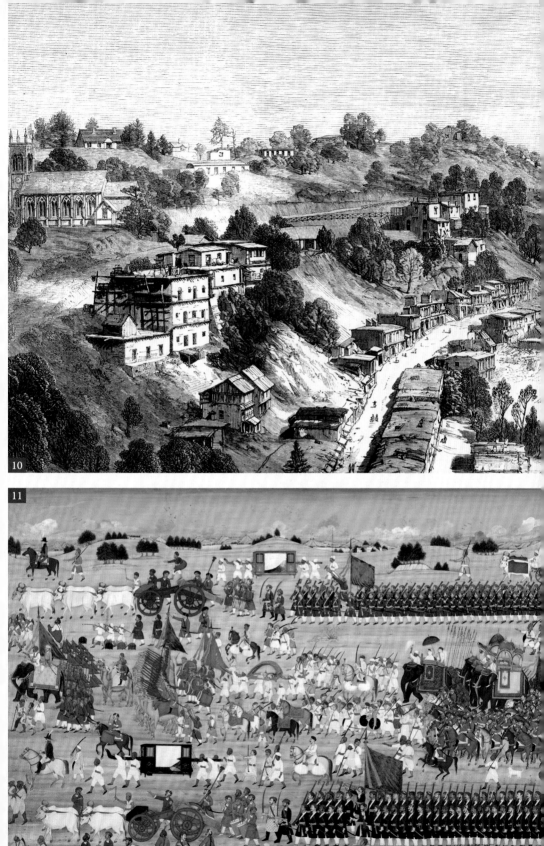

12

Gardner's twelve years of 'apparently aimless wandering' began with forays into what are now Turkmenistan and Uzbekistan. In 1824, while negotiating the badlands east of Samarkand [12], he and his companions were chased south into Afghanistan. On behalf of a claimant to the Kabul throne, he there took command of 800 Afghan irregulars [13] and married a princess.

The 1826 massacre of his young family launched Gardner on the greatest of his journeys, a 2000-kilometre circuit of the high Hindu Kush and the unknown Pamirs. Not until fifty years later would the Pamirs be properly explored. Fired by Gardner's story, Colonel T. E. Gordon painted his Wakhi guide on the Great Pamir in 1874 [14]. Later, a British-led Afghan Boundary Commission recorded the site of their winter camp at Bala Murghab on one of the Oxus's upper tributaries [15].

13

16

17

In the eastern Pamirs, Gardner and his followers relied on the hospitality of Kyrghyz pastoralists [16] and local chieftains. Without maps (there weren't any) or a compass, Gardner was understandably vague about this section of his itinerary. Only when he emerged into the deserts of Chinese Xinjiang did he encounter a known location in the walled town of Yarkand, now Shache [17].

To nineteenth-century geographers the most intriguing section of Gardner's mountain odyssey was the last. Having crossed the Himalayan spine to Ladakh and Kashmir, he returned to the Hindu Kush and was the first to penetrate the unknown mountains of Kafiristan (now Afghan Nuristan). With their European complexions and Islamophobia, the Kafirs [18, 19] were an ethnological curiosity. Gardner struggled to comprehend their beliefs but admired their carpentry and building skills [20].

18

19

20

21

22

Gardner's 1830 reappearance in Afghanistan anticipated the First Anglo-Afghan War. His travel notes would be lost when Alexander Burnes [21] was massacred. Gardner too fell foul of the occasionally armour-clad Durrani nobility [22] and spent nine months in detention near Kandahar [24]. And in Kabul, after assuming the unlikely role of an Afghan prince, he was pardoned by Dost Mohamed Khan, the unsmiling emir whom the British would dethrone [23].

23

24

25

For Gardner, as for the British invaders, the Khyber Pass afforded the best exit from Afghanistan. Guarding its approaches, the fort of Jamrud [25] was built by the great Sikh general, Hari Singh Nalwa, in 1836. He would die in its defence and Gardner would witness one of many Sikh-Afghan battles here.

Driven from Kabul by the British, Dost Mohamed fled north to 'the Valley of Urghundee' [26] near Bamiyan before

surrendering. Exiled to India, he would eventually be reinstated, but only after an entire British army had been wiped out, the British puppet had been overthrown, and a second British invasion of Afghanistan had been mounted.

26

27

Until Gardner's itineraries had been substantiated no explorer could be certain of being the first anywhere. George Hayward [27, with sporting trophies] consulted Gardner, as did Thomas Douglas Forsyth [32, with Indian servant], but neither reached the Pamirs. Sir Henry Rawlinson [28] and Sir Henry Yule [29] had their doubts; and it was left to Sir Owen Tudor Burne [31] to vouch for Gardner's character and for the self-effacing Ney Elias [30] to provide first-hand evidence of his achievement.

28

29

30

31

32

34

36

35

33

Coveting service in the Punjab,
Gardner followed in the footsteps
of other foreign adventurers.
Generals Jean Baptiste Ventura [33]
and Jean Francois Allard [34] were
ex-Napoleonic officers who now
commanded the Sikhs' European-
modelled corps, the *Fauj-i-khas*.

In 1832, the philandering General Paolo
Avitabile from Naples [35] was about
to become governor of Peshawar, and
the Quaker, Dr Josiah Harlan from
Pennsylvania [36], the governor of
Gujrat.

37

Stretching from Afghanistan to Tibet, the Sikh empire was the creation of Maharaja Ranjit Singh [38]. By the age of 20, he had captured the city of Lahore, united the fractious Sikh militias and established an inclusive but highly personal form of direct rule.

Crucial to this success was the remodelling of his formidable army. At the height of his fame the saffron-robed maharaja [39] was portrayed in the midst of his European-officered cavalry and infantry.

Pre-eminent among the Sikh maharaja's courtiers were three Dogra (Hindu) brothers from Jammu, Gulab Singh, Dhyan Singh and Suchet Singh [37], here shown in playful mode with their children, musicians and a dancer.

38

39

Though deeply distrustful of the Dogra brothers, Gardner was in the employ of the devious Dhyan Singh [40] when in 1839 the old maharaja died [41], here with Hira Singh, Dhyan Singh's son, at his side. In the ensuing power-struggle both Dhyan Singh and Hira Singh perished. But Gulab Singh, the eldest Dogra [42], manoeuvred his way through both the anarchy and the first Anglo-Sikh War to emerge as maharaja of Kashmir, with Gardner as his commandant of artillery.

service, Army or Navy'. Furthermore, by citing his accent and other evidence, they were convinced that he was not an American at all but 'an Irishman born in the town of Clongoose'.

On just two counts were Pearse/Cooper and Grey/Garrett in agreement: that Gardner definitely had some connection with Ireland and that during this period he somehow acquired a knowledge of gunnery. The other sources endorse these propositions and enlarge on them. Edgeworth, while confirming the Gardner family's American domicile, implies that 'Clongoose' in Ireland was where Alexander completed his education. Durand, on the other hand, maintains that he was educated entirely in what he calls 'the Ould Country', attending 'a well-known Jesuit College, near Maynooth' after having previously 'served five or six of his early years in the American Navy.' This naval interlude might explain why his education lasted into his twenties. No other source mentions the US Navy; but that he did indeed learn about gunnery while aboard ship seems likely.

Pearse, following Cooper, has Gardner returning to America in 1812. But on this transatlantic crossing, as on the previous one, he fails to say whether he travelled as a passenger or as a member of the crew. 'Landing at New Orleans in the month of March,' he received a letter from his second brother (the one who had not gone to Russia but whom Grey and Garrett mischievously confuse with the one who had). The letter conveyed the sad tidings that their father had died. After visiting an uncle in Philadelphia, Gardner 'immediately embarked on the career of adventure to which his inclination led him... and sailed for Lisbon,' says Pearse. It was now 1813.

In reference to the same round trip to America, Edgeworth says that the ship Gardner sailed in was a Portuguese brigantine and, in his always post-Pearse dates, he ascribes the voyage to 1823. The decade-long discrepancy between Edgeworth and Cooper/Pearse is thus announced; as noted, it resulted in Edgeworth's concertina-ing the 'twelve years of apparently aimless wandering' into just two. Only when Gardner presents himself in Lahore in 1832 do the accounts become more or less synchronised.

Arriving in Lisbon after his return trip to America, Gardner claims to have visited Madrid to dispose of some Spanish property inherited by his mother. He then remitted the proceeds of the property's sale to his elder brother in Astrakhan, and retaining just enough for his own travelling expenses to join this brother, he set sail again, this time down the Mediterranean.

> While preparing for this journey [continues Pearse], Gardner made the acquaintance of a man called Aylmer, whom he describes as very clever and an experienced traveller, and, moreover, a relation of the Principal of Gardner's old Jesuit school in Mexico. Aylmer was a Jesuit himself, and had no difficulty in persuading Gardner to join him in a journey which he was about to make to Alexandria and Cairo. ... Early in the year 1813 they accordingly set out from Madrid together and arrived in due course at Cairo.

Naturally Grey and Garrett here smelled another rat, in fact several. It was all so improbable and confusing as to be scarcely worthy of comment. They note only that in Edgeworth's account Mrs Gardner's Spanish inheritance fades from the reckoning. Like Major Haughton, like the town of San Xavier and the whole American upbringing, 'the *chateaux en Espagne* do not materialise,' they sneer. Yet Edgeworth, too, makes mention of 'Mr Aylmer', though in this case he is someone 'connected with the Principal of Clongoose' rather than the Principal of San Xavier.

By now the conflict of evidence must have had even Pearse wondering where, if anywhere, lay the truth. To the mystery of Gardner's naval interlude was added that of his Irish education at 'Clongoose' and the shadowy but evidently influential figure of Father Aylmer of the Society of Jesus. Well might Grey and Garrett scoff. Yet to anyone inclined to take Gardner seriously it will come as no surprise that 'Clongoose' and Aylmer are far from fictitious.

'Clongoose' was almost certainly Clongowes. It is situated nine miles west of Dublin in the rich farmland of County Kildare and within a few minutes' drive of the 'well-known Jesuit College near Maynooth' mentioned by Durand. Enquiry reveals Clongowes as the site of Clongowes Wood Jesuit College, and Maynooth as that of St Patrick's College. Both these institutions still exist. Schuyler Jones, in dogged pursuit of the elusive colonel, once contacted them. The resulting correspondence was, he says, 'interesting, but unfruitful'.

Of the two, the Royal College of St Patrick, or 'Maynooth College', is the older and has been, for most of its existence, exclusively clerical. Founded in 1795, it now awards pontifical degrees and is considered 'the national seminary of Ireland'. Gardner could have attended it, although as someone proud to have resisted Catholicism and, in Pearse's words, never likely to allow 'religion to come much between him and worldly objects', he seems an unlikely candidate for the novitiate. Clongowes Wood Jesuit College, on the other hand, is a boarding school for boys and of some distinction. Alumni have included the novelist James Joyce, who features the school in *The Portrait of the Artist as a Young Man*, the Taoiseach Michael O'Higgins and the Ryanair boss Michael O'Leary. But Clongowes Wood College opened its doors only in 1824, making Gardner's attendance impossible even within the timeframe adopted by Edgeworth.

It appears, however, that the buildings of Clongowes Wood, then known as Castle Browne, had previously housed pupils and had actually been acquired for a school in 1813. The school opened there in the following year. By 1816 it had 194 pupils and, according to its records, in the same year it welcomed as its new rector the Rev Charles Aylmer SJ.

Happily this Charles Aylmer, a native of nearby Painstown, has attracted some documentation. Born in 1786, a year after Gardner, Aylmer had been educated at the Jesuit college of Stonyhurst in Lancashire (England). Discovering there a vocation to join the priesthood, he had then been despatched to Sicily in 1809.

The reason for Aylmer's Mediterranean voyage was that at the time, and adding greatly to the confusion over the status of places like San Xavier del Bac and Clongowes, the Jesuit order was in serious disarray. A papal bull had officially suppressed the Society of Jesus in 1773. In Mexico, Franciscan friars had briefly taken over San Xavier del Bac and in Ireland all Jesuit establishments had been closed down. But by the early 1800s the papal bull was being ignored and the Jesuit order steadily reinstated. Protestant countries like England had paid little attention to the ban anyway, and as the Napoleonic conquests were rolled back, other parts of Europe followed suit. In Sicily, for instance, the Jesuits were reinstated in 1804 and the island itself came under British occupation from 1806. Hence would-be Jesuits from the British Isles increasingly looked to Palermo's seminary when preparing for Holy Orders. Ireland, on the other hand, retained the Jesuit ban. For Irish youths like Charles Aylmer a vocation carried the added attraction of an opportunity to see foreign parts.

Aylmer's 1809 voyage to Palermo was made in a very small sailing vessel. It carried just seven passengers, six of whom were Jesuit novices from Ireland. They went from Liverpool by way of Portugal and Gibraltar, and since Pearse insists that Gardner sailed into the Mediterranean with Aylmer, it is tempting to conclude that the colonel himself was the seventh passenger. Unfortunately this possibility must be resisted; the date given by Pearse is four years later than that given by the Jesuits. Yet an incident described by Bartholomew Esmonde, one of Aylmer's shipboard companions, does have a strangely familiar ring.

> Before leaving the Burlings [their first landfall on the coast of Portugal], our captain exercised us in the use of our muskets in order to prepare us to meet privateers, as ours was a running ship without convoy. At length the breeze freshened up and carried us down the coasts of Portugal and Spain to Cape Trafalgar, rendered famous by the victory and death of Lord Nelson [four years earlier]. Thence we bore down for the straits [of Gibraltar] (called by sailors 'The Gut'). Before we entered them we were stopped and boarded by an English frigate, the *Hyperion*. Her officer, who came to examine our papers and the men's protections, obliged us to lie by while he performed what he called his duty. Among our sailors was one unfortunate Irishman who was set down in the ship's register as 'subject of Great Britain' but who now declared himself to be an American citizen and produced an American protection as such. But on being questioned more closely he had the ill luck to produce a paper specifying that he was a British subject, had served several years in the English Navy, and had received his discharge during the last peace. This settled the business and the poor fellow was instantly taken from us.

Nothing more is heard of this 'poor fellow'. His name is not revealed and it may anyway have been an alias. He was obviously a member of the crew rather than a passenger. It is not clear whether he was indeed American, nor why, if he wasn't, he was 'instantly taken from us'.

It does, though, establish that as early as 1809 Charles Aylmer's path had crossed with that of someone of ambiguous nationality who could well have been Alexander Gardner. And if indeed it was he, his connection with the Co. Kildare Jesuits may be explained. He could have spent the previous two years at sea as suggested by Durand and as supported by his own testimony about having 'formerly served in a ship of war'. Then, on the strength of his acquaintance with Aylmer and his colleagues, he could, after the affair in the straits of Gibraltar, have passed the next three years supplementing his education among the pro-Jesuit fraternity of Co. Kildare. This would be consistent with both Edgeworth and Durand and with the longer version given by Pearse on the strength of Cooper's memorial.

But it is, of course, mere speculation. He might simply have been an Irish lad born and brought up in Clongowes, as Garrett and Grey would maintain. There he could have met Aylmer before the latter left for Palermo, and there too he could have picked up all he knew about the Jesuit establishments in the Americas and Sicily. Certainty is ever at a premium where Gardner is concerned. Perhaps what this entire episode best illustrates is simply the confusion that must attend any life recollected in extreme old age, related for the most part verbally, summarised piecemeal by assorted witnesses, interpreted by a biographer who never met his subject, and finally savaged by later researchers convinced that the subject in question was an outright blackguard.

According to Pearse, in 1813 Gardner and Aylmer travelled east together not simply to Palermo but on to Cairo and beyond. The facts suggest otherwise. Father Aylmer is probably best known for a letter he wrote from Rome in July of the following year, by when Pearse would have him on the Black Sea. The letter described a papal audience at which the ban on the Jesuits was finally rescinded. 'I could not refrain from tears ...' wrote Aylmer to his colleagues back in Ireland, 'Oh truly how sweet is victory after a long fought battle!!!'

To be fair, Aylmer drops out of Gardner's narrative as suddenly as he drops in; Pearse's belief that the two men continued to enjoy one another's company was just an assumption. But while he was in Cairo, Gardner did team up with three or four other footloose adventurers. Attracted to Egypt following that country's conquest by Napoleon and then by the British, they all claimed militarily useful skills and they compared the terms currently on offer to foreign mercenaries in Egypt with those they might expect in Qajar-ruled Persia, Tsarist Russia and, increasingly, the Sikh-ruled Punjab. Two of them were German mineralogists but only one is named. He was called either 'Datterwitz' (Edgeworth), 'Dotterweiss' (Durand), 'Dallerwitz' (Pearse), or 'Dottenweiss or Dotterwich' (Grey and Garrett). There was also 'a highly accomplished Frenchman' named 'Rossaix' (Pearse) or 'Musaix' (Edgeworth). 'The conversation that Gardner had at this time with M. Rossaix led him, many years later, to enter the Maharaja's [ie Ranjit Singh's] service,' says Pearse.

In view of Gardner's habit of naming only real people, it is safe to assume that most of these gentlemen did actually exist. Datter-witz, in particular, would make a later appearance, although in the opinion of Grey and Garrett, this proved nothing. The name had simply been 'borrowed by Gardiner to affix to one of his imaginary travelling companions'.

Imaginary or not, the whole group left Cairo, crossed the Sinai Desert and entered Syria. Near Jericho they caught up with a cara-van returning from the Mecca *haj*. 'Organised by some Armenian merchants', the caravan's complement of 3000—'a medley of Asiatics, chiefly pilgrims; a mendicant set, but very sturdy,' says Gardner— offered a modicum of security. Desert raiders might be deterred, although the petty pilferers among their fellow travellers were not. The foreigners therefore made common cause with a small group of Christian, Turkish and Arab merchants 'who had effects which they did not choose to lose'. Together they camped apart, 'letting it be known that any prowlers would be fired upon'. There was no question of hiding their identity or blending in with the pilgrims. This being one of the few occasions when Gardner rode with others of European descent, they were doubtless conspicuous in the high boots, long coats and black stove-pipe hats favoured by contemporary travellers to the East. Indian and Persian artists invariably depicted Europeans in just such garb, regardless of their calling or the climate.

At Erzerum in eastern Turkey, Datterwitz and his fellow German received adverse news about the job prospects in Persia. They opted instead for Gardner's destination of Astrakhan. All accordingly left the haj caravan and rode for the Black Sea coast at Trebizond (Trabzon). From there they sailed in a Russian vessel to Circassia, just north of the Caucasus in what is now Georgia. Gardner sent word to his brother of their imminent arrival and, without incident, they entered Russian territory. By the time they reached Astrakhan, it must have been mid-1814.

According to Pearse, what followed was an improbable three years of dedicated study that would whet the colonel's interest in everything from gems to gunpowder.

> Finding that the salaries of mineralogists were very high, and that there was considerable demand for superintendants (presumably of mines), Gardner applied himself studiously to all the books he could gather together, so that his brother might be able as soon as possible to testify honestly to his acquirements.

It is not clear what became of the Germans, but Gardner lived with his brother throughout this interlude and was confident that the brother's recommendation would secure him a lucrative assignment. He also recorded his gratitude for 'some training in the rudiments of geology and chemistry acquired from his lamented and honoured father'. A 'settled and promising life' in Tsarist employ now beckoned. Russia's gain could have been Turkestan's loss. The idea of continuing further east to the Sikh kingdom of the Punjab seems to have vanished like a mirage.

Then, on the unusually precise date of 14 December 1817, unforeseen tragedy struck. In Pearse's words, 'his hopes were shattered and his home broken up by the sudden death of his brother, who was killed by a fall from his horse'.

Lobbying for the promised posting and trying to realise his brother's fortune took up much of 1818. Neither was successful. The job offer was withdrawn and the brother's estate was mired in litigation. Disgusted and disheartened, Gardner toyed with the idea of again returning to America.

He changed his mind 'when he met one day a German called Sturzky'. Edgeworth calls him Schrotsky. He was not the German mineralogist who had accompanied Datterwitz from Cairo but he had now teamed up with the self-same Datterwitz. Both men had just relinquished posts in the Russian service and were again bent on trying their luck in Persia. For want of a better plan, Gardner went along with them.

Their diagonal voyage from the north-west extremity of the Caspian Sea to its south-eastern corner was made in a small merchant vessel and was beset by calms and contrary winds. In December 1818 they finally tramped ashore on Persian soil near Astrabad (now Gorgan). There Gardner and Datterwitz again parted. It seems that news had reached them from Rossaix, the French officer they had met in Cairo. Blazing the trail that Allard and Ventura, then Court and Avitabile, would follow, Rossaix had made his way to the Sikh-ruled Punjab and was now 'receiving large pay at Lahore'. To the cash-strapped Gardner, this was enough. He and the mysterious Sturzky abandoned the Persian plan and headed east.

Near the Perso-Afghan border their path crossed with that of an envoy returning from the Persian court to his native Kokand, one of the Central Asian khanates in the Ferghana plain of what is now Uzbekistan. This man painted such a rosy picture of the opportunities on offer in his homeland that Sturzky and Gardner again changed their minds. Instead of the Punjab, they now set their sights on Turkestan. But almost immediately, says Pearse, Gardner was laid low with an unidentified fever.

> Sturzky therefore took a friendly leave of him, and departed with [the Kokand envoy]. This took place within a few miles of Herat, and

Gardner entered that city on the following day, and remained there a short time until cured of his fever. He then proposed to visit Khiva, and possibly to rejoin Monsieur Sturzky.

Thus it was that, in January 1819, astride a rough-coated pony, in the company of another pilgrim kafila and finally rid of European associates, the 34-year-old Gardner had passed beyond the confines of civilisation and crossed the snowy outliers of the Hindu Kush to launch himself on the first of his great journeys into Turkestan.

In Khiva he did re-meet Sturzky. He was the man to whom Gardner turned for financial help after satisfying Khiva's inquisitors with that confession of his American nationality. But Sturzky was by then a broken man. Faring badly among the Uzbeks, he had been forcibly converted and deprived of whatever he had earned. He trailed back to Astrakhan with Gardner and is heard of no more.

The twelve years of 'romance and vicissitude' that followed, of 'aimless wandering' amid 'arduous and terrible incidents', have been described. Gardner's presentation to Maharaja Ranjit Singh of the Punjab in 1832, and the enlistment that followed, brought an end to this life of high-plains drifting and Himalayan scrabbling. In the service of India's most powerful native state, he would no longer be a free agent or a solitary witness. The tempo of his tale changes. It becomes markedly less erratic if just as contentious; so does the critique of it.

Despite Grey and Garrett's best efforts to prove otherwise, the Lahore news-writer's report of Gardner's first audience with Maharaja Ranjit Singh contained only one revelation: that he had arrived in Lahore with a companion called Kanara. Grey and Garrett identify this man with someone whose real name was Kennedy or Kerry. He was also known as Canora, Khora and Kinaila and spent 14 years in the Sikh army. Like Gardner, Kanara would claim to have been born in America—or very specifically 'in Northumberland Town, Philadelphia, St John's Street, odd [numbered] side'. He had served three years in Egypt before drifting east and was indeed 'about 35 years' of age, having been born in 1799. From the precision of his American address and his thick Irish accent, Grey and Garrett deduced that he must have been primed by Gardner and that, like him, he was really a British deserter of Irish birth. He could well have left the employ of Sultan Mohamed Khan of Peshawar with Gardner, and he too was destined for distinguished service in Sikh employ. But in 1848 he would die the hero's death that would elude Gardner. During the bloodletting at the Sikh court that preceded the Second Anglo-Sikh War, he was murdered while defending his guns from the mutinous soldiery. The fact that Gardner never mentions him proves nothing. He served mainly on the frontier, was seldom in Lahore and, apart from their joint induction, the two men's paths rarely crossed.

In respect of the confession by both men that they had 'formerly served on a ship of war, but not being satisfied with their position, quitted it, and proceeded from Bombay to Peshawar', that too proved nothing. Once upon a time Gardner probably had served on a ship of war, though whose ship is anyone's guess. Grey and Garret assumed it was one belonging to the British Navy or the East India Company, and this was almost certainly the impression that Gardner and Kanara wanted to give. To convince the maharaja of their gunnery skills and secure a command in his artillery, it was vital to lay claim to some relevant experience. Twelve years freebooting in Inner Asia would not have been good enough; a spell tending the latest European ordnance on the gun-deck of a man o' war would have been ideal.

Only the fact that they had supposedly quitted their ship in Bombay troubled Grey and Garrett. Wondering how the two 'deserters' could possibly have traversed a large chunk of what was already British India without once being detected or arrested, they proposed that they must in fact have come ashore in Karachi and travelled up the Indus, so avoiding British territory. But Ranjit Singh might also have wondered how they had got to Peshawar undetected. Thus, had they indeed landed at Karachi, they would surely have admitted it. Otherwise the only possible explanation was that they hadn't deserted at all and were not therefore wanted by the British government.

Gardner's later immunity from British justice in respect of desertion, the most heinous of crimes, would bear this out. Charles

Masson, the much put-upon archaeologist who was indeed a deserter, bartered both his independence of movement and his treasure trove of archaeological findings for a pardon, yet would still be dogged by the stigma of desertion till his dying day. Gardner, on the other hand, though well known to numerous British officers, would never once be publicly accused of desertion. In fact, he would eventually find sanctuary under British rule and then be allowed to hold a sensitive command as the only non-Asiatic in the employ of the Kashmir government.

In short, Grey and Garrett's contention that he was a renegade looks to have rested less on the evidence to hand and more on the estimate they had already formed of his 'despicable' character. Events in the Punjab would imminently confirm these suspicions. But of the two most persuasive arguments for accepting the gist of his story as factual, they make no mention at all. The first line of argument has been well aired by Schuyler Jones.

> ... for anyone who would claim that Gardner's travels in Central Asia were fabricated, there is a serious difficulty to be explained away: it is one thing to claim to have visited all those places, it is quite another to sit down and construct a false journal—hundreds of hand-written pages—compete with dates and places. It is a considerable labour and there is no indication that Gardner ever tried to sell his manuscripts or even to publish them. On the contrary, he freely gave them to people he met. He seems, moreover, to have been a man of action who would have had little patience with such work.

In other words, if it was all a fiction, why did he bother? And even if much of his story was actually relayed by word of mouth, why pad it out with so much contestable detail and so many improbable incidents? Why not show a greater regard for consistency, corroboration and general plausibility? It was as if his intention was not to convince but simply to relive fading memories.

The second argument against his story being fabricated takes a more comprehensive view of his life. As of 1832 and his entering Sikh employ, Gardner's career can indeed be substantially corroborated.

His role may sometimes have been exaggerated but his movements are accepted and the horrific events he describes are a matter of record. Moreover, his testimony is cited in several contemporary histories. If post-1832 he may be regarded as a reliable witness, then the same confidence might reasonably be extended to his pre-1832 career.

His critics, of whom Grey and Garrett were by no means the first, were themselves inconsistent. The earlier exploits were dismissed as outright fantasy while the later exploits were generally considered credible, though far from creditable. Hence, instead of questioning the colonel's good faith, they now found grounds to question his whole character. Was he, as he liked to think, 'invariably actuated in my inward soul by feelings at once honest and upright'? Or was he, at bottom, a rank opportunist, someone whose crimes and complicity in the atrocities of the period were proof of such depravity that, even if he was neither a liar nor a deserter, he was beyond all indulgence and deserving only of irredeemable ignominy?

6

The Lion of the Punjab
1832–39

Until his arrival in Lahore, the march of history had rarely impinged on Gardner's career. Napoleon merits just a single mention in the *Memoirs*, Wellington none at all; political upheavals feature merely as opportunities or inconveniences. Evading the bustle of events seems to have come as naturally to the colonel as giving a wide berth to centres of population. Frontiers were crossed without comment; itineraries evolved without plans. Over the silent wastes he had jogged in his bearskin burnoose as impervious to the fortunes of nations beyond the horizon as to the icy blasts off the Bolor-tagh.

But as of 1832, all this was about to change. The man now known as 'Gordana Sahib' would find himself scorched by a political inferno. In a life overloaded with adventure, his fourteen years in the service of the Sikh Empire would prove the most uncomfortable of all.

Lahore offered all that he craved. Staggering wealth was there for the taking, along with ample occasion for indulgence and ever more horrific assignments. But they came laced with extreme danger and soured by intrigues and treachery of Byzantine intricacy. A host of new characters, both Asian and European, crowd the colonel's narrative; all are identified and many of them documented. The places he is sent are found on the map, the commissions he undertakes feature in the history books, and the company he keeps lives on in notoriety. Out of an often baffling obscurity in the lands to the west of the Khyber Pass, he had cantered into the lurid limelight of the last of India's great native empires.

An empire is supposed to decline and fall; the process can take centuries and be replete with achievements to rival those of its heyday. The Sikh Empire imploded. Already at its zenith when Gardner arrived in 1832, it had degenerated into a bloodbath by the time he left in 1847 and had vanished altogether by 1849. If its rise had been meteoric, its fall was cataclysmic. Half a century in the making, it would be obliterated in a decade.

To survive in this setting of escalating carnage, Gardner was not ill equipped. A congenial exterior, a fearless disposition, a lack of scruple and an acute instinct for self-preservation would prove useful assets. But what he lacked was any regular military experience. Maharaja Ranjit Singh valued ex-Napoleonic officers like Ventura and Avitabile, stern disciplinarians who had fought on the battlefields of Europe and were familiar with the latest tactical manoeuvres. Gardner knew a bit about ballistics but had yet to command a battery or serve with regular troops. By way of induction an unnamed French officer had lately been set the challenge of hitting a white spot on an acacia tree on other side of the wide Ravi River. The maharaja was advised by General Ventura that success could only be a matter of luck. 'But the Maha Raja adhered to his own opinion; the experiment took place; the officer missed the tree, and lost his hope of emolument'. If Gardner were not to be similarly dismissed, he badly needed to back his pretensions as a master-gunner by making an instant impression.

Opportunity graciously obliged. Shortly after his audience with the *Sher-e-Punjab* or 'Lion of the Punjab', one of Ranjit Singh's titles, Dhyan Singh, the man Gardner calls the 'Prime Minister', drew him aside to inspect a brace of new cannon. Presents from Lord William Bentinck on the occasion of a British governor-general's first visit to the Punjab in 1831, the guns had been unpacked but had yet to be fired. According to Durand's account, the problem concerned the two boxes of shrapnel shells supplied with them; no one knew how to prime them. According to Pearse, it was the guns themselves. Either way, Gardner strode forward to investigate and was lucky enough to happen upon some technical data.

> I found in one of the tumbrils [ie gun carriages], enclosed in a bundle
> of fuses, a small printed slip of paper giving instructions as to time of
> burning, time of flight, etc.

It was promising. He studied the instructions, lit a few fuses, and
finding the results corresponded with the paperwork, announced to
Dhyan Singh that 'there seemed to be no further difficulty'.

> Accordingly one of the guns, with its tumbril, etc, was given over next
> day into my charge and I was ordered to get ready to fire three or four
> shells at different distances in the presence of Maharaja Ranjit Singh.
> I took a few soldiers in hand, and in a few days' time all this was done
> with a degree of success unexpected even by myself, the shells bursting
> exactly as required at 600, 800, 1000, and 1200 yards.

The maharaja was delighted. With a clap of his hands and a glint in
his single eye (the other had been lost to smallpox in his youth), he
proceeded to bombard Gardner with questions.

> Much as I had heard of the insignificance of his appearance, it at first
> startled me; but the profound respect with which he was treated, and
> the extraordinary range of subjects on which he examined me, speedily
> dispelled the first impression.

Other visitors would form a similar opinion. Lithe but never large,
Ranjit Singh was now 52 and visibly shrinking. Ravaged by a combination of experimental aphrodisiacs and fiery liquor, he looked his
best on a horse. At closer quarters the pock marks, the grey whiskers
and the closed eye-socket were all the uglier for a disproportionately
large forehead that no turban could entirely conceal. To Emily Eden,
who sketched the maharaja in 1838 while accompanying her brother,
the next British governor-general, to Lahore, the 'Lion' resembled
nothing so much as 'an old mouse'. But, perhaps because he had
forgotten how to read or write, his appetite for information was in-

satiable and his memory phenomenal. Judging men and events with unerring insight, he saw more with his one eye than others with two.

'The Maharaja was indeed one of those masterminds which only require opportunity to change the face of the globe,' confirmed Gardner. Born in 1780, Ranjit Singh had succeeded to his father's command of one of the numerous *misls*, or factions, into which the Sikh warrior class had been divided when the tenth and last of the Sikh Gurus had died in 1708. Aged only nineteen, he had engineered the capture of Lahore and, two years later, added the Sikh holy city of Amritsar. In the same year, 1801, he was anointed maharaja of Lahore. Although this title clashed with the egalitarian principles of the Khalsa (a term comprehending the generality of initiated Sikhs to whom the last Guru had entrusted temporal responsibility), one by one the other misls were obliged to submit.

Their loyalty was often suspect; but Ranjit's reputation for inclusive government, wise rule and military success soon attracted a far wider following. Muslims and Hindus were as prominent as Sikhs in the offices of state. The army rapidly expanded to include Pathans, Gurkhas, Dogras and Purbiahs (Biharis from British India), not to mention the European contingent. Thanks to Ranjit Singh, the Sikh Empire was a notably multi-faith, multi-caste and multi-ethnic enterprise; but thanks to Ranjit Singh, it was also overly dependent on the charisma of its remarkable creator.

Typical of those drawn to Ranjit's Lahore was Dhyan Singh. As the instigator of Gardner's test-firing of the new cannon, the 'Prime Minister' was as delighted with the outcome as was the maharaja. Dhyan Singh was the second of those three Dogra (ie Hindu Rajput) brothers from Jammu who were by now as close to the maharaja as any of his Sikh retainers or his immediate family. All three brothers commanded large numbers of troops; in addition, the dapper and impeccably mannered Dhyan Singh acted as the maharaja's principal adviser at court, while the glowering Gulab Singh served as his feared enforcer in the hills, and the elegant Suchet Singh added a touch of glamour 'as a gay courtier and gallant soldier'. Gardner had managed not just to impress the 'Lion of the Punjab' but to ingratiate himself with the most powerful pride in the realm. 'Ever after,' he says,

'[Dhyan Singh] acted as my patron and steadfast friend. His brothers, Raja (and afterwards Maharaja [of Kashmir]) Gulab Singh and Raja Suchet Singh, also befriended me.'

On the strength of his marksmanship and these patrons, Gardner was immediately inducted into the Sikh army. Durand records that he was given command of two guns, a salary of 750 rupees a month and the revenue of two villages. Gardner himself, as quoted by Pearse, says it was actually 'eight horse-artillery guns, two mortars and two howitzers' and that, as well as a salary, he received 'a considerable present' plus the expectation of hefty sweeteners from such officers as he might subsequently instruct. For a man who in Peshawar had reportedly been retained on 3 rupees a day, it was wealth indeed. The nest-egg that would be so coveted by his daughter Helena began to accumulate as of this appointment to command one of the Sikh army's thirty-odd batteries of horse-drawn artillery.

> Thus matters continued for three or four months, when I was ordered to proceed with my park of artillery, to which was added a force of 800 regular infantry and 400 'Ghorcharahs', or irregular cavalry, to join General Ventura.

Jean Baptiste Ventura had reached Lahore ten years earlier in the company of another officer, Jean Francois Allard. The pair complemented one another nicely. Tall, saturnine and scholarly, Ventura was a native of Modena in Italy; Allard, short, silver-bearded and genial, came from St Tropez. Both had served with distinction in Napoleon's armies and had fought at Waterloo. But being excluded from the subsequent amnesty because of their republican views, they had then hawked their talents in Egypt and Persia. From there, following the trail laid by Rossaix, they had continued east through Afghanistan to try their luck in India.

The maharaja had at first suspected them of being British agents. He was reassured only after extensive enquiries and numerous trials like that just undergone by Gordana Sahib. Impressed by their professionalism, he had then directed Allard to form and train a cavalry brigade and Ventura to do the same with an infantry brigade. Unlike the irregular cavalry that had traditionally made up the bulk of the maharaja's forces, these troops wore uniforms, carried standard weapons and were disciplined, drilled and deployed in accordance with European practice.

Augmented by artillery units like that now commanded by Gardner, they formed the nucleus of Ranjit Singh's new model army, the Fauj-i-khas. In the previous century similar brigades had been trained by European officers—de Boigne, Reinhardt and Perron as well as Skinner, Thomas and the other Gardner—to serve sundry Indian princes; but Ranjit Singh had been the first to contemplate reorganising his entire army along these lines. The Fauj-i-khas had been the template, and Generals Ventura and Allard its pioneers. In 1827, they had been joined in this enterprise by two more ex-Napoleonic officers, one the portly Neapolitan Paolo Avitabile and the other Claude Auguste Court, a less conspicuous figure whose talents lent themselves to the designing and casting of the superior artillery pieces in which the maharaja took such pride. Gardner's foundry skills as later exhibited in the service of Kashmir would be acquired from General Court.

In 1831, Ventura had commanded the troops that had defeated Syed Ahmed and his jihadist followers at the battle of Balakot. Gardner, of course, had been on the other side in that battle and had anyway arrived too late. Their paths had not crossed. But in 1832, Ventura was engaged in extending the empire along the right bank of the Indus in the extreme south of the Sikh dominions. There, Gardner joined him and, after what he calls 'some trouble', the two districts of Rojhan and Sabzalkot were subjugated.

Both these places lay on the frontier with Sind, an arid and poorly defended land ruled by three quarrelsome emirs and on which the maharaja had long fixed his covetous gaze. So had his inveterate enemy Dost Mohamed Khan and his Barakzai brothers in Afghanistan. And so too, it seemed, had the British. A few months earlier, the then Lieutenant Alexander Burnes had made his debut on India's north-western extremity by sailing up the Indus from near the modern Karachi through Sind to the Punjab.

Ostensibly the purpose of this voyage was to reciprocate Ranjit Singh's generous gift of some Kashmir shawls for Britain's King William IV. In return, a royal equipage comprising a state coach and horses was to be despatched to Lahore. Built in Bombay and modelled on the conveyances in the Royal Mews at Whitehall, the coach was lightly sprung, ornately gilded and lavishly upholstered. The horses—four colossal mares and a stallion, all of the shaggy-hooved Shire variety used in Britain for hauling beer carts—had also been carefully chosen; as England's nearest thing to an elephant, the Shire horse was expected to make a favourable impression on an equine connoisseur like the maharaja. More to the point, neither the elegant carriage nor the heavily-built horses could possibly withstand the 700-mile overland trek to Lahore. They could only be delivered by boat, so turning the presentation into an ill-disguised pretext for investigating the navigational potential of the mighty Indus and its tributaries.

With some difficulty, and for the loss of one of the decidedly Trojan horses, Burnes had delivered the equipage in Lahore. He had then aired the foregone conclusion of his superiors in the Indian Political Department that the river was nothing if not a natural conduit for trade. The grains and fruits of the Punjab and Afghanistan could be exported down it and the manufactures of India and Britain imported up it. All that was needed were reciprocal commercial treaties with the powers along the river, some customs posts and pilotage arrangements, one or two British-manned riverside outposts, and bigger boats—plus some pacificatory measures to stop the Sindis from contesting their passage.

The maharaja was moderately enthusiastic about the nautical aspects of this scheme. He toyed with the construction of a navy and was especially keen on the idea of vessels that could ply against the current. The British played along and promised him a paddle steamer; but according to Gardner, the maharaja was not of a mind to wait.

> Having heard of steamers, Ranjit Singh desired to have one; and believing that a foreigner could do anything, asked General Ventura if he was a good blacksmith, and desired him, without waiting for a reply, to make him a steamer at once.

Ventura objected. As an amateur antiquarian like Charles Masson, in 1830 the general had begun excavating the great Buddhist stupa at Manikyala near Rawalpindi. He had better things to do with his spare time. Yet 'since it was as much as his position was worth', he reluctantly agreed to proceed with the boat on payment of a sum of 40,000 rupees. Then 'he came to me', says Gardner, 'and begged my aid'.

> I read up all I could about paddle-boat building, and succeeded in turning out a wondrous sort of two-decked barge with paddle-wheels to be worked by hand. ... Ranjit Singh clapped his hands, as was his wont, in ecstasy with the boat, in the sides of the lower decks of which I had made port-holes which bristled with swivel guns. This boat was launched on the Ravi [River], but with the utmost efforts of the exhausted wheel-turners, would not go more than ten yards or so up the stream.

Ranjit Singh was overjoyed that it went at all; 'he had equalled the achievements of the West in science, and that was all he desired,' noted Gardner. The ship's designers were equally elated. Since the cost of the boat had been barely 2000 rupees, Ventura and Gardner pocketed the rest of the 40,000 rupees and proudly boasted of being responsible for 'the first and only "steamer" built for the Sikh monarchy'. Its maiden voyage, though short, would be long remembered.

> I had built fore and aft cabins, and [the maharaja] filled them with nautch-girls [dancers and courtesans] and there was a great *tamasha*. ... The picnic was not unaccompanied by strong drinks and I received at the end of the celebration a further present of a shawl and 300 rupees.

Quite when this all happened is not stated. Since the inspiration came from Burnes's 1830–1 voyage, it must have been soon after Gardner's arrival in 1832.

But navigation had been only half the story behind Burnes's Indus voyage. In India, trade seldom followed the flag; it more often preceded it; and just as the coach and horses disguised a British bid to open the river to commerce, so the promotion of riverine trade disguised a British bid for political and strategic advantage.

With the capture of Delhi and the defeat of the Maratha confederation, the most formidable in India, in the early 1800s, the British, though still technically servants of the East India Company, had almost completed their conquest of India. Only peripheral opponents remained, and they not for long. The Nepalese were defeated in 1815 and the Assamese in 1824. Along the skirts of the Himalayas, that left only the extreme north-west—Sind, Punjab and, because the Afghans still claimed Peshawar and the neighbouring tribal regions, Afghanistan.

In the Company's lately adopted summer capital at Simla (Shimla), itself only a few days march from the Sikh frontier, British strategists had begun to agonise over what they perceived as the vulnerability of their north-western approaches. Thirty years earlier, following his conquest of Egypt, Napoleon had threatened to invade India via Persia and Afghanistan. Now, in the 1830s, it was Tsarist Russia that supposedly nursed designs on India, albeit by urging its Persian allies to press their claim to much of Afghanistan. With support from St Petersburg a Persian army was already laying siege to Herat. If successful, an eastward extension of Persian territory could be expected to provide a 'covered way' for Russian influence to reach up to and over the Hindu Kush. Dost Mohamed might then choose to throw in his lot with St Petersburg and even Ranjit Singh might succumb to Russian blandishments. Disaffected peoples within India itself would also look to the Russians. However hypothetical and far-fetched, the prospect was enough to induce a blimpish paranoia among the Simla sahibs.

Ever since the British had acquired Bombay in the seventeenth century, their presence in India had relied heavily on control of the sea-lanes. Having now to confront a major European power on India's landward approaches was the stuff of military nightmares. As they tossed in their beds, the generals drew imaginary 'natural' frontiers along the banks of the Indus—or, better still, along the crests of the Hindu Kush—and conjured up friendly 'buffer' states beside and beyond them. Simultaneously, political agents, like the roving Burnes, began probing the passes and deserts while exploring the sympathies of those who aspired to control them. Russian agents did likewise. Such were the opening moves in the hundred year's cold war of Anglo-Russian alarms and espionage that became known as 'The Great Game'.

Among the intervening powers in the 1830s, the foremost were of course Ranjit Singh's expanding Sikh Empire and Dost Mohamed Khan's less cohesive but resurgent Afghan emirate. Either would do as a buffer—but probably not both, given their mutual hostility. On the whole the British preferred the Sikhs. Over the previous quarter of a century their relations with Lahore had gone from cordially suspicious to suspiciously cordial. The maharaja appreciated the all-conquering record of the Company's army and, once their mutual frontier had been settled along the line of the Satluj River, resigned himself to expanding elsewhere. Thus, Peshawar had first been snatched from the Afghans by the Sikhs as early as 1818 and Kashmir in 1819. Although Peshawar itself was still governed by the Barakzai brother, Sultan Mohamed Khan, he now held it as Lahore's feudatory rather than Kabul's—as Gardner had already discovered.

Naturally, Dost Mohamed Khan in Kabul resented these Sikh encroachments. Kashmir meant as much to the Afghans as it does today to Pakistanis; and Peshawar had been under Afghan rule for the best part of a century. Like Kabul, its population was mainly Pashtun (Pathan) and overwhelmingly Muslim; it commanded access to the Khyber Pass, Kabul's outer portcullis; and it was in Peshawar that in 1809 the first ever British mission to Afghanistan had been entertained by the Afghan court. For Dost Mohamed, the repossession of Peshawar, whether by force or by some British-brokered agreement with Lahore, was an imperative.

Ranjit Singh, on the other hand, had no intention of relinquishing Peshawar, even to oblige his British allies. He was, however, sorely troubled by the reluctance of the Pathan tribes in its hinterland—Afridis, Waziris, Yusufzais, etc—to submit to Sikh rule, and especially so since the tribal belt extended to Sind, which he coveted even more now that the British were showing an interest in it.

Such was the situation along the west bank of the Indus in late 1832 when Gardner and his troops were urgently recalled from their operations in the south under Ventura. They were to head back upriver through the Derajat (between Dera Ghazi Khan and Dera Ismail Khan) to the always-troublesome town of Bannu. Near there, in the fort of Lakki, noted Gardner, a Sikh force of 2000 irregulars and four small guns under the command of Sardar Tara Singh was being besieged by 'some thousands of well-armed and mounted Bannu-ites, assisted by 4000 or 5000 wild mountain Waziris on foot'.

There was no doubt that Gardner's much bigger guns and his 1200 cavalry could tip the balance. But first they had to get there. Hauling guns into mountain terrain was never easy. Roads barely existed in the outlying foothills of the Hindu Kush and when crossing a pass near Pezu there was 'almost a complete lack of water'. They persevered regardless and the besieged were duly relieved. Then came the retribution.

> In the course of about four months we managed to cut down, burn and destroy all the grain crops, and to level and destroy the forts, villages, gardens, fruit-trees, orchards, etc., of all the most refractory and of those who refused to pay their fixed annual stipend or revenues.

This was standard practice. For the next three years, Gardner, still serving under the Sikh commander Tara Singh, was engaged in little else. Collecting overdue revenues, punishing recalcitrant tributaries and enforcing the authority of the Khalsa were ongoing administrative chores in a young empire.

May 1835 brought the only distraction. In an attempt to win back Peshawar by force, Dost Mohamed Khan at the head of a formidable army had descended the Khyber Pass and dug in along a wide front at the entrance to the pass. Ranjit Singh, while playing for time by 'amusing [Dost Mohamed] with proposals', summoned his own forces. Thus, Tara Singh's orders in Bannu were suddenly countermanded. Still with Gardner's artillery in tow, he headed for Peshawar. There he joined the rest of the European-led Fauj-i-khas and took up a position in the plain below the Khyber Pass. Positioned on the right wing of the main Sikh army, they had an excellent view of both it and the Afghan forces.

The spectacle made a greater impression than the fighting. It was Gardner's first glimpse of the army of the Khalsa in all its glory. It would also prove to be Ranjit Singh's last chance to lead it in battle. Compared to European armies drawn up in anonymous and regiment-ed squares, Indian armies favoured fluidity, exhibition and colour. Bridles, like daggers, were encrusted with gems, and saddle cloths overlaid with silks. Chiefs and commanders, whether on horseback or atop richly caparisoned elephants, wore whatever finery took their fancy. 'The great Maharaja actually insisted that they should be so dressed and always took defaulters to task,' says one authority. 'Gold, jewels, velvets, silks, muslins and shawls were profusely used ... White, red, green and yellow were the most popular colours.'

Turbans came in similar shades and were invariably topped with plumes 'much in the same way as the Highland chiefs of Scotland place a heron's feather in their bonnets,' thought another observ-er. Nowhere, though, is there any mention of tartan. Gardner had evidently yet to discover a reason to advertise his Scottish ances-try. Instead, conforming to his surroundings as usual, he no doubt adopted some variation of the costume ascribed to Generals Court and Avitabile—'a long green coat ... ornamented with a profusion of lace and ... oblong buttons of solid gold, trousers of scarlet cloth with a broad gold stripe down the seams, a green velvet cap with a band also of gold lace and a tassel, and an embroidered belt to which a bejewelled sabre was attached'.

According to Gardner, the Sikh army ranged against Dost Mo-hamed numbered 80–100,000 of whom about 20,000 belonged to the European-style Fauj-i-khas. Both figures were an exaggerated guess, although not that wide of the mark. Estimates at the time put the strength of the regular units of the Sikh army at 40,000; three-quarters were infantrymen dressed much as their British coun-terparts in blue trousers and scarlet jackets; and all sported beards, this being a requisite of Sikh employ. If Gurkhas, their headgear was the shako (the tall cylindrical hat with a brim-like visor favoured by both French and English), and if Muslims or Sikhs, it was the turban (with loose ends hanging to the shoulders). The artillery were similarly attired while the regular cavalry cut a dash in crimson jackets with matching turbans 'ornamented in the centre with a small brass half-moon, from which springs a glittering sprig about two inches in height'.

But these 40,000 were just the regular troops, those in the permanent pay either of the state or of feudatories like the Dogra brothers. About as many again, who might also be attached either to the maharaja or his feudatories, were classed as irregulars. They included no artillery but more cavalry (or *ghorcharas*); and anything approaching a uniform was here exceptional. Since these irregular units had long 'constituted the elite of Sikh army, [they] were the most gaudily dressed'. Velvet shirts topped with chain mail were standard, with waistbands embroidered with gold and with more gilt embroidery on the slippers which constituted their only footwear.

For a whole month this dazzling array was engaged in daily skirmishing and cannonading with Dost Mohamed's equally numerous host. The Sikh losses Gardner put at a hundred or so a day, mostly cut to pieces by the *ghazis* (holy warriors) of the Afghan cavalry, each of them 'with his little green Moslem flag'. Afghan losses were supposed greater thanks to the superiority of the Sikh artillery. But still Gardner felt more like a spectator than a participant.

> The firing and fighting took place along the whole front, and there being but ... three short miles between the armies, and the Afghan position being on rising ground, every movement on either side was plainly visible to the other.

Finally, on 11 May, the balance of numbers was deemed to have swung in the Sikhs' favour. To Gardner's delight, the news prompted a distribution of cash. All outstanding back-pay plus a month's wages in advance was immediately distributed to the entire army. Completed in an astonishing four hours, the hand-out was regarded as the surest means of giving the troops something to fight for. Simultaneously the order was issued for a pre-dawn advance along the entire front.

This was done, but the Sikhs had not advanced above a 1000 yards when the words 'Fled!' 'Fled!' were loudly vociferated by the whole army... In fact Dost Mohamed with all his troops and *ghazis* had retreated during the night into the Khyber, and when day broke not even a single tent or Afghan was to be seen.

What Gardner called 'one month's sparring, coquetting and skirmishing' had served its purpose, although it scarcely handed Ranjit Singh 'the undisputed occupation and mastership of the Peshawar valley' as he supposed.

The army was then dispersed, Gardner being sent back to Bannu to again chastise the Waziris. Later in the year his unit was reunited with the main body of the army for the annual celebration of the Dussehra festival at Amritsar. And there, for reasons unexplained, his career took what would prove a fateful turn.

It was about this time [1835] that the Prime Minister, Raja Dhyan Singh, took me from Maharaja Ranjit Singh's service and placed me in full command of his and his brother's artillery, which was attached to the already organised Jammu contingent of 7000 to 8000 men.

Though still serving alongside the Sikh army, Gardner had suddenly been transferred. Now in the employ of the Dogra brothers of Jammu rather than the maharaja of Lahore, he saw the move as a promotion. His monthly income including salary, allowances and other perquisites remained at about 700 rupees a month; and, according to Herbert Edwardes, a later acquaintance, it came with a further sweetener, namely 'a native wife given to him by Raja Dhyan Singh out of his own household'.

Providing European officers with desirable Indian wives was normal practice. An obliging wife was supposed to cement the foreigner's loyalty to the Khalsa and, if required, provide information about her husband's possible dereliction of duty or treasonable contacts.

Gardner had almost certainly acquired one wife on entering Ranjit Singh's service. Ventura and Court had done likewise, while Avitabile supported a whole bevvy of wives. This second Mrs Gardner simply signified his change of allegiance from Ranjit Singh to Dhyan Singh. For any European entering Sikh employ, marrying a bibi was as obligatory as growing a beard and refraining from smoking and eating beef. (Mercifully, be it said, these obligations to conform to Sikh practice did not extend to adopting the title of 'Singh'.)

Yet to the ever sceptical Messrs Grey and Garrett, mention of the new wife being a member of Dhyan Singh's household (they carelessly call it 'Gulab Singh's household') could only mean that the lady in question was one of the Dogra raja's discarded mistresses. On no better evidence, others have assumed she was a Dogra princess. Her name is not known. Gardner himself barely mentions her and, if there were any children, they too go unrecorded. Her significance lay in cementing Gardner's loyalty to the man who, on Ranjit Singh's death, would attempt to mastermind one of history's bloodiest successions.

Happily, and despite being overlooked by Pearse, there survives a telling character sketch of Dhyan Singh by Gardner himself. It begins by describing the 'Prime Minister' as a veritable paragon, 'active, enterprising, brave, energetic and intrepid to a degree; unconscious of all personal danger, but ever ready to repulse any'. He was, too, 'of a most determined and resolute disposition, but when required to yield, no one could do so with better grace; the master of a most winning, gentle, affable, sedate, yet manly and commanding address ... laconic in speech, impatient of delay, ... polite to all, and occasionally humorous, witty and sarcastic'. And so on for two fulsome pages. Then comes the put-down.

> But though he may be said to possess, as he certainly did, all these and many other qualities, still the good traits in his mysterious character seemed to be but a well-assumed and well-worn, befitting, mystic cloak to screen a Machiavelian spirit, made up of a most diabolical, wily, deceptive, crafty, dissembling, faithless, subtle, deep, dark, designing and ruthless disposition. And all for what? Ambition!

Despite some essential re-punctuation, these rambling sentences with their surfeit of synonyms leave no doubt that it was indeed Gardner who penned them. He would write to similarly devastating effect of the other two brothers, Gulab Singh and Suchet Singh, and of Dhyan's Singh's son, Hira Singh. Contemporaries, whether Sikh or British, would generally concur with his verdicts. Devious indeed were the Dogras of Jammu under whose command Gardner would spend the rest of his life.

In charge of Dhyan Singh's artillery Gardner continued in the field throughout 1836–7 and into 1838. Another Afghan attempt on Peshawar, this time led by Dost Mohamed's son, resulted in the defeat of a Sikh army at the battle of Jamrud and claimed the life of Hari Singh Nalwa, Ranjit Singh's most fearless general. Once again all available forces were rushed to the Peshawar valley and once again the Afghans slipped back up the Khyber rather than risk a decisive confrontation. There followed a campaign under Gulab Singh against the Yusufzai tribes to the north (which 'gave our whole contingent plenty—nay, handfuls—of work night and day for six months'), followed by the brutal suppression of the Sudhans of Poonch in the Kashmir hills and then a final swipe at the still unsettled Waziris in and around Bannu.

It must have been mid-1838 by the time Gardner returned to La-hore. The monsoon had yet to arrive and within the walled city the air hung heavy. At that time of year even night temperatures seldom dropped below 30 degrees Celsius. Lahore held its breath. But the only storm clouds on the horizon were not of the seasonal sort and were decidedly menacing. The Great Game was about to turn nasty.

On behalf of the Russian Tsar a Polish captain, Ivan Vitkevitch, had just spent the winter in Kabul. His unexpected appearance there had been as a red rag to the British bull. Now, six months later, a high-powered mission from the British governor-general had arrived in Lahore and was locked in negotiations with the Sikhs. Everywhere the rumours were of war. And to make matters worse, Maharaja Ranjit Singh was visibly fading.

'He is by no means firm on his legs when he walks ... and still has a slight hesitation in his speech, the consequence of a paralytic stroke,' noted a member of the British deputation. By the end of the year the maharaja was 'much worse' following what may have been another stroke. He could barely speak, and by January 1839 the same observer was of the opinion that 'he cannot last much longer'.

The timing could hardly have been worse. In the critical months leading up to what the British would call the First Afghan War, the key figure in their plans was about to take to his death-bed and his empire to be plunged into turmoil.

Of the causes of the Anglo-Afghan war and its conduct, Gardner would be highly critical. So would everyone else. To those, like Edgeworth, Cooper and Durand to whom the colonel would relate his life-story, the events must have been familiar enough, in fact too painfully familiar to bear repetition. Besides which, Gardner's part in the war was negligible. He was neither privy to the negotiations that preceded the British invasion of Afghanistan nor directly involved in the war's prosecution. He presumably first learned what was afoot either from rumours about the purpose of the governor-general's mission or from the fears being voiced by the now Captain Alexander Burnes. Burnes passed through Lahore in June 1838: and since it is not clear that their paths ever crossed again, it can only have been on this visit that Gardner famously lent him—if indeed he did lend him—his precious account of Kafiristan.

At the time Burnes was beating a red-faced retreat from Kabul en route to a probable dressing-down in Simla. For six months he had been trying to persuade Dost Mohamed Khan that British trade and British protection could alone guarantee Afghan sovereignty. Above all, he had insisted that any overtures from Russia must be repudiated on the grounds that, if Dost Mohamed Khan was set on regaining Peshawar, only the British stood a chance of persuading the Sikhs to hand it over. A mercurial figure of undoubted talents, Burnes had formed a high opinion of Dost Mohamed and an even higher opinion of his own standing in Kabul. He loved the city, relished the pageantry of its court and had become besotted, it was said, with the attentions of its choicest 'houris'. He was also convinced that the desired understanding between Dost Mohamed and the British was within his grasp. To conclude it, all he needed was the whole-hearted support of India's new governor-general and his advisers.

This had not been forthcoming. Burnes might charm the Afghans, but his unauthorised proposals had cut no ice with those who mattered most in British India. Claude Wade, the political agent at Ludhiana, the British listening post on the Anglo-Sikh frontier, resented Burnes's meddling and saw no prospect of Ranjit Singh relinquishing Peshawar. Sir William Hay MacNaghten, the blue-spectacled pedant and chief secretary to the governor-general who had been deputed to lead the current mission to Ranjit Singh, railed against the Russians while rubbishing the idea of prejudicing Anglo-Sikh amity for a shaky alliance with Dost Mohamed. And George Eden, Lord Auckland, the new governor-general, while basking in the affection of his two spinster sisters, saw only what his staff placed in front of him—and dithered.

Burnes might just have got his way but for the arrival in Kabul in December 1837 of the Tsarist agent Vitkevitch. To counter Vitkevitch's overtures, Burnes had confidently offered Dost Mohamed the plum of Peshawar and promised 300,000 rupees towards the defence of Herat against the Persians. But for MacNaghten and Wade this was the final straw. Burnes had gone too far. He had been promptly recalled and his dealings disowned. Instead of a British alliance, Dost Mohamed was to be offered a British exile.

For it so happened that an alternative claimant to the Afghan throne was conveniently to hand. This man was the stately Shah Shuja. A pensioner under British protection at Ludhiana, Shah Shuja had been deposed thirty years earlier by the father of Prince Habib-ulla, Gardner's old comrade-in-arms. Since then, Shah Shuja's claim had three times been rejected on the field of battle, though never renounced. For a fourth attempt he was certainly game; yet he was woefully ill-equipped. He needed everything—recognition, cash, allies and an army.

Under the alliance being brokered with the ailing Maharaja Ranjit Singh by the MacNaghten Mission in the mid-summer of 1838 he got all four. The East India Company would provide recognition, funds and some troops. Ranjit Singh, in return for the uncontested possession of Peshawar and one end of the Khyber Pass, would furnish more troops, plus supplies and transit rights across the Punjab. And of course Shah Shuja promised the British an Anglo-friendly regime in Kabul and an end to Afghan raids over the Khyber.

What was called the Company's 'Army of the Indus', though more accurately described as the 'Army for Afghanistan', began assembling at Ferozepur in the latter half of 1838. Gardner seems not to have attended the grand ceremonial send-off when Auckland and his sisters finally met the maharaja. Dhyan Singh was present, but his troops were not involved. Nor, in the event, was most of the Sikh army. As a result of last-minute negotiations, the main invasion force was to march to Afghanistan via Sind rather than across the Punjab. The role of the Sikhs, on whose promised support MacNaghten had counted, was reduced to that of mounting a diversionary attack via the Khyber. Even this was soon watered down. The units of the Khalsa army to be used had to be Muslim contingents so as not to inflame Afghan hostility. They were slow to materialise, and by the time they did assemble in Peshawar, the main British invasion force had already taken the Afghan city of Kandahar and was heading for Kabul.

Meanwhile Ranjit Singh was dying. He passed away on 27 June 1839. The British were left to fight their own war in Afghanistan with little help from their allies. Lahore was anyway convulsed by the succession crisis. The extinction of a dynasty was about to begin, and no outsider would be more implicated in the bloodletting that ensued than the obliging 'Gordana Sahib'.

7

Blood and Blunder
1839–43

The Hon. Emily Eden, the more caustic of Governor-General Lord
Auckland's sisters, reported that Ranjt Singh had a grand total of
thirty-two wives. In December 1838, in the course of the Lahore
meeting between the maharaja and the governor-general, the Eden
sisters had been the only members of the gubernatorial entourage
to be admitted to the royal *zenana*. Riding over to the palace (more
sedate transport had been declined with the immortal 'I can't stand
much elephant') the Eden girls met just five of these 'thirty-two Mrs
Runjeets'. Four were adjudged 'very handsome' (high praise from
Emily Eden), two 'would have been beautiful anywhere', and all had
'immense almond-shaped eyes'. Of the full complement, some also
had offspring. But since the maharaja had long been trialling every
conceivable cure for senile impotence, the question of whether these
children were in fact his, and if so which of their mothers counted
as official wives, had become a source of lively debate.

To settle the matter, Ranjit Singh, shortly before he died, had
named as his heir his eldest and only undisputed son, the 38-year-old
Kharak Singh. Emily Eden rather liked Kharak Singh and had engaged
in a mild flirtation with him. The heir apparent had not responded. In
fact he rarely responded to anyone; others always spoke up for him.
'They never let him open his lips,' wrote Eden. He was not incapable

of speech, just painfully slow to articulate. Joseph Cunningham, the historian of the Sikhs, put him down as 'an imbecile', and Gardner provided an explanation: 'Kharak Singh was a blockhead and a slave to opium [who] passed his whole time in a state of stupefaction'.

Kharak Singh's mother had died a few years earlier, which removed one possible supporter of his cause; but he did have a wife, the formidable Chand Kaur, and together they had a son, Nau Nihal Singh, who was more popular and competent than either of them (see Ranjit Singh's family tree on page 138). Ranjit Singh's plan seems to have been that Kharak Singh, as soon as he proved himself incapable as maharaja, would simply step aside to make way for the claims of his more articulate offspring. In the meantime, and to give Kharak Singh a chance of confounding the critics, on his deathbed the old maharaja had exacted a promise from minister Dhyan Singh. Dhyan Singh was 'to act as Kharak Singh's guardian and protector and to treat him in every way as the only son and heir of his old master'. Simultaneously the minister was elevated to the post of *wazir*, or vizier, in effect ministerial plenipotentiary for the whole empire. With authority equivalent to that of a regent, Gardner's immediate superior was now rather more than a 'prime minister'.

This plan for the succession, though sound, was not, however, fool-proof; for, blockhead that he was, Kharak Singh made no secret of his resenting Dhyan Singh's guardianship. He longed to be rid of both him and his Dogra brothers, and he found a like-minded backer in one Chait Singh. A fellow Sikh, Chait Singh was keen to take on Dhyan Singh and then the viziership. In addition—and aside, that is, from the problem of there being far too many Singhs—the masterplan had a still greater flaw. Dhyan Singh, ever a slave to what Gardner stigmatised as 'Ambition!', had hatched a 'diabolical ... deceptive ... dissembling ... deep, dark, designing [etc, etc]' stratagem of his own.

The focus of this counter-plan was another youthful Singh, in this case Hira Singh, who, as well as being vizier Dhyan Singh's son (see Dogra family tree on page 140), was the teenage Adonis on whom the old maharaja had doted to the exclusion of all others. Whenever Ranjit took to his gilt encrusted throne, Hira Singh was invariably to be found seated beside him, the only person not of the blood royal elevated above the level of the floor. Even Hira Singh's father, Dhyan Singh, squatted, usually behind this royal tableau.

Young Hira Singh could do no wrong. His ill manners went uncorrected and his outbursts unpunished. Moreover 'it was he and he alone that could lull the old chief to sleep.' Or as William Osborne, Emily Eden's nephew and Auckland's military secretary, put it, 'his influence over Runjeet Singh is extraordinary, and though acquired in a manner which in any other country would render him infamous, here he is universally looked up to and respected.' Dearer to Ranjit Singh than either his own son (Kharak Singh) or his grandson (Nau Nihal Singh), it was this 18-year old Hira Singh who had been paraded as the chosen one—and it was he who remained the chosen one in the deep designs of his father and uncles.

> [The Dogras'] dream [says Gardner] was that Hira Singh, the heir of their family, or at least the most promising of its rising generation, might eventually succeed to the throne of Ranjit Singh. Those to be swept away were the male members of the Maharaja's family and all those ministers, advisers and chiefs who would not join the Dogra party...
>
> In the course of a few years this programme was carried out in all its essential features.

But 'the torrent of blood which [the Dogras] caused to flow' did more than achieve the plot's essential features; it would eventually account for both its instigator, the devious Dhyan Singh, and then its presumed beneficiary, the effeminate Hira Singh. Yet at the time, opines Gardner with one of his rare rhetorical flourishes, 'the veil of futurity hid these events from their eyes'. Of all the Europeans in Lahore's employ, only he, Alexander Gardner, was both privy to the plan and witness to its grisly outcome. History was unfolding under his nose, and with a fine sense of his privileged position, he was determined to make the most of it. 'I will now relate how it was that all these murders were brought about directly or indirectly by the Dogra brothers.'

Fifty years later editor Pearse, when embarking on this sanguinary

Family Tree of
Maharaja Ranjit Singh

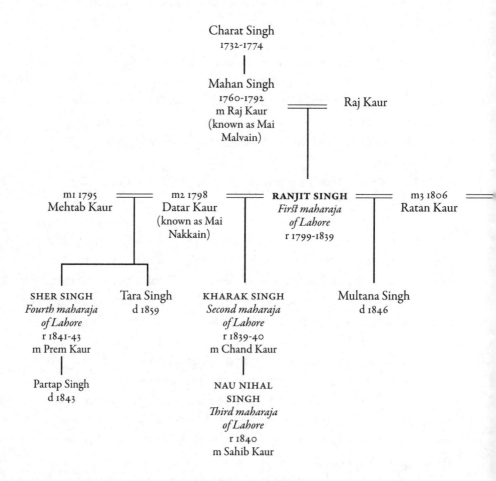

Charat Singh
1732-1774

Mahan Singh
1760-1792
m Raj Kaur
(known as Mai
Malvain)

Raj Kaur

m1 1795
Mehtab Kaur

m2 1798
Datar Kaur
(known as Mai
Nakkain)

RANJIT SINGH
*First maharaja
of Lahore*
r 1799-1839

m3 1806
Ratan Kaur

SHER SINGH
*Fourth maharaja
of Lahore*
r 1841-43
m Prem Kaur

Tara Singh
d 1859

KHARAK SINGH
*Second maharaja
of Lahore*
r 1839-40
m Chand Kaur

Multana Singh
d 1846

Partap Singh
d 1843

NAU NIHAL
SINGH
*Third maharaja
of Lahore*
r 1840
m Sahib Kaur

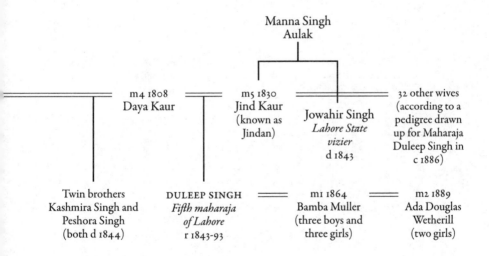

Manna Singh
Aulak

m4 1808
Daya Kaur

m5 1830
Jind Kaur
(known as
Jindan)

Jowahir Singh
*Lahore State
vizier*
d 1843

32 other wives
(according to a
pedigree drawn
up for Maharaja
Duleep Singh in
c 1886)

Twin brothers
Kashmira Singh and
Peshora Singh
(both d 1844)

DULEEP SINGH
*Fifth maharaja
of Lahore*
r 1843-93

m1 1864
Bamba Muller
(three boys and
three girls)

m2 1889
Ada Douglas
Wetherill
(two girls)

Family Tree of the Dogra Rajas of Jammu

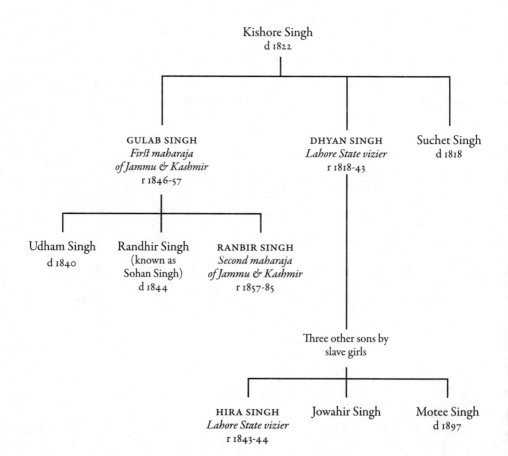

Kishore Singh
d 1822

GULAB SINGH
*First maharaja
of Jammu & Kashmir*
r 1846-57

DHYAN SINGH
Lahore State vizier
r 1818-43

Suchet Singh
d 1818

Udham Singh
d 1840

Randhir Singh
(known as
Sohan Singh)
d 1844

RANBIR SINGH
*Second maharaja
of Jammu & Kashmir*
r 1857-85

Three other sons by
slave girls

HIRA SINGH
Lahore State vizier
r 1843-44

Jowahir Singh

Motee Singh
d 1897

catalogue of 'crimes and tragedies', would rate it 'unparalleled save in the darkest period of the downfall of Rome or in the early days of the French Revolution'. Gardner makes no such claim. He simply invites his audience to follow his narrative and judge for themselves. He certainly magnified the carnage and he very probably exaggerated his own part in events. But his vantage point was indeed unique. Even Grey and Garrett would grudgingly admit that he was present throughout, and that since his account was verified by others, 'it must, we imagine, contain a fair amount of truth'.

More obviously, it also contains enough twists and turns to test the most patient reader. Such inconsistencies are best explained in the colonel's own words. The Dogra brothers 'played the awful game with deliberate and unswerving pertinacity,' he says.

> Their only thought was that the way to the throne had to be cleared of all obstacles, [but] at the same time an outward show of fealty to the Khalsa, and of loyalty to the sovereign line of succession, had to be maintained. The slightest suspicion might have been fatal, yet prompt action seemed to be the least dangerous course, and the first blow fell quickly.

It fell, in fact, less than four months after Ranjit Singh's body had been cremated along with several of his devoted womenfolk. By then, October 1839, up in Afghanistan the flames of war were dying down. The British-led Army of the Indus had successfully stormed Ghazni and made a triumphant entry into Kabul. The Khyber Pass had also been forced, Dost Mohamed had fled the scene and Shah Shuja, the British puppet, had been installed in his place. With the Union Jack now fluttering atop the Hindu Kush, it was as if the forward march of Albion's Indian empire had leap-frogged clean over the Sikh kingdom in the Punjab. The flotillas which had begun to ply the Indus came laden not with muskets and bullion for the Sikhs but with stores and ammunition for the occupying army in Afghanistan. On a variety of pretexts, British officers who were criss-crossing the Punjab en route for Kabul or Simla gave Lahore a wide berth, as if its affairs were no longer of consequence.

The Sikhs, lately supposed the lynchpin of the tripartite alliance signed by Auckland, Shah Shuja and Ranjit Singh, were now being marginalised. Consequently they felt threatened. The genial relations that had once subsisted between Ranjit Singh in Lahore and Colonel Wade in British Ludhiana deteriorated. Wade himself was replaced even as the precarious balance of power in Lahore was destabilised by all the Anglo-Afghan comings and goings.

Among the various court factions, suspicions grew. Mischievously, vizier Dhyan Singh put it about that the now Maharaja Kharak Singh and the ambitious Chait Singh were in direct touch with the British. Supposedly they were offering to place the Punjab under Calcutta's protection in return for Calcutta guaranteeing its support for their anti-Dogra cause. Whether or not this was the case, the rumour proved counter-productive. The Sikh Khalsa felt betrayed by its own maharaja, while some elements in the Sikh army, plus the next-in-line to the throne (Nau Nihal Singh) and his mother (Chand Kaur), aligned themselves with the Dogras. Thus, whether or not Kharak Singh was betraying the Khalsa, he was himself being betrayed by both his son and his wife.

In search of allies of his own, the unhappy maharaja then looked to General Ventura and the rest of the foreign contingent in the Khalsa army. But this too backfired. Since the foreigners were supposed to be on good terms with the British, it only confirmed suspicions about the new maharaja's double-dealing. Gardner, however, was not approached. Being now in the exclusive employ of the Dogra rajas, he found himself numbered among Kharak Singh's opponents and well placed to observe their manoeuvres.

The quarrel, when it flared, did so in open durbar. An irate Chait Singh acting on behalf of the maharaja challenged Dhyan Singh's authority and muttered a parting 'See what will become of you in twenty-four hours.' The imperturbable Dhyan Singh replied with a smile: 'Your humble servant, sir: we *shall* see.' Like the ides of March, the time had come but not yet gone.

That night Gardner was ordered to load his guns and position them at the palace gates. Then 'Dhyan Singh asked me if I would like to accompany him and of course I accepted the invitation.' Armed with daggers and the odd musket, the assassins numbered fifteen in all, among them the three Dogra brothers, the nineteen-year-old Nau Nihal Singh and the now Captain 'Gordana Sahib'.

> It was near midnight when we entered the palace, and no sooner had we left the gate ... than a voice accosted us. [Dhyan Singh responded with a pre-arranged password] and without uttering a whisper we stealthily crept our way in the dark up a flight of stairs, over a place called the Badshah-i-Takht, and thence to the immediate vicinity of the royal apartment.

Here a shot rang out. On seeing a figure bolt into the night, Suchet Singh, the youngest of the Dogra brothers, had fired. For his 'imprudence' he was rewarded by Gulab Singh, the largest of the brothers, with an earthy expletive and 'a tremendous cuff on the ear'.

The shot alerted the two companies of the palace guard. But they too had already been suborned; it was enough this time for Dhyan Singh to identify himself. 'He simply showed his right hand (on which he had two thumbs) and put his finger to his lips.' The guards pointed to an open door and then dropped to the ground, pretending sleep.

> There was a light in the room. Dhyan Singh approached and entered it, followed by the whole party. Lo! there sat Maharaja Kharrak Singh on his bed washing his teeth. The adjoining bed, which belonged to Chait Singh, was empty... He had gone out on hearing the shot fired.

While Nau Nihal Singh and four others held the restive maharaja down, the rest of the party went in search of Chait Singh. He was discovered clutching a sword and cowering in the corner of an ante-room.

> The eyes of Dhyan Singh seemed to shoot fire as his gaze alighted and fixed itself on his deadly foe [continues Gardner]. Gulab Singh was for interposing to do the deed of blood himself... but Dhyan Singh roughly shook him off and, dagger in hand, slowly advancing towards his enemy, said, 'The twenty-four hours you were courteous enough to

mention to me have not yet elapsed.' Then with the spring of a tiger the successful counter-plotter dashed at his enemy and plunged his dagger into his heart, crying out, 'Take this in memory of Ranjit Singh.' Dhyan Singh then turned round, his face radiant with gratified purpose, and courteously thanked us for our aid.

To Gardner this was all in a night's work. But to critics like Grey and Garret such cold-blooded murder would be evidence of the rankest villainy. 'Comment on the mentality of a European who so calmly confesses having been concerned in such an atrocious deed is, we imagine, superfluous.'

With Chait Singh dead, it remained only to dispose of Kharak Singh. Initially the plotters pledged their continued allegiance to the speechless maharaja and maintained their action was 'entirely a state proceeding'. But with his power-hungry son (Nau Nihal Singh) and faithless wife (Chand Kaur) ranged against him, there was no question of letting the maharaja retain the reins of power. Instead, he was deposed on the grounds of treason and incompetence, smuggled into a locked chamber and left there to moulder. Broken and betrayed, he is said to have become first ill and then deranged. He died nine months later. Gardner insists that on Dhyan Singh's orders he was actually poisoned, his food having been laced with a lethal mixture of white lead and mercury.

Kharak Singh breathed his last on 9 November 1840. From the moment Dhyan Singh had renounced his pledge to Ranjit Singh, he had stood no chance. But Nau Nihal Singh, as his successor, did at least ensure that his father had a state funeral. The pyre was lit in the Hazuri Bagh, the great courtyard adjacent to the palace and the site of Ranjit Singh's cremation. Most of the principal figures at court attended. As to what followed, there would therefore be many witnesses if precious little consensus.

From the Hazuri Bagh, after conducting the last rights, Nau Nihal Singh hastily absented himself to perform the usual post-funerary ablutions in a nearby watercourse. Out of respect for his dead father he then returned on foot and in the company of Gulab Singh's eldest son, Udham Singh. The two young men paused beneath the deep stone archway that opened onto the courtyard, possibly to share a joke. 'As they emerged from it, a crash was heard.'

> Beams, stones and tiles fell from above, and the Maharaja and Udham Singh were struck to the ground. The latter was killed on the spot, and Nau Nihal Singh was struck to the earth. He was injured in the head, but presently attempted to rise. The Prime Minister [Dhyan Singh] rushed up and ... Nau Nihal Singh was carried into the palace, the doors were closed, and admission denied to all.

Two hours later, Dhyan Singh re-emerged. The doors were now thrown open to reveal the life-less corpse of Nau Nihal Singh spread-eagled within. He had reigned for a matter of hours, or as Cunningham would put it, 'the same day dazzled him with a crown and deprived him of life'. With the passing of its third maharaja in eighteen months, the edifice of the Sikh Empire was looking as precarious as the Hazuri Bagh gateway.

Gardner's telling of these events, though accepted as reasonably accurate, leaves many questions unanswered. In part this is because there are two versions of his testimony, the shorter being that offered by Pearse in the *Memoirs* and the longer that prepared by Major George Carmichael Smyth for his *A History of the Reigning Family of Lahore*. Smyth's book, which Pearse knew but used only sparingly, was published in 1847 at a time when the events in question were still fresh in the mind. It was compiled, says Smyth, 'chiefly from the notes of a Captain Gardner of the Seik artillery'; and that this was in fact the case is evident from that profligate prose portrait, already quoted, of Dhyan Singh's diabolical character.

Gardner's relationship with Carmichael Smyth is not entirely clear. They would be in correspondence from at least 1845, and they seem to have actually met in Ludhiana in late 1846, at which point Smyth incorporated some more Gardner material in the appendices of his book. As usual, all Gardner's information seems to have been willingly provided without any expectation of reward. It may, though, have been meant to explain and, if necessary, exonerate his part in the 'crimes and tragedies'. And in the hands of Major Smyth, it was used to make another point.

Smyth, who had spent 26 years in India and would soon retire as a major-general, was convinced that the demise of Nau Nihal Singh, the last in the uncontested line of descent from Ranjit Singh, sounded the death knell of the Sikh Empire. To him, and to the many other British officers of a similar opinion, the obvious response was for the British to intervene—or 'adopt coercive measures'—before the bloodletting got out of hand. Events at the time could not have been more favourable. In Afghanistan, the cities of Kabul and Kandahar were now secured, as was Dost Mohamed Khan (he had given himself up the day before Kharak Singh died and was about to be escorted into exile in India). With an under-employed army on one side of the Punjab, and another assembling to relieve it on the other side, the components for a British pincer movement on Lahore were already in place.

Sir William MacNaghten in Kabul went further. Now the man in charge of the British occupation there, he argued that the death of Ranjit Singh's last certain heir rendered the existing alliance between the British and the Sikhs null and void. Hence any accusations about bad faith towards such an old and trusted ally as the Khalsa could now be discounted. He also urged that, as a *quid pro quo* for British intervention in the Punjab, the city of Peshawar, plus the west bank of the Indus, should be transferred from the Sikhs to Shah Shuja, so awarding to a British-run Afghanistan precisely the territories that an Afghan-run Afghanistan had been denied.

But at the time these views failed to win official support and no action was taken. London, appalled by the cost of the Afghan occupation, was demanding not action but austerity; Auckland, as usual, was dithering. The moment passed, and within a matter of weeks it was too late. By then Lahore was rent by what amounted to civil war; and by the end of the year the Army of the Indus was itself facing extinction. A British intervention in the Punjab would indeed materialise, but not for another four years.

Writing in the aftermath of all these events, Major Carmichael Smyth used Gardner's gory account of the intrigues at the Sikh court to prove that he, Smyth, had been right all along. Without the great Ranjit Singh, the Sikh Empire was beyond redemption. The former maharaja's would-be heirs were hopelessly divided, his armed forces likewise, and the Dogras would go to any lengths to keep them so. Dispensing with Kharak Singh was, perhaps, inevitable; but doing away with his more promising son and successor amounted to national suicide. Auckland should have acted there and then. Had he done so, the British would have been spared not one war but two, and against the most determined army they ever encountered in the East.

This being Smyth's reading of the situation, he supposed that Nau Nihal Singh's fatal encounter with the gateway had not been an accident. Yet Gardner himself barely hints at foul play. Unusually, he confesses to having been absent at the critical moment. Dhyan Singh had ordered him to leave the funeral ceremonies to go and round up forty of his gunners 'dressed in fatigues'. He was never told why they were needed and, by the time he returned with them, 'the catastrophe had just occurred'. He was then ordered to dismiss them. Something untoward may have been afoot; but precisely what he never discovered.

After close questioning of those present, Gardner was more confident about the disaster itself. Thirty years later, in 1871, Sir Henry Durand, the lieutenant-governor of the Punjab to whom Gardner related one version of his life-story, would be mortally wounded when entering the town of Tonk. Passing through a monumental archway like that of the Lahore Hazuri Bagh, his elephant dislodged a chunk of masonry and brought the whole structure down on top of the lieutenant-governor. Quite plausibly an identical accident had accounted for Nau Nihal Singh. But Gardner's informants were insistent that the five elephants that attended the young maharaja had been sent back 'to wait at a little distance' and that he had therefore been on foot at the time.

Yet if an elephant was not responsible, who was? The obvious answer was Dhyan Singh. He could have directed someone with a crow-bar to conceal himself on the gateway's ornate superstructure with orders to dislodge one of the stone beams at the critical moment. But this too made no sense, since the only person to be killed outright was Dhyan Singh's own nephew, that is Udham Singh, the son of the elder brother and co-conspirator Gulab Singh. Possibly no one had foreseen that Udham Singh might enter the gateway with Nau Nihal Singh. Or possibly the collapse really was a freak accident.

Gardner was more suspicious about what happened in the two hours afterwards. Apart from Dhyan Singh and the palanquin-bearers who carried the wounded maharaja into the palace, no one, not even his mother, was allowed near Nau Nihal Singh. And of the five palanquin-bearers, all of whom were normally attached to Gardner's artillery, 'two were afterwards privately put to death, two escaped into Hindustan [i.e. north India] and the fate of the fifth is unknown to me'. One of them, however, confided in Gardner. According to this man, Nau Nihal Singh had suffered only a minor head wound from the shower of tiles and masonry. It was just above his right ear and it left a bloodstain no bigger than a rupee coin on the coverlet of the palanquin. Yet when the lifeless corpse was exposed two hours later, 'blood in great quantities, both in fluid and coagulated pools, was found around the head of the cloth on which the body lay'. Perhaps an artery had burst, perhaps a third party had burst it for him. The reliable Cunningham offers the most judicious verdict: 'It is not positively known that the [Dogra] Rajas of Jummoo designed to remove Nao Nihal Singh; but it is difficult to acquit them of the crime, and it is certain that they were capable of committing it.'

With no other legitimate descendants of Ranjit Singh in the field, attention now turned to Maharani Chand Kaur (that is, Nau Nihal Singh's mother) and to several lesser contenders, all of whom, though not of the blood royal, could claim to have been born of one of Ranjit Singh's womenfolk and, 'from time to time, for reasons of his own', to have been acknowledged by Ranjit as princes.

Foremost among the latter was Sher Singh, a dashing but dissolute 30-year old, moderately popular with the troops and well thought of by the British. Dhyan Singh had already identified Sher Singh as his next candidate for the *gaddi* (or throne): but at the crucial moment Sher Singh was absent on his estates and in no hurry to return. He wanted time to organise support. Dhyan Singh obliged by suppressing the news of Nau Nihal's death for as long as possible. All of which again argues against the tragedy at the gateway having been meticulously 'designed'.

While Sher Singh was biding his time, Maharani Chand Kaur sprang a surprise. She let it be known that her daughter-in-law, in other words the deceased Nau Nihal Singh's widow, was expecting a child. If a boy, he would be Ranjit's great-grandson and so the undisputed heir to the throne. The news caused a sensation and had an immediate effect on Chand Kaur's standing. According to Gardner, she now 'claimed the regency of the kingdom pending the birth of her grandchild' and duly won the qualified support of the outwardly legitimist Dogra brothers. In case no heir actually materialised, she also floated the idea that she might adopt the effeminate and somewhat forgotten Hira Singh, which would have gratified his father, Dhyan Singh. No less quixotically, it was suggested that she marry Sher Singh, her obvious opponent. But these were little more than manoeuvres designed to knit together whatever flimsy strands of legitimacy were available. In the event, there would be neither a birth nor an adoption and least of all a marriage.

With the kingdom now under the supposed authority of Chand Kaur as sovereign regent with Sher Singh as vice-regent and Dhyan Singh as vizier, in January 1841 Sher Singh himself at last headed for Lahore. Meanwhile Dhyan Singh had seen fit to retire to Jammu, there to nurse his deep designs and await developments. That left Lahore in the hands of Chand Kaur and her supporters, principally Gulab Singh and Hira Singh plus the 3000 Dogra troops who were temporarily placed under Gardner's command. All withdrew behind the high walls of Lahore's fort-cum-palace, itself comprising the north-western quadrant of the well walled city. A trial of strength looked unavoidable, with Gulab Singh and Gardner best placed in terms of the city's fortifications and Sher Singh best prepared in terms of manpower.

In this and subsequent tussles for control of the throne three elements would emerge as critical. A claimant needed the support of the army—or at least such units of it as could be mustered in the vicinity of Lahore; he or she also needed the acquiescence, but not necessarily the recognition, of the British; and he or she needed the connivance of one or other of the Dogra rajas of Jammu, Dhyan Singh and Gulab Singh. (Suchet Singh, the youngest of the Dogra brothers, Gardner dismisses as irrelevant. He was 'the bully at court and the desperado of the Punjab; a capital soldier but no officer ... and a most licentious debauchee and shameless defiler of women').

To woo the army Sher Singh issued what was known as a 'five brother' proclamation. This entitled every trooper to bring to the impending conflict four of his kinsmen and thus claim five shares in the expected booty. 'Such was the ancient custom of the Khalsa army,' says Gardner, 'and the magnitude of the assembly on this occasion may be imagined: to the very horizon the plains and hills [immediately east of Lahore] were one blaze of camp-fires'. Sher Singh could count on the army.

His relationship with the British was less clear. Their outright support was withheld pending an indication that his claim had been accepted in Lahore. But he was definitely the preferred British candidate. He therefore welcomed reassurances that the Khalsa's long-standing British allies wanted only a strong government in the Punjab, and he made no attempt to interfere with the passage of British troops to and from Kabul.

The great unknown was the attitude of the Dogra rajas. Certainly Dhyan Singh had acted as Sher Singh's impresario and had given him every encouragement. On the other hand, Dhyan Singh's son Hira Singh and brother Gulab Singh had thrown in their lot with Maharani Chand Kaur and the forces defending the fort. On opposite sides in the dynastic struggle, it appeared inevitable that the brothers would have to oppose one another in battle. Yet not so, claims Gardner; 'for it is a well known fact that in all important intrigues, it was the policy of the two brothers, by appearing to divide, to side with and lead the two opposing parties ... with the intention of destroying both claimants'.

Assuming there was such an understanding, the impetuosity of would-be Maharaja Sher Singh almost frustrated it. On 13 January (1841) the defenders in the fort were alerted by 'one of the most tre-

mendous roars that ever rose from a concourse of human beings'. It
came from a mound at Mian Mir where the army was encamped all
of two miles from the Lahore fort, and it could mean only one thing:
Sher Singh had finally arrived. It was followed by more cries, some
hailing him as maharaja with Dhyan Singh as his vizier, and others
demanding 'Death to Chand Kaur and the Dogras'. Dhyan Singh's
voice was not, however, among those baying for blood. He was still
in Jammu, a hundred miles to the north. Sher Singh was under orders
to do nothing till he arrived, and Dhyan Singh was playing for time
in the confidence that the longer he delayed, the greater would be
the impact of his eventual intervention.

Back in Lahore, for forty-eight hours nothing happened. Encamped among his restive hordes at Mian Mir, Sher Singh strained
at the bit and fretted. His suspicions about Dhyan Singh's continued
absence were compounded by the army's demands for ever more
excessive financial incentives. There was a real danger that support
would melt away without a quick assault on the fort and its fabulously
endowed treasury.

It was a different story within the fort. There feverish preparations
were underway to resist any assault. The approaches to the fort's gates
were blocked with carts; above them, guns loaded with grape-shot
were hauled to each of the upper forts; and higher still, the parapets
were lined with Dogra sharp-shooters. 'My women and all the others,
excepting the queen,' says Gardner, 'had been hidden previously in
disguise in various parts of the city... The poor queen [Chand Kaur]
was so sick with terror at the uproar made [by the enemy], no doubt
to overawe us, that she caused another lakh of rupees to be given
hurriedly to the doubtful city troops of the regular army, who held
the gates of the city'. Outnumbered by about four to one, Gardner
admits that resistance indeed 'seemed useless'. Only a grim-faced Gulab Singh, the most battle-hardened of the Dogra brothers, showed
no sign of alarm. Calm, active and resourceful, Gulab Singh was at
his best in such a crisis.

As the third morning dawned, Sher Singh's patience snapped.
Unable to restrain his supporters any longer, he ordered the massed
ranks of his largely Sikh forces to fan out and encircle the city. Gardner

watched the advance with mounting alarm.

> Every gate was immediately opened to them by the soldiers, who, having
> pocketed three lakhs from the queen, had made an equally profitable
> bargain with Sher Singh. Destruction stared us in the face: we had
> red-hot cannon-balls ready to blow ourselves and the whole city into
> the air, if the worst came to the worst.

The besieged were not just outnumbered but hopelessly outgunned.
By Gardner's calculation, two heavy siege trains, each of forty guns,
were laid against the fort, while the road in front of it bristled with
another eighty horse-drawn artillery pieces. Giving a total not far
short of that credited to the entire Khalsa army at the time, this
estimate was less a guess than a wilful exaggeration. As always with
Gardner, desperate times brought forth daring words. But as the
only foreigner in the Dogra camp, he was in his element. The 'siege
of Lahore' would be his moment of truth as an artillery commander.

Entrance to the inner fort was via the Hazuri Bagh courtyard,
its outer gate being that which had collapsed on Nau Nihal Singh
and its inner gate giving access to the palace apartments. The outer
gate fell without a shot being fired. Presumably its defendants had
been bribed to open it. With a mob of cavalry, Sher Singh himself
cantered into the courtyard and, taking cover, demanded that Gulab
Singh surrender.

But it was at the inner gate that Gardner had decided to make his
stand. Carts were piled up against it and behind them he positioned
two cannon. A peep through a crack in the gate's woodwork was not
reassuring. Facing it were 'fourteen guns deliberately loaded, planted
within 20 yards, and aimed straight at the gate'.

Gulab Singh answered Sher Singh's challenge by demanding that
it was he, Sher Singh, who should surrender. Ear pressed to the gate,
Gardner heard the exchange and awaited the outcome.

> There was a brief but breathless pause, and I had not time to warn my
> artillerymen to clear out of the way when down came the gates over our
> party, torn to shreds by the simultaneous discharge of all the fourteen

guns. Seventeen of my party were blown to pieces, parts of the bodies flying over me. When I had wiped the blood and brains from my face, and could recover a moment, I saw only one little trembling *Klasi* [*khalassi*, gun attendant]. I hurriedly asked him for a port-fire, having lost mine in the fall of the ruins. He had just time to hand it me, and I had crept under my two guns, when with a wild yell some 300 Akalis [fanatical Sikh 'Immortals'] swept up the Hazuri Bagh and crowded into the gate. They were packed as close as fish, and could hardly move over the heaps of wood and stone... Just at that moment, when the crowd were rushing on us, their swords high in the air, I managed to fire the [two] guns, and literally blew them into the air.

A second salvo mowed down the artillerymen in the courtyard; they had held their fire 'paralysed by the destruction of the Akalis'—or simply fearful of killing more of them. The Dogra sharp-shooters on the fort's parapets now found their range and began pouring a hail of bullets onto the surging crowd in the courtyard below. It was as if the tide of battle had turned the moment Gardner had discharged his guns. 'Then Sher Singh fled,' he reports, 'and grievous carnage commenced'.

Sher Singh had fled the Hazuri Bagh, although not the city. The storming of the Lahore Fort dragged on for another four days. A second gateway into the palace was defended much as the first; and just as the Dogra sharp-shooters picked off the attackers, so enemy snipers picked off the defenders from the tall minarets of the adjacent Badshahi mosque. The great Mughal mosque was known to be doubling as a powder magazine. When Sher Singh himself took up a position there, Gardner was all for turning his guns on it and 'blowing him and the building into the air'. He was deterred by Gulab Singh's caution and by the news that the subterranean passages connecting the mosque to the fort had been packed with explosives. Blowing up the one would likely bring down the other.

Hammered by Sher Singh's artillery, the fort, originally built by

Akbar in the seventeenth century, was crumbling anyway. Sikhs whose loyalty to Gulab Singh was suspect made their escape through its breached walls; raiding parties sent out to spike the enemy's guns returned through other breaches. With enemies within as well as without, it was greatly to Gulab Singh's credit that the fort held out at all.

Gardner gives the number killed in the Hazuri Bagh as '2800 soldiers, 200 artillerymen, and 180 horses'. Carmichael Smyth, possibly on Gardner's authority, prefers overall totals for the whole five days: 4786 men, 610 horses and 320 bullocks among Sher Singh's attackers, and only 130 killed or wounded among Gulab Singh's defenders. Gardner himself emerged unscathed, which was unusual. He would later claim to have been wounded on five occasions during his service in the Punjab, but this, it seems, was not one of them.

More predictably, he also emerged as the hero of the hour—and in this case, not simply in his own estimation. Gulab Singh himself would later confess that, thanks to the Hazuri Bagh action, he had formed 'a high opinion of Gardanah [sic] as a thorough-going friend, and ... [one who] always stuck by him when ... others deserted him'. Coming from a Dogra whom Gardner reckoned even more of a monster than Dhyan Singh, the testimonial may not have been worth much. But just as, in a crisis, Gulab Singh was a good man to serve under, so Gardner was a good man to have at one's side. Their relationship would be a long one and, in the opinion of critics like Grey and Garrett, a highly compromising one.

On 18 January (1841) the arrival of the elusive Dhyan Singh from Jammu was at last announced. Like a composer taking the podium after a faultless performance of his latest work, he promptly moved centre stage and was feted by all. The guns fell silent; the horse-trading began. 'Our bombardment was over and the [Dogra] brothers arranged terms of peace,' says a relieved Gardner.

On the face of it, the new order of precedence that emerged from the peace terms was indistinguishable from the old. Dhyan Singh would continue as vizier, Maharani Chand Kaur as 'titular head of the State', and Sher Singh as maharaja. But the dealings behind these arrangements left no doubt that the balance of power had swung firmly in the Dogras' favour. For his loyalty to the maharani during the siege, Gulab Singh was appointed her protector; he duly obtained a handsome settlement for her, including a large tract of hill territory that just happened to adjoin his own and over which he promptly took charge.

To Sher Singh, he was equally magnanimous. According to Gardner, in the course of the siege Gulab Singh had entered the palace treasury and helped himself to Ranjit Singh's most treasured possession, the famous Koh-i-Nur diamond. The Dogra raja now formally presented the stone to the new maharaja as a token of his loyalty. In return he accepted a reward of more hill territory yielding an annual income of 200,000 rupees. He then filled sixteen waggons with treasure and coin from the treasury before departing the fort under cover of darkness and under a safe passage guaranteed by the new maharaja. Nothing is said of Gardner's share in this bonanza. It seems likely, however, that not a few choice baubles came his way to take pride of place in the stash of treasure for which Helena would seek.

For Dhyan Singh, the rewards were of a different order. Long the power behind the throne, he was now the acknowledged king-maker. Sher Singh, though often resentful of his vizier's machinations, continued to rely on his influence over the troops, on his record as Ranjit Singh's closest advisor and on his hold over his now immensely enriched brother, Gulab Singh. The vizier's 'Ambition!' appeared to have been satisfied. But if recent events had demonstrated anything, it was that real power was being siphoned away from the court and the zenana and appropriated by the massed ranks of the army.

Disgusted by the endless vendettas and genuinely concerned for the fate of the Khalsa, the Sikh regiments had begun to express their grievances through informally chosen *panch*es or *panchayat*s. Each of these five-man committees—one authority calls them 'army soviets'—represented the rank and file of a different unit or regiment. As the market for military muscle grew, especially under Sher Singh, so did the expectations of the panches. Their pay and perquisites, though invariably in arrears, had to be increased to get them to fight, increased again to get them to stop fighting and increased once more to get them to disperse. Throughout the siege Sher Singh had been as much at the mercy of his own soldiery as he had of the Dogra sharp-shooters in the fort. With no legitimate successor to the throne, the panches saw themselves as the true heirs of Ranjit Singh and the sworn defenders of the Khalsa against all rivals—be they power-hungry Dogras, acquisitive British imperialists, make-believe maharajas or embezzling paymasters.

Or indeed francophone generals; for the days of Ranjit Singh's foreign contingent were now numbered. First to go was Allard; he had died in 1839. In the reprisals that followed the death of Nau Nihal Singh, General Court was obliged to seek refuge in Ventura's heavily fortified residence; he then fled to British India, returned to his mutinous command in 1842 and would flee for good in 1843. Ventura, one of Sher Singh's staunchest supporters, would leave at the same time. And Avitabile had thrown in the sponge six months earlier. Having spent the last two years of his eight-year 'reign of terror' over Peshawar in endeavouring to oblige Afghan-bound Britishers while under constant pressure from his mutinous troops, the overweight governor finally extracted his fortune, married off his cloistered handmaiden to his cook, and headed back to Naples.

Lesser officers, whether Indian or European, fared worse. Ventura's *aide-de-camp*, a man called Foulkes, was burnt alive by his Sikh troopers; his first name, though unstated, must surely have been Guy. This was in 1843. A year earlier, when many of the cash incentives promised at the time of siege were still outstanding, the troops took matters into their own hands. According to Smyth, who was primed by Gardner:

[They] murdered many of their officers and *munshi*s [paymasters who were usually non-Sikhs], shooting some, cutting down others and even burning some of them alive, rolled up in scarves. ...With such deadly enmity did they pursue the munshis in particular that even in the streets of Lahore they were heard to declare that they would kill every man, woman and child who could either read or write Persian, the language in which the munshis kept the pay accounts. ... Houses were sacked and burnt, and their inmates tortured and ill-used in a manner that is fearful to think upon. This may serve to shew the state and condition of the Sikh army at the time when the Panches established themselves as its representatives.

The so-called 'Anarchy' of 1841, the first of several, lasted only a matter of weeks. There followed a lull which Maharaja Sher Singh greeted by 'passing his time in drinking-bouts and every debauchery,' says Gardner, '... and for the space of a year and a half, nothing of great importance befell him'. Gulab Singh, along with Gardner and the Dogra artillery, suppressed a mutiny in Kashmir with heavy bloodshed and were later directed to Peshawar to liaise with the British, though they got no further than the Indus. Maharani Chand Kaur also left Lahore, having been effectively pensioned off.

But the apparent calm was misleading. Lahore seemed peaceful only because elsewhere there was outright war; Sher Singh kept his throne because his challengers were otherwise distracted. East and west, from the deserts of Afghanistan to the snowy wastes of Tibet, nemesis was never busier.

Gardner explains what was happening in this wider world with a story. Though undated and very probably apocryphal, it has a ring of plausibility about it. While encamped on the west bank of the Indus near Attock, he and Gulab Singh learned that a European was approaching. It turned out to be a Major Henry Lawrence 'dressed, not very successfully, as a Pathan' and whom Gardner had met on a recent excursion into Peshawar. Lawrence had come in person and at considerable risk because he had some worrying news for the Dogra. Gulab Singh laughed. He too had news, but he would divulge it only if Lawrence spoke first.

> The bargain was struck, and Lawrence led off by telling Gulab Singh that his expedition to Tibet had utterly failed, and that his agent, Wazir Zorawar Singh, with 9000 soldiers, had been cut off nearly to a man.

> 'I also have some news,' said Gulab Singh in his turn, and then told Law-

rence the horrid truth that all was over with the British in Kabul, and
that Akbar Khan [son of Dost Mohamed] was pressing [British-held]
Jalalabad with terrific vigour.

In this momentous exchange, it was Gulab Singh who would have
the last laugh. The Dogra invasion of western Tibet had been under-
taken as part of Gulab Singh's empire-building in the hills. Having
detached the tundra that was Ladakh from Lahore's direct rule, he
had given his governor in the Ladakhi capital of Leh a free hand.
This Zorawar Singh had then overrun Baltistan and Gilgit to the
north-west of Kashmir before picking a quarrel with the Tibetans
and driving deep into what was Chinese territory. The Chinese
objected; the British upheld these objections, and Gardner, though
never at his most convincing on the Himalayan region, would surely
have seconded both.

But before a withdrawal could be arranged, a combination of the
Tibetan winter and the more frost-hardy Tibeto-Chinese troops made
short work of the shivering Dogras. In mid-December at altitudes
of over 12,000 feet, they were not so much defeated as deep-frozen.
For lack of fuel, the wooden stocks of their muskets were burned,
and for lack of stocks, gloveless flesh stuck fast to bare gun-metal.
The Chinese just 'left them to perish, huddled in heaps behind rocks
or at the bottoms of ravines'. A very few survivors made it over the
highest Himalayan passes to a British-Indian hill-station, and it was
from there that news of the disaster had reached Calcutta and then
Major Lawrence in Peshawar.

In fact, word of what had overtaken the invaders may have arrived before word of their original incursion. If so, it made failure
after such an un-trumpeted success more palatable. Gulab Singh
would anyway repair the damage by repelling a counter-invasion of
Ladakh and tightening his hold on the Kashmir valley. The Dogra's
Tibetan disaster could be swept under the carpet. Britain's Afghan
catastrophe could not.

After two years of British rule in Afghanistan, troop reductions
and complacency played a major part in what would be British
India's worst ever defeat. So too, when the retreat was sounded in

Kabul, did the same harsh winter of 1841–2 that claimed so many Dogra lives in Tibet. But it is hard to avoid the conclusion that in Afghanistan the main culprit was a dearth of those sterling qualities, like leadership, discipline and military competence, on which the British most prided themselves.

One of the first casualties had been the now Sir Alexander Burnes, MacNaghten's right-hand man in Kabul. Lynched by a mob incensed by his appetite for Kabul's fleshpots, Burnes had been driven from his burning house and hacked to death. It was in the chaos that accompanied this attack that there supposedly perished all trace of those travel notes lent him by Gardner.

That was in early November 1841. Emboldened by this success, Afghans of every persuasion then poured into the capital and began piece-meal assaults on the sprawling British lines. Treasury, arsenals, storehouses and numerous strong points were picked off. By December the 'rebels' numbered 50,000. Akbar Khan, Dost Mohamed's son, escaped from captivity in Bukhara to take overall command; and one by one the British-held cities fell. With the investment of Ghazni to the south and of Jalalabad, astride the road to the Khyber Pass, the escape routes were closed. Starving, short of ammunition, frozen by night and knee-deep in slush by day, the once proud 'Army of the Indus' stared defeat in the face.

Macnaghten, the man most to blame for the situation, must also shoulder the blame for what followed. He opted for evacuation and on 14 December the remnants of the army, plus several thousand camp-followers, trudged out of Kabul under a decidedly unsafe safe-conduct. Even Akbar Khan had no chance of enforcing it in the ghazi-controlled defiles that led to the Khyber and the safety of Peshawar.

It was this 'horrid truth' that Gulab Singh shared with Henry Lawrence on the banks of the Indus. Lawrence was already aware of the plight of Jalalabad's garrison and was desperately trying to effect the despatch of a small relieving force. But of events in Kabul he may have been poorly informed; and this begged the question of how Gulab Singh could be so well informed.

Gardner, a man who could sniff a rat when all about him were

choking on attar of roses, thought he knew the answer. He had no
doubt that Gulab Singh was in secret communication with the Afghans' Barakzai leadership. Sultan Mohamed Khan, one of the exiled
Dost Mohamed's many brothers and the man under whom Gardner
had served in Peshawar ten years earlier, had been at Gulab Singh's
side during the siege of Lahore. Moreover, Gulab Singh was now
'in constant communication with Mohamed Akbar Khan [Sultan
Mohamed's nephew and the current Afghan leader] ... [and] was
receiving daily letters from Kabul'.

The Dogra not only knew what was going on in Kabul but was
colluding with the rebels. To frustrate the British relief effort, Gardner had been ordered to spirit away the ferry-boats on the Indus and
so delay the four ill-equipped British regiments that were hastening
across the Punjab in the hope of relieving the Jalalabad garrison. With
little help from the Sikhs, this rescue mission got only as far as Ali
Masjid in the Khyber Pass and then ran out of supplies.

Lawrence should have paid more heed to Gardner. According
to Herbert Edwardes, Lawrence's disciple and future biographer,
Gardner had warned that the relief force would never reach Kabul.
'This is the time to break your strength,' he advised, 'to raise insurrection here and there, draw off your force in different directions,
and then act.' But the advice went unheeded. To a man, the Army
of the Indus blundered.

Lawrence was only a junior political officer at the time, and he
was not sure what to make of Gardner. 'An adventurer who described
himself as an American', Gardner had reportedly been a lieutenant in
the navy, 'yet, somehow or other, had also been educated at a Jesuit
college...and finished under Gulab Singh'.

> [He] had wild moods of talking, letting the corner of dark things peep
> out, and then shutting them up again with a look behind him, as if life
> at Jammu [ie with Gulab Singh] was both strange and fearful.

Lawrence was intrigued. He would retain an interest in Gardner, seek
his advice, borrow from his life-story and then disown him.

Meanwhile retribution against the Afghans had to wait another four months. The retreat from Kabul had turned into a rout, and not until William Brydon, the sole survivor to have evaded both death and capture, had famously limped into Jalalabad was the scale of the disaster revealed.

By May 1842, when a 40,000-strong 'Army of Retribution' did finally trundle across the Punjab to storm back up the Khyber and re-take Kabul, Gulab Singh (and Gardner) had moved on. 'His heart was in Tibet,' says Cunningham, and a revolt in his hill territories east of Kashmir proved more urgent. From there he was unexpectedly summoned back to Peshawar. The British had decided that the support of his Dogra troops was essential to the retaking of Afghanistan. They were even prepared to bribe him with the offer of Jalalabad. Gulab Singh still prevaricated, and to such an extent that the British too suspected that he was 'in league with Akbar Khan for the destruction of the army of an obnoxious European power'.

On the assumption that Gardner accompanied Gulab Singh back to Peshawar, neither of them can have been directly involved in the ominous turn of events back in Lahore. There, in June 1842, the name of Maharani Chand Kaur joined the growing list of dynastic casualties. According to Major Smyth, four of her female attendants were responsible. 'They dashed out her brains with a heavy stone while they were engaged in dressing her hair'.

Smyth, presumably on information gleaned by Gardner, blames Sher Singh. Smarting from her refusal of his marital advances, the maharaja had supposedly bribed her attendants to bludgeon to death someone who might yet revive her challenge to his authority. 'But the event served the interests of Gulab Singh still more ... inasmuch as it gave him undisturbed possession of all the property of the deceased Chand Kaur.' Worse still, the murder brought an end to the brief respite in the blood-letting at the Sikh court. It signalled a return to the Dogra-engineered power struggles that had brought Sher Singh to power in the first place.

At this point in his narrative as pieced together by Pearse, Gardner takes the opportunity to introduce two new contenders for the throne. Smyth does likewise but with much more circumstantial detail. The first of the contenders was just five years old in 1843, by name Duleep Singh. No one supposed this little boy was really of the blood royal. It was common knowledge that his father was a *bhishti*, a water-carrier, and his mother the daughter of Ranjit Singh's former dog-walker-cum-court-jester. The dog-walker had nevertheless chided the old maharaja into taking an interest in his daughter, one Jind Kaur or Jindan; and as is the way with impotent old roués, Ranjit Singh had derived some pleasure from being associated with 'a girl who might pass for his great-grand-child'. He had found suitable foster-parents for the little girl, and in due course Jindan had re-appeared at Ranjit's side as an exceedingly lively teenager and a jester of sorts in her own right.

In this charade Jindan herself was far from innocent. Noted for 'pertness, forwardness, and something even worse' as well as for her precocious charms, she 'enlivened the night scenes in the palace .... by putting to shame any who were in any degree less depraved or less shameless than herself'—or so says Smyth, although 'to give a detail of these affairs and scenes acted in the presence of the old Chief himself and at his instigation would be an outrage to common decency.'

Exceptionally popular at these nocturnal orgies had been Jindan's faithful re-enactions of her assignations with the water-carrier. The maharaja took a particular delight in them and when in due course Jindan brazenly announced that she was carrying a child, even the water-carrier—the real father—had offered his congratulations 'as though [the now ailing maharaja] were really the father of the babe'.

To those ever on the look-out for a new pretender, especially one who promised to have a long minority, this tenuous association with the great Ranjit Singh was enough. Dhyan Singh had been first off the mark. By way of insurance against the day when Sher Singh no longer served his purpose, he had already taken under his doubtful protection the scandalously dissolute Jindan and her unsuspecting infant, Duleep Singh.

The second of the new contenders was very different. It was actually a Sikh threesome, and they too took an interest in the little Duleep.

But these Sindhanwalias—two uncles and a nephew—also had a blood claim of their own in that they shared a common ancestor with the old maharaja, albeit four generations back. After the death of Nau Nihal Singh, the Sindhanwalias had made the mistake of backing the claims of Chand Kaur against those of Sher Singh and had been obliged to flee as a result. Two of them took refuge in British India, where they were well received; and it was under British pressure that in 1843 Sher Singh agreed to rehabilitate them.

Not only were the Sindhanwalias readmitted to court but 'for a time there was great familiarity between Lehna Singh [one of the uncles], Ajit Singh [the nephew] and the Maharajah [Sher Singh], and the three frequently caroused together'. Vizier Dhyan Singh at first approved; but when he felt his influence with the maharaja waning, he began to have second thoughts. Another masterplan was taking shape; and 'with that strange foreboding which seems to attend the coming of terrible events,' noted Gardner, 'there was a general uneasiness in the air'.

As usual Gardner credits Dhyan Singh with being the mastermind behind the mischief, although the Sindhanwalias would appear at least as guilty. In what was essentially a case of triple-bluff, Dhyan Singh started the trouble by signing a secret pact with the Sindhanwalias for the disposal of the maharaja and his replacement with the little Duleep Singh. They then revealed this pact to its victim, Sher Singh. The maharaja, whose subtlety of mind was not great, was easily persuaded of the need for counter-measures; and who better to execute them that the loyal Sindhanwalias? Accordingly another secret pact was signed, this time between the maharaja and the Sindhanwalias, for the disposal of Dhyan Singh and his decorous son and heir, Hira Singh.

Trusted now by each of their targets, the Sindhanwalias bided their time. On 15 September 1843 the maharaja was due to inspect some of the family troops at his summer residence outside Lahore. He failed to show up. Fully armed for the occasion, uncle and nephew then went in search of him. They found him entertaining some wrestlers and 'reproached him in a jocular manner for keeping them waiting'. In equally familiar terms, the Sindhanwalia nephew proudly offered for inspection 'a handsome double-barrelled fowling piece' that he had lately acquired. The maharaja leant forward to take it and 'as Ajit Singh handed it to Sher Singh, he, by an almost imperceptible and apparently unintentional movement, brought its muzzles to bear on the breast of the maharaja and fired both barrels almost together'

> The unfortunate Sher Singh fell back in his chair, a corpse... His head was immediately cut off and such of his servants as made a show of resistance were shot or cut down.

A similar fate befell Sher Singh's twelve-year-old son, once a particular favourite of the Eden sisters. According to Gardner, all Sher Singh's womenfolk were also murdered.

> I for one was on the alert directly I heard the shots fired [claims Gardner], and went at once to find Dhyan Singh, who had already gone to see Maharaja Sher Singh in consequence of some dark rumours that reached him. He found Ajit Singh [Sindhanwalia] fresh from his deeds of blood and half-way on his return journey to Lahore.

Presuming that all was going to plan, Dhyan Singh accompanied the regicides back to Lahore. It now remained only to enthrone the little Duleep Singh and declare a *fait accompli*. In the meantime it was essential to maintain secrecy. Vizier Dhyan Singh therefore agreed to proceed to Lahore in the company of the Sindhanwalias and with only a small personal escort.

> Suspicion seemed to flash across the Minister's mind, for he glanced at his escort as if to see how many men he had with him; and finding that he was greatly outnumbered, he found that he had no option...

Entering the fort, even Dhyan Singh's escort was detained. 'The hitherto wary minister was now caught in his own toils,' says Cunningham, 'and he became the dupe of his accomplices'. Looking about him, he noticed the battlements were crawling with men. He enquired about their purpose and, as he did so, one of the Sindhanwalia's soldiers 'shot him in the back and despatched him with a sword'. The Machiavelli of Lahore had made a fatal miscalculation.

Though by now four maharajas had passed away in as many years, far worse was this demise of the vizier. Without the man who, for good or ill, had been directing affairs for half a decade, and without he whose authority alone reached back to the illustrious age of Ranjit Singh, the Sikh Empire had taken another lurch towards its rudderless demise.

The court was losing its authority. A five-year old maharaja, his capricious mother and the effete Hira Singh would be hard-pressed to restrain the army's ever more assertive panches. The loose cannon that was Gulab Singh already commanded most of the empire's hill districts. And the British, triumphant at last in Afghanistan but keen to disengage there, were again well placed to intervene in the Punjab.

As Avitabile, Ventura and most of the other foreign contingent made plans for their escape, Gardner was left pondering his own position. Without Dhyan Singh, his patron of the last eight years, he had every reason to follow suit. But he chose to stay on. Gulab Singh was still in the field and apparently keen to retain him. 'There was no necessity to leave that I saw. I was always treated with honour and respect.'

Possibly he was also encouraged to stay on from an unlikely quarter. The recent meeting beside the Indus with Major Lawrence had led to an exchange of letters which convinced Lawrence that Gardner could be a useful source of intelligence on the intrigues in Lahore. Others would simply suppose that, for one already so mired in blood-shed, the prospect of still worse atrocities held no horrors. Yet Gardner was clearly shocked by the death of Dhyan Singh. Instead of reviling the monster beneath the 'mystic cloak', he paid his final respects by applauding the minister's more obvious qualities.

> Thus perished the wise and brave Dhyan Singh, whose fall was deplored by the whole army: but it was [about to be] avenged and that quickly.

8

Dark and Disgustful
1843–45

Prior to the crisis of 1843 there was a reasonable chance of the Sikh Empire weathering the intrigues that beset it. Maharaja Sher Singh had outlasted both of his predecessors; under him relations with the British had if anything improved; and the army, though much more assertive than in Ranjit Singh's day, remained a cohesive entity. But now, with the passing of Sher Singh, instead of stabilising, the state plunged into a vortex of recrimination and chaos. There would be no going back.

The assassinations of the maharaja and his son had taken place on 15 September (1843), with that of Vizier Dhyan Singh following later the same day. Gulab Singh being busy in the mountains, that left Dhyan Singh's son, the effeminate Hira Singh who had once been Ranjit Singh's favourite. Since he had also been the Dogras' original candidate for ultimate power, the Sindhanwalias could ill afford to overlook him. They had in fact intended to dispose of him at the same time as his father. But it so happened that at the crucial moment young Hira Singh had been visiting the main body of the army just outside Lahore. Though as yet unaware of his father's murder, he ignored a summons from the palace forged in his father's name and, when word of the assassinations reached him, incited the army's panches to exact vengeance. With commendable expedition he then marched on the city itself, in whose palace the Sindhanwalias were holed up.

In the words of Muhammad Naqi, a not impartial court official who penned the little known but contemporary *Tarikh-i-Punjab* ('Punjab Chronicle'), 'that sun of glory, that star of beneficence and guardian of the kingdom, Raja Hira Singh, entered the city with a mighty following four hours after dusk'. Leading the vanguard of Hira Singh's 'mighty following' was Paolo Avitabile; and for what would prove the last engagement fought by the old maharaja's foreign generals, Avitabile was that night joined by the unsmiling Jean Baptiste Ventura. It was Ventura who took charge of the ensuing siege, throwing himself, says Naqi, 'like an angry lion upon the foxes within'.

Other veterans, like Suchet Singh, youngest of the Dogra brothers, hastened to support this Punjabi version of the 'army of retribution'. Guns again played on the fort's pocked defences, and inducements to defect again changed hands. On the 16th one of the Sindhanwalias was shot dead as he lay wounded. Then on the 17th, Ajit Singh Sindhanwalia, the man directly responsible for the deaths of both Sher Singh and Dhyan Singh, attempted to escape by leaping from the walls. He landed within reach of some attackers, one of whom decapitated him 'with a single swift blow of his sword, and thus', in Naqi's wishful words, 'forever quenched the spark of mischief'. The fort then fell to Hira Singh and the attackers. It was all over in forty-eight hours.

Gardner's part in this second siege of Lahore is not known. It was evidently less pivotal than in the first, although he was certainly present. In particular he marvelled at the conduct of Dhyan Singh's young widow, a lady of whom he must have known from the wife 'given to him by Rajah Dhyan Singh out of his own house'. To urge on the avenging assault, this 'exquisitely beautiful' maid had publicly vowed to delay her husband's obsequies by refusing to mount his pyre until she had herself beheld the heads of his murderers. Nor would she be disappointed, resolved a suddenly gallant Gardner. And nor was she; for 'I myself laid their heads at the feet of Dhyan Singh's corpse that evening'.

Fort and city were then again ransacked, a bonanza from which Gardner no doubt reaped further pecuniary advantage. Carmichael

Smyth, primed by Gardner, claims that 'betwixt thirty-five and forty lakhs of rupees [3.5–4 million] were abstracted from the treasury', adding that 'it was not more than an eighth part of what Hira Singh took himself'. From the royal dispensary 'essences and scents were spilt like water and many tonics, rare medicines and precious wines were wasted,' says Naqi.

> In a single night all the bazaars and streets of the city were sacked by the licentious soldiery and the people suffered untold miseries... atrocities were perpetrated and irreparable havoc was wrought ... Doorless shops gaped like the wide eyes of lovers. The people were bereft of all protection.

According to Naqi, it was only thanks to 'the work of that great and noble hand', in other words Hira Singh, that the plunder was halted, order restored and a durbar held to decide on the empire's future governance.

With all the Sindhanwalias accounted for (the last member of the clan had fled back across the Satluj to British protection), three parties now vied to fill the power vacuum. None of them contested the actual succession. All accepted as a *fait accompli* the Sindhanwalias' elevation to the gaddi of the seven-year old Duleep Singh, and all now reaffirmed their loyalty to the little boy. A long minority by a doubtful claimant who showed few signs of precocious ability suited their purposes. Gulab Singh could continue his empire-building in the hills using Gardner and others to represent his interests at court. His nephew Hira Singh could wrestle with the military panches until such time as their demands exhausted the funds available to satisfy them. And those closest to the throne could endeavour to mount a challenge based on the young maharaja's fragile claim to legitimacy.

The last of these three parties was that of Jindan or Jind Kaur, the still young and outrageously manipulative daughter of the water-carrier who, as queen-mother, was now known as the rani or maharani. Around her gathered a coterie of Dogra-hating officials including Jowahir Singh, her brutish brother, and Lal Singh, an impressive looking Brahmin and former treasury clerk who was soon assumed to be one of her lovers. In the next few years both these men would in turn attain the all-powerful vizier-ship.

At first, though, that office was claimed by Hira Singh on the strength of his father's long tenure and the support currently afforded him by the army. To Gardner's way of thinking Hira Singh was a disaster. More capricious and vindictive than his father or his uncle, he yet lacked their fixity of purpose and their genius for unfathomable intrigues. Instead Hira Singh relied, even more than the Rani Jindan, on his own Brahmin accomplice and lover, one Pandit Jalla, a man described by Gardner as 'of the most repulsive cast of countenance, and of a most tyrannical and ambitious spirit'. It was an opinion shared by others, not least by the remaining European officers, nearly all of whom now finally left Lahore much to Gardner's disgust. Sikh veterans and chiefs within the army's ranks felt equally slighted. Ranjit Singh had moulded an empire in which neither creed nor caste was a bar to advancement and office. But five years after his death, the empire's essentially Sikh character had been so diluted that the Khalsa was poorly represented in the councils of state. Instead an assortment of Hindu Dogras and Brahmins, Pathan and Punjabi Muslims and members of the menial castes (like the rani and her brother) were wielding power. The claim by the military panches that it was they, the grassroots of the army, who alone represented the Khalsa's ideals of dedicated service in a common cause had some substance.

While such discontent simmered within the ranks, Hira Singh and his Brahmin *éminence grise* picked off likely challengers. Jowahir Singh, brother of the Rani and uncle of the maharaja, was imprisoned for supposedly making overtures to the British; Raja Gulab Singh was invited to make his obeisance yet somehow delayed doing so; and his brother Suchet Singh issued a quixotic appeal to the army, then fled the scene and was treacherously slain. Meanwhile two twenty-something princelings, Kashmira Singh and Peshora Singh, made their own move. Both were considered adoptees of Ranjit Singh, having been named by him in honour of the provinces (ie Kashmir and Peshawar) conquered in their birth years. But it was the fort of Sialkot, hard by Gardner's eventual resting place, which was their stronghold. There they made their stand and were soon besieged.

All this occupied the best part of a year (1844), during which Gardner, having been dismissed by Hira Singh, was confirmed as the equivalent of a colonel in charge of a six-gun detachment of Gulab Singh's artillery. In this role he claims to have personally recaptured Sialkot from Kashmira and Peshora Singh and to have very nearly saved Suchet Singh from his assassins. 'I was one day too late,' he says—rather as he had been with Syed Ahmed at Balakot.

But like the narrative of his Himalayan travels, his account of the year 1844–5 takes too many yeti-like strides and omits more than it reveals. Perhaps editor Pearse was over-zealous in simplifying what was admittedly a most confusing sequence of events. More probably both Pearse and Gardner were keen to pre-empt too close an examination of this most torrid of interludes. The political turmoil was bad enough and the personal turmoil even worse; for it was at this point that Gardner was called upon to perform that 'black, heinous, and even disgustful and revolting' deed, as he himself called it, that would haunt his reputation ever after. Discretion being again the better part of candour, the reader of the *Memoirs* is offered in its stead doubtful triumphs, near-miss excursions, a new alibi and yet more decapitated heads.

The next of these grisly trophies would give Gardner the greatest satisfaction, bearing as it would the 'repulsive countenance' of Pandit Jalla. By late 1844 vizier Hira Singh and the Pandit had forfeited the support of the panches. The treasury was practically bare and the emoluments—gold bangles, double pay, one-off bonuses, etc—promised to the troops who had evicted the Sindhanwalias and were now harrying Hira Singh's other opponents had still to be paid out. The heavy-handed treatment of Kashmira and Peshora Singh, neither of them a serious threat and both of them relics of the revered Ranjit Singh, had alienated men who had once fought alongside them. Worse still, the killing of Suchet Singh offended all who, like Gardner, remembered that womanising 'desperado of the Punjab' not as 'a threat to every husband' but as a man whose derring-do and utter indifference to danger had delighted a generation. As the one remaining member of the Dogra brotherhood, Gulab Singh had felt Suchet Singh's loss most acutely. But like the army, he blamed

the evil influence of Pandit Jalla more than the easily swayed Hira
Singh. The pandit was likened to a snake lodged in the bosom of the
Khalsa. He had to go.

Yet petitions to that effect were repeatedly parried and promises
broken. Pressure from the army did lead to the release of Jowahir
Singh, who resumed his anti-Dogra agitation alongside his sister,
the rani; but Pandit Jalla stayed on. By juggling with troop deployments and making timely disbursements he clung on till December
1844. The final straw seems to have been his attempt to restore the
treasury's revenues by increasing the receipts due from the empire's
jagir-holders and dispossessing those who failed to pay up. This was
seen as an affront not just to those *sirdars* (ie the Sikh nobility) affected but to all who served in their name. Disaffection everywhere
led to a closing of ranks. Factions within the army rediscovered their
shared loyalty to the Khalsa, while court opponents of the Dogras
made common cause with those army officers, Gardner included,
who were in Dogra employ. The rani inflamed opinion further by
claiming that Hira Singh and the pandit had abused her and insulted
the young maharaja. Meanwhile Gulab Singh, the one man who had
materially profited from every action to date, wooed the panches with
promises of the still greater remuneration that he alone could afford.

'Eventually Hira Singh and the Pandit [Jalla] were compelled to
take refuge in the late Raja Dhyan Singh's house in Lahore,' reports
Gardner, 'but subsequently fled with 1200 men.' They were reportedly
heading for Jammu with the idea of winning over Gulab Singh, one
of whose sons was with them. But overtaken at nearby Shahdara, and
with vizier Hira Singh still refusing to surrender the detested pandit,
'after a running fight of nine miles they were all caught and slain'. Hira
Singh had outlived his father by just fifteen months.

> The army then entered the city of Lahore and commenced killing all
> the Dogras [says Gardner]. My life, being, as I was, in command of the
> troops of that race [ie the Dogras], was imperilled; but some Akalis,
> who knew that I was an old officer of Ranjit Singh, took me under their
> protection, and from motives of personal safety I became a complete
> Akali in costume and habits.

The Akalis were the warrior fanatics of the Khalsa and the most irregular of its irregular units. Gardner got to know them well. He was
probably the only foreigner ever admitted to their ranks and would
write an intriguing biographical sketch of Phula Singh Nihang, the
most revered of their leaders. A freebooter 'like the Robin Hood of
English history', the legendary Phula Singh had delighted the Sikhs
with his exploits. He had intimidated British visitors, thought nothing of defying even the great Ranjit Singh and answered to no one.

To an outsider with Gardner's long experience of Asiatic alibis,
adopting the attire of an Akali may not have been too demanding. They 'wear but little clothing and are sometimes divested of
it altogether,' noted Dr William MacGregor, one of several British
soldier-historians of the Sikhs. Despising both body armour and
silken finery, the Akali in action opted for a long indigo shirt, plus
a waistband from which dangled the keenest of curved scimitars.
Gardner already boasted the upswept whiskers and wild-eyed stare
that were *de rigeur*. The only challenge must have been the Akali's
distinctive turban with its tapered peak, somewhat like Wee Willie
Winkie's nightcap, along which were threaded razor-sharp quoits of
diminishing diameter for use as discus-like projectiles.

Accustomed to brandishing the trophies of war as a way of ter-
rifying the citizenry, the Akalis severed the heads of those slain at
Shahdara and paraded them round the streets of Lahore.

> I myself, dressed as an Akali, carried the Pandit's head in my hand ...
> [and] after the Akalis had triumphantly carried about the heads of the
> dead princes [ie of Hira Singh and his cousin] for more than a fortnight,
> I managed with great difficulty to secure the heads and to send them
> to Jammu to Gulab Singh. The heads were then cremated.

Thus passed the season of good cheer that the ever-watchful British
across the Satluj were celebrating as Christmas 1844. New Year found
the army panches in Lahore locked in heated debate as to whom to
back next. Gulab Singh was the obvious choice, he alone commanding
the resources with which to reward them. Yet these same resources,
including the jagirs and treasure he now claimed as the estates of

Dhyan, Suchet and Hira Singh, also furnished a strong incentive for undertaking punitive action against him.

Accordingly, and with the full encouragement of the rani and Jowahir Singh, in February 1845 a large section of the army under the nominal command of Lal Singh, the rani's favourite, headed for Jammu and its well-endowed raja. There Gulab Singh, having already lost two brothers and two sons in the Lahore blood-lettings, was inclined to be conciliatory. He nevertheless marshalled his men and buried his treasure. The advancing forces would dub him 'the golden hen' as their search parties rummaged the neighbourhood for these hidden nests. According to Gardner, he 'thirsted for vengeance on the Sikh nation' and was already in treasonous contact with both Dost Mohamed in Kabul and Major George Broadfoot, Calcutta's newly appointed and decidedly bellicose political agent in Ludhiana.

Gardner, being, as he certainly was, in Gulab Singh's employ, must indeed have felt his life 'imperilled'. His patron had been declared a rebel, and with the exception of a Transylvanian doctor and a Spanish engineer, he was the only non-Asian officer left in Lahore. Briefly he may indeed have tagged along with the Akalis. More fatefully he turned his attention to the palace and the royal party within.

There Jowahir Singh, although not yet officially installed as vizier, was acting as if he was. Backed by his sister, the rani, and emboldened by the priceless asset that was the young maharaja, Jowahir Singh had launched a vendetta against his former enemies and especially those of the Hira Singh regime who had been responsible for his earlier imprisonment.

Foremost among these was Jodha Ram or Jodha Misser, another Brahmin who had lately succeeded to the command of Avitabile's battalions. Jodha Ram was said to be either the father-in-law or the adopted brother of the deceased Pandit Jalla, and his reputation was just as unsavoury. At his hands Jowahir Singh had suffered personal humiliation (with a shoe beating) and then worse (he had been imprisoned and tortured). He wanted Jodha Ram dead. Failing that, he wanted him disfigured in the most mortifying fashion that penal custom sanctioned. But fearful of antagonising the crack troops whom the Brahmin now commanded, he could not himself be seen to wield the sword. He needed someone else to do the job—and then take the blame; and as luck would have it, his choice fell, like a hangman's noose, on the shoulders of the currently friend-less artilleryman he knew of as Gordana Sahib. The colonel's hitherto charmed existence amid the carnage in Lahore was about to be fatally compromised.

Of what transpired between Gardner, Jowahir Singh and Pandit Jodha Ram in early 1845 not a word is to be found in Pearse's edition of the Gardner *Memoirs*. Jodha Ram is nowhere mentioned, and Gardner's only meeting with Jowahir Singh is said to have taken place no sooner than September of that year. The nine months prior to it slip by with news of Peshora Singh's fate in far-off Attock but no record at all of events in Lahore. And it is the same in Carmichael Smyth's Gardner-informed account of the period. Jodha Ram's name is notably absent, while that of Jowahir Singh features mainly in connection with the uprising that had claimed the life of Hira Singh and with another uprising, ten months later, that would claim the life of Jowahir Singh himself.

One might, therefore, reasonably suppose that when, some three quarters of a century later, a cache of news reports dating from the year in question came to light, the dusty storerooms of Lahore's Punjab Records Office would have been the scene of some distinctly unlibrary-like excitement. For once again Charles Grey and Herbert Garrett had struck lucky. Catalogued as files 165 and 166, the faded missives in the Records Office contained two entries that were so damning as to be barely credible.

The first, dated 23 February 1845, recorded how Jowahir Singh, though distrustful of all around him and 'quite unable to act for himself', had nevertheless 'ordered the mutilation of a Brahmin officer [Jodha Ram] who had offended him' and that he had also, at about the same time, 'employed several persons, one of whom is a Mr Gardiner, a deserter from some European regiment, to raise three regiments amounting to about 900 men'.

In the first of the reports the fate of the Brahmin and the news of

Gardner's employment were not connected; but in the second, which was undated but evidently only a few weeks later, they definitely were.

> At Lahore Sirdar Jowahir Singh has for some days prepared to defend the fort, and told his new levies they were his only hope, at the same time giving each man a present. The instrument of this man is the European Gardiner, now created a Colonel, mentioned in an earlier letter. I learned today that this man is believed in the Punjab to be a deserter from a man-o'-war in Bombay. I also find that a report that I did not mention before is authentic. It is that with his own hands he cut off the fingers, nose and ears of Jodha Ram, lately mutilated by order of the sirdar [Jowahir Singh].

Reading this, Grey and Garrett appear to have been genuinely horrified, their disgust being leavened only by ill-concealed delight. The anonymous writer of the news reports was probably not the same as he who had recorded Gardner's arrival in Lahore thirteen years earlier; nor had it occurred to him, any more than it had to his predecessor, that the statement about Gardner being a deserter from a European regiment or some Bombay man-o'-war was almost certainly a timely fabrication. Grey and Garret didn't entertain the idea either. On the contrary, they once again insisted that here were what they called 'solid and unimpeachable facts!' Not only was Gardner a 'deserter', an 'imposter' and a 'liar' but, shame to tell, a blood-stained butcher to boot.

Yet Grey and Garrett, no less than Pearse and Carmichael Smyth, cannot have been unaware that the Lahore news-writer's reports were no longer exactly news-worthy. By the 1920s the outrage described had in fact been common knowledge for decades. Cunningham had referred to it in his magisterial *A History of the Sikhs* published in 1849, the respected *Calcutta Review* had shuddered to relate it in gory detail in 1846, and in 1847 Gardner himself had admitted his involvement in a long and rambling apologia.

The question raised by the discovery in the Punjab Records Office was not, therefore, whether Gardner had been a party to such a dastardly act but whether those, like Smyth and Pearse who had suppressed all mention of it, could be trusted as witnesses to the rest of his career. Grey and Garrett thought not. They accused editor Pearse in particular of uncritical partisanship and deplored the gullibility of all the distinguished referees who, swayed by Pearse, had lent their names to the Gardner 'legend'. Clearly a man responsible for cutting off bits of a fellow officer should never have been hailed as 'one of the finest specimens ever known of the soldier of fortune' (Sir Henry Durand), let alone as 'deserving the attention of our rising manhood in the British Isles' and an exemplar of 'what men of British race can do under stress of trial and suffering' (Sir Richard Temple).

Yet, as Gardner himself would put it, 'truth and falsehood are often found curiously mingled and confounded, and even misplaced and exchanged'. Conjecture could turn into hearsay and hearsay into fact; just as imperceptibly, reality could be undermined by innuendo, and innuendo by falsehood. Things weren't always what they seemed, even when on the record. Cunningham had played safe. He had merely referred to Jodha Ram's having been 'barbarously mutilated ... by depriving him of his nose and ears'; the order came from Jowahir Singh but Gardner's role went unmentioned; perhaps Cunningham was unaware of it, perhaps he was simply unsure of it. Captain Herbert Edwardes writing in the *Calcutta Review* had had no such doubts. Grey and Garrett would quote—and often misquote—Edwardes at length. The date of his article was 1846 (not their '1847') and the relevant passage, though damning enough, contained more than a germ of truth.

Jodha Ram gave offence to the new minister [Jowahir Singh] and was given over to one of those cruel sentences which Runjit Singh was accustomed to call mercy. But Jodha Ram was a Brahmin, and no Hindu would do the deed which would secure to himself damnation through a hundred generations. The Kotwal [police superintendent] of the city of Lahore—a Mussalman [Muslim], and no very particular person, who had for years been the municipal instrument of violence—was therefore ordered to cut off the ears and nose of the wretched man. He too refused; and we blush to record that the only man in Lahore who could be found to execute the barbarous decree was a European. Mr

Gardener, or Gordana, in the Sikh artillery took a razor and with his own hands in cold blood, without personal enmity of any sort, inflicted the punishment which Sikhs, Hindus and Mussalmen had shrunk from in disgust. But then he was made *a colonel*; and as Walpole observed, 'Every man has his price. The only thing is to find it out!'

Bursting with righteous indignation, the only thing neither Edwardes nor the news-writer had found out was the precise status of the culprit. Although the system of ranks and promotion within the Sikh army did not directly correspond with that familiar to the British, Gardner had certainly enjoyed both the responsibilities and the pay of a commandant or colonel for at least a decade. If he was rewarded at all for his part in Jodha Ram's mutilation, it was not with promotion but with command of the 900-strong bodyguard he was raising for Jowahir Singh.

But as to the punishment itself, Edwardes was right. Since the laws of the country forbade the death penalty, other forms of physical subtraction were standard. According to the dependable General Allard, 'a criminal sometimes has his nose or ears cut off, but never his head. It is also not uncommon to cut off the criminal's hands.' These were judicial punishments, and repeat offenders might be subject to all of them, plus the cutting of their Achilles' tendons. The 'mercy' lay in their being spared death and in their entitlement, once incapacitated, to a small pension. However disgusting to European sensibilities, Gardner had not been pursuing a personal vendetta against the pandit. He had acted under orders and in strict accordance with Sikh custom.

By chance a copy of Edwardes' *Calcutta Review* article as abstracted in the *Delhi Gazette* would eventually catch Gardner's eye. He would light upon it during a visit to the home of Martin Honigberger, the Transylvanian physician who was the only other non-Asian resident in Lahore at the time; and it came as a nasty shock. An action of which the colonel was by no means proud was now in the public domain; worse still, it was being misrepresented. Realising the dire consequences, he lost no time in trying to set the record straight. The result would be the longest surviving rant he ever wrote—some seventy foolscap pages in the only surviving copy, each of them covered in his eccentric prose and mostly devoted to a wordy 'defence' of his 'barbarous' action.

But this unexpected document, surely one of the most bizarre productions ever to find its way from the East India Company's records into those of the India Office and then the British Library's archives, was quite unknown to Grey and Garrett or to Pearse. In fact it seems to have eluded everyone else interested in Gardner's story, past or present. For one thing, the 'defence' is filed amid a clutch of other intelligence reports, mostly of minor interest; and for another it came rather late in the day, not being finalised until, at the earliest, late 1846. This was nearly two years after the event, by which time Jowahir Singh and Jodha Ram were history and the situation in the Punjab was so radically different as to be barely recognisable.

By then the first of the two Anglo-Sikh Wars had already been fought. The Sikh Empire had been brought under a form of indirect British rule, Lahore teemed with British troops, and the Anarkali Tomb, the spacious former residence of General Ventura and now the headquarters of the British protectorate, echoed to the barked orders and blithe conceits of a British Indian administration at its mission-conscious zenith. None of which, it need hardly be said, would bode well for a be-turbaned colonel of uncertain nationality with a chequered past, a hole in his throat and a lot of explaining to do.

Back in February 1845, with his foreign colleagues dispersed, his former patron (Dhyan Singh) dead, and his current patron (Gulab Singh) besieged in Jammu, the fugitive Akali who answered to the name of Gordana had been forced to undertake some serious stock-taking. In a revealing letter filed along with his 'defence' he would claim that, despite his employment by Jowahir Singh, his salary had been more than halved. Under Ranjit Singh and Dhyan Singh he had received 250 rupees a month and 120 rupees for provisions, fodder and an active service allowance. To these were added another 120 'for the expenses of my wife etc etc', 50 for 'horses, mules, camels and carriage etc' and

50 more as the yield of a village in Lahore and some wells at Jammu previously granted him as a jagir. That made 590 rupees a month, a sum which other perquisites and presents bumped up to around 700 rupees. It was a considerable income, equal to 8400 rupees a year or, depending on one's favoured equivalence table, anything from £74,200 to £2.7m in today's values. But following Dhyan Singh's death the monthly total had shrunk to under 250 rupees. 'I cannot support myself and [my] family with about 20 servants etc etc on this salary,' he plaintively concluded.

Whether the 'family' or the 'wife etc etc' here mentioned included any more children is not revealed. Nor are any Lahore offspring listed elsewhere. But the fact that he still had any income at all was plainly thanks to Jowahir Singh. As colonel of the three battalions raised to protect the rani and her brother, Gardner at least had a command; indeed with Jowahir Singh's May 1845 appointment as vizier, he was back in the service of a 'prime minister'. Unfortunately Jowahir Singh was no Dhyan Singh. A heavy drinker and an even heavier-handed operator, he lacked the resources to win over the army and he lacked the guile to exploit divisions within its ranks.

These divisions were starkly revealed during the summer of 1845. In April the cash-rich Raja Gulab Singh was finally extricated from his Jammu stronghold and brought to Lahore to make his submission. Supposedly he came as a contrite prisoner; yet by the time he arrived he was posing as an eager ally. Half the army relished the prospect of depriving him of his wealth by way of punishment for his defiance; the other half, won over by his blandishments, relished the prospect of relieving him of his wealth as the price of their support in his putative bid for the viziership. It was a situation of which the deceased Dhyan Singh would happily have taken advantage. But Jowahir Singh, by claiming the viziership for himself, precluded all room for manoeuvre. Moreover by relying on Gardner's troops for his security, he was effectively defying the regular army and scuppering any chance of winning favour among its anti-Dogra elements. In the end Gulab Singh got off with a hefty fine, which he could well afford, and promises of compliance, which he had no intention of honouring. 'The golden hen' then scuttled back to Jammu to dig up his treasure nests and await events.

A greater blunder was Jowahir Singh's reported involvement in the murder of Peshora Singh. As the last of those two siblings who had supposedly been adopted by Ranjit Singh (the other, Kashmira Singh, had just perished in a fracas that could have been contrived by almost anyone), Peshora Singh, though 'vain and of slender capacity', enjoyed considerable respect. Gulab Singh afforded him a degree of support; and the troops sent to winkle him out from various places of sanctuary found good reasons not to press him too closely. According to Cunningham, it had been the failure of Avitabile's former brigade to bring Peshora Singh to book that had resulted in the brigade's new commander, in other words Jodha Ram, being sentenced to the razor.

However this may be, Peshora Singh seemed to lead a charmed existence. Having captured the great fort of Attock on the banks of Indus, he even made so bold as to declare himself maharaja. This was too much for Jowahir Singh, whose position depended entirely on his nephew's claim to the succession and his sister's claim to be acting as the little boy's regent. He therefore directed troops, not from Lahore but from the ever troublesome Yusufzai and Derajat regions, to besiege the Attock fort. In August 1845 Attock duly surrendered. Peshora Singh was then ordered to be taken to Lahore with every prospect of ultimately being rehabilitated. But before he could be moved he was dead, treacherously slain by one of his captors and his body reportedly chopped up and fed to the river's fishes.

The perpetrator of this crime was assumed to have acted with a view to ingratiating himself with Jowahir Singh. Equally he could actually have been instructed to act thus by Jowahir Singh. Such was certainly the view taken by a large section of the army. Jowahir Singh's authority was now called in question, and the army panches demanded he render an account of his part in the affair. He refused; the army insisted; and the vizier retorted by 'combining cowardice with debauchery, in which he was plunging deeper every day'. This was the view of Francois Henri Mouton, a French officer dismissed by Pandit Jalla but who now resurfaced in Lahore as a military adviser to General Tej Singh, one of the rani's supporters. Meanwhile Gardner once again found his loyalties stretched. Though still ensconced in the Lahore Fort, his new battalion was as often facing inwards as outwards. Formed to defend Jowahir Singh, it found itself expected to confine him. In effect, under pressure from the seniormost council of panches, the vizier's bodyguard had become his goalers.

This stand-off lasted into September. It was then that Gardner was summoned for what in the *Memoirs* he calls his 'one interview' with Jowahir Singh. '[I] could hold out no hope, but told him to behave like a man and face the peril,' he says. Jowahir Singh took this to mean that he had no choice but to submit. He acted accordingly. On 21 September he and the rani, accompanied by the young maharaja, ascended a troop of royal elephants and processed out of the fort, followed by an escort of 400 cavalry and 'two elephant-loads of rupees with which to tempt the army'.

Of what ensued there are several versions. They differ only as to the details, with Gardner's version being as vivid and credible as any. In a scene that would long be remembered as the last of the Sikh Empire's great tragi-pageants, the royal cavalcade was greeted by 'an ominous salute that ran along the immense line of the army [as] 180 guns were fired'. There followed a silence no less ominous during which the entire army seemed to hold its breath. It was broken only by the trampling feet of the royal cavalcade, says Gardner.

Dhulip Singh was received with royal honours; his mother, the Maharani Jindan, in miserable terror for her brother, was seated on her golden howdah, dressed in white Sikh clothes and closely veiled. As soon as the procession reached the middle of the line, one man came forward and cried out 'Stop', and at his single voice the whole procession paused... Four battalions were now ordered to the front, and removed Jowahir Singh's escort to a distance. Then another battalion marched up and surrounded the elephants of the royal personages... the Rani's elephant was commanded to kneel down, and she herself was escorted to a small but beautiful tent prepared for her close by.

Then a terrible scene took place. The Rani was dragged away, shrieking to the army to spare her brother. Jowahir Singh was next ordered to descend from his elephant. He lost his head, attempted to parley, and a tall Sikh [belonging to General Court's division] slapped his face and took the boy Dhulip Singh from his arms, asking him how he dared to disobey the Khalsa. Dhulip Singh was placed in his mother's arms, and she, hiding herself behind the walls of her tent, held the child up above them in the view of army, crying for mercy for her brother in the name of her son. Suddenly, hearing a yell of agony from a well-known voice, she flung the child away in an agony of grief and rage. Fortunately he was caught by a soldier, or the consequences might have been fatal.

Meanwhile the bloody work had been done on the hated Minister. A soldier, who had presumably received his orders, had gone up the ladder placed by Jowahir Singh's elephant, stabbed him with his bayonet, and flung him upon the ground, where he was despatched in a moment with fifty wounds.

Another eyewitness, Sardar Sarup Singh, himself a Sikh trooper, would recall the aftermath of the assassination even more graphically.

By this time myself and some others of our battalion had run up, and we saw the Rani Jindan rushing out of her tent and throwing herself down on her brother's corpse. She did not mind their swords or bayonets; one man kicked her in the side, another pushed her with the butt of his matchlock. She was mad, raving mad at the time, and she cared for nothing. Her face and arms and long hair were smeared with her brother's blood, and she raised up her arms and cursed us all... She tore open her dress, and beat her breasts, and pulled out her hair in handfuls. Then she kissed her brother's head—she could not have kissed his face as it was all hacked—and she wiped the blood off her face and arms with her hair. She glared round like a tigress and screamed out to the Sardars that she would take care to wreak her revenge.

So ended Jowahir Singh's nine months of precarious ascendancy. By being implicated in the elimination of Peshora Singh he had signed his own death-warrant. Or so it seemed. Yet a doubt remained. With little to suggest that he had been directly involved in events in Attock, the finger of suspicion swung from Lahore to Jammu. 'No one ever doubted the murder of Jowahir Singh was planned by Gulab Singh of Jammu', recalled Sardar Sarup Singh when echoing the verdict of his fellow cavalrymen many years later. 'When Gulab Singh heard what had happened [to Peshora Singh at Attock] he got letters written which caused the report to be spread from Attock to Lahore that all this [had been] done by the direct orders of Jowahir Singh; and that is why Jowahir Singh was killed.' To the many for whom it was axiomatic that no calamity could overtake the Khalsa without a Dogra brother being involved, Gulab Singh had to be the culprit. His distancing himself from events in Lahore now looked like open defiance. And this being the case, Gardner's advice to Jowahir Singh to face the music may have been less than disinterested.

On the other hand, these were, as the colonel might have put it, 'Barbarous Times'. To the tally of three maharajas murdered in quick succession had now been added that of three viziers murdered just as rapidly. Indeed such were the blood-lettings to which Lahore was becoming accustomed that the amputation of the nose, ears and digits of an obstreperous Brahmin must have seemed eminently forgettable, if not entirely merciful.

For once the elimination of a vizier brought little in the way of public recriminations. This time there was no indiscriminate killing, no ransacking of the city or parading of trophies. The murder, recalled Cunningham, 'partook of the solemnity and moderation of a judicial process, ordained and witnessed by a whole people.' In keeping with this decorum, Jowahir Singh's corpse was given the full honours of a *sati* cremation. The Rani Jindan and her son returned to the fort unharmed. And neither the succession nor the rani's regency was challenged. Traumatised and leaderless, the kingdom soldiered on, clinging to the memory of the never vanquished Ranjit Singh and to the conviction that its army remained a match for any.

Though increasingly exposed, the Khalsa was as yet anything but cowed. Rather was it, like a tiger brought to bay, at its most dangerous. Within six weeks of Jowahir Singh's demise, the army was on the move. The Sikh kingdom was finally going to war with the Honourable East India Company.

DECADE OF DOWNFALL

1839	27 June	Ranjit Singh died of natural causes
	8 October	Chait Singh Bajwa stabbed to death by Dhyan Singh
1840	5 November	Kharak Singh poisoned by Dhyan Singh (probably in league with Nau Nihal Singh)
	5 November	Nau Nihal Singh and Udham Singh both killed by falling masonry
1842	9 June	Chand Kaur stoned to death by her maid servants (probably under the orders of Sher Singh)
1843	15 September	Sher Singh shot by Ajit Singh Sindhanwalia
	15 September	Partap Singh beheaded by Lehna Singh Sindhanwalia
	15 September	Dhyan Singh shot by one of Ajit Singh Sindhanwalia's horsemen
	20 September	Ajit Singh Sindhanwalia and Lehna Singh Sindhanwalia both killed by the Sikh army for their role in the murder of Sher Singh and Partap Singh
1844	27 March	Suchet Singh killed by the Sikh army under Hira Singh's orders
	7 May	Kashmira Singh and Attar Singh Sindhanwalia both killed by the Sikh army under Hira Singh's orders
	21 December	Hira Singh, Pandit Jalla and Sohan Singh all killed by the Sikh army as reprisal for the murders of Kashmira Singh and Attar Singh Sindhanwalia
1845	11 September	Peshora Singh strangled to death by Fateh Khan Tiwana and Chattar Singh Attariwala supposedly under Jowahir Singh's orders but probably the work of Gulab Singh
	21 September	Jowahir Singh assassinated by the Sikh army for his supposed role in the murder of Peshora Singh
	18 December	Battle of Mudki commences
	21 December	Battle of Ferozeshah commences
1846	10 February	Battle of Sobraon commences
1848	15 May	Jind Kaur exiled to Benares
	22 November	Battle of Ramnagar commences
1849	13 January	Battle of Chillianwala commences
	21 February	Battle of Gujrat commences
	29 March	Duleep Singh deposed by the British

The causes cited for the First Anglo-Sikh War are so numerous and for the most part so contested as to be scarcely worth rehearsing. Contemporaries on both sides could seldom agree on them, and anyway Gardner himself would claim not to have been involved in the fighting. The blame for the conflict can best be described as shared. Each side accused the other of aggression; yet there were Sikh sirdars who held the Sikhs responsible and British *sahibs* who held the British responsible. Both sides could be accused of contravening the existing treaty; likewise both could reasonably claim to be defending what was rightfully theirs.

Sir George Campbell, soon to be a political officer in Ludhiana and later lieutenant-governor of Bengal, would put it well in his *Memoirs of My Indian Career*: 'it is recorded in the annals of history, or what is called history [and] which will go down to posterity, that the Sikh army invaded British territory in pursuance of a determination to attack us. And most people will be very much surprised to learn that they did nothing of the kind.' The Sikhs did cross the Satluj River, which was the frontier, but only to entrench themselves in pockets of territory on the southern side that still owed allegiance to the Lahore durbar. 'They made no attack on our outlying cantonments, nor set foot in our territory,' says Campbell.

Nor did they actually initiate hostilities. In fact no one did. It was more a case of spontaneous combustion. The two most formidable armies in India drew nigh to one another; neither had an over-whelming superiority or a very clear idea of what might be achieved; nor was there any great animosity between them. But enough of the would-be combatants on both sides were either spoiling for a fight or resigned to it. In this situation, defensive manoeuvres were easily misconstrued as offensive deployments, and demonstrations of firepower as range-finding preludes to an all-out bombardment. 'A collision must have occurred sooner or later,' says Campbell; the Sikhs had crossed the river, the British felt challenged to expel them, 'and so war came.'

More crucial than the various grievances given as pretexts for the war was the prevailing political climate on both sides. Of that in La-hore a graphic account is provided by Dewan Ajudhia Parshad in a rare

Persian text entitled *Waqai-i-jang-i-Sikhan* ('Events of the Sikh War').
As a senior official since the days of Ranjit Singh, the *dewan* wrote
of the near-anarchy in Lahore from first-hand knowledge, although
for the actual fighting he relied on the accounts of acquaintances
who were involved. The latter material is the less convincing. The
dewan, though himself a military man—he had succeeded Ventura
in command of the Fauj-i-khas—held the rank and file of the army
in some contempt and would insist that 'the Khalsa kingdom was
destroyed by the Khalsa army'. By way of contrast, reference may be
made to some 'Personal recollections of Sikh soldiers and Sardars'
as assembled (but never published) by John Fitzgerald Lee under
the title *Old Broken Links*. One at least of the grey-bearded veterans
interviewed by Lee in the 1890s had served under Gardner, and all
provide ample corroboration of the colonel's own account of the
wartime treachery in Lahore. For the destruction of the Khalsa
kingdom they blame their officers along with the Lahore court that
was directing them.

The British perspective is distorted by a similar ambivalence. As
the governor-general's political agent at Ludhiana, the fire-breathing
Major George Broadfoot did more than anyone to precipitate the war.
Bagoo Mull, one of Fitzgerald Lee's veterans, remembered Broadfoot
as 'the Red Sahib with the spectacles'; the Afghans remembered him
as 'the black-coated infidel'. Campbell thought him 'arrogant and
overbearing', Cunningham considered his every act, 'conceived in a
spirit of enmity', and another British contemporary described him as
'punishing faults with a severity many would have deemed ferocious'.
Heavily-built and of ruddy complexion, Broadfoot had distinguished
himself in the defence of Jalalabad during the Afghan War. By way of
reward he was then given political responsibilities, for which he had
no training, in connection with the Sikhs, of whom he knew nothing.
His views and actions were nevertheless endorsed by Lord Hardinge,
the governor-general. They were also given a much wider currency by
publicity-conscious officers like Henry Lawrence, who would assume
responsibility for the post-war settlement of Sikh affairs, and Herbert
Edwardes, Lawrence's doting disciple and biographer.

But this quasi-official line with its emphasis on Sikh provocation was cautiously contested by the likes of Cunningham (who during the war served as an aide-de-camp to the commander-in-chief and then to the governor-general), by Carmichael Smyth (he who was Gardner's mouthpiece) and by Campbell (who would rubbish the whole idea of a 'Sikh invasion'). Cunningham in particular would incur the wrath of British officialdom. His masterly *A History of the Sikhs* was heavily censured for its criticism of the war's genesis and conduct; as a result, his exceptionally promising career was fatally blighted. His death, two years after the book's first publication, would be attributed to this professional persecution.

Much of the confusion on both sides stems from uncertainty about the precise relationship between the British authorities and the contestants for power across the frontier. As early as March 1845 the then hard-pressed Gulab Singh in Jammu had written to the governor-general offering his support for a British invasion of the Punjab. In return he sought a British promise of recognition of his independent rule over Lahore's hill country. The offer was not accepted at the time but, revived in the run-up to the war, it would ensure the neutrality of Lahore's most powerful feudatory throughout the actual hostilities.

In similar vein the late Jowahir Singh was also supposed to have been in clandestine contact with the British. More certainly a channel of communication had since been opened between the closest advisers of his sister, the rani-cum-regent Jindan, and Captain Peter Nicholson, who was Broadfoot's assistant political agent at Ferozepur, the nearest British listening post to Lahore. According to Gardner and most other observers, the rani, along with her Brahmin generals Lal Singh and Tej Singh, lived in fear and trembling of the army's rebellious panches. Being without the treasure to appease them and being equally suspicious of Gulab Singh's intentions, the rani and her generals conceived the bold idea of neutralising the entire army by sending it to extinction at the hands of the British. Gardner quotes an 'old Sikh motto' by way of explanation. The best way to dispose of a snake, went the motto, was to 'throw it into your enemy's bosom'.

The snake was the evilly disposed, violent, yet powerful and splendid

Sikh army. It was to be flung upon the British, and so destroyed. Thus did the Rani Jindan in her turn plan to avenge herself on the murderers of her brother Jowahir Singh.

But for the plan to work, the rani needed to goad the army into action, then withhold supplies and reinforcements from it and caution its commanding officers against taking advantage of any British reverses, while simultaneously priming the British with the intelligence that would ensure its defeat. Hence, if this was indeed the situation, the war would not be between the British and the Sikh Khalsa but between a coalition consisting of the Sikh court and the East India Company on the one hand and the rank and file of the Sikh army on the other.

Naturally, Dewan Ajudhia Parshad contests this reading of the rani's treachery. As a loyal official and commander, his sympathies lay with the rani, with the imposing Lal Singh, her intimate adviser, and with the stocky Tej Singh, who was now designated her commander-in-chief. Citing endless examples, the dewan accuses the army of corrupting the political administration, flouting the directives of the court and terrorising the populace.

> In the cantonments, too, there was no semblance of discipline or order. The soldiers, after receiving their pay, absented themselves without leave. ... Parades took place in name only ... Not more than a quarter of the total number appeared ... No sergeant dared call the roll ... The officers, in fear for their lives, quietly submitted to the will of the troops.

In vain did 'the brave and resolute' Tej Singh strive to remind the regular soldiery of the *Fauj-i-ain* of the discipline they owed to the memory of Ranjit Singh. They paid no heed. The final straw came with the spread of this rebellious spirit to the ranks of the dewan's Fauj-i-khas comprising the European-style regiments raised and trained by Ventura and Allard. The Fauj-i-khas had lately been stationed at Lahore to guard the treasury and powder-magazine and to act as a disciplined counter-weight to the mutinous inclinations of the rest of the army. But here too insurrection now surfaced when the officers of the Fauj-i-khas, under pressure from the panches of the Fauj-i-ain, agreed to the brigade's redeployment to distant Peshawar. The men felt betrayed and 'after this altercation and mutiny, the *Fauj-i-khas* became like the other brigades of the Sikh army, flouting the authority of their officers...' says the dewan.

All of which would have been music to British ears. In Ludhiana it was reported that 'Sikhs all over the Punjab had gone mad and had set their house on fire'. The danger of the conflagration spreading to the Sikh territories that lay south of the Satluj, to the few Sikh states that were already under British protection and even to the ranks of the Honourable Company's *sepoy* army, was supposed real enough. Accordingly Broadfoot, the political agent, saw fit to claim that British sovereignty over the cis-Satluj pockets of Sikh territory was as absolute 'as over the district of Hoogly [a suburb of Calcutta]', all of which, says Campbell, was 'very near to political annexation'. The political agent also took the disturbances to be a handy pretext for strengthening the British presence on the frontier. Calcutta was alerted to the need for reinforcements. Boats for a pontoon bridge that would make an invasion of the Sikh kingdom possible were assembled, then hidden.

Downstream in Ferozepur, itself the subject of an earlier annexation, Captain Nicholson was more concerned with the plight of the rani. Thanks largely to the scurrilous reports of news-writers who knew what their British paymasters wanted to hear, the rani was supposedly sustaining her reputation as a *femme fatale* by presiding over a court in which depravity knew no bounds. Even the good Dr Honigberger, when treating her for ophthalmia, supposed the affliction 'the consequence of the many abortions she had experienced'. The British press would call her 'the Messalina of the Punjab' and her early November appointment of her favourite, Lal Singh, as vizier seemed in character. But in later life Lal Singh would insist that his dealings with the Rani had never been other than political. She was not conventionally beautiful, he recalled, but 'had eyes that could charm like those of a snake and a voice sweeter than that of a bird'. These assets she cleverly deployed and 'was proud of the influence she possessed over men in making them subservient to her will and caprices'.

A case in point arose on 23 November (1845). According to Nicholson's informant in Lahore, that was the day on which the army planned to kill the rani. Till then she had had some success in persuading the troops to evacuate Lahore and in convincing their panches that the British were bent on overthrowing the Khalsa; all were therefore agreed on the need for a counter-offensive. An adage to the effect that the elephants of the Khalsa would one day bathe in the Ganges was resurrected, as was another about 'the army of the Guru' occupying the throne of Delhi. There was also much excitement about the booty to be expected from the capture of Ludhiana, Ferozepur, Ambala and even Benares. But on 22 November, as the first troops moved out heading for the Satluj frontier, their generals, notably Lal Singh and Tej Singh, were still 'sitting in *aram* [at ease] in Lahore' and seemed 'disinclined to take a step in the business'. Treachery was already suspected, the finger of suspicion being pointed at the rani. She, however, was undaunted and offered to meet her accusers the next day at the sacred site of Ranjit Singh's cremation. 'It will probably be a massacre or a march,' wrote Nicholson.

In the event it was a march, albeit an uncoordinated one. The rani, exercising all her powers of persuasion, upbraided the troops for their disloyalty, offered them four month's pay, and in return exacted a solemn pledge that they would disperse from Lahore and henceforth obey their officers. From one who had charmed Ranjit Singh himself, it proved to be enough. But as word filtered through about British reinforcements heading for Ferozepur, the pledge counted for nothing. 'Signs of insolence on the part of the soldiers reappeared,' says Ajudhia Parshad; rejecting the temporising of their officers, the men drafted their own orders and marched to the frontier with Tej Singh, their commander-in-chief, trailing behind and Vizier Lal Singh, in command of the irregular cavalry, going off at a tangent.

> In short, the whole army on this side of the Sutlej was to be mobilised. They would cross to Ferozepur, seize the treasure lying there and, until they occupied Delhi, they would observe the strictest Hindu vows. They would take the revenue of London itself from the British.

9

Charge and Discharge
1845–47

The total strength of the Sikh army on the eve of the First Anglo-Sikh War has been put at just over 150,000. Of these less than half were regulars, 54,000 of them being infantry, 6000 cavalry and maybe 4000 artillerymen (for the now approximately 380 field guns). The other half of the Khalsa army, according to Fauja Singh Bajwa's meticulous analysis in the *Military System of the Sikhs*, was comprised of irregular units, among them some 20,000 cavalry (the colourful ghorcharas) and numerous infantry contingents, many in the service of leading feudatories like Gulab Singh of Jammu.

Beyond the Satluj this host faced an even larger army. The combined forces of the East India Company were perhaps twice as numerous. They too were composed largely of Indian troops (*sipahis*, sepoys), and though commanded by Europeans and augmented by numerous Royal (ie all-British) regiments, they were not better armed or drilled than the Sikhs. Thanks to General Claude Auguste Court and his gunsmiths, the Sikh cannon were actually of larger calibre and, thanks to Gardner and others, their management and marksmanship would prove, if anything, superior. Those on both sides who anticipated a titanic struggle were right. When, after the war, Herbert Edwardes would describe Britain's empire in India as having been hanging by a thread, no one would presume to challenge him.

Naturally only a fraction of each side's troops would be called on to fight. As demonstrated by Gardner's earlier punitive-cum-peace-keeping operations, the Sikh kingdom's existence depended on the widespread application of force. With ever rebellious Pathan tribes on its long western frontier, a new British presence in Sind to the south and a lot of recalcitrant chiefs within, it could ill afford to denude existing deployments. Cunningham's estimate of no more than 40,000 Sikh troops crossing the Satluj, though one of the more conservative, is generally reckoned the most accurate.

The British were nevertheless outnumbered. With their own forces distributed across an entire subcontinent, they had at the time only some 20,000 men within easy reach of the Sikh frontier. These were divided between the cantonments of Ferozepur (7000), Ludhiana (5000) and, 150 miles in the rear, Ambala (7–10,000). Any additional reinforcements from places further afield like Delhi and Meerut would take weeks to arrive. Broadfoot, despite doing his best to provoke the Sikhs, and regardless of the warnings from Nicholson in Ferozepur, had consistently pooh-poohed the likelihood of a large-scale Sikh advance. Anticipating only uncoordinated incursions, he had stockpiled sufficient ammunition and provisions for sporadic engagements but not for a sustained campaign.

From a Sikh point of view it was therefore imperative to take advantage of their army's initial superiority and the enemy's temporary disarray. By striking hard, promptly and in force, the Khalsa had every chance of turning the long-term odds in its favour. Conversely, by neglecting to do any of these things, its high command had a fair prospect of engineering a speedy defeat. Thus, in the palace as in the ranks, hopes ran high when in early December the bulk of the Lahore troops moved out. They headed south till the minarets of the Badshahi mosque finally dipped below the horizon behind them; then by various routes they marched the fifty-odd miles to the Satluj.

Indistinguishable in this mass of men and guns converging on the river, of lumbering bullock trains and swaying camel carts, of camp-followers, fodder-merchants and mobile bazaars, there trotted through the dust storm raised by the mighty concourse three heavily bearded strangers. One was the Spanish engineer Hurbon or Hurbons, 'a fine solider' according to Gardner, 'who did all the castrametation [entrenchment and fortification] which so surprised the British army'; another was the Frenchman Mouton who was attached to General Tej Singh as a cavalry officer and tactical guru; and the third was Gardner himself. He commanded a horse battery, and presumably his reputation for opportunistic allegiances and scruple-free amputations rode with him. Not, though, it seems, for long.

According to the colonel himself, his war was over before it began. 'I started originally with the army,' he explains, 'but was recalled by the Rani, and she specially insisted that I was wanted to hold Lahore against the Khalsa.' He was to bring back with him no Sikhs, only such Muslim troops as were serving under him. 'My orders were simple: "No Sikhs are to return; manage that and the rest shall be as you like."' Though the order came from the rani, it could as well have come from Gulab Singh in Jammu, for whom Gardner says he was once again 'acting as agent and factotum'. Either way, and with an irony typical of the whole war, Lahore was to be held by non-Sikhs on behalf of the court and its least dependable feudatory, and denied to the Sikh army that was supposed to be fighting in its defence.

Precisely when Gardner was recalled is a matter of debate. He himself implies that it was before crossing the Satluj or reaching the front. Yet a report by Mouton, which was published in Paris immediately after the war, suggests a rather different story. According to Mouton, the Khalsa's Muslim gunners and their colonel withdrew only after fording the Satluj on 12 December 1845 and after the first battle, that of Mudki, on 18 December. During the nocturnal retreat from that rather indecisive affair, says Mouton, 'the colonel of the artillery abandoned seventeen guns and fled away to Lahore taking all his men with him'. By way of justification Mouton then adds that the rani had previously written to the non-Sikhs of the artillery to the effect that 'when the Sickes should come to blows with the English, they should abandon them and come to Lahore, where she would recompense them for their devotion to her cause.'

Mouton fails to identify who the colonel in question was. Moreover the accusation about a colonel and his men having abandoned their guns and fled is contradicted by British reports about the Sikh gunners at Mudki displaying 'reckless bravery and devotion to their guns'; indeed 'they never left them and died rather than yield', says a Colonel Robertson. But the number of guns later recovered by the British was exactly the seventeen mentioned, and Gardner is very specific about all the men he brought back being Muslims. It looks like one and the same incident; and if it was, and if he was indeed the colonel referred to, one can understand his reticence. Whether he had 'fled' or withdrawn, he stood exposed as a deserter. Having done so on the rani's instructions, he was revealed as a traitor to the army in which he served. And having fought at all, he would be deemed *persona non grata* by the British and might be subject to a post-war deportation order like that which would bring Mouton himself back to Paris to tell his side of the story. As so often the holes in Gardner's narrative prompt greater doubts than the colourful fabric they perforate.

The Muslim gunners, he adds, 'were enchanted at the recall, and on our return I was, as it were, governor of Lahore'. Mouton disagrees, asserting that the gunners were not at all enchanted; on the contrary they were disbanded and arrested, and their houses 'were looted by [the rani's] people'. Similarly Gardner's claim to have been 'as it were, governor' of the city would cut no ice with Grey and Garrett. They were surely right in suggesting that he exaggerated his role; in fact, on his own admission, 'the only duty imposed on me was to protect the Maharani Jindan and her child, and to get the dreaded Khalsa army destroyed somehow.' But of this, his first admission that he too was actively engaged in sabotaging the Sikh war effort, he would say no more. Discretion was again proving the better part of candour.

Meanwhile the destruction of the army was not going entirely to plan. On Sunday 21 December, four days after the indecisive clash at Mudki and by which time more Sikh troops had crossed the river, the Khalsa's forward army was entrenched at a village called Ferozeshah (some twenty miles from Ferozepur) and was there challenged by the main British force under Sir Hugh Gough, its commander-in-chief. A veteran of the Peninsular War, Gough had marched from Ambala with Sir Henry Hardinge, the governor-general. Also a Peninsular veteran, Hardinge now assumed the role of Gough's second-in-command.

They brought more guns and reinforcements and they were joined by some of the Ferozepur contingent, including Captain Nicholson with news of the latest Sikh dispositions as supplied by his informants in Lahore. Numbering some 18,000, including 5000 Royal troops, the British at last felt sufficiently confident to take the offensive.

The Sikh troops were simply relieved to find that the decision to give battle no longer rested solely with their faint-hearted commanders. At the time of Mudki, Commander-in-Chief Tej Singh had been fifty miles away in Lahore, and Lal Singh (commanding the ghorcharas) had taken flight after the first exchange of fire. 'He fled, hid himself in a hayrick' and later 'in an oven belonging to an old bakeress in Ludhiana'. But Gardner, by now safely back in Lahore, was wrong in supposing Lal Singh would stay in hiding for another two weeks. At Ferozeshah the vizier-general and his cavalry were in fact back on the right flank of the Sikh position; and even Tej Singh was about to make his long-awaited appearance. None of which, of course, was other than bad news for the 25,000 Sikhs and the 103 guns that awaited their commanders' doubtful directives amid Ferozeshah's scrub-strewn fields.

With his penchant for over-statement, Herbert Edwardes would call Ferozeshah 'the Waterloo of India'. In truth it was neither as decisive nor as conclusive. The outcome hung in the balance for two days and, though the Sikhs would ultimately retreat, even the British would hesitate to claim victory. What took both sides by surprise was the ferocity of the encounter. As Cunningham put it from his vantage point as one of Gough's ADCs, 'the resistance met was wholly unexpected and all started with astonishment'.

Guns were dismounted and their ammunition was blown into the air; squadrons were checked in mid-career; battalion after battalion was thrown back with shattered ranks, and it was not until after sunset that portions of the enemy's position were finally carried. Darkness, and the obstinacy of the contest, threw the English into confusion; men of all regiments and arms were mixed together; generals were doubtful of the fact or extent of their own success, and colonels knew not what had become of the regiments they commanded or of the army of which they formed a part.

And that was just during the first hours of contact. On what the calendar showed as the longest night of the year, the unthinkable followed: the British turned tail. With his forces exhausted, bewildered, frozen and unfed (their 'teeth chattering on empty stomachs' as one man put it), and with both ammunition and water in short supply, Gough felt obliged to order a retreat. The Sikhs had already regained the entrenchments from which they had earlier been driven and now themselves took the offensive.

Soon the makeshift camp to which the British had removed was at their mercy. Amid scenes of utter confusion, the Company's men threw themselves down on the cold ground and licked the drops of condensation from their guns to slake their thirst. Fires merely attracted the enemy's sharp-shooters; the wounded were left uncared for. Casualties had been heavy, including no less than five of Gough's ADCs. Captain Nicholson would file no more reports from Ferozepur, and Major Broadfoot would no longer sweep them aside in Ludhiana; both were among the nearly 700 dead whom the British had left behind, along with twice as many wounded.

As Gough and Hardinge canvassed the opinions of their fellow officers about withdrawing all the way from Ferozeshah to Ferozepur, they experienced the empire-builder's nightmare. A battlefield defeat worse than any in Afghanistan was staring them in the face. 'It seemed that we were on the eve of a great misfortune,' recalled Captain Robert Napier (later Field Marshal Lord Napier of Magdala). Hardinge prepared to go down in history as the governor-general whose underestimation of the Sikhs had sealed the empire's fate. He ordered the burning of state papers and of his own correspondence. He also 'bade his son Charles Hardinge farewell, presenting him with his sword—which once belonged to Napoleon and which he had been given as a gift by the Duke of Wellington—before sending him away from the field'. A mass withdrawal, though the less desperate option, invited an even more inglorious defeat than staying put in a fight to the death. Either way, the effect would be catastrophic—and not just for Gough's Satluj army.

British rule in India rested on the giant presumption of invincibility. Kick away the presumption and the whole edifice would crumble. The Khalsa's belligerence had been encouraged by the British disaster in Afghanistan; a similar disaster in the Punjab would ignite revolt within the Company's sepoy army and fuel dissent throughout the subcontinent. Britain's Indian dominion was as vulnerable as the Jeremiahs claimed. And just a decade later, the British bluff would indeed be called in what Raj historians would dub 'the Indian Mutiny'. But at Ferozeshah, Gough and Hardinge contemplated just such a conflagration within weeks. To them the darkest night of the year felt more like the long dark night of the soul for Britain's Eastern enterprise.

Dawn on 22 December found nothing changed. The situation was as bad as expected and the shortage of both powder and ball was confirmed. But at least the Sikhs had not pressed their attack. Around 07:00 hours the British line wearily re-formed, bayonets were fixed and a do-or-die advance was sounded. As they edged forward in the cold light of day, scarcely a shot was heard. To eke out their ammunition the British sepoys were under orders not to fire. And as for the Sikhs, they were simply not there.

As described by Dewan Ajudhia Parshad, the Khalsa's nocturnal deliberations had been just as doom-laden as those of the British. 'The darkness of that night was as the life of the vanquished,' says the dewan. 'Raja Lal Singh was wounded and a fugitive... Those who were left in the Sikh camp discussed whether they should disperse, or collect their artillery and set up the *dera* [camp] elsewhere. But hourly their numbers were dwindling.' The men abused their officers for not pressing the attack, and the officers berated their men for refusing orders. What now of the panches' pledge to the rani, asked the officers? What of the boasts about capturing the throne of Delhi, 'destroying London' or bathing in the Ganges? 'And not one of those foolish Sikhs, unless he could recover his obsession by chattering with his comrades, could offer a reply,' sniffed the dewan.

And what too of Lal Singh? The dewan had failed to mention that his good friend the vizier had set the tone. It was Lal Singh who had refused to take advantage of the British plight that night;

and, if the vizier-general was now a fugitive, it was because he had again absconded. 'During the [night's] disorder, Raja Lal Singh, the commander-in-chief fled away from the camp with all his irregular cavalry and [the] gunners of sixty guns, taking the route to Lahore', reports Mouton. Others followed his example. By daybreak all save a handful of diehards had already decamped from the killing fields of Ferozeshah.

For a second time the British duly overran the Sikh entrenchments, now largely deserted. Exhausted as much by the plundering and the grave-digging as the skirmishing, and still desperately short of ammunition, they then again bivouacked in confusion—and then again found themselves facing annihilation. For in mid-afternoon clouds of dust billowing above the horizon announced the approach of the Sikhs' reserve army. Commander-in-Chief Tej Singh had finally arrived.

The moment was well chosen for an easy Sikh triumph. There was no question that Tej Singh's fresh troops and his formidable guns could make short work of Gough's maimed and depleted army. When the Sikh artillery opened up along a broad front, the British replied with blanks; shot was too precious to be expended in hope. Governor-General Hardinge again divested himself of a trophy, this time the star on his breast. 'He evidently never expected to leave our square alive ...', recalled Colonel Robertson, 'things looked very black indeed.' But the real question was whether Tej Singh actually intended to engage. Hardinge assumed that his sudden appearance meant that he did; past form and reliable intelligence suggested that he didn't.

The form-book was right. On various pretexts—that his forces were about to be cut off in the rear (Carmichael Smyth), that he was needed at the river by the remnants of the Ferozeshah forces (Dewan Ajudhia Parshad), that he took off 'to bring up the reserve' (Gardner), or that punishing the British was never his object (nearly everybody)—whatever the excuse, Tej Singh opted for a hasty retreat. Blinking in disbelief, the British were left to continue their military build-up and claim the honours in one of history's most dubious victories.

✳

It was not the end of the war. During January (1846) the focus shifted upriver to Ludhiana, from where a smaller Sikh force was eventually driven off, and then back towards Ferozepur for the final *coup de grace*. This would be launched by the British on the banks of the Satluj at Sobraon on 10 February. But by then the tables had well and truly turned. Gough now headed the strongest army ever fielded by the East India Company. For two months the roads from Delhi and Meerut had been choked with traffic as more men, supplies and armaments wound their way to the front. Ferozepur and Ludhiana now being deemed safe, all their troops had joined the throng; a considerable detachment from the British force stationed in Sind was also approaching; and what cheered Gough and his men most was the sight of an elephant-drawn siege-train of nineteen enormous guns plus 4000 wagons laden with supplies and munitions. Herbert Edwardes, the soldier-scribe ('India's Waterloo', etc), accompanied this convoy from Delhi; and at about the same time Major Henry Lawrence, Edwardes's hero and the sahib whom Gardner had met disguised as a Pathan on the Indus back in 1842, had been summoned to take over the late Broadfoot's role as the army's political officer. Not unlike self-righteous vultures, the Punjab's future arbiters were gathering.

That the Sikhs would submit could now be taken for granted. During a series of secret exchanges with both the Lahore court and Gulab Singh of Jammu, the British had hammered out what Cunningham calls an 'understanding'. In exchange for guarantees that (1) the young maharaja would retain his throne, (2) the rani would retain the regency and (3) Gulab Singh would be rewarded for his forbearance with a separate principality in the hills, it had been agreed 'that the Sikh army should be attacked by the English, and that when beaten it should be openly abandoned by its own government; and further, that the passage of the Sutlej should be unopposed and the road to the capital laid open to the victors'. But just in case the military men still clung to their myths, Cunningham then added his own gloss. 'And under such circumstances of discreet policy and shameless treason was the battle of Sobraon fought'. Small wonder Cunningham and his great history would be officially condemned.

That the Sikh army would indeed be 'beaten' could also be taken for granted. While the British had more than made good their earlier losses, the Sikhs had been left to fend for themselves, In January the panches had sent a 500-strong deputation to Lahore to plead for the powder and supplies the troops so badly needed. 'For three days they had been living on grain and raw carrots,' says Gardner, who had the unenviable job of keeping this deputation at bay. Since the rani 'feared justly for her personal safety at the hands of these desperate men', he guarded her with four battalions and, when she finally consented to give the deputies an audience, he stage-managed the event to perfection.

As well as the presence of a 'very large personal guard', he made sure the rani was suitably screened behind a curtain, that the little maharaja was on display in front of it, and that he himself stood in close attendance on both. To the news that Gulab Singh had already sent supplies, the men roared in derision. 'No, he has not. We know the old fox; he has not sent breakfast for a bird (*chiria-ki-haziri*).'

> Further parley ensued [continues Gardner], the tempers of both parties waxing wroth. At last the deputation said, 'Give us powder and shot.' At this I saw some movement behind the *purdah*... I could detect that the Rani was shifting her petticoat; I could see that she stepped out of it, and then rolling it up rapidly into a ball, flung it over the screen at the angry envoys, crying out, 'Wear that, you cowards! I'll go in trousers and fight myself!' The effect was electric. After a moment's pause, during which the deputation seemed stunned, a unanimous shout arose. 'Dhulip Singh Maharaja, we will go and die for his kingdom and the Khalsa-ji!' and breaking up tumultuously and highly excited, this dangerous deputation dispersed, and rejoined the army. The courage and intuition displayed by this extraordinary woman under such critical circumstances filled us all with as much amazement as admiration.

By chance, fifty years later when John Fitzgerald Lee was interviewing Sikh veterans for his 'Old Broken Links' archive, he was told almost precisely the same story. In Lee's translation of the testimony of Sardar Sarup Singh, the rani is given more choice derogatives—'you pigs, sons of female dogs, cowards, sheep, sons of white livered run-aways', etc—and she backs her jibe about their donning petticoats with the assurance that 'the English don't kill women'. But otherwise the story is identical. Given that none of Lee's informants could read a word of English and were anyway most unlikely to have obtained a copy of the just-printed *Memoirs*, Gardner's critics might well have marvelled at this corroboration of what otherwise looked like one of the colonel's wilder flights of fantasy.

Double-crossed by their sovereign, their officers, their supposed ally (ie Gulab Singh) and even their enemy, the troops of the Khalsa, as they laboured at the trench-digging and bridge-building to create their last redoubt at Sobraon, still clung to the Khalsa's twin pillars of faith and fatherland and to the never-tarnished memory of the great Ranjit Singh. Gardner, although sympathetic to their plight, felt they had brought all their troubles upon themselves. Like others, he blamed their unruly conduct, their interference in politics, their pay demands and their arbitrary assassination of Jowahir Singh. He agreed that Tej Singh and Lal Singh, their tweedledum-and-twee-dledee commanders, were 'contemptible poltroons', each as incompetent as he was deceitful; and he, more than anyone, had fathomed the depths of Gulab Singh's duplicitous character, 'one of the most repulsive it is possible to imagine'.

But the spirited rani was more to his taste. And whether he was Lahore's 'governor' or not, his residence and responsibilities in the city left him little choice but to favour her cause. As an accessory to the plot to betray the army, his one hope had to be that it would succeed. Being also in the employ, and so the confidence, of Gulab Singh brought no conflict of interest on this score; Gulab Singh was more eagerly undermining the army than anyone. And finally the colonel, like everyone else, could not but act with an eye to his own very uncertain future.

Rarely troubled by principle or scruple, in retrospect Gardner's whole career could be seen as a quest for survival, albeit spiced with such adventures and rewards as came along. But during the prolonged death-throes of the Khalsa, the necessity for self-preservation had assumed a whole new dimension. It engendered a cynicism seldom to be found in his earlier travels and it called for a level of double-dealing of which there is no hint in the *Memoirs* or in any of the other accounts of his life.

As if to mask this omission, the narrative in the *Memoirs* now becomes perfunctory and disjointed. Editor Pearse has preserved its first-person standpoint, but the materials available were patchy (Cooper's verbatim notes evidently began to dry up at this point; Durand's account already had). The colonel, in short, was becoming evasive. Such discretion was out of character, and it was possibly not of his choosing. For, on the evidence available, it appears that he was already compromised with the Sikhs to the extent that some years previously, he had opened his own line of direct communication with British India's officialdom. While those around him were betraying one another as well as the troops in the field, Gardner had taken up his well inked pen as if to stab them all in the back.

Major Carmichael Smyth provides the first clue. Smyth's appetite for inside information on the sanguinary events that had led up to the war may have been innocent enough. The facts were well known, and much of his *History of the Reigning Family in Lahore* could, and would, be classed as embroidery. Additionally, Smyth made handsome acknowledgement of his debt to Gardner in both his Introduction and his appendices. But in doing so he implied that Gardner could be considered a reliable source on the grounds that he 'has for several years past supplied important information to the British Government without betraying his own [government?]'. Smyth's introduction was written sometime in 1846, when the rest of his book was already in manuscript. On the assumption that 'several years' must mean more than two, Gardner's dealings with the British must have dated back to 1843 or earlier.

In a footnote to the above, Smyth goes further. 'To give an idea of Captain Gardner's knowledge of Seik affairs ['Captain' here because, though 13 years a colonel, he was now drawing only a captain's salary], I may mention that Major Lawrence, in writing to me from Katmandoo, observed "If I was in Broadfoot's place I should like to have

Gardner at my elbow."' Lawrence's letter to Smyth had presumably been written in late 1844 when Broadfoot had first been appointed political agent in Ludhiana with responsibility for Anglo-Sikh relations. Never one to underestimate his own abilities, Lawrence, after having helped to orchestrate the reinvasion of Afghanistan, had by then been packed off to Nepal as British Resident. He had not taken kindly to this change of scene. He would indeed have preferred to have been in Broadfoot's place; and, had he been so, he could think of no one better to have at his side than Gardner.

Henry Montgomery Lawrence was, of course, the man Gardner had met in the winter of 1841–2, first in Peshawar and then again, with Gulab Singh, on the banks of the Indus when news of the British disaster in Kabul had been exchanged for tidings of the Dogra defeat in Tibet. Now, four years later and following Broadfoot's death at Ferozeshah, Lawrence was at last where he felt he should have been all along, assigned to Governor-General Hardinge's staff as Broadfoot's successor and a shoo-in for the choice role of supremo in Lahore in any post-war settlement.

On the face of it, Gardner had backed the right man. Lawrence would indeed mastermind the post-war treaties with Lahore and for the next two years oversee the affairs of the Punjab. There his reputation for inspirational leadership would rise to mythic heights, only to be exceeded by immortality when, as Sir Henry Lawrence, British Resident in Lucknow during the 1857 'Mutiny', he died a hero's death and was duly canonised in the annals of the British Raj.

But a 'thin and attenuated figure' with a long straggly beard, unkempt hair and evangelical convictions, the Major Lawrence of 1846 was not to every man's taste. He 'shrank from frivolity and display', says his devoted amanuensis Edwardes, and if he was known to his friends as 'Pat', it was as much in recognition of his 'fiery' temper as of his Irish origins. His frequent excursions into print, though often anonymous, designedly never remained so, and his outbursts of pique antagonised superiors including his brother, the future Governor-General John Lawrence, and Lord Dalhousie, Hardinge's immediate successor. Apostolic and industrious, he was also impressionable and self-regarding. The best of allies one day, he could be the most implacable of opponents the next. Any relationship between such a god-fearing scion of the raj and a free-thinking mercenary with a dubious past could only be one of convenience, not conviction.

It suited Gardner to lay claim to intimacy with Lawrence. In the *Memoirs*, the sources for which mostly post-dated Lawrence's Lucknow apotheosis, 'Sir Henry' is always referred to as 'my well-known and honoured friend'. 'I have often since [our first meeting] expressed my admiration of that great and good man,' says Gardner, 'and of the tact and ability he brought to bear on his political duties'. The 'ability' was universally acknowledged but the 'tact', not a quality normally awarded to Lawrence, seems to have referred to whatever arrangement the two had reached on the banks of the Indus.

At first the relationship had scarcely been controversial. In 1842 the Anglo-Sikh alliance still stood and had been bolstered by the Tripartite Alliance in respect of operations in Afghanistan. Sharing intelligence was presumably to be encouraged between allies. Moreover the only early evidence of Gardner supplying Lawrence with information comes from a work of fiction. First published anonymously in the *Delhi Gazette* in 1842, 'The Adventurer in the Punjab' was immediately reissued as *Some Passages in the Life of an Adventurer in the Punjaub* and in 1844 republished, now under Lawrence's name, as *The Adventures of Bellasis*. Favourably noticed and extensively quoted in the same year by an anonymous reviewer (who was in fact Lawrence himself), it was finally retitled and re-published yet again in 1845 as *Adventures of an Officer in the Service of Runjeet Singh*.

The book, in two volumes, describes the career of a footloose adventurer who sounds familiar. Though English-speaking, this 'Colonel Bellasis' insists he is not in fact English and makes a great mystery of both his true identity and his chequered past. A seasoned free-lance, he had evidently reached the Punjab after prolonged service in and around Persia. He had no Napoleonic credentials and no real experience of military command; yet, on Lawrence's own admission, Bellasis's Punjab exploits had been 'suggested to the author by his intercourse with some of the foreign officers in Ranjit's service, though not intended to represent any *one* of them'. At the time when Lawrence was writing the story it is doubtful whether he had ever been to Lahore. As an assistant political agent in Ferozepur and then in Peshawar he may have contacted foreigners like Allard and Ventura but he scarcely knew them. Avitabile in Peshawar he did know but, over-weight and scandalously prone to indulgence, Avitabile would have been an unlikely model for the paragon of manly virtue that was Bellasis.

That left Gardner. Whether out of 'tact' or authorial possessiveness, Lawrence's book never mentions a debt to Gardner. Yet Edwardes, as Lawrence's mouthpiece and biographer, testifies that the two men became more than mere acquaintances in the course of their 1842 meetings. Gardner, through the wife 'given to him by Raja Dhyan Singh out of his own house' and 'his living always among the natives', knew what was going on 'behind the scenes and heard a good deal of the intrigues that were on foot,' says Edwardes. While conferring with Lawrence he could be positively garrulous.

> He had wild moods of talking, letting the corners of dark things peep out, and then shutting them up again with a look behind him as if life in Jummoo [ie in the service of Gulab Singh] was both strange and fearful.

More obviously, in the *Memoirs* Gardner claims that at least one of Bellasis's fictional triumphs was simply lifted from his own life-story. On his first arrival in Lahore back in 1832, he recalls, 'an incident occurred which is described in the work called 'Adventures of an Officer', by the great and good Sir Henry Lawrence'. It concerned a mere jostling of horses. Gardner, like Bellasis, emerged triumphant from the scuffle and a certain Nand Singh, a pushy Sikh trooper, was sent 'rolling on the ground'. Gardner could have made up this incident; he could even have purloined it from Lawrence's book. But it was so inconsequential, so identically described and so vulnerable to accusations of plagiarism that crediting the original incident to Gardner is surely the most plausible explanation.

In the light of Carmichael Smyth's mention of Lawrence's high opinion of Gardner and of the 'several years' during which Gardner had supplied Lawrence with 'important information', the two men must have stayed in touch after their meeting on the Indus. Gardner was flattered by Lawrence's interest; and Lawrence was badly in need of Gardner's insights. Miffed that his services during the reinvasion of Afghanistan had not been rewarded with at least a c.b., Lawrence had been shunted to postings at Ambala and nearby Kaithal before being packed off to Kathmandu in 1843. He was thus more removed from events at Lahore than ever. He had missed the years of anarchy that included the assassinations of Maharaja Sher Singh and vizier Dhyan Singh in 1843, of Hira Singh and Pandit Jalla in 1844 and of Jowahir Singh in 1845. He also missed the rise of the mutinous sentiment in the Sikh army and of course he as yet knew nothing of the controversial part played by Gardner in executing Jowahir Singh's 'disgustful' sentence on Jodha Ram. Times had changed. His 'Adventurer in the Punjab' evoked an earlier age, one in which Ranjit Singh still ruled and romance lent a certain glamour to a figure like Gardner/Bellasis. Lawrence was in for a few surprises.

Yet to someone like Lawrence, for whom career and convictions went hand in hand, the summons from Hardinge to join him on the Satluj could not have been more welcome. Almighty Providence had at last heeded his prayers; a fair field would yet be his. By late January 1846 he was at the governor-general's side to welcome the news of the Sikh defeat at Ludhiana and await the final showdown at Sobraon.

Neither Gardner nor Lawrence actually fought at Sobraon. On the fateful day, 10 February 1846, Gardner was still in Lahore, while Lawrence, though present, was acting in a purely political charac-ter. The outcome of the battle was anyway a foregone conclusion. Tej Singh, much to the disgust of Colonel Mouton, his tactical adviser, had refused to launch an attack before the British had been reinforced. He had then opted to mount the Khalsa's last stand not from a well-established position on the river's higher north bank but from a sandy bridgehead on the opposite shore. This effectively split the Sikh army in two. Half the troops, including Lal Singh with nearly all the cavalry and much of the artillery, would be little more than spectators on the northern shoreline; the other half would be marooned on the southern shore and facing the might of the British advance along a two-mile front from which the only line of retreat lay back over a long and highly vulnerable boat-bridge. To strengthen the bridgehead itself, Hurbon devised an elaborate system of parapets and entrenchments, but these defences were far from continuous and the sandy soil that yielded so obligingly to the spade would be a death-trap for the heavy guns. Manoeuvring them proved almost impossible; at every discharge their carriages sank deeper and their aim became more erratic.

> The English had all the advantage of the position [says Mouton]... while we had only a badly constructed bridge on the biggest river in the Punjab to fall back upon, which too was in danger of being threatened by flood. At the first repulse the whole army would thus fall into the river, and the war would finish miserably, thus bringing all our resources to an end.

Written with the wisdom of hindsight, this was indeed what happened. Tipped off by Tej Singh as to the Sikh front's weakest points, Gough's troops were concentrated accordingly and, after a three-hour bombardment, advanced *en masse*. Even the habitually restrained Cunningham was impressed.

> The field was resplendent with embattled warriors, one moment umbered in volumes of sulphurous smoke, and another brightly apparent amid the splendour of beaming brass and the cold piercing rays of polished steel.

Far from discouraging the Sikh troops, strategic suicide and official betrayal seemed only to have made them more resolute. But bravery alone was not enough. 'The soldiers did everything and the leaders nothing,' says Cunningham. 'Hearts to dare and hands to execute were numerous; but there was no mind to guide and execute the whole.' Hurbon's breastworks proved effective enough, but in the space of a few hours the extremities of the Sikh line were turned and the British began closing in from the rear. As usual Tej Singh was the first to flee. From a bomb-proof shelter specially erected for his protection, he made straight for the bridge, crossed it, removed enough pontoons to render it useless to those who would follow, and then fled to Amritsar.

Once turned, the Sikh position could have been designed—and probably was—to ensure maximum slaughter. Pressed ever closer, the pride of the Khalsa's troops fell back on the river and then on the sabotaged bridge. Some swam, others attempted to wade. The British gave no quarter. As men and horses plunged into the blood-stained waters, the difference between being shot or drowned became academic. Of the estimated 10,000 Sikhs who lost their lives at Sobraon, more were carried away by the river than left on the battlefield. The British fatalities were put at 320, which was less than half those at Ferozeshah.

> It was at one o'clock in the afternoon that the defeat was complete [says Mouton], but no one gave himself up to the English. Many were drowned. Their arms were piled upon the bank, guns, ammunition, wagons and drums were all lying pell-mell.

Meanwhile, downstream at Ferozepur, a large British detachment crossed unopposed. Mouton was in favour of sending the Sobraon survivors and those held in reserve to cut them off; but 'it was in vain that I appealed to these barbarians in the name of honour and fatherland'. The impossibility of continuing a war conducted by treacherous generals using 'a brave but undisciplined army' was self-evident.

Gardner, however, claims that there was still hope for the Sikhs. For within hours of Sobraon, Gulab Singh had finally taken the field. He made straight for the British camp, now on the road to Lahore at a place called Kasur, though whether he intended to fight or submit was unclear. Gardner hastened from the rani's side to join him there ('How is Her Majesty?' asked Gulab Singh) and together they presented themselves to Lawrence as the British political agent. It was the first time the three had met since the Afghan War.

> I had about 500 men [says Gardner], Gulab Singh some 2000, and

20,000 or 30,000 men within hail. Now here were the Sikhs crossing [back over the Satluj], and the British at Kasur, who were therefore in a most critical position, as they were between the Sikh and Dogra armies. Of course Gulab Sing had a double move [ie was playing a double game]; and Lawrence seemed to be anxious ... Though Sir Henry tried to pump me, I only said, and could say, as an honest paid servant of my masters, 'Keep up a bold face and look to your right; the Dogra force may be secured to act as light infantry in case of any further trouble'.

Trouble being the last thing Gulab Singh wanted, he ordered Gardner to hold four cannon in readiness for a possible Sikh counterattack. The counterattack failed to materialise. Acting on behalf of the rani and the court, the Dogra chief then offered his services as an intermediary between the British and the Sikh army. As per the earlier 'understanding', the terms of surrender had anyway been pre-arranged. On 18 February the young maharaja personally made a humiliating submission. Two days later the British entered Lahore. Presumably Gardner's last minute caution had been intended solely to impress Lawrence, and in this it seems to have had the desired effect.

However erratic their correspondence over the previous three years, the flow of intelligence reports between Gardner and Lawrence becomes well attested for the period immediately after the Kasur meeting. While still supplying 'behind the scenes' material for Carmichael Smyth's book, Gardner was given the task of reporting direct to Lawrence on such matters as the security of Lahore, the disposition of the scattered Sikh forces, the progress of their disbandment and especially the location of their remaining artillery. Written with the colonel's usual disregard for syntax, some of these reports survive in the Henry Lawrence papers in the British Library; and in one in particular there lurks a possibly revealing, if cryptic, aside (here italicised):

... and several have purchased matchlocks etc *perhaps you could oblige me with the Adventurer in which I wrote some notes—I have given Major Smith a few more sketches—as a continuation to the former—But I mean if encouraged to commence anew a large and compleat work*—Tej Singh has taken on a number of old artillerymen...

Picking this apart, 'the Adventurer' may be taken as a reference to Lawrence's Bellasis book, while 'Major Smith' is clearly Carmichael Smyth. The letter is undated but internal evidence suggests it relates to the period immediately after the British takeover of Lahore, so March or April 1846. Reference to Gardner's intention 'to commence anew a large and compleat work' (on the Sikh Empire? on his own life-story?) is intriguing enough; but the letter also raises the whole question of the relationship between Smyth, Lawrence and Gardner. Gardner had evidently annotated a copy of Lawrence's book and had submitted it to him for comment. In due course these annotations would indeed be published in the appendices of Smyth's *Reigning Family*. And since they were mostly corrections or criticisms, the hyper-sensitive Lawrence must surely have raised objections. He may have concluded that Smyth and Gardner were out to discredit him; he may even have felt that they had pre-empted his undertaking a similar work of his own.

Two years later Lawrence would take his revenge. Writing anonymously in the *Calcutta Review*, a journal founded by his friend Sir John Kaye and which he was well known to favour with his views, he dished out a review of Smyth's book that for sheer bile would be hard to equal. The *History of the Reigning Family of Lahore* was 'a hash' got up by Smyth and 'a Mr Gardner late of the Sikh service'. 'Concocted to suit the prurient appetites of a particular class of reader', it was 'a mass of contradictions ... of errors palpable to the meanest understanding... erroneous facts and crotchety opinions.'

> It deserves no quarter [concluded Lawrence], serving as it does as a handle for the enemies of England and the calumniators of our noble army...

Gardner came in for the fiercest of criticism. His tales of 'blood and bestiality' at court were quite unsubstantiated, for 'not only is Mr Gardner, in general estimation, a disreputable person but he had no access to the Durbar of Lahore—which in no sense recognised him as a gentleman—and could only report the idle rumours of hangers-on and low [life] adventurers like himself'. Yet it was precisely this same low-life adventurer whom Broadfoot might have done well to 'have at his elbow' and to whom Lawrence had formerly turned for 'important information'. The *Calcutta Review* (ie Lawrence) quotes both these references to himself as they appeared in Smyth's book and fails to contest either. It merely notes that whatever 'Major Lawrence' wrote from Kathmandu was not what he might have written from Lahore—and that anyway the information provided by Gardner was worthless.

> [For] it is no secret that Colonel Lawrence [he had been promoted in 1846] *never* had any opinion of Gardner's character and that, for a year or more before he caused him to be discharged from the Sikh service, he had ceased to place the slightest reliance on his reports.

Clearly there had been, to put it mildly, a falling out. Gardner says nothing on the matter. In the *Memoirs* Lawrence remains 'my friend' and is last noticed as one of two British officers to whom Gardner gave a conducted tour of the Lahore palace. Robert Napier, the other, 'asked me if I could manage to procure him a sight of the Rani'. Knowing Rani Jindan was equally curious about the British, Gardner made the necessary arrangements; 'and thus it was that the beautiful head and neck appeared once or twice over a wall'. Napier was highly gratified, Lawrence probably not.

For several months after this triumph, Gardner continued to enjoy the regard of the British. He was welcomed as the curiosity he undoubtedly was and found a ready audience for his tales of adventure in Inner Asia among Lahore's occupying British troops. Not even Lawrence believed he was other than American, albeit an 'Irish-American'. And according to Gardner, it was not Lawrence who demanded his eventual discharge but the still powerful Tej Singh.

The falling out with Lawrence could have owed something to Gardner's disappointing performance as an informant; it could also have owed something to Lawrence's pique over the Gardner-Smyth book collaboration. Much more convincingly, though, it stemmed from an ugly rumour, soon confirmed as fact, which no upright sahib, least of all Lawrence, could possibly ignore. For the past two years a horribly disfigured Brahmin had been accosting any passing Lahori with the time—and ears—to listen to his sorry tale. The Brahmin's name was Jodha Ram; and his physical deficiencies, he claimed, had been inflicted by Gordana Sahib, the very man who had lately been responsible for the queen-regent's protection and was now the toast of the British officers' mess.

Lawrence must have become aware of the rumour about Jodha Ram soon after arriving in Lahore in the spring of 1846. He would later claim that it was common knowledge at the time, and Herbert Edwardes, his disciple and future biographer, stated it as fact in the 1846 *Calcutta Review*. No doubt Lawrence was as horrified as Grey and Garret would be; indeed he had probably primed Edwardes with the information in the first place. But no action seems to have been taken until nearly a year later. At that point—February 1847—Jodha Ram lodged an official complaint and was awarded compensation. And Gardner, with heavy heart, took up his pen to lodge his long-winded 'defence'.

One explanation for the delay might be that Gardner had remained in the employ of the Lahore Durbar throughout 1846 and had continued to supply Lawrence with intelligence reports. In May, for instance, he reported on complaints that an Englishwoman, the much admired wife of Colonel Henry Charles Van Cortlandt, was seeing too much of the rani and sowing discord between her and her vizier Lal Singh. Van Cortlandt, himself Anglo-Indian, had formerly served under Ranjit Singh but had fought with the British at Ferozeshah and Sobraon. Now back in the employ of the Khalsa despite Lawrence's contemptuous opinion of him, he had been given command of a battalion and would eventually take over the troublesome Dera Ismail Khan district. Gardner would claim that Van Cortlandt invited him to join him in the Derajat but, possibly because by then Gardner's dismissal was already looking probable, he would decline. Had he accepted, he would have been well placed to participate in the Second Anglo-Sikh War when it broke out in neighbouring Multan in mid-1848. Van Cortlandt and his formidable Susanna would emerge from that war as heroes. Gardner would play no part in it.

For in October 1846, instead of the sweltering deserts along the lower Indus, Gardner had resumed active duty in the cool of the hills. He was deputed to Kashmir and would not return until the end of the year. In what seems to have been his first visit to the famous valley since his hasty transit of it back in 1828 he accompanied the forces of Gulab Singh in the awkward task of detaching Kashmir from the rule of the Lahore Durbar.

This was in fulfilment of the complicated post-war settlement. Following victory at Sobraon, the British had secured signatures to two separate treaties. The first treaty, that of Lahore, was made with the Sikh durbar on 9 March. In return for British recognition of the authority of the existing government—Duleep Singh as maharaja, the rani Jindan as regent, Lal Singh as vizier and Tej Singh as commander-in-chief—the durbar was obliged to surrender all claims to territory south of the Satluj, to make over to the British the rich lands of the Jalandhar Doab between the Satluj and the Beas River, and to pay an indemnity of 15 million rupees. Since there was no prospect of such a colossal sum being raised, it was reduced to 5 million, with all the hill country between the Ravi and Indus, including Kashmir, being ceded as security for the balance. Another clause hinted at the fate of this hill-country by guaranteeing the 'independent sovereignty' there of Gulab Singh of Jammu.

The second treaty, that of Amritsar, was signed exclusively with Gulab Singh a week later and confirmed this arrangement. The last of the Dogra brothers and his heirs were to enjoy their independent sovereignty on the same terms of British oversight as had been imposed on the Lahore Durbar in the heavily pruned lands that remained under the Durbar's control. Moreover, 'in consideration of the [Kashmir] transfer', Gulab Singh was to pay the British government 750,000 rupees.

Technically this was not a sale; since the territory in question had just been transferred to the British as surety for the original indemnity, the payment could be seen as part-settlement of that indemnity. But to many observers it looked as if Kashmir and all its Himalayan dependencies had simply been knocked down to the only serious bidder. The British had no wish to assume responsibility for Kashmir themselves, and only 'the Golden Hen' had the resources to buy them out. Cunningham was not alone in calling the transaction 'dexterous ... but scarcely worthy of the British name and greatness'. Nor was it to the liking of everyone in Lahore. When Gulab Singh attempted to assume his new fief, he was rebuffed by Kashmir's incumbent governor acting, it was claimed, in the interests of his former superiors in the Sikh capital. Hence arose the need for the military intervention in Kashmir of late 1846.

The expedition taking Gardner away from Lahore and its ugly rumours was unusual in that it involved troops from all the interested parties—British, Dogra and Sikh. Against some spirited resistance this combined force overran the Kashmir Valley and defeated Sheik Imam-ud-din, the incumbent governor, in an assault on the hilltop fortress of Hari Parbat just outside Srinagar. Sadly Gardner's surviving reports of the campaign relate only to the expedition's return journey and contain no account of the actual fighting. Instead they deal in considerable detail with the misconduct of the victors—'compleatly robbing and plundering and pulling down the Houses or Hamlets of the poor inhabitants are amongst some of the least or slightest transgressions,' he noted.

Coincidentally, these reports also introduce a fellow officer of some interest to Gardner sleuths. This was a certain 'Colonel Canora', who appears to be the same Khora/Canara/Kinaila/Kennedy as he who, fourteen years earlier, had reportedly been Gardner's companion when he first presented himself in Lahore. Canora, also a gunner who claimed to be American, had spent most of his years in Sikh employ on the frontier. He had not been called on to fight in the first Anglo-Sikh War but he did take part in the Kashmir campaign; and there according to one of Gardner's reports to Lawrence, he had been offered an inducement to join 'a private Sikh combination against the British'. Nothing came of this 'mutinising', as Gardner calls it.

Canora remained true to his salt, although Gardner rather wished he hadn't; for if he had taken the bribe they might have been able to trace it to its mutinising source.

Eighteen months later, at the outset of the Second Anglo-Sikh War, Canora would again be approached, would again refuse, and would this time die in a hail of bullets. For embracing death rather than surrender his cannon to a possible enemy, he would be handsomely memorialised by Captain James Abbott, Lawrence's representative in the Hazara district (and the man after whom Abbottabad was named): 'Thus died a man who, whatever the defect of education and infirmities of nature, closed his career with an act of gallantry and loyalty unsurpassed by anything I have read in history'. To Gardner such a plaudit would have been most acceptable, though not the price.

It was a difficult time for foreigners in Sikh employ, in fact not much safer than before the British arrived in Lahore. Men like Van Cortlandt, Canora and Gardner were caught in a web of conflicting allegiances. With disaffection rife even among those Sikh troops that had not been disbanded, the loyalty of their men could no longer be depended on. Intrigues at court only made matters worse. And Edwardes, Abbott and the rest of Lawrence's so-called 'young men', however assiduous in upholding the authority of the Lahore Durbar, lacked experience of the Punjab. Moreover, under the terms of the Lahore Treaty, they could count on the presence of British troops only until the end of 1846. Time was running out. Worse still, a clause common to both the Lahore and Amritsar treaties stipulated that:

> The Maharajah engages never to take, or retain, in his service, any British subject, nor the subject of any European or American state, without the consent of the British Government.

Besides providing convincing evidence that the British (ie Lawrence) had as yet no objections to Gardner serving the Khalsa, it would appear that the British believed him to be precisely who he said he was (the mention of 'any American state' could well have been tailored specially for him). Indeed the consent of the British government to his continued employment may be taken as proof that there were

no grounds for suspecting he had ever deserted from the East India
Company's armed forces. Had such grounds existed, he would have
been detained, tried and would by now have been embarking on a
hefty sentence.

But the condition of British consent to his employment also had a
downside. In Sikh eyes it prejudiced his standing. Thus Gardner and
his friends laboured under the double stigma of being seen as British
collaborators by those they commanded, while lacking the security
that a lasting British presence might have ensured.

As well as accusing the Khalsa troops in Kashmir of terrorising
the local population and nursing 'mutinising' designs against the
British, Gardner's reports to Lawrence dwell on the authenticity of
certain letters handed over by the defeated Kashmir governor Sheikh
Imam-ud-din. These letters, purportedly from vizier Lal Singh—or
'the Red Lion' as Gardner translates his name (so making it sound
like a pub)—pre-dated the campaign and seemed to direct the governor to resist Gulab Singh's occupation of his Kashmir fief. They
thus appeared to exonerate the governor and implicate 'the Red
Lion'. But Gardner was suspicious not only of their provenance but
also of Commander-in-Chief Tej Singh's part in the affair. Had Tej
Singh also been a party to the plot to resist Gulab Singh? Or was
he merely drawing attention to it in order to discredit Lal Singh?
Or had perhaps that arch-schemer, the now Maharaja Gulab Singh
of Jammu and Kashmir, contrived the whole affair to discredit the
Lahore government in the eyes of its British sponsors?

Gardner offered no answers to such questions and Raja Lal Singh
duly paid the price. Tried by a panel of investigators headed and
appointed by Lawrence, 'the Red Lion' was sent into a perpetual
exile which began in the city of Agra under a loose form of house
detention. His asylum there being within striking distance of the Taj
Mahal, John Lang, an Australian lawyer and journalist, tracked him
down sometime in the 1850s. Lang took Lal Singh for the adopted
Sikh he had long claimed to be and found him excellent company.
Together they excavated a mass grave in the compound of the raja's
handsomely appointed garden-house. Lal Singh had no complaints
about either his treatment or his domicile. Archaeology apart, his

current hobby was surgery. 'A skilful operator' in the opinion of Agra's medical fraternity, he 'could take off an arm or a leg with surprising dexterity'. As if to prove the point, a table in his house was spread with surgical instruments—'saws, knives, scalpels of every size and shape'—plus two richly inlaid swords of the finest Damascus steel. The swords had belonged, said the raja, to the Dogra father and son, Dhyan Singh and Hira Singh. Having proved so effective in removing heads, the raja proposed having them adapted for operations of a more life-saving nature.

Lal Singh's trial in December 1846 had been quickly followed by another Anglo-Sikh accord. The preamble to this Treaty of Bhairowal declared that, since the Sikh durbar had made 'atonement' for Vizier Lal Singh's infringement of the Lahore Treaty by deposing him, the British government had acceded to the durbar's 'anxious' request for 'aid and assistance to maintain the administration of Lahore state' until such time as Maharaja Duleep Singh came of age. In effect, British troops would stay on till 1854, when the little maharaja would be 16, and so would a British agent or resident (currently Lawrence) with vastly increased powers 'to direct and control all matters in every department of the State'.

At the same time, and presumably because of her close relationship with Lal Singh, Rani Jindan, the Queen-Mother/Regent, was dropped from the Council of Regency and offered an annual pension of 15,000 rupees. This she accepted; but her influence over her son continued to concern the British and during the Second Anglo-Sikh War she too was packed off into exile. After a year's detention in Chunar Fort near Benares/Varanasi, she escaped. She obtained sanctuary in Nepal and was finally reunited with her son in Calcutta in 1861, thirteen years after their parting in Lahore. Duleep Singh, who had been deposed before he had ever been enthroned, took her back to England, his own place of exile, and provided for her until she died two years later in a house off Kensington High Street. The property was then acquired by the Catholic Church and was no doubt carefully sanitised since, as *The Tablet* shuddered to report, under the rani it had been 'the scene of Hindoo religious ceremonies, and even sacrifices'.

Although almost none of Gardner's reports to Lawrence is dated, one of the last in the file mentions his 'upwards of 16 years' service', of which only 'the last two years' had been spent in Lahore. This would date the report to no earlier than 1847 and probably to February or March of that year. It can scarcely have been later, for in April Commander-in-Chief Tej Singh gave the colonel his marching orders. He was summarily dismissed from the Sikh service, deprived of his jagir, and ordered to leave the kingdom within twenty-four hours. Tej Singh, whom he had long regarded as his enemy, was acting on the basis of Pandit Jodha Ram's accusation and with the full backing of Lawrence. But perhaps unaware of this, it was apparently to Lawrence that Gardner made his great appeal. Ensconced in British Ludhiana, the colonel finally put pen to paper for his long and little known 'Defence'. It would be the nearest thing to an apologia for his entire career that he ever wrote.

10

A Self-Communing Life
1847–60

The manuscript identified among the papers of Sir Henry Lawrence as 'Col. Gardiner's defence of his having mutilated Jhoda Misser' is not for the faint-hearted. Unsigned by Gardner himself, it is a copy and is certified as such by Lawrence's brother John. John Lawrence, a more thorough and less idolised administrator than Henry, had been given charge of the districts between the Satluj and Beas Rivers that had just been ceded to British India under the Lahore Treaty; he also acted as Henry's stand-in at Lahore during the latter's absences. The humble copyist of the document is not named and perhaps deserves better. His neatly written copperplate may be taken as reasonably faithful to the original and is almost certainly more legible. The resultant document is not, though, easier reading. Gardner's random capitalisation has been retained, as has his erratic punctuation, his parenthetic embellishments and his extravagant way with adjectives. Some sentences run into one another, others expire in mid utterance. Sparks of eloquence and embers of the colonel's schooling may be detected, but they lie smothered in verbiage.

Yet, for better or worse, this is at least raw Gardner. Here speaks the man himself, without the benefit of Pearse's or Carmichael Smyth's assiduous editing and without the narrational adjustments that Cooper and Durand may have felt obliged to make. Fortuitously the colonel gets to be heard in his own words at the most crucial moment in his career. With his back to the wall and his reputation in tatters, he reflects on his chequered past and gives vent to the lessons learnt and the conclusions to be drawn in so far as they explain what led to the affair concerning the man known as Jodha Misser or Jodha Ram.

The document, although written with only one obvious break, can be divided into three sections. The first deals with the dilemma of how to reconcile the habits of a solitary life passed in constant peril with the norms of 'so-called civilised' society; any traveller just back from some unfancied corner of the globe will recognise the difficulty. The second section, written apparently in continuation of some previous correspondence, clarifies and corrects various statements about the catastrophic blood-lettings that had led up to the First Anglo-Sikh War. And the third explains in detail how it was that Gardner came to bear the blame for Jodha Ram's 'disgustful' fate. Each section is sufficiently distinct to hint at independent composition, possibly at a different date and in a different context. Yet the second section contains enough references to the first, and the third segues so naturally from the second, as to preclude the possibility of any of them having been inadvertently included. However disjointed, the Defence must be treated as an integrated composition, and any deductions about its date and intended recipient must apply to all three sections.

The title chosen for the whole apologia anticipates the first of the three sections:

> A Sample of some curious Moralizing Notions
> and Ideas of the World as
> imbibed by a person long separated
> from the World and for 26 years
> leading a <u>Self communing Life</u>.

In truth the 'Self communing Life' may not have been intentionally underlined; the double lines beneath it could be just a graphic device to distinguish the title from what follows. But the '26 years' is about right. Counting back from the arrival of the British in Lahore in March 1846, it dates the start of his self-communing life to 1820.

According to the *Memoirs* it was actually 1819 when he first took off from Herat into Turkestan as a solo adventurer, but given Gardner's usual indifference to dates, a year's discrepancy in over quarter of a century is no great matter. So far so good, then.

By way of an opening salvo, there next comes the following part-paragraph, here re-punctuated (or more often de-punctuated) and with some spellings adjusted:

> The World is at best but one large mass, one great revolving Circle, of frail, vain, foolish and almost unaccountable and incomprehensible Contrariety and inconsistency. Genuine truth and pure ideas are to be met with, and found in general, only as plausible and superficial terms and as but thin, vain and false tinselly coatings embodying nothing but the nucleus of vanity and falsehood. By the Laws, manners and Customs of one Country, acts are acknowledged crimes or discrepancies which in other climes are and may be considered, and are extolled as, virtues. Just much the same as the monthly or daily Fashions of Paris and London change and revolve with the opinion and fancy, so does the nature, light and opinion of things and worldly matters keep incessantly changing, shifting and revolving throughout the whole World, forming that one great circle of contrariety.

... and so on, for the next twenty-one pages. The phrasing is often confusing but the drift is clear. 'Notions imbibed from a long residence out of all European or ... civilised life and what I term the sole self-communing life' convince him 'that I have a just claim to consider myself innocent ... in the eyes of my God and Creator...'

In rather less words Cunningham makes much the same point when defending Gulab Singh's appalling record of perfidy and oppression. A man 'must be judged with reference to the morality of his age and race, and to the necessities of his position'; if such allowance is made, even Gulab Singh will 'be found an able and moderate man, who does little in an idle or wanton spirit, and is not without some traits of good humour and generosity of temper'.

Gardner would not be so kind about his long-term employer; but nor would his own conduct stand up to conventional scrutiny.

The actions of a lone introvert were not to be viewed in the light of polite society's rules but 'in the real, unmasked, plain, candid, naked, original and genuine light of the Inward man'. Only conscience could be relied on to 'brush away the cobweb, or allow the thought to strike, that substantial truth and reality is a thing much differing ... from the spurious and bad substitute which is made to represent it by the frail and changing opinions of the World'. In other words, society's cyclical and self-deluding fads could safely be ignored. As per the last sentence of this opening section, 'It is not in forms or names but in the purity of a Man's Sentiments that he shows or holds his religion or his reverence to God'.

Though decidedly out of character, such appeals to 'the Almighty', 'the Creator' or some non-denominational 'Godhead' feature quite prominently throughout the Defence. They may even provide a clue as to who it was supposed to be read by. As usual the document is neither dated nor addressed; but in the second section there appear several second-person references to the intended reader. For instance, the sentence 'I have sent *you* a pretty good account of [the panches] in some of the blank pages of the Proof sheets I sent you, or returned you, just before I left Lahore for Cashmeer' would suggest that the Defence formed a part of Gardner's ongoing contribution to Carmichael Smyth's book. With reference to Nau Nihal Singh, Gardner confirms that the young maharaja's untimely end occurred when entering the Hazuri Bagh 'through the gateway or long portal I showed *you*', which could again be intended for Smyth; and *a propos* of Mundee (or Mandi), a place supposedly producing diamonds, it 'is just in the Hills above *you*', which could indicate that Smyth was out on tour.

On the other hand, Smyth, whose appetite for scandal was not easily sated, never mentions the Jodha Ram affair or the extenuating circumstances that attended it. Since he several times acknowledges his debt to Gardner, one can only assume that he was quite unaware of the colonel's character having been called in question. Nor, supposing Gardner had enlightened him, would that long disquisition on the 'self-communing life' have been apposite to Smyth's book. The Defence is found only among the Lawrence papers; and its wording

appears tailored not to the muck-raking purposes of Smyth but to
the high-minded principles of Henry Lawrence, a man who made no
secret of being in daily communication with his Creator. Lawrence
had also been one of the two officers whom Gardner had shown round
the Lahore palace, so gratifying their desire for a glimpse of the rani;
no doubt Gardner also took the occasion to point out the Hazuri
Bagh 'gateway or long portal', now known as the Roshnai Darwaza
(Gate of Light), which shed its masonry on poor Nau Nihal Singh.

Lawrence, however vehemently he denied it, had once thought
well of Gardner. He had been happy to listen to him, had encouraged
him to provide intelligence and had reckoned him reliable. Gardner
in turn respected Lawrence. Yet, no less certainly, he would have been
aware that his dismissal by vizier Tej Singh would at the very least
have required Lawrence's approval. On all counts, therefore, it was
logical that the Defence should have been written for the eyes of 'the
great and good Sir Henry Lawrence'.

Further, the fact that the Defence was attested by Lawrence's
brother John may help to date it; for when John was in Lahore, it
was usually because Henry was absent. Henry's poor health (he had
contracted a recurrent fever while in Burma), combined with his
interventionist style of direction and his reluctance to miss out on
any opportunity for personal heroics, meant that he was absent much
of the time. In May 1846 he was in what is now Himachal Pradesh
overseeing the belated surrender of the rock-top fortress of Kangra.
By an odd coincidence Kangra's fort had been the stronghold won for
Ranjit Singh by the dashing Colonel Bellasis in Lawrence's *Adventurer*. Real-life events suddenly promised to authenticate Lawrence's
fiction and afford a chance of replicating one of Ranjit Singh's more
notable conquests; he had insisted on taking personal command. In
October/November '46 he had likewise insisted on accompanying
the expedition to Kashmir, and in August '47 he repaired to Simla
prior to taking nine-months leave in Britain. As the map to which
Gardner refers would have made clear, Simla is indeed located just
across the hills from the little town of Mandi, near which the still
gem-obsessed Gardner had got wind of a diamond mine.

The 'proof sheets' referred to in the Defence document could have been those of Carmichael Smyth's *History of the Reigning Family of Lahore* but could equally have related to the latest edition of Lawrence's *Adventurer* (or possibly his proposed sequel to it). Thus Gardner goes into some detail to correct a statement that it was an elephant that brought down the Hazuri Bagh gateway on top of Nau Nihal Singh. Once again it is only Lawrence who blames an elephant. Smyth needed no correcting on this point because, primed by Gardner, he had never blamed an elephant in the first place.

And there are other examples. Yet in a footnote to the Hazuri Bagh incident in Smyth's book and in its appendices, Smyth does reprint almost word for word Gardner's version of the Nau Nihal Singh affair as it appears in the Defence. Both footnotes and appendices were last minute additions evidently made by Smyth soon after writing the Introduction to his book. The introduction is datelined 'Jullunder, 5th January, 1847', which, if Smyth was indeed the Defence's intended recipient, would fit with its reference to his 'coming to Jullunder'. But if he wasn't the intended recipient, several explanations spring to mind. Gardner may have roughed out parts of this second section of the Defence for Smyth's edification and have sent it to him before composing the other two sections. As already noted, he and Smyth seem to have delighted in exposing Lawrence's fallibility at every opportunity. And just possibly Lawrence's notoriously cavalier attitude to paperwork (his latest biographer talks of his tent being strewn with reports and his children playing among them) may somehow have contributed to the confusion. The only thing that seems sure is that, whatever the provenance of this second section of the Defence, it too was intended for Henry Lawrence. It also confirms the dating of the whole Defence to after the Bhairowal treaty of December '46, after the flood of petitions, Jodha Ram's included, that the Treaty prompted, and probably to the time of Gardner's dismissal in April '47 or possibly even August '47, by when Lawrence was in Simla.

After so much uncertainty, the final section of the Defence, which is the longest as well as the most relevant, also proves the most straightforward. In justifying his treatment of Jodha Ram and in response to Edwardes's accusation in the *Calcutta Review* that he had accepted a colonelcy for it, Gardner might reasonably have cited the penal climate that prevailed at the time. General Avitabile had famously asserted his authority in Peshawar by ringing the city with gibbets and leaving his victims dangling from them for weeks. Gulab Singh was rumoured to have boiled his prisoners alive while skinning their womenfolk, also alive, in their presence. Ventura, too, could be a brutal disciplinarian; and the British preference for flogging rather than imprisonment and for instant death in the case of suspected mutineers was not much better.

But Gardner, while disputing a fickle world's right to judge any aspect of his conduct, never apologises on the grounds that cruelty was commonplace. Rather was the mutilation of Jodha Ram 'black, heinous, and even disgustful and revolting to my own mind'. If he insisted that he had 'little to answer for', it was not because his action was in any way acceptable but because he had been left with no choice in the matter. It was 'a compulsory deed in its fullest sense,' he claimed—provided, he adds facetiously, 'it may be called compulsion to have not only one but four muskets on full cock placed and levelled at a man's head, ready to blow or send him into Eternity without a moment left for reflection...'

But how had it all come to this? How, after fourteen years of serving the Khalsa, after a dozen campaigns and being wounded, he says, 'in five different engagements', had he been manoeuvred into such an impossible situation?

Incredibly the whole affair had started with a minor local difficulty. Soon after Jowahir Singh had come to power in January 1845 'a next door neighbour of mine ... seeing the turn of affairs, found means to petition and get an order to take possession of my house, on which I felt myself obliged to go and seek protection from the new Durbar and Jowahir Singh.' Gardner had not previously met Jowahir Singh but he did know Jiwan Singh, who was Jowahir Singh's right-hand man and acted as his treasurer and enforcer. Jiwan Singh presumably got the expulsion order reversed, and in the process Gardner came to the attention of Jowahir Singh. Soon after, Jowahir Singh commissioned him to raise the two battalions of infantry and the corps of artillery on which the new regime would come to rely.

As commandant of what was effectively the palace guard, Gardner's duties included the safe-keeping of prisoners, especially 'the State ones or those from whom large sums of money were expected'. One of these unfortunates was a certain Khuda Bakhsh. On instructions from Jiwan Singh, Gardner was ordered to so work on this individual that he would confess to his transgression and make tangible amends to the tune of 50,000 rupees.

By pretending to take Khuda Bakhsh's side in the matter Gardner did as he was told, and with such success that Jiwan Singh applauded his persuasive techniques. The prisoner was then released, Jiwan Singh and Bakhsh became firm friends and Bakhsh was appointed Lahore's *kotwal*, or magistrate and chief of police. Meanwhile Gardner returned to his military duties. 'I thought nothing more of the affair and was daily busily employed in managing to get up and rectify as quickly as possible my new corps etc'.

Three weeks later, in the middle of the night, he was summoned to the palace. Jowahir Singh was there in person along with four of his cronies; he was perfectly sober at the time, insists Gardner, despite 'a Bottle of Champagne and another of Sherry on the table beside him'.

> He kept unusually Quiet and Seemed deep in thought. At last he broke silence by calling me close to him—and even closer than I de-sired—[and] in a cool, deep, low but earnest and enquiring tone asked me what Countryman I was. Then [he] asked me Several questions respecting how Europeans in general obeyed all or any orders given them and [how] they were noted and remarkable for doing so in the strict word of the sense.

As if to illustrate the unreliability of non-Europeans, a servant who had misread a sign from Jowahir Singh to fill his sherry glass was then taken away to receive 500 lashes, 'beneath which the man became senseless and actually nearly lost his life'. Next it was Jiwan Singh's turn to be put to the test. He got off with a dressing-down, literally since it included the loss of his cloak. Then it was Gardner's turn. Would he as a foreigner obey an order whatever its consequences? Indeed he would, he replied; but only if he reasonably could. A lump of white arsenic was then produced and thrust across the table.

Would he swallow it?

> A thought struck me at the moment that he [Jowahir Singh] must be
> only really trying me, and with the confidence of this thought, I really
> took out of his hand the piece he offered me; it seemed to weigh a good
> ½ ounce. He asked me to eat or swallow it. I immediately answered with
> a resolute and even a firm tone that I was ready to obey his orders and
> only waited for them.

The two men then glowered at one another in silence. Gardner's
defiant stare was, he says, 'as piercing if not more so than even [Jowa-
hir's]'. It was no comfort that his inquisitor 'reminded me much of the
present Maharajah Gulab Singh in doing his utmost to strike terror
and dismay into all around him.' The silence continued. Another
thirty seconds passed very slowly. The muscles of Jowahir Singh's face
then 'softened' and the ordeal was over. Jowahir Singh took back the
arsenic, two more servants were flogged to within an inch of their
lives, and Gardner was sent home.

For this show of fidelity he was awarded 500 rupees and promised
the charge of two districts. Jiwan Singh commandeered the districts
but Gardner kept the cash.

> I assure you ... I breathed somewhat more freely when I got out of the
> precincts of the Fort than within them and ... really think that, had
> I acted other than I did that night, I should not be alive to relate the
> fact now...

It was during another nocturnal conclave some days later that the
fate of the Brahmin Jodha Misser/Jodha Ram was first aired. He
too was being held in detention and in this case Jowahir Singh was
not disposed to accept blood-money. Two years earlier the boot had
been on the other foot. Jowahir Singh had been Jodha Ram's prisoner
following a supposed attempt to undermine the Hira Singh regime
by smuggling the young maharaja to the British in Ludhiana.

Whether or not there was such a plot, as Jowahir Singh's gaoler
Jodha Ram had shown no mercy. Exposing his own back, Jowahir

Singh now pointed out the scars left by the branding irons with which the Brahmin had tortured him. He then produced 'two handfuls of rough hunker stones or pebbles' that he claimed the Brahmin had made him swallow and that 'he had voided during many days with the utmost pain and detriment to his health and constitution and [which] very nigh caused his death'. Jodha Ram had so tortured Jowahir Singh without the knowledge of Hira Singh and without the sanction of the rani or the young maharaja (ie Jowahir's sister and nephew). He must be punished accordingly and swiftly. The matter was urgent because Jodha Ram's Brahmin supporters were publicly demanding his release while inciting the men of his former command (ie Avitabile's Division) to mutiny.

Opinions were then canvassed among the assembled company, death being the preferred option. But as when determining the fate of his attackers in the Pamirs, Gardner made the mistake of sounding a note of caution. The sentence must be decided by either the rani or Jowahir Singh, he ventured, and they would do well 'under the present circumstances [to] be careful of exciting the public mind or soldiery'.

> I no sooner said this than [Jowahir Singh] changed his countenance, and in a few more minutes, he, seemingly not well pleased with the advice, gave me permission to retire.

Another twenty days elapsed. It must now have been March 1845. Gardner had done his best to warn Jodha Ram of his fate and had forwarded petitions pleading for a mitigated sentence. Meanwhile Jowahir Singh had grown more confident than ever of attaining the vizership.

Again Gardner was roused from sleep, this time in the small hours of the morning and with a flurry of orders; he was to deliver the prisoner under guard to the kotwal Khuda Bakhsh, he was personally to escort this party with two companies of troops, and finally, on pain of death, he was to conduct them to the *chabutra*, a raised platform in one of the city's open *chowk*s (courtyard at a road junction) that served Lahore as a place of official condemnation and public punishment. There he was to 'remain on the spot ... until the Hands,

The bloodbath that followed the death of Maharaja Ranjit Singh also claimed his son, Maharaja Kharak Singh, and grandson, Nau Nihal Singh [together, 43], plus the former's consort, Maharani Chand Kaur [45, on balcony], and his principal adviser Chait Singh [44]. As the fourth maharaja in as many years, Sher Singh [45] fared no better. Despite his jewelled accoutrements [including the Koh-i-Nur diamond on his arm, 46] he was massacred on the same day as Dhyan Singh [45].

47

48

Gardner's hour of glory came in 1841 when he and his gunners repelled an attack on Lahore's fort-cum-palace [47] by the about-to-be-maharaja, Sher Singh.

The 1859 albumen print [48] shows the palm trees of the Hazuri Bagh courtyard, where the action took place, with the minarets of the Badshahi mosque in the background.

The location of the Lahore Fort in the north-west corner of the walled city is well shown in a wood-work model [49] which was destined for pride of place, along with the Koh-i-Nur diamond, at the 1851 Great Exhibition in London.

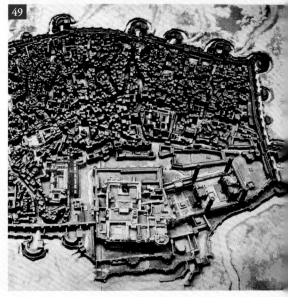

49

50

In 1843, after a two-year reign, Maharaja Sher Singh was slain by the Sindhanwalia *sirdar*s, notably Ajit Singh and Lehna Singh [51]. They appear here with the five-year-old Duleep Singh, supposedly a product of the great Ranjit Singh's final years, whom they recognised as maharaja.

The Sindhanwalias were soon eliminated by Hira Singh and his Brahmin adviser, Pandit Jalla [52]. But Hira Singh, welcoming the prospect of a long minority, also recognised the young maharaja.

This opened the way for an unsteady regime in which the queen-mother, the outrageous Maharani Jind Kaur [50], acted as regent, with her brother Jowahir Singh as *vizier* [53], here in conversation with the surviving Dogra, Gulab Singh, who was biding his time. Gardner, during these critical last months of the Sikh Empire, found himself heavily compromised by serving each of these contestants in turn.

51

52

53

54

55

Five years of king-making intrigue and unprecedented blood-letting emboldened the rank-and-file of the Sikh army to take matters into their own hands. Guarding the Lahore armoury [54] with its curious assortment of medieval chain-armour and modern rifles was often Gardner's task. Meanwhile, the maharani and her courtiers, notably Vizier Lal Singh [55] and Commander-in-Chief Tej Singh [56, with his son and nephew], were suspected of inviting the British to intervene and so destroy the mutinous army.

56

NAHUNG.

After the 1844 assassination of Jowahir Singh, Gardner claims to have gone to ground as an Akali Nihang. The most fearsome and fanatical of Sikh irregulars, the Akalis rode into battle with assorted weapons [57] that might include razor-sharp discs strung on their turbans or even a bow and arrows [59].

Regular troopers of General Allard's cavalry carried a lance and pennant [58], while the infantry trained by General Ventura wore a uniform like that of the British sepoys [60]. Officers took pride in magnificently wrought swords, like that [61] of Colonel Francois Henri Mouton, Lal Singh's tactical adviser during the First Anglo-Sikh War.

62

In the First Anglo-Sikh War, the Sikh guns proved superior to those of the British in both calibre and marksmanship [61]. Gardner had commanded several batteries but claimed to have taken no part in the war. Instead he served as effectively 'governor of Lahore', where the only other remaining foreigner was Martin Honigberger [64], a Transylvanian doctor. Provocative statements by the bespectacled Captain George Broadfoot [63] provoked the conflict, in which Broadfoot himself was an early casualty.

63

64

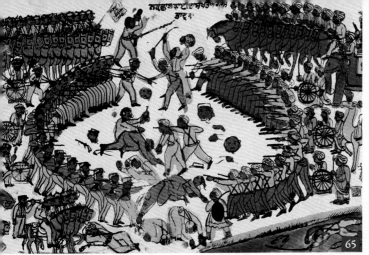

The First Anglo-Sikh War (1845–6) began with a modest battle at Mudki [66] and ended with a catastrophic Sikh defeat at Sobraon [67]. In between, the most ferocious fighting [65] was during the indecisive encounter at Ferozeshah. In the second war (1848–9), the British tasted defeat at Chillianwalla [68] but finally triumphed at Gujrat.

69

70

71

Though seriously compromised, Gardner was the only foreigner in Lahore to weather the transition from Sikh to British rule. For this, as for his subsequent dismissal, he was indebted to the later Sir Henry Lawrence [69], who with a dedicated band of disciples, including his brother George [70, standing] and his later biographer Herbert Edwardes

72

(sitting), would oversee the administration of the Punjab until John Lawrence, another brother [71], took over.

On the entablature of the 'Lawrence Testimonial', a massive silver candelabrum paid for by public subscription [72], Sir Henry and Maharaja Duleep Singh are seen presiding over a post-war demobilisation of Sikh troops [74]. Already Sikh, Dogra and British troops were campaigning side by side, most notably in Kashmir to remove its defiant governor, Sheikh Imam-ud-din [73].

75

Expelled from Lahore in 1847, Gardner prospered in British India as a saltpetre contractor but was recalled by Gulab Singh, now ruler of Kashmir, to command the state's artillery. He remained in the Kashmir service for the rest of his days, mostly under Maharaja Ranbir Singh [75, in durbar] who inherited his father's throne, along with the sumptuous state barge [76], in 1857.

76

77

As a local celebrity with a fund of improbable memories, the old colonel in the tartan turban was much sought after by visitors to Kashmir. They included the American Charley Longfellow, son of the poet, and the English artist George Landseer, nephew of Sir Edwin Landseer. As well as taking Gardner's portrait, Landseer captured the charm of Kashmir in river scenes [77] and al fresco tableaux in the mountains [78].

78

79

606

Entertainments in Kashmir, whether
in the Shalimar Gardens [79] or more
privately [80], included performances
by the Valley's renowned nautch-
girls in which the colonel himself
sometimes joined. In 1864, the Simla
photographer Samuel Bourne captured
him in informal mode with Dogra
artillerymen [82], with two Sikh
bodyguards being in attendance [81].

81

80

3190

82

84

This photo of Gardner [83] was found in an album of photrographs dated 1870–72 containing scenes in Kashmir and a portrait of Sir Henry Durand [4]. The two men met in 1870. Durand was so intrigued by this 'soldier of an olden time' that he immediately published the first connected account of Gardner's life-story.

After one last improbable venture—gun-running into Xinjiang—the colonel died in Jammu in 1877.

He was buried in the graveyard of the church of the Holy Trinity in Sialkot [84], the nearest consecrated ground, and this despite his having lived much of his life as a Muslim and been highly critical of Christian 'missionizing'.

Having failed in two attempts to realise her father's fortune, Helena Botha née Gardner died in Dublin in 1947. Her tombstone is in the city's Deansgrange cemetery [85]. The epitaph reads:

IN LOVING MEMORY
HELENA HOUGHTON CAMPBELL BOTHA
Daughter of
COLONEL ALEXANDER GARDNER
Born in Kashmir
Died in Dublin
January 19th 1947

Overleaf This pastel portrait of Colonel Alexander Gardner by George Landseer was thought to have been lost. It was drawn in the 1860s, exhibited in London in 1876 and rediscovered in 2011.

85

Nose and Ears of the Misser should be cut off'. He had till 'the first quarter of the day, or 9 o'clock am, had struck' to see the sentence conducted; if by then it had not been carried out, both he and Jiwan Singh would 'suffer like punishment or even death'.

✳

As day broke, the critical, not to say chaotic, nature of the situation became ever more apparent. Gardner was not unprepared. Over the years many other distasteful tasks had come his way. In Turkestan he had robbed his enemies and then sold them into slavery. In Afghanistan he had all too often killed them with only his word that he did so 'in self-defence'. He had certainly been a party to the murder of Chait Singh (Maharaja Kharak Singh's associate). He had also taken unseemly pride in parading around sundry decapitated heads. No one who had spent most of the past fourteen years in the service of either Dhyan Singh or Gulab Singh could claim to be other than steeped in blood. 'Disgustful deeds' came with the job; they were seldom optional and never predictable.

From the wretched Jodha Ram he might have little to fear, but from Jowahir Singh, Jiwan Singh and their associates he had excellent reason to suppose his life was in real danger. The officer charged with seeing he carried out the sentence confided in him that he was also charged with ensuring he never left the chabutra alive if he failed. Nor was it only Gardner's life that was at risk; his men were also in danger. And not just from Jowahir Singh and his associates; for while the latter might be determined that the sentence be executed, Jodha Ram's supporters were determined to prevent anything of the kind. These included a mob of fellow Brahmins, all with drawn swords, and a growing number of Sikhs from Jodha Ram's/Avitabile's brigade. As all mounted the chabutra, a pitched battle looked just as likely as a swift amputation.

We were in all about 350, which the crowds of armed Brahmins and Sikhs against us far exceeded ... [This] was sufficient to cause the *kotwal* to turn as pale as a sheet and he even became stupid and half paralysed

through fear, and it was really on this account that a great and most
injurious delay was occasioned in procuring a Barber to execute the deed.

Barbers were possessed of razors and reckoned the most adept at
wielding them. Lahore being a Sikh kingdom where shaving was
frowned on and haircuts forbidden, they may also have welcomed
the work. Whether they also had scruples about mutilating a twice-
born Brahmin, Gardner does not say. Yet one barber was no sooner
procured than he was 'lost in a scuffle'. His replacement then 'actually
fainted and became utterly senseless through fear of being himself
murdered'. And by the time a third appeared, it was the kotwal who
was so 'disenabled' by fear of the consequences that he couldn't bring
himself to issue the order.

Barber No 3 got started regardless. But he had proceeded no
further than shaving the relevant areas of Jodha Ram's head when 'a
terrible crush was made by the armed multitude on all sides; swords
were drawn in every direction and the ranks of our two Companies
were actually broken'. It was at this point that Jowahir Singh's trusty
troopers raised their guns and levelled them, four pointing at Gardner
and Jodha Ram and two at the kotwal.

> Another half moment would have decided [the matter], at least for
> us, had I not myself (for I cannot, nor would I, deny telling the truth
> to save my own as [well as] the lives of perhaps many that day), drew
> my sword and took hold of the barber's hand. With the razor in his
> trembling hands we managed between us to effect the purpose as well
> or as quickly as possible.... In two moments more, myself as well as
> two or three more Servants of Jowahir Singh were on our Horses and
> had to make our way with the assistance of about fifty Bayonets out of
> the multitude, who now seemed as if panic Struck or requiring time
> to form a resolute push.

The deed was done; and under the circumstances he had taken the
only possible option. 'Pray, would it not be too intrusive [to ask],'
he begged, surely of Lawrence rather than Smyth, 'what would or
should be the proper part I should have acted on that occasion or

emergency?' He disputed the claim that he had done what no Hindu, Muslim or Sikh would do; that was rubbish. So was the claim that he had been made a colonel for his services; 'instead of gaining anything I consider I have lost everything by it'. He knew those responsible well enough to believe that they would indeed cut him down, and in particular he blamed Jiwan Singh for organising the whole affair and representing him to Jowahir Singh 'as a great desperado'. In the end it was either Gardner's neck or the ears, nose and fingers of Jodha Ram. As he put it in the last sentence of the Defence, there was nothing else he could have done.

> I had only the choice left me of keeping quiet and losing my life or act the part I did and lose my character with the World. But surely there must be thinking men, who will judge and think before they speak.

So far as is known, Gardner's version of events as given in the Defence document was never contested. No doubt he had heightened the drama and exaggerated the danger. He particularly resented the accusations that he had acted 'in cold blood' and been rewarded for his services. But all this was beside the point. He had accepted responsibility and that was enough to justify his removal under the Punjab's new dispensation. He could expect no mercy from an administration which, though still headed by Jowahir Singh's young nephew, was directed by paragons of British rule who deemed him a traitor to the moral principles and racial conceits they held so sacred. The 'thinking men', if there were any, stayed silent. Gardner was stripped of his rank, deprived of his jagir and given twenty-four hours to leave the kingdom.

He went only as far as Ludhiana. Disgraced by the British, if not technically dismissed by them, he crossed the Satluj to the nearest place in directly administered British territory. There he was neither charged as a former deserter from the Company's ranks, which he certainly would have been if there had been any official suspicions on that score, nor much troubled by the stigma of the Jodha Ram affair. According to editor Pearse, who gives no hint of the affair and whose resumé of the remainder of Gardner's life is little more than notes, he 'occupied his leisure by giving to Colonel Carmichael Smyth the information which the latter embodied in a work entitled *The History of the Reigning Family of Lahore*'. In fact, by April 1847 it may have been too late to make any further additions to Smyth's 'curious and little known work'; it was published in the same year.

It was also very nearly too late for Lahore's reigning family. In November 1847 Rani Jindan was packed off into exile. Then in April 1848 that slow-burning rebellion against both the British and Lahore's complicit durbar which the history books call the Second Anglo-Sikh War broke out in Multan. This time the war was fought largely in the western Punjab but spread up the Indus to Peshawar, Rawalpindi and the Hazara hills. In a battle of heavy casualties the British came off badly at Chillianwalla but in another they won convincingly at Gujrat.

It was all over by early 1849—all over in terms of the fighting and all over for the kingdom of Lahore. The regency was wound up; young Duleep Singh was packed off into exile, having been deposed without ever having been enthroned; the Koh-i-nur diamond, of which Ranjit Singh had earlier deprived Shah Shuja, was forfeited to Queen Victoria: and what remained of Ranjit Singh's great kingdom was absorbed into directly administered British India. The last of India's native empires was no more. Had the Jodha Ram affair never come to light, Gardner would have been out of a job anyway.

But seldom job-less for long, in reality he seems to have embarked on two new ventures almost simultaneously. Soon after reaching Ludhiana, 'he was permitted to enter the service of Gulab Singh, now created an independent sovereign as Maharaja of Jammu and Kashmir'. 'Permission' was required because of that clause in the Amritsar Treaty obliging the Kashmir maharaja not to employ any European or American without obtaining British authorisation. Such clearance was normally refused, yet for Gardner it was evidently forthcoming. Far from being under a cloud, he seems to have retained the regard of John Lawrence, if not of Henry, both of the brothers being on the three-man Board of Administration which had taken over the running of the Punjab.

Grey and Garrett tell a slightly different story. They confess to not knowing what became of Gardner after 1847 but suppose he re-entered Gulab Singh's service 'probably in 1851'. In that year Henry Steinbach, a Prussian officer who had been in and out of Sikh service since 1836 and had since commanded 'a couple of battalions and some guns' for Gulab Singh of Kashmir, resigned in a fit of pique and was reportedly succeeded by Gardner. Gardner was certainly in Srinagar in 1853. It was then that his 'kenspeckle' figure heading the Kashmir troops at the maharaja's weekly parade was noticed by two young Scottish officers, the first in what would become a notable succession of British visitors intrigued by the man in the tartan turban.

Such sightings apart, his movements during the decade 1847–57 are indeed shrouded in uncertainty. A possible clue was unearthed by Grey and Garrett. Beneath the great dome of the Anarkali Tomb, where the Lawrence administration had originally set up shop and where the Punjab Records were now housed, those two archival terriers came upon a letter from something called the 'Indus Commercial Establishment'. Assuming they copied it correctly, the letter was dated 'Multan, 5ᵗʰ October, 1850' and signed 'A. Gardiner'. (Grey and Garrett use both the Gardner and the Gardiner spelling.)

> I most respectfully beg to state [read the section of the letter they transcribed] that being a native of Philadelphia, the capital of Pennsylvania, in the U.S. of America, I must consequently consider myself an American citizen. I have paid out large sums of money in erecting saltpetre works, and propose leaving here in 30 days to establish myself permanently at Bombay.

Though too concise to be other than an edited extract, there can be little doubt that this letter was indeed from the colonel. Multan, in the extreme south of the Punjab, was now of course British, and circumstantial evidence places Gardner there. A propos of slave-dealers in the Hindu Kush, for instance, the *Memoirs* include a 'Note by Colonel Gardner', the delightfully inconsequential nature of which argues in favour of its authenticity.

I subsequently knew at Mooltan a most respectable Lohani fruit merchant who was proved by his own ledger to have exchanged a female
slave-girl for three ponies and seven long-haired, red-eyed cats, all of
which he disposed of, no doubt to advantage, to the English gentlemen
at that station.

If there were 'English gentlemen' in Multan at the time, this cannot
have been earlier than the Second Anglo-Sikh War and was probably
after it. The new British Board of Administration in Lahore had by
then appointed a district commissioner in Multan, he being none
other than Michael Pakenham Edgeworth. One of John Lawrence's
dedicated 'young men', Edgeworth was also the man responsible for
publishing the first somewhat garbled abstract of Gardner's travels.
According to Edgeworth's journal now in The Bodleian Library,
Oxford, the colonel's notes on which the abstract was based (minus
'two volumes' lent to Burnes) had been entrusted to Edgeworth in
Multan, probably in October 1851. Clumsily edited, they appeared
two years later in the much respected *Journal of the Asiatic Society
of Bengal*.

Grey and Garrett failed to make this connection with Edgeworth's
presence in Multan, let alone with the red-eyed cats. They contented
themselves simply with noting that the letter's mention of Gardner
being a native of Philadelphia 'puts another nail in the coffin of the
mysterious birthplace "on the shores of Lake Superior"'. Subsequently,
however, on Gardner's own admission, Philadelphia had been the
home of his uncle and younger brother. Since the purpose of the saltpetre letter was simply to clear his position as a non-British resident
with the British authorities, he presumably offered 'Philadelphia' as
a more convincing place of birth than some nameless township on
the Great Lakes which he had left at the age of five.

Whether Gardner in 1850 made good on his expressed intention of
establishing himself in Bombay is not known. If he did, it must have
been less than 'permanently' since he is supposed to have succeeded
Steinbach in Kashmir the following year.

More revealing is the letter's mention of that investment in the
saltpetre business. Saltpetre, or potassium nitrate, is obtained from

salty encrustations of guano nitrates and is an essential ingredient in gunpowder. India had been supplying the British munitions industry with this ammonia-reeking substance since at least the mid-eighteenth century, and because its weight and bulk meant it was best moved by boat, the Gangetic regions of Bengal and Bihar had been the main source. Gardner reasoned that what was so profitably moved by barge down the Ganges could also be profitably moved down the Indus. Admittedly the unpleasant business of saltpetre extraction was a far cry from the sparkle of rubies and diamonds that had previously haunted his imagination. But it drew on his combination of mineralogical training gained in Russia and gunnery experience in the Punjab and it was surely an agreeable change from being at the beck and call of a vindictive durbar.

Grey and Garrett assert that he had originally headed for the southern Punjab to buy up 'a number of unserviceable cannon balls from the munitions captured by the British during the last Sikh War'. Multan, the much-besieged city where that war had started, offered any recycler of military materials rich pickings. Hence, in the least likely of his many avatars, Gardner had set up as a munitions contractor and established the 'Indus Commercial Establishment', or I.C.E., an acronym that wishfully defied Multan's reputation as one of the hottest places on earth.

The potential of saltpetre seems soon to have side-lined the attractions of recycling cannonballs; but in either case considerable investment was called for. A government license was needed for salvaging projectiles and a government lease for scraping up saltpetre deposits. However much the colonel's reputation may have suffered in Lahore, and however meagre his final salary there, at least some of the wealth accumulated during his long years of service was evidently intact and was now put to good use.

Moreover the saltpetre business prospered. A subsidiary of I.C.E. trading as 'Messrs A. Gardner and Co' is credited with having shown the government 'how a large revenue might be raised from lands seemingly worthless, and [from] a source that had been neglected'. In May 1855 a long report on the 'Mode of Manufacturing Saltpetre in the Punjab' appeared in *The Lahore Chronicle*. Submitted by Donald

McLeod, the Punjab Governing Board's financial commissioner, it
was datelined Multan, signed by 'A. Gardener' and amply authenticated by his usual disregard for syntax. Much of it is technical. The
best deposits are to be found in the vicinity of ancient settlements,
and the collection and processing (by boiling and leaching the saline
desert crust) is described as arduous and labour-intensive. At the time
Gardner reckoned that about 3000 families were involved in the Punjab's 6–700 saltpetre 'factories'; and of these about a hundred were
operated by A. Gardner and Co., mostly in and around Multan and
in neighbouring Sind. Since, as well as leasing the saltpetre fields, the
contractor had to pay advances to his workforce, Gardner reckoned
his investment in what he calls a 'permanently sinking or sunken
fund' ran to 'about 20,000 rupees'. That was nearly three times his
annual income as a colonel in the service of the Sikhs. The industry
had enormous potential, he believed; but it needed more government
support in the form of longer leases and better arrangements for
shipping the stuff onward to Karachi and Bombay.

Five years after this report in *The Lahore Chronicle*, another appeared in the *Bombay Times*. 'Mr A Gardner, who was formerly, for
many years, in the Seik service,' still held the leases to all the saltpetre
deposits in Multan and neighbouring districts. 'It was he who first
commenced the manufacture of the article some eight years ago [so
in 1852]' and thanks in large part to an unexpected bonanza, his
business was now 'yielding a clear profit of 75 per cent'. The bonanza
could well have resulted from the demand for gunpowder created by
the 1857 Indian Mutiny/First War of Independence; but the *Bombay
Times* credited it to the Crimean War, during which 'the price of the
article rose enormously, one hundred per cent above its ordinary value'.

Impeccable timing and a strong gambling instinct look to have
paid off. Gardner had struck lucky just when his fortunes were at their
lowest ebb. The nest egg that would pay Helena Botha's annuity and
be reckoned at one million sterling may not have come entirely from
the glittering troves that once filled the Lahore treasury. It may have
originated in the stench that issued from the open-air encampments
of Multan's saltpetre farmers.

No further reports on the Punjab's saltpetre industry have come to light. During the summer months, A. Gardner and Co. must anyway have managed without A. Gardner; officers serving the Maharaja of Jammu and Kashmir were expected to be in Kashmir during the 'season'. Moonlighting in Multan would have been possible only during the winter months, when the Kashmir court was in Jammu. Presumably Gardner got out of I.C.E.—or I.C.E. got out of the saltpetre business—in the early 1860s when the going was good.

One cannot but wonder, though, about his returning to Kashmir at the behest of Gulab Singh. Why, one might ask, would a successful saltpetre contractor who was now near, if not well past, retirement age have chosen to spend his remaining years in the service of the scheming tyrant whom he feared above all others? 'Ambitious, avaricious, and cruel by nature,' Gulab Singh, says Carmichael Smyth on Gardner's authority, 'exercised the most ruthless barbarities, not in the heat of conflict or the flush of victory only, nor in the rage of an offended sovereign against rebellious subjects; he deliberately committed the most horrible atrocities for the purpose of investing his name with a terror that should keep down all thoughts of resistance to his cruel sway'.

But equally, why would such a monster want the services of a tarnished commandant whose days of active service were over and who was on record as calling the said monster's character 'the most repulsive it is possible to imagine'? If Gardner's relationship with Henry Lawrence was surprising, that with Gulab Singh verged on the sadistic. Yet as events continued to show, each man harboured a degree of respect for the other. Gardner conceded that Gulab Singh's calculating nature made him 'the very best of soldiers' and Gulab Singh, like Lawrence, reckoned Gardner a useful man to have at one's side.

By now, 1860, Gardner was either 80 years old (as per his original date of birth in the Sialkot parish register), 75 (as per Cooper and Pearse) or 59 (as per the amended entry in the Sialkot register). Carrying the scars of fifteen wounds and unable even to drink without his forceps, he might reasonably have repaired to some British hill-station and got on with the 'large and compleat work', presumably his life-story, that he had mentioned to Lawrence in 1846. He owed

Gulab Singh nothing and he had known Kashmir only when it was ravaged by cholera, as during his first short visit in 1828, or when terrorised by troops, as during his second in 1846.

Martin Honigberger, his Transylvanian doctor-friend in Lahore, had also toyed with the idea of offering his services to Gulab Singh in Kashmir. He had subsequently opted for Dehra Dun in British territory and for the company of the considerable family he had already established there. Gardner may well have been tempted to follow him. In the absence of any further mention of his own wife—she who had been given him out of Dhyan Singh's household—it does not appear that she accompanied him on his precipitate exodus from Lahore, nor is she ever heard of again. In Kashmir, as in Lahore, his new assignment would mean a new ménage.

Pearse says Gardner was given command of one of Gulab Singh's infantry regiments and all the Kashmir artillery. His salary was '500 rupees per month' plus 'the revenues of some villages bestowed upon him by the Maharajah'. As a result he lived in considerable style 'after the native fashion' and enjoyed 'a comfortable income' for his remaining years'. Nothing is said of his involvement, or of his whereabouts, during the imminent Indian Mutiny/Great Rebellion of 1857, but this is not surprising. The conflagration barely affected Kashmir. Gulab Singh remained loyal to his British sponsors and Gardner's saltpetre business was probably reaping its own reward.

Four years earlier in 1853, two identical twin brothers, Thomas and John Gordon from north-east Scotland, both of whom would become Indian army generals, had cast their eyes over the maharaja's infantry and artillery during a visit to Srinagar. They were impressed.

[The troops were] under the instructional command of Colonel Gardner, a military adventurer who had made his way into the Punjab from Central Asia in 1831 and entered the service of Runjit Singh in 1832 as colonel of artillery... We saw him head the troops at the Maharajah's weekly review, held after the manner of the 'Salamlik' parade at Constantinople.

Yet two years later, in 1855, Gardner had been back in Multan where, in between writing that letter to Mcleod in Lahore about the saltpetre business, he had again pressed his travel notes as previously loaned to Edgeworth on a new acquaintance. This was Henry George Raverty. An army officer who had fought in the Second Anglo-Sikh War, Raverty was in the process of learning Pushtu and would eventually produce a compendious work on Afghanistan. Gardner hoped that such an authority might be able to improve on Edgeworth's garbled editing of the travels as published in the *Journal of the Asiatic Society of Bengal*. But Raverty had had time to 'only glance' at Gardner's jottings. 'Some things struck me as being rather marvellous,' he later recalled, 'and there were 'some errors'. But considering that the pages he saw had largely been reconstructed from memory, the originals having perished with Burnes, errors were to be expected. Raverty recommended that the travel notes be re-examined in the light of his own forthcoming publication and 'their accuracy tested'.

Much the same thought would soon occur to other Central Asian authorities. The jury was still out on Gardner's improbable itineraries of the 1820s. After thirty years of well authenticated service in the Punjab and now Kashmir, a big question mark remained over his origins and his previous exploits. Claims and counter-claims as to whether he was who he said he was, and had been where he said he had been, would ricochet around him for the remaining years of his long life.

II

Last Words
1860–77

To Gardner's relief, Kashmir's greatest loss during India's Mutiny/ Great Rebellion proved to be Maharaja Gulab Singh. He died of natural causes—something of a record for one of the dreaded Dogras—in 1858, having already handed over the reins of power to Ranbir Singh, his only surviving son. It may well have been this transition that persuaded Gardner to withdraw from the saltpetre business. The new maharaja, out of respect for his father, retained Gardner's services and confirmed his salary and jagirs. An affable autocrat of scholarly tastes and only mildly sinister ambitions, Ranbir Singh posed no threat to his commandant of artillery. He regarded the old colonel more as a mascot than a general and was happy to indulge his eccentricities of dress and behaviour. Gardner responded with a sometimes embarrassing loyalty. Multan was losing whatever appeal it ever had. Kashmir was now his home; retaining a bolt-hole in British India was no longer necessary.

By the 1860s, with the Mutiny quelled and the scapegoat that was the East India Company blown away with it, India eased into the long dog days of the Raj. Wars gave way to 'expeditions'. There would be no mobilisation comparable to that for the Afghan War or the two Sikh Wars until the World Wars of the twentieth century. Nor, as had happened prior to the Mutiny, would trouble be invited by annexing native states on the flimsiest of pretexts. Considerably more of India was now under direct British rule than wasn't. The surviving princely states (including Kashmir and the few Sikh statelets south of the Satluj) could be left unmolested, like tousled stands of natural woodland among well-ploughed fields. Britannia rested content with her imperial estate. It remained only to assess its extent, realise its productive potential and ensure its defence.

Steam locomotives—Gardner called them 'smoke-breathing hors-es' in one of his epistles—began to chug along the new tracks being laid from Calcutta and Bombay up to Delhi and Lahore. Surveyors had already triangulated their way across the plains and were now pushing their map-making on into Kashmir and the mountains. Telegraph wires followed. The empire was being consolidated, communications improved, frontiers defined and demarcated. The contentious Durand Line between India (later Pakistan) and Afghanistan would be the work of Mortimer Durand, son of the Sir Henry Durand to whom Gardner was about to confide one version of his life-story. Another of Durand's sons, Algernon, would be despatched to Gilgit on Kashmir's northern frontier. A definition of Kashmir/Ladakh's eastern frontier with Tibet had already been attempted by Alexander Cunningham, brother of the now deceased historian of the Sikhs and himself the founder of the Archaeological Survey of India.

Kashmir's frontiers were of particular concern. Quite apart from their importance to arm-chair strategists directing the Anglo-Rus-sian shadow-boxing known as 'The Great Game', the temptation of scrambling across these frontiers into the 'forbidden' lands of Tibet and Turkestan was proving irresistible to trophy-bagging sportsmen and publicity-conscious explorers. A generation earlier the adoption of Simla as India's summer capital had introduced heat-crazed Britons to the delights of the mountains. Now Kashmir was seducing them with more mountains, better shooting, cheaper shopping and less official supervision, not to mention lotus-filled lakes, punt-able riv-ers and golf-ready swards. As of 1860 the Valley and its hills became the Raj's pre-eminent playground. Here the White Man could put down his burden, revert to what Kipling called his 'childish ways' and have a bit of fun.

There was not even a permanent British official in Kashmir to police the holiday-makers' activities. The Amritsar Treaty had contained no provision for a British Resident, and successive maharajas would stoutly resist all requests to admit one. Instead, a civilian of no great distinction was despatched to Srinagar every summer. Sometimes known as the commissioner, his job was merely 'to act as referee between the large body of English visitors and the subjects of His Highness the reigning Maharaja'.

It was in this role that Frederick Cooper, the career-blighted 'butcher of Amritsar', came to Srinagar in 1864. Hearing tell of Ranbir Singh's only foreign commandant, Cooper issued his invitation and the tartan-clad Gardner duly presented himself. A Captain Segrave was on hand to record the event.

> I can perfectly recollect my first interview with him. He walked into Cooper's reception room one morning, a most peculiar and striking appearance, clothed from head to foot in the 79th tartan but fashioned by a native tailor. Even his *pagri* [turban] was of tartan, and it was adorned with an egret's plume, only allowed to persons of high rank. I imagine he lived entirely in native fashion; he was said to be wealthy, and the owner of many villages.

With this apparition Cooper arranged a series of interviews. From the notes which resulted, some of which Gardner approved, and from other notes prepared by Gardner himself, Cooper began reconstructing his life-story. This unfinished work, like the notes on which it was based, is now lost; but thirty years later, both the notes and Cooper's draft were indeed extant and it was on them that Pearse would substantially base the colonel's *Memoirs*.

It may also be significant that Gardner's meeting with Cooper was the first occasion on which he is described as wearing tartan. The Scottish Gordon brothers, who would surely have picked up on it when they watched him take the salute in 1853, have nothing to say on the matter, nor had the outfit been previously mentioned by Lawrence, Edwardes or anyone in the Punjab. Since the 79th Highlanders—or more correctly the 79th Cameron Highlanders—had not served in the Anglo-Sikh Wars or anywhere else in India at the time, this is not surprising.

But the 79th had been sent post haste to India when the Mutiny/ Great Rebellion broke out. Reaching Calcutta in November 1857, the regiment was in the thick of the action at Allahabad, Cawnpore (Kanpur) and Lucknow in 1858 and then spent three years in the Punjab and on the North-west Frontier. There the regimental summer quarters were at Murree and Abbottabad, astride the main bridle-path to Kashmir. It must thus have been in around 1860–2 that bolts of the regiment's distinctive tartan began finding their way onto the shelves of Srinagar's bespoke tailors and from there to the cutting table and the colonel's wardrobe.

In the same year of 1864 when Gardner met Cooper, he came to the attention of Owen Tudor Burne. Burne accompanied Sir Hugh Rose, the then commander-in-chief in India, as his military secretary during a winter visit to Kashmir. The maharaja's officials were deeply suspicious of the visit. They supposed the commander-in-chief's presence meant that the British were preparing an invasion. In fact Rose and Burne were more interested in Kashmir's deer-stalking; thirty years later Burne would claim that he could remember every hillside. In his published *Memories* he would make no mention of Gardner. Yet he clearly spent some time in his company since in another context he would claim a close acquaintance and deliver the most fulsome and unexpected of endorsements.

Also in Kashmir in 1864 was Alexander Hill Gray, a roving observer with an obsession about Tibet. As a keen practitioner in the new art of photography, Gray had encumbered his Himalayan travels with boxes of fragile glass plates and the latest in the way of gigantic cameras. It is known that Samuel Bourne of the leading Simla photographers Bourne and Shepherd photographed Gardner on at least two occasions in 1864, but it could equally have been Gray who was responsible for the most famous image of the colonel. The photo, which would serve as the frontispiece of the *Memoirs*, certainly dated from about this time because Cooper expressed regret that it failed to do justice to the colonel's animated delivery—to 'the vivacity of expression, the play of feature, the humour of the mouth, and the energy of character portrayed by the whole aspect of the man as he described the arduous and terrible incidents of a long life of romance and vicissitude'.

By an odd coincidence Alexander Hill Gray was a former pupil of Stonyhurst College, the Jesuit establishment in Lancashire to which the fathers of Clongowes had turned when the Society of Jesus was proscribed in Ireland. Though Gardner seems not to have been aware of the connection, he shared Gray's sartorial tastes and in particular he coveted the cut of Gray's shooting jacket. No doubt he reasoned that what worked so well in tweed could only be improved in tartan. As recorded in *Sixty Years Ago*, the title of Gray's disastrously condensed account of his own half-forgotten 'wanderings', the meeting of the two men is notable for containing Gardner's only admission, outside the 'Defence' document, of the Jodha Ram affair.

A man who called upon me in Srinagar, living not far from me, [wrote Gray] was undoubtedly the most singular character I ever met with, a Colonel in the Rajah of Cashmere's Army; and of perhaps sixty years of age. It was to a plaided Norfolk jacket (made especially for the Himalayas) to which he had taken a fancy, that I was indebted for the acquaintance of Colonel Gardner, who made known to me some parts of his most extraordinary life. Of American extraction, he with two other adventurers had offered their services to more than one princeling in Central Asia, before entering the service of Runjeet Singh, the King of the Punjaub...

Any one who has read the history of this Prince must have remarked that a favourite brutality of his was ordering a prisoner's nose to be cut off. A Brahmin prisoner was brought before him on one occasion, and knowing the dread the Hindoos possess of being punished in the next world for any injury done to a Brahmin in this, Runjeet Singh asked in open court if there was no one among his courtiers (who were Hindoos) ready to cut off this man's nose? Whereupon Colonel Gardner, as he himself told me, immediately offered to do what was wanted, and with his sword cut off the Brahmin's nose on the spot.

On another occasion, says Gray, Gardner had volunteered to capture
'some Rajah in the Himalaya' who was in arrears with his tribute. It
was a tricky assignment and one for which Gardner stipulated that,
if successful, he be allowed to 'marry the captive Rajah's daughter'.

> Runjeet Singh consented and the Colonel informed me that the girl
> duly became 'one of his wives'! He bade me warn the officers who were
> at that time 'doing' Kashmir not to break into his abode as he kept a
> ferocious dog that was dangerous (his seven wives were there)!

> Of course during these years Gardner passed as a Mussulman and used
> to carry a Koran on his breast. When narrating to me his extraordinary
> life, I ventured to ask him if he would re-embrace Christianity again,
> but he put me off by muttering something like 'Oh, I don't know.'

> This remarkable man had, as he himself says, 'a maggot in his brain'—
> even when I met him in 1864 when he was 79 years of age.

Gray must himself have been at least 80 when he wrote his *Sixty
Years Ago*; and if Gardner's memory could occasionally play him
false, then so could Gray's. In the space of a few short paragraphs,
the colonel's 'perhaps sixty years of age' at the time of their meeting
had become '79 years of age'. Gray had also confused Ranjit Singh
with Jowahir Singh in the nose-cutting affair, he had wrongly supposed Ranjit Singh's courtiers were all 'Hindoos', and in respect of
the recalcitrant hill rajah's daughter, he had somehow mistaken the
dashing but unfortunate Prince Habib-ulla Khan of Afghanistan for
'the one-eyed mouse' who so successfully ruled the Punjab for forty
years. Surprisingly Gray acknowledges Pearse's *Memoirs*, although
he clearly didn't read them closely. The man with 'a maggot in his
brain' is borrowed from Pearse, as probably is the '79 years of age'.
But as the photograph suggests, his original 'perhaps sixty years of
age' is perfectly understandable. Guessing the age of a man who was
habitually enveloped in tartan, topped with a turban and obscured
by an abundance of whiskers can never have been easy.

While in Kashmir, Gray had an unlikely competitor in the por-

traiture business. This was the 30-year old George Landseer, nephew
of Queen Victoria's favourite painter, Sir Edwin Landseer. Trading
on this family connection, the younger Landseer had already exhibited at the Royal Academy, and it was possibly as a stand-in for his
uncle that he had followed the trail to India beaten by earlier com-
mission-hungry artists like the Daniells, Zoffany and Chinnery. He
arrived immediately after the Mutiny and, like the 79th Highlanders,
reached Kashmir in the early 1860s.

When Gray met him, Landseer was busy with a series of portraits
of Maharaja Ranbir Singh. The two men nevertheless found time to
swap sporting trophies, with Gray offering 'a specimen of the rare
Markhor' and Landseer responding with a set of antlers shed by a
barasingha ('twelve-pointed' stag), Kashmir's very own 'monarch of
the glen'. Nothing is said of Landseer having painted Gardner; presumably the commission had not yet materialised. But the colonel's
portrait did feature in Landseer's Bond Street exhibition of 1876 and
would be described by the *Art Journal* as 'remarkably striking'. The
whiskers are here much whiter and woollier than in the photographs
and the eyes sadder. His turban lacks its egret-plumed *kalgi*, and his
age is as hard to guess as ever.

A notable feature of all these encounters is that, while happy to
accept British hospitality, Gardner appears not to have repaid it.
Living in native style, whether in Srinagar or Jammu, he guarded
the privacy of his domestic arrangements and actively discouraged
visitors. Even the whereabouts of his residences were not generally
known. The guard dog and the numerous 'wives' and retainers emerge
from what he himself vouchsafed, not from first-hand observation.

In 1865 an added reason for this reclusive behaviour may have
been the impending arrival of the baby Helena. Whatever his age,
the colonel now had the time to take any parental responsibilities
seriously. Bibi Kali was 'his favourite wife' and it was she who gave
birth in that year. Precisely when is unclear. The date of birth given
on Helena's later baptismal certificate is 15 November 1865. Yet in
May of that year Gardner had written seeking medical advice for 'his
infant' from the Reverend William Jackson Elmslie, a missionary
physician who had opened Kashmir's first dispensary. Either the

advice was being sought for an embryo, or the baptismal clerk had made a mistake, or Helena had had at least one older sibling who did not survive.

Elmslie worked for the Church Missionary Society, with whom Gardner had already had a run-in. In the previous July the evangelising Rev Robert Clark of the CMS had made his first Kashmiri convert. The news, along with Clark's insistence on permanently residing in the heart of the city, had provoked widespread protests from the Muslim population. Cooper, and then his stand-in as referee between the British community and the maharaja, became involved. The maharaja, however, preferred to use Gardner's good offices. It was thus the colonel who was given the task of informing Clark that he must leave the Valley. The maharaja's government, Clark was told, 'would have nothing whatever of Christianity in Cashmere'. Clark left; Elmslie stayed on.

Such anti-evangelical sentiments coincided with the colonel's personal views and were shared by many British officials of his generation. Missionary disdain for India's devotional practices, allied to rumours of forced conversions, had been among the grievances that had inflamed the Mutiny/Great Rebellion. Gardner heartily disapproved of all confessional excesses and especially those of Christian missionaries—the 'Padree-Missioners' who 'Dick Turpin-like' drew forth their 'pocket pistol Bible' and called 'Halt. Stand and deliver—Your life or your religion'. He thought they should stick to useful activities like famine relief and agricultural advice. Elmslie, a broadminded Scot who winced at Clark's confrontational approach, was on the right track with his dispensary.

In July 1866 the good Doctor Elmslie heard again from Gardner and this time in person.

Colonel Gardiner, an Englishman, or rather, I believe, a Canadian, who is in the pay of His Highness, came to ask me to vaccinate his little child. He told me the people had now the greatest confidence in my surgery and medicine, but that they dislike the missionary element in my work, the feature of it which I love the most.

Immunised, if not baptised, baby Helena was then whisked backed into the cramped confines of Srinagar's maze of canals and dank alley-ways. Elmslie would leave no record of visiting her there and presumably never did.

Nor was Elmslie called on to attend when, two years later, Bibi Kali was taken ill. Her death seems to have been sudden and perhaps not surprising given Srinagar's unhygienic reputation. Gardner never spoke of his loss. He let it be known that he had a daughter but not that she had only a foster-mother. 'Living in native fashion' meant that purdah was observed in the colonel's household; he was never seen in the company of his family and rarely hinted at its composition. Of Bibi Chirang, who assumed responsibility for Helena when Bibi Kali died, no more is known than of the other wives and women who make a fleeting appearance in Gardner's story.

Little Helena, with a parent old enough to be her great-grand-father, must have been a candidate for the same seclusion and oblivion as they. When fate determined otherwise it looks to have been the result of the chance encounters that belated celebrity was now bringing the colonel's way.

While Gardner was rediscovering the pangs of parenthood and reliving his adventurous youth for the benefit of Frederick Cooper, his travels had begun to attract some interest in wider geographical circles. Raverty had had to turn down the re-editing of the itineraries shown him in Multan, but Edgeworth's version was in print and, by way of the Bengal Asiatic Society's journal, had found its way into the hallowed reading rooms of London's Royal Geographical Society. It was probably there that the two greatest Central Asian authorities of the day poured over the garbled text and it was in the Society's publications that their misgivings were usually aired.

Sir Henry Yule, a polyglot scholar who was then working on a definitive edition of Marco Polo's travels, was the more dismissive of the two. In an introduction to an 1872 reprint of John Wood's *Journey to the Source of the River Oxus*, he admitted that 'the travels and adventures of Colonel Gardiner are of such an extraordinary character that, had they ever been placed in a readable form before the public, he would long ago have enjoyed a world-wide reputation'. Sadly they had not; Yule had only Edgeworth's abstracts to go by, and since 'geography, like Divinity, has its Apocrypha', he felt obliged to 'include under this head the diary of Colonel Gardiner'. Though much the same criticisms could be made of Polo's narrative, Yule declared he could make nothing of the 'diary'. The itineraries were too disconnected and yeti-like, while 'the phantasmagoria of antres vast and deserts idle, of scenery wild and uncouth nomenclature' were frankly incredible. Despite numerous attempts over a number of years to make some sense of the abstracts, all had ended in 'mystification and disappointment'. They were like the 'memoranda of a dyspeptic dream'.

The most Yule would concede was that Gardner 'was a real person' and that he 'had acquaintance with ... Badakshan and the Pamirs to a degree far surpassing that of any European or native traveller whose narrative has yet been published'. This, under the circumstances, was surprising. The Pamirs section of the travel notes was one of the most questionable in the whole Gardner saga. It had of course been part of the documentation lent to Burnes and lost at Kabul. Yule had before him only Edgeworth's erratic rendering of Gardner's hazy recollection of events three decades earlier. Yet, in the present state of knowledge, he hesitated to refute even this.

Sir Henry Rawlinson, the other great authority, was about to become president of the Royal Geographical Society. He was best known for his work on the cuneiform inscriptions of Iraq but had served in Kandahar during the British occupation of Afghanistan, knew Persia well and now advocated forward moves in 'The Great Game' to counter Tsarist advances in Central Asia. During the 1860s and '70s Rawlinson adverted to Gardner repeatedly. He too had his reservations. 'The remarkably curious and very little known' paper that had appeared in the Asiatic Society's journal claimed Gardner had travelled 'in a zig-zag fashion' through all the countries between Samarkand and Kashmir; 'but he kept his journals in the most erratic fashion and no doubt exaggerated grossly'. Since his narrative read more 'like a romance than as a journal of actual adventure', it was 'hardly of any use'. Rawlinson's only hope was that 'age had somewhat tempered the exuberance of his [the colonel's] fancy' and that he might yet work up his travels into something intelligible.

Such were Rawlinson's thoughts in 1866. But six years later he was changing his tune. The old colonel had certainly been in Badakshan, he now thought, probably in the Pamirs and had unquestionably seen much of the terrain between Kashmir and Chitral. Hence Rawlinson's assertion that '[Gardner] actually traversed the Gilgit valley from the Indus to the Snowy Mountains and finally crossed into Chitral, being in fact the only Englishman [sic] up to the present time to have performed the journey throughout'.

Oddly it was not just the itineraries that Rawlinson found persuasive but Gardner's obsession with natural curiosities and monumental ruins—Yule's 'antres vast' and 'phantasmagoria'. Others, including Grey and Garrett, would see these fanciful diversions as discrediting the whole narrative. But Rawlinson thought they authenticated it. As an archaeologist he had no problem with monumental ruins. Rocks that emitted perpetual fire were commonplace in Azerbaijan, and he knew for a fact that there was a Chinese account of 'a magical horse who dwelt in a cave on Mount Pho-li, south of the Oxus' and that corresponded 'signally well' with the legless horse of Gardner's story.

Though wrong about Gardner's nationality—whatever it was, it wasn't English—Rawlinson knew that he was still alive in 1872. He knew too that Cooper, who had just died, had been working on Gardner's story. He also knew of Durand's account; and he was confident that several other travellers already in the field might any day shed new light on the matter. Indeed, he and the RGS had commissioned one of these travellers to make special enquiries.

In the late 1860s the mountains of Kashmir and the deserts beyond were unexpectedly turning into a major arena of exploration. Inner Asia was becoming as exciting as Darkest Africa. Lives were being lost there, medals won and reputations built, in the race to be the first to traverse unknown passes, trace infant rivers and generally obtain the sort of information that Gardner had never bothered with.

Numerous factors lay behind this surge of interest. The British were alarmed over the increase in Tsarist activities in western Turkestan. They were also intrigued by the emergence of an independent Khanate in Chinese eastern Turkestan under a man called Yakub Beg. In addition Kashmir's maharaja was forever encroaching on his mountain neighbours' territory with potentially embarrassing consequences. And, in the name of sport, assorted travellers were infringing sovereign rights wherever their quarry or their fancy took them.

Gardner, a man from travel's other side, indeed an interloper even among interlopers, scarcely belonged in the company of serious explorers. Yet he found himself much in demand. His advice was sought and his memory plumbed by men as diverse as the infuriating Hungarian ethnologist, Dr Gottlieb Wilhelm Leitner, and the suave diplomat, Sir Thomas Douglas Forsyth. Precisely where his travels had taken him was now a matter of some moment. Until the old colonel's claims could be tested, no one could be sure of being the first anywhere.

Briefed along these lines by Rawlinson, the 29-year old George J. Whitaker Hayward headed for the mountains in 1868. Hayward had offered to go anywhere. Formerly an officer in the 79th Highlanders and now a self-declared explorer, he would go to the ends of the earth provided he could be sure of making a name for himself. He was as tough, athletic and obsessed as they came. Rawlinson had suggested Inner Asia and saw Hayward as the perfect match for it. 'If any Englishman can reach the Pamir...', Mr Hayward is the man,' he told the RGS.

It was exploration's halcyon age. In Australia they were looking for Burke and Wills; in Africa, Stanley was about to start searching for Dr Livingstone; and in Asia, Hayward was to go in search of the Pamirs. Gardner's whereabouts were no mystery, but only the exploration of the Pamirs would reveal whether his account of them was credible. It would also provide reliable information on the bleak tract, only a few hundred miles across, which was all that now separated Kashmir territory from the advancing Tsarist domains.

Hayward did his best. His first attempt of 1868–9 took him from Kashmir to Ladakh and on through the mountains to Yarkand in eastern Turkestan. Initially he travelled in the disguise of a Pathan.

The idea for the disguise, as for the itinerary, probably came from Gardner. Hayward certainly consulted the colonel, although he was abruptly distracted by the news that another traveller, a tea-planter called Robert Shaw, had stolen a march on him. Catching up with Shaw, and so becoming joint winner in the race to be the first Englishman to clap eyes on Yarkand, took priority.

Hayward and Shaw finally met in the wastes of eastern Ladakh, then spent most of the next six months within hailing distance of one another. Seldom, though, did they actually communicate. Shaw saw Hayward as a gate-crasher who was jeopardising his hopes of selling tea to the Yarkandis, and Hayward saw Shaw as little better than a pedlar whose deferential attitude to their Turkestani hosts was undermining his own chances of a safe-conduct to the Pamirs. Both were right; and both were disappointed. After a long and anxious detention in what the Chinese called Xinjiang they were at last dismissed and allowed to retrace their steps. They did so separately.

In 1870, Hayward prepared to try again. In a series of grizzly excursions—he usually refused to carry a tent and thought nothing of walking fifty miles a day—he had whiled away the months since returning from Yarkand by charging round the borders of Kashmir. In August he was back in Srinagar where he evidently rented a house. There at an open window a passing stranger one day noticed not only Hayward but the unmistakeably raffish figure of Gardner. A new assault on the Pamirs by way of Gilgit was under discussion. Primed and more determined than ever, Hayward took off again in November 1870.

Eight months later he was dead, hacked to death on a mountainside in Yasin. Yasin was a semi-independent enclave to the north-east of Gilgit and only a watershed short of the Pamirs. Rawlinson was devastated by the news. 'Now all is changed. Mr Hayward lies cold in death... under a heap of stones on a bleak hillside.' When Rawlinson spoke, there was scarcely a dry eye in the RGS's auditorium.

Gardner, on the other hand, may not have been devastated. Hayward, like Gardner himself in 1846, had accused the maharaja's troops of genocidal atrocities perpetrated on the hill peoples along Kashmir's uncertain northern frontier. He rightly feared the consequences of this disclosure, and his murder may well have been orchestrated to discourage other critics. But Hayward's indiscretion had left Gardner—a Kashmir pensioner who had acted as Hayward's guru—in an embarrassing situation. It looked as if he had abetted one of the maharaja's sternest critics. The tragic news from Yasin was therefore not unwelcome. Meanwhile the mysteries of the Bam-i-dunya and the Bolor-tagh, of Badakshan's ruby mines, the ravenous wolves of the Pamirs and the primitive Akas along the Alai would have to wait.

Some idea of Kashmir's international popularity at the time may be gained from the identity of the passer-by who had spotted Gardner at Hayward's window. He was in fact a fellow American, Charley Longfellow. A playboy adventurer, Longfellow was also the son of Henry Wadsworth Longfellow, the much loved, much-parodied author of *The Song of Hiawatha*.

Of all those who claimed acquaintance with the colonel in his declining years Longfellow junior seems to have been the man most drawn to him. He knew him only slightly and was not inclined to probe his past; but he accepted him as an American, was amused by his foibles and repeatedly mentioned him in his correspondence. This may in part be explained by Longfellow being a semi-invalid. He had been badly wounded in the American Civil War and had just been carried most of the way from Simla to Kashmir. Once in the Valley he stayed put, sticking to water-borne sight-seeing and writing a decidedly dry account of all that interested him.

As logged in this unpublished account and in letters to his sister, Longfellow's three and half months in and around Srinagar in late 1869 were entirely leisurely. He read, including the Koran and a life of The Prophet lent him by the missionary Dr Elmslie, he sketched and he socialised. His stay coincided with visits by Shaw (the tea-planter proved 'a quiet fellow') as well as Hayward; it spanned the maharaja's return to his summer capital after a three years' absence (he came so seldom because his visits always prompted floods); and it ended with an official visit by Sir Donald McLeod, lieutenant-governor of the Punjab (and formerly the Punjab commissioner who had taken an interest in Gardner's saltpetre venture).

All these visitations occasioned social gatherings. It was while inspecting an exhibition of Hayward and Shaw's sporting trophies from Yarkand that Longfellow first spied Gardner. A month later he noticed him behaving oddly at a dinner given by the maharaja for the Valley's summer visitors. On this occasion, when the British commissioner (ie Cooper's successor) rose to speak, Gardner did so too and, says Longfellow, 'in a husky voice from age and liquor kept helping the Commissioner out in his speech'.

> He [ie Gardner] is a character, says he is 85, is active, has a fine white beard and wears Oriental dress, except that last night he appeared in turban, a wonderful Byronic shirt and brown dressing gown with brass buttons and a great red sash.

Gardner's extemporising had been the one bright moment in an otherwise excruciating evening.

A week later, Longfellow attended a review of the Kashmir forces. Seated beneath an enormous yellow umbrella, the maharaja talked throughout the march-past and never once looked up. Perhaps he knew what to expect. First came the cavalry, whose officers attempted to salute simultaneously with both hands. It meant dropping the reins, 'upon which their horses usually tried to bolt'. 'Then came the artillery—that is the men; they had no guns—led by Col. Gardiner on foot, who stepped off as springily as a man of 30 ...' The gunners, though boatmen when off-duty, were much the best dressed and a credit to their colonel. 'The entertainment ended by the band mutilating God Save the Queen.'

As autumn drew on and the leaves of the giant chinar trees turned a deep crimson, the commissioner announced that the season was drawing to a close: all Europeans must leave the Valley by 15 October. In fact some stayed on a bit longer because Lieutenant-Governor McLeod was running late. Longfellow returned his books to Elmslie's library, then came away with Richard Burton's three-volume *Personal Narrative of a Pilgrimage to al-Madinah and Meccah*. He was in no hurry to leave.

October 14 brought a Hindu festival during which 'the old man with the cotton wool beard'—presumably Gardner—joined the dancing girls on stage. Finally came Lieutenant-Governor McLeod, just in time for Halloween. The festivities in his honour were the grandest Longfellow could remember. His Highness wore yellow silk with a turban of many colours and Gardner 'a red coat with green epaulettes and a gold turban'. There were only fifteen foreigners left in the Valley and the dinner was all the better for it. 'No speeches or toasts,' noted Longfellow, 'Old Gardner furious that HH's health hadn't been proposed.' Afterwards they adjourned to a terrace overlooking the river. Illuminated boats glided by and the opposite bank was a wall of trellis festooned with lamps.

Longfellow took leave of the Valley three days later, accompanied by the good Dr Elmslie. 'Never saw Kashmir look so pretty,' Longfellow scribbled in his diary, 'clean air, trees turning brown, yellow and red … and the snow covered mountains gleaming white in the distance.' He left with regret and many a backward glance. He could understand why 'the old man with the cotton wool beard' had chosen to end his days there.

By now, late 1869, little Helena had just turned four. The idea that she should have a European education could have come from Gardner himself but more probably came from one of his passing acquaintances. As well as Hayward and visitors like Gray, Landseer, Leitner and Longfellow, in 1869 Gardner evidently formed a relationship with Colonel Charles Lionel Showers, as attested by the substantial bundle of Gardner papers found among those of Showers himself in the Cambridge archives. Here can be found the most impenetrable of all the colonel's productions: a sarcastic eighteen-page critique of British rule entitled 'A letter from the people and Baba Loke ['father figures'] of India to their long lost Arryan Brethren & Pater Familias, Dear John Bull of Englishstan'. Pearse would include a later and less outspoken version of this 'Letter' in the *Memoirs*, but the hastily written original was entrusted to Showers. Indeed it may well have been solicited by Showers, himself an abrasive and controversial figure who, like Gardner, had fallen foul of the Lawrences and their supporters.

Also entrusted to Showers were a 'sketch' of Kashmir's mountain dependencies (Gilgit, Chilas, Skardu and Leh), another on 'Kaffiristan and the Kaffirs', and some 'notes, explanations and remarks' relative to a route map of the entire region covered by Gardner's earlier travels. All these documents would have been of interest to the unfortunate Hayward, who in April 1870 had asked Showers to return them to Gardner. Presumably Hayward wanted to consult them before embarking on what would be his last journey, and presumably Showers was unable to oblige; for it was thanks to their fortuitous preservation among Showers's papers that the Kafiristan sketch was eventually transcribed by Dr Schuyler Jones in the 1970s.

But there exists no record of the nature of the relationship between Gardner and Showers. It was probably professional rather than personal. More likely candidates for having prompted Gardner to send Helena to school in Murree are the Rev Dr William Jackson Elmslie and Major-General Sir Henry Marion Durand.

Elmslie, as a missionary, would have alerted Gardner to his duties in respect of Helena's education and recommended the Murree convent. Despite being polar opposites in the matter of religion, Gardner respected Elmslie and trusted his advice. But Elmslie may not have had a chance to give it, for he never returned to Kashmir. Shortly after leaving the Valley with Charley Longfellow in 1869 he died under somewhat questionable circumstances. It looked like poisoning; and because he, like Hayward, had aired criticisms of the Kashmir government, the finger of suspicion was again pointed at the maharaja. The British government, however, took no action. Alienating somewhere as strategically sensitive as Kashmir to mollify the families of meddlesome missionaries and irresponsible explorers was out of the question.

Sir Henry Durand, for one, would have opposed an investigation. Durand's only visit to Kashmir immediately preceded Helena's departure for Murree in 1871 and must have involved considerable informal contact with Gardner. Moreover a recommendation from the lieutenant-governor of the Punjab would have been more than enough to have ensured Helena's admission to the Murree school.

Gardner and Durand had become acquainted in the early summer of 1870. Durand, as the newly appointed lieutenant-governor, had paid an official visit to Srinagar which replicated almost exactly that of his predecessor McLeod. The only differences were that there were more holiday-makers about and the formal dinner in the maharaja's palace was this time accompanied by both speeches and toasts. In his own address Durand lavished praise on Ranbir Singh, concluding with the statement that 'the Queen had no subject more loyal than the present Maharajah'. According to a guest (who preferred to be anonymous but has since been identified as one J. Duguid), Durand then 'called on Colonel Gardiner to reply'.

> The colonel, one of the most extraordinary men in India, has from his boyish days gone through adventures of every romantic and daring character [reported Duguid]. ... He replied briefly, and ended by saying he had been present at the late Maharajah's [ie Gulab Singh's] death, whose last words to his son were 'Should only one Englishman be left in the world, trust in him'.

'Some present were disposed to think this concluding sentence an embellishment of the gallant colonel's invention,' adds Duguid—just as some might have thought the same of Durand's concluding words about the queen having no more loyal subject than the maharaja.

That Durand had singled out Gardner to second his formal address suggests that the two had already met. 'A stalwart man ... and one of our ablest administrators', Durand had fought in the Afghan War, the Second Anglo-Sikh War and the Mutiny. Nearing the untimely end to his own distinguished career, he seems to have been immediately impressed by Gardner. He listened to his tale and prepared notes for a fulsome memoir which were published, without any of the usual caveats, in *The Friend of India* in 1870. A quarter of a century ahead of Pearse's *Memoirs*, Durand's *Life of a Soldier of the Olden Time: An Unwritten Page of History* was the first to describe the colonel's career in a connected fashion and the first to substantiate those 'adventures of every romantic and daring character'.

There is no mistake about the high heart, the undaunted courage, the unflagging will... [ends Durand's article]. That such a man has been so little mentioned in the history of the times is a marvel. But we must remember he was a man without a country, though England or any country might be proud to claim him. Faithful to his standard, whatever it was, obeying without question military orders, he presented and presents perhaps one of the finest specimens ever known of the soldier of fortune.

Although anything but the last word on Gardner, these were very nearly Durand's last words. In what seemed to be a curse on all who took up the colonel's case, the lieutenant-governor was dead within a few months, felled by the collapse of that elephant gate at Tonk in January 1871. Cooper had not lasted much longer, nor Elmslie, and McLeod passed away in 1872 when he was dragged from the platform at Gloucester Road station by a steam-powered forerunner of the London Underground.

Pearse himself must have heaved a sigh of relief when he wrote his own last sentence. What he calls 'the vicissitudes of Gardner's papers' had by then accounted for two more 'very high authorities on Central Asian geography', both of whom 'had unhappily died while the papers were in their possession'. One was presumably Sir Henry Yule (died 1889), and the other more certainly 'Mr Ney Elias,' who expired when the *Memoirs* were going to press. Pearse's somewhat Delphic last word on Gardner could well have been intended as a caution to any other would-be biographers: 'To those who have in them the divine spark of enterprise these pages may not be without a suggestion and a lesson.'

Sir Henry Yule's verdict on Gardner's travels has already been noted. For that of the unlikely sounding Mr Ney Elias there is only Pearse's word; but assuming the verdict to have been reproduced in good faith, one can understand why Grey and Garrett would later ignore it altogether. Elias was unequivocal: Gardner had certainly been in both Badakshan and the Pamirs. More to the point, so too had Elias. Of all those who ventured an opinion on the Gardner itineraries, he alone had actually retraced the colonel's route across the Pamirs. Where Hayward had failed, the elusive Ney Elias had succeeded.

Even Elias's nephew and biographer could not explain why he was called 'Ney'. He was 'Elias' because he was of Jewish parentage, an identity not many contemporaries in India either shared or envied. Once hailed as 'the mute inglorious Milton' of Inner Asian travel, Elias was also a perfectionist and a loner. He saw more, yet made less fuss about it, than any other pioneer. Self-effacing to the point where modesty itself became a form of vanity, he once scorned the offer of a minor honour and was thus never elevated to the knighthood that crowned the careers of most successful explorers. In such company he found plain 'Mr' sufficient distinction.

Like Gardner, Elias was an outsider, and like Gardner he came to India's borderland circuitously and from the wrong direction. His first great journey had taken him from Beijing to Moscow by way of the Mongolian steppe, the Gobi Desert and most of Asiatic Russia. That was in 1872 at a time when Gardner was still gracing the maharaja's parades and Helena was at school in Murree. In 1873 the RGS awarded Elias one of its two gold medals, the other that year going to H. M. Stanley. There then followed a surveying assignment in Burma that took him to Thailand, Laos and China before he was posted to Leh in Ladakh in 1876. There his flickering star was eclipsed by the comet-trail left by Hayward and Shaw.

In 1870, while Hayward was planning his Gilgit-Yasin approach to the Pamirs, Shaw had returned to Yarkand along with Thomas Douglas Forsyth, a member of the Indian Civil Service with a particular interest in Anglo-Russian relations and once one of Henry Lawrence's 'young men'. Like Shaw, Forsyth saw Indian trade with eastern Turkestan, now under its break-away khan, Yakub Beg, as the ideal foil to Russian designs on the country. In the event, the 1870 expedition was no more successful than that of 1868; but it did prompt a reciprocal overture from Yakub Beg and in 1873 Forsyth had tried again.

This time Forsyth headed the largest and most lavishly provided mission yet despatched across the Himalayas. The British were finally taking eastern Turkestan (or Chinese Xinjiang) seriously. As well as a geologist/botanist and a bag-piper, the mission's British complement included a survey captain, a political officer, a surgeon-major and, as second-in-command, Lieutenant-Colonel T. E. Gordon, one of those identical twin brothers who had watched Gardner parading his Kashmir troops twenty years earlier. With Yakub Beg's reluctant blessing, Gordon and surveyor Henry Trotter made a short foray into the Pamirs and enquired into the murder of Hayward. Neither quest produced convincing results. Hayward's vendetta with Maharaja Ranbir Singh was ignored and the Pamirs were pronounced no obstacle at all to the advance of Tsarist forces. Nor was anything said about Gardner's claims to have traversed the region. In what was essentially a political and strategic initiative, the doubtful utterances of some land-lubbing equivalent of the Ancient Mariner could seemingly be ignored.

Thus it was left to the always-solo Ney Elias to conduct the first British exploration of the Pamir region. It had to wait until 1885. Elias's poor health necessitated a spell of home leave, and in the interim Yakub Beg's oppressive rule in eastern Turkestan was contested by China's resurgent Qing dynasty under the Qianlong emperor. When Elias finally headed west from Xinjiang into the Pamirs it was thanks to a Chinese passport. He was there, and in neighbouring Badakshan, for eight arduous months. 'The first Englishman to cross the Pamirs', he discovered the 24,000 foot Mustagh Ata, reconnoitred more than a dozen passes over 13,000 feet, explored the headwaters of the Oxus River, surveyed each of the possibly 'eight Pamirs' and 'was also the first actually to visit ... Shignan and Roshan.' Like Gardner he also found wolves more numerous than Kyrghyz and heard tell of ruby mines. No living European possessed a better knowledge of the region. Elias's verdict on Gardner's claims may therefore be taken as conclusive. It also embraces Gardner's earlier movements in Asia and, though by no means wholly favourable, is worth quoting as Pearse gives it.

> There appears to me [ie Elias] good internal evidence that as regards the main routes he professes to have travelled, Gardner's story is truthful. When he tells us that he visited the east coast of the Caspian, North-

ern Persia, Herat, the Hazara country, even Khiva; that he spent some time in and about the district of Inderab [with Prince Habib-ulla], and afterwards passed through part of Badakshan and Shignan, thence crossing the Pamirs into Eastern Turkestan, I see no reason to doubt him. At the time he speaks of, such journeys were almost as practicable for Europeans as for Asiatics. Most of the countries in Central Asia were in a more or less disturbed and lawless condition—much more so than in later years—but that was a condition which affected Asiatic and European alike ... The times were, on the whole sufficiently favourable to render belief in the main features of his narrative possible; and it is, in a sense, the truth of the general narrative that enables us to excuse the untruth of many of the details.

In other words, had Gardner not travelled over a great part of the ground he professes to describe, it would not have been possible for him to interpolate the doubtful portions of his story. He could not have known enough of the surrounding conditions or even the names of places and tribes, nor have met with the people whose clumsy inventions he at times serves out to us. It is necessary, for instance, that a man who could never have read of the Pamir region should have at least visited that country or its neighbourhood before he could invent or repeat stories regarding Shakh Dara or the Yaman Yar, or be able to dictate the name of Shignan.

Twenty years after his death, Gardner had finally been vindicated. Publication of Elias's verdict would add enormously to the credibility of the *Memoirs* and ensure a mostly favourable reception for them. Not till twenty years after that would Gardner be un-vindicated by the arbitrary editing of Messrs Grey and Garrett.

12

Afterlife

Not all of those who met the colonel in Kashmir left any record of him, and not all those who left a record can be identified. As noted, Colonel Showers was among the former, and so too, even more regrettably, was Sir Robert Henry Davies. After numerous postings in northern India, it was Sir Robert who succeeded Durand as lieutenant-governor of the Punjab following the collapse of Tonk's elephant gateway. He was also, of course, the family man to whom young Helena's English upbringing was about to be entrusted.

Davies's 1871 appointment to the lieutenant-governorship had been preceded by a spell of duty in Lahore ten years earlier. His first wife having died, there in 1860 he had married Mary Frances Cautley, and there in 1862 had been published his report 'on the trade and resources of countries on the north-western boundary of British India'. The report included observations on the saltpetre industry, for which Gardner as the province's most articulate contractor was almost certainly consulted. And since the new Lady Davies was destined to be solely responsible for Helena's English residence until the lieutenant-governor's 1877 retirement, it may be assumed that Gardner thought as highly of her as of her husband. It would be nice to think he may even have attended their wedding—as Sir Robert would Helena's. And nicer still if any of this threesome had put pen to paper about their relationship.

Of the many who did leave a record of meeting the colonel, the most mysterious must be the elderly churchgoer responsible for the mouth-wateringly entitled *Rough Notes Made in the Years 1868, 1869, 1870, 1871, 1872 and 1873 in Syria* etc. A stickler for anonymity, the *Rough Notes*' author withheld his own name and, for no obvious reason, those of nearly all he met. But unlike 'Rev. R.', 'Mr. C.' and 'Col. H.', Gardner is at least identified. 'A noted character hereabouts [ie in Kashmir]', the book awards him 'a long and chequered life' which first embraced a spell at sea (when 'according to his own account he acted the part of a smuggler, and something more'), and then the companionship of 'four wives, the youngest about 25, by whom he has one child, a little girl at school in Murree'. The date of the author's meeting with Gardner is given as August 1872, so confirming Helena's removal to Murree but conflicting with reports of Bibi Kali's having died in 1867. Like others, the writer looks to have relied more on second-hand report than first-hand testimony.

The last published sighting of the old colonel came a year later in October 1873. By then Helena was transferring from her Murree kindergarten to boarding school in England while Thomas Douglas Forsyth was making the most of his mega-Mission's stay in eastern Turkestan. Attracted by the excitement over the latter, Andrew Wilson, an experienced journalist and editor of the *Times of India*, undertook a mountain tour billed as 'from Chinese Tibet to the Indian Caucasus through the Upper Valleys of the Himalaya'. The tour would yield several articles for *Blackwood's Magazine*, these being subsequently incorporated in a book, *The Abode of Snow*.

Naturally Wilson's itinerary had to include Srinagar and its most sought-after resident. Primed by Durand's *Life of a Soldier of Olden Times*, Wilson tracked down the colonel, confirmed his American origins and urged him to share some of his memories.

There was something almost appalling to hear this ancient warrior discourse of what have now become almost prehistoric times, and relate his experiences in the service of Ranjit Singh, Shah Shuja, Dost Mohammed and other kings and chiefs less known to fame. If (as I have no reason to believe) he occasionally confused hearsay with his own experience, it could scarcely be wondered at considering his years, and there is no doubt as to the general facts of his career. Listening to his graphic narrations, Central Asia vividly appeared as it was half a century ago...

Wilson says nothing about the colonel's health at the time, or his appearance. But nor does he mention him undertaking any parade duties. Now aged either 72 (the amended registry) or 88 (the *Memoirs*), he presumably walked less 'springily' and talked less 'animatedly'.

There had in fact been one scare already. At about the same time as Andrew Wilson was interviewing him, Sir Henry Rawlinson of the RGS received a letter from a Mr Campbell Terries informing him that Gardner had suffered a paralytic stroke and died. This Terries was apparently a nephew of the colonel, and his statement was 'probably untrue', thought Rawlinson.

There could, though, have been more to it than met the eye. In what can hardly have been a coincidence, it was another nephew, both of them presumably offspring of Gardner's anonymous sisters, who prompted Rawlinson's comment. The second nephew was a Mr Kiernan who dabbled in the weapon's trade and lived at Brondesbury Villas in London's heavily Irish borough of Kilburn. His identity is known because he had just sent a rather delicate request to the secretary of state for India. Kiernan wanted to know whether, under the terms of Forsyth's impending treaty with Yakub Beg in eastern Turkestan, a consignment of muskets and rifles for 'the king of Yarkand' would be permitted to pass through India. Such an unusual enquiry was promptly referred to the authorities in India. Meanwhile Kiernan was asked to explain.

He did so in a letter of 29 June 1874. The guns, Kiernan claimed, had been requested on behalf of the Yarkand ruler by Kiernan's uncle, 'Col Gardner of Seereenugger Cashmere'. He was an old soldier in the service of the maharaja of Kashmir and had given a promissory note for £15,000 as part-payment for the guns. If the India Office wanted further reassurance, reference could be made to the many distinguished officers who knew Gardner, including 'Sir Henry

Durand... Lieut-Governor of the Punjaub'.

Since Durand had now been dead for three years, either Gardner was going gaga or this Kiernan was taking advantage of him. In time the paper-trail would lend support to the latter. From the four-way correspondence between London, Calcutta, Lahore and Kashmir, it emerged that Gardner was indeed now frail and less coherent than ever. Though aware of the transaction, he apparently thought it concerned only a sample shipment and not the 10,000 rifles for which Kiernan had quoted. On the other hand Kiernan, and probably Terries, entertained an ulterior motive of their own. According to a Captain Henderson, who interviewed both Gardner and Kiernan in Jammu, Kiernan 'thought that his uncle was a rich man and that something was to be got out of him'. He was even proposing that the colonel's pension be commuted into a one-off payment of '£1000 or so' so that he, Kiernan, could then transfer the money and the old man to London and his own stewardship.

> To find him however living in a mud hut in the middle of Jammu has opened his eyes... [continued Henderson]. Poor Colonel Gardner is very much shaken with his journey here [ie from Srinagar to Jammu], and it is very difficult to get anything like a connected story out of him.

It had ever been so. Connected stories were as alien to the colonel as pithy prose. But if Henderson believed Gardner to be impoverished, it was he who was wrong. The 'mud hut' in Jammu was presumably just a temporary *pied a terre*; moreover, as well as the £15,000 promissory note, the mud hut's occupant had just sent Kiernan £500 to be invested in a consignment of other goods for eastern Turkestan. Obviously the colonel's state pension was neither his only income nor any indication of his real worth. It was Kiernan, not Henderson, who was right about his resources. Kiernan was, though, misled as to his state of mind. Gardner was quite capable of managing his own affairs. He had no intention of ending his days in Kilburn or anywhere else other than the state of Kashmir.

'There is something "shaky" in the transaction,' minuted the assistant secretary in the India Office's Political and Secret Department by way of summarising the affair. The muskets might actually be intended for the maharaja of Kashmir; for if they were really for Yakub Beg, it was highly improbable that, when the Forsyth Mission was still in Turkestan, its ruler had not asked Forsyth for the guns instead of attempting importation through such an irregular channel. The assistant secretary—he was none other than Sir Owen Tudor Burne, the commander-in-chief's military secretary back in 1864–5—then sprang his own surprise:

I know Colonel Gardner well. He is a most distinguished old man who has been thro' the whole of Central Asia experiencing the most extraordinary vicissitudes that ever fell to the lot of one man. He is now superannuated in the service of the Maha[raja] of Cashmere and is fond of relating his adventures to all who will listen to him. ... He wrote most valuable memoranda on the geography of Central Asia – memoranda which I was able to read in 1865 in Cashmere and discovered to be of incalculable value. Unfortunately he sent them home by the hands of a gentleman who lost them. O.T.B.

Since there were no Kashmir sightings of Gardner in 1875 or 1876, it is probable that he never returned to 'Seereenuggur' after this gun-running episode. Instead he stayed in Jammu, though surely not in a mud hut. Whether or not partially paralysed by the rumoured stroke, an annual 300-mile trek back and forth through the mountains would have tested the constitution of anyone the wrong side of seventy.

Pearse claims that Gardner continued to write at length about Indian affairs and Anglo-Russian relations until his death. As remembered by his fellow pensioners of the Kashmir artillery—those old servicemen who relayed their memories to George MacMunn and so to the visiting Helena in 1898—'the old man with the cotton wool beard' spent his last days reliving the past with the help of the headgear arranged on his table. When he died in his bed in January 1877, there, alongside his trusty throat-forceps, lay Arb Shah's *keffiyeh*, a Turkoman's tall black 'flowerpot' and an Uzbek's bearskin burnoose with maybe a Chitrali cap or two, a fez and of course a ten-gallon tartan turban complete with its egret's plume kalgi and jewelled clasp.

✳

Helena's hopes of resuming the quest for her father's missing fortune were never realised. After failing to locate the treasure in 1898, she and Christiaan Lourens Botha returned to Africa and were married. They had a daughter in 1901 and according to the *Rand Daily Mail* 'did much entertaining in Johannesburg'. By 1908 they were in Cape Town where, to a ladies' civic reception, Helena 'wore blue crepe de chine with chemisette and sleeves of Irish lace and a plumed horsehair hat of the same shade'. Of the hat in particular her father would have approved. Two weeks later, at a state ball, she 'looked very well' in more blue silk and cream lace. But as the First World War loomed, the marriage began to break up. In 1919 Helena (by then 53) and daughter Margarita (then 18) booked a second-class cabin from Capetown to Southampton. A divorce followed, along with a settlement that enabled Helena to live in Nice on the French Riviera.

From there in July 1933 came the news that she was planning a second visit to India. Syndicated reports to that effect were widely circulated and appeared in newspapers published in places as far apart as Cannes and California. The visit was this time billed as 'an expedition' and with every prospect of success. 'DAUGHTER WILL SEEK FORTUNE IN KASHMIR', headlined, for instance, the *Freeport Journal-Standard*; 'Millions of Dollars in Jewels Sought by Adventurer's Heir'. The earlier visit had been frustrated, explained Helena, because 'my friends lost their courage and I had to give up the search'. At the Lahore bank she had 'found only a package containing my father's will'. 'This time I am determined to find the gems because I am convinced the treasure does exist.' She said she needed the proceeds to provide for her children, two by her first husband, the Bavarian lieutenant Max Gerl, and Margarita by Judge Botha.

Of all these newspaper reports the most informative was that carried in Barcelona's *La Vanguardia* of 9 August 1933. Presumably Helena had responded to enquiries from the paper in English, her answers being then translated into Spanish—and now back into English. As the only known version of how her father and mother had first met, the following extract is still worth quoting.

"My mother, it would appear, was a Sceiik's [ie Sheikh's] daughter from
Turquestán, whose tribe carried out continuous raids on Cachemir,
until it was exterminated by my father." (Mrs Gardner-Botha says).
"Only four women remained alive, and the most beautiful one, Kali,
my mother, was taken to my father's harem. She passed away two years
later, and I was brought up by my father's second favourite, Cirang Bibi."

All of which recalls Alexander Hill Gray's story about the recalcitrant hill raja to whose daughter Gardner had similarly laid claim.
But nowhere else in the Gardner literature is 'a Turkestani Sheikh'
mentioned, either as the object of one of the colonel's campaigns or as
Helena's grandfather. The date too is problematical. Two years before
Bibi Kali's death would be 1865, which was after Gray met Gardner,
indeed the year in which Helena was born, supposedly in November.
Gardner's men could have been sent on some unrecorded raid that
summer; apart from his first meeting with Elmslie in May, there are
no other reported sightings of him in 1865. Yet if Bibi Kali was not
a Kashmiri but a Turkestani of some distinction, it seems odd that
Helena never divulged this information to Pearse—and even odder
that the colonel himself never thought it worthy of mention. With
its overtones of his earlier Afghan wife, it looks like another case of
wishful displacement. The presumption must be that Helena, now
68, had inherited a tendency to fantasize.

Embroidering her parentage could have been meant to lend more
glamour to her quest. If so, it failed. The press reports may have been
intended to raise funds for the trip; and if so, they too failed. For
instead of Kashmir, her next removal was to Ireland. The Second
World War was no doubt in some way responsible. By 1940 Helena
was living, and Margarita was dying, in Dublin. At the Mayfair Hotel, 30 Lower Baggot Street, Helena lived on alone till the age of 81.
According to her tombstone in the Deansgrange cemetery, 'HELENA
HOUGHTON CAMPBELL BOTHA, daughter of Colonel ALEXANDER
GARDNER, Born in Kashmir, Died in Dublin, January 19th 1947'.

Later in that same year of 1947 India and Pakistan would attain independence. Kashmir instantly became a bone of contention between
the two successor states, with Ranbir Singh's descendant opting to

join India while his Muslim subjects, abetted by Pakistan, contested the decision. Where all this left the Gardner hoard of plate and coin, of Damascene swords, bejewelled poignards and whatever else fancy might suggest, is anyone's guess.

It is not inconceivable that Gardner entrusted his wealth to the maharajas' state treasury for safekeeping, in which case its fate is doubly mysterious. For, held in numerous steel trunks in the vaults of a bank in Srinagar, the Kashmir State Treasure seems itself to have now disappeared. The trunks were opened in 1984 and their contents, including thousands of diamonds and emeralds, hanks of pearls and pieces of solid gold furniture were valued at half a billion rupees. Numerous claimants stepped forward, among them the Indian government, the Jammu and Kashmir state government, the Pakistan government, the descendants of the maharajas and at least one body representing the Sikh community. But their claims have never been settled and meanwhile the trunks have reportedly vanished.

Were Gardner's baubles part of this treasure trove, there might also be a problem about which of his heirs could claim them. The death of Helena's daughter Margarita in 1940 ended the Botha line of descent; but the offspring of Helena's children by her Bavarian lieutenant, Max Gerl, could presumably register a claim. There were two Gerl children: Alfreda Maria Gerl born in 1891 and Frederick Alexander Gerl in 1892. Frederick Alexander was adopted by Christian Lourens Botha. He grew up in South Africa, married there and had a daughter, Helen V. Botha, in 1930. His sister Alfreda Maria may also have been adopted by Botha and she eventually had three husbands. Hence anyone with a recent ancestor called Willoughby Lee, Salzmann or Beckley, with time on their hands, a romantic bent and the funds to take on several governments, might yet be in with a shout.

If the last word on the Gardner treasure has yet to be written, so has the last word on the colonel's credibility. For a man with a back-story beginning in the eighteenth century and reaching half-way round the world, it is appropriate that there is an after-story running through the twentieth century and resonating no less widely. In fact the colonel's standing in the eyes of posterity has been soaring and plummeting with the precipitous frequency of a Himalayan trail ever since he was laid to rest in the Sialkot cemetery. Helena's 1898 visit to Kashmir had been as much about redeeming her father's reputation as realising his fortune, and just so, the aborted expedition of 1933 looks to have been meant to serve the same dual purpose.

From a low point at the time of the 1898 visit, Gardner's fame had taken off with the publication of the *Memoirs*. The reviews had been numerous and could hardly have been more favourable. The *New York Tribune*, for example, thought the book 'ought to become a classic'. Gardner, 'an extraordinary man', had seen 'much which had for centuries been unknown to white men'. He belonged 'in the gypsy tradition' of 'fearless, romantic vagrancy' and of 'intercourse, founded on real sympathy, with the strange tribes of the earth'. In fact he was 'a man after Sir Richard Burton's heart', and it would 'be hard to exaggerate the fascination of his biography'.

The *New York Times* preferred to compare him with Captain Dugald Dalgetty of Drumthwacket, the free-booting hero of Walter Scott's novel *A Legend of Montrose*. *The Guardian* delved even deeper into fiction: he was 'an adventurer of the good old cut-and-thrust kind who may fairly take his place alongside Ivanhoe, D'Artagnan and Amyas Leigh [of Charles Kingsley's *Westward Ho!*]'. The same paper applauded his loyalty to whoever employed him, and despite his 'holding in fine contempt our latter-day theories regarding the sacredness of human life', declared him 'a hero after his own fashion – a man Carlyle would have loved to have written an essay on'. Carlyle's loss was proving a bonus for the reviewers. Quoting at length from the book, they clearly relished writing about the man as much as reading about him.

Not all were agreed on Pearse's handling of the narrative, however, and those few who were aware of the Jodha Ram affair were generally as uncomplimentary about the editor's suppression of it as they were about Gardner's involvement. But even the well-informed *Standard* concluded that, distasteful though his actions sometimes were, the colonel was 'a remarkable man in many ways'.

Several also regretted Gardner's failure to make scientific observations and advance geographical knowledge. In this respect
Major-General Sir Frederic Goldsmid put them right in a wordy but
thoughtful review running to fifteen pages in the *Imperial and Asiatic
Quarterly Review*. Goldsmid's point was that 'personal incident' left
the colonel with almost no opportunity for scholarly diversions.
Accounts that were 'handicapped by adventure', like Gardner's, were
nevertheless essential to sparking interest in geographical science and
making exploration exciting. It was altogether wrong to criticise him
for not meeting the exacting standards of a specialist fraternity to
which he never aspired.

Goldsmid's review ended by applauding the inclusion in the *Memoirs* of 'some instructive and well compiled notices of the white officers
of the Maharaja Ranjit Singh'. Attached as appendices, these thumb-
nail sketches of Ventura, Allard, Court, Avitabile and some fifteen
others had been written by Pearse on the basis of a list provided by
Gardner. It was by no means a comprehensive list but it was the first
of its kind and generated considerable interest. To a reading public
that assumed the age of the freelance adventurer in India had ended
with the eighteenth century it came as a revelation; and, to at least
one reader, as an inspiration. Unwittingly, Gardner's list and Pearse's
elaboration of it were about to stimulate the research that would be
the colonel's undoing. As a result, his reputation, riding high at the
turn of the century, would plunge to an all-time low.

Appropriately enough, the dissenting note was first sounded in
Lahore. In the early 1920s Herbert Garrett, then vice-principal of the
Lahore Government College, persuaded the administration to open
the Punjab archives so that the records of the Sikh kingdom could
be sorted and studied. Garrett organised teams of researchers, and
in 1923 was himself appointed Keeper of the Records and director
of the Punjab archives. The scrutiny and cataloguing got underway
immediately.

At the time, the Punjab was reeling from the fall-out of the 1919
Amritsar Massacre. In the worst atrocity perpetrated by the British
during India's entire freedom struggle, some 500 Punjabis celebrating the feast of Baisakhi had been mown down by troops under

the command of Brigadier-General Reginald Dyer. Dyer believed he had been fulfilling instructions from Sir Michael O'Dwyer, the lieutenant-governor. Neither man had apologised for the massacre or been censured for their conduct. By 1920, Dyer was in fact being lionised as the 'saviour of the Punjab'; a public subscription raised for his benefit in London topped £26,000. The province was consequently in turmoil, at a time when elsewhere in India Mahatma Gandhi was expanding his *satyagraha* ('truth-force') campaign to demand immediate *swaraj* ('self-rule'). On the back foot for once, the British were keen to curry favour in a province from which the army was substantially recruited. Opening the archives looks to have been intended as a sop to Punjabi sentiment.

One line of archival research had already been suggested. Citing the list of 'white adventurers' in the *Memoirs*, and in particular Gardner himself, a letter had been published by the Allahabad-based *Pioneer Mail* to the effect that it was disgraceful 'such men should suffer oblivion without some attempt being made to discover more about them'. This had prompted a reply from another unnamed correspondent who was based in Lahore and claimed to have been collecting materials on Ranjit Singh's 'white officers' for thirty-five years. In particular he had obtained highly compromising information about Gardner from an informant who had actually known the colonel. Gardner, he could now reveal, was 'a fairly tough customer'. Much of his story was 'fishy', his birth near Lake Superior was 'humbug', and the atrocities in which he had been involved were 'almost beyond belief'. Eighteen months later in the Calcutta-based *Englishman* the same writer returned to the fray. Some points in his previous letter were corrected and more details supplied, along with one particularly compromising accusation that really was 'beyond belief'.

There is no irrefutable proof that this nameless correspondent was Charles Grey, the man who would publish *European Adventurers of Northern India 1785–1849*; but it looks to be a certainty. Grey had indeed been in India for 35 years. He had been living in retirement in Lahore since 1918 and admits to labouring in the archives for six years before his book saw the light of day in 1929. An amateur antiquarian but no scholar, Grey had previously spent ten years as a

non-commissioned officer in the army and thirteen in the employ
of the North-Western Railway. He was older than Garrett but less
accomplished, less articulate and more given to inaccurate quotation
and ill-substantiated conclusions. 'Fishy' and 'humbug' were terms to
be expected from an officious railway clerk, not from a professional
archivist.

Additionally, running through the newspaper articles and the
book, there was an unmistakeable consistency of both content and
sentiment. The same accusations—of Gardner being Irish-born, a
military deserter and never a person of any consequence in Lahore—
were repeated in all of them; and the same discreditable incidents
were cited—the murder of Chait Singh, the parading of the severed
heads and of course the mutilation of Jodha Ram.

The one exception happened to be the most questionable accusation of all. Though adverted to in the *Pioneer Mail* and elaborated
on in the *Englishman*, it somehow never featured in the *European
Adventurers*. Here it is given as it appeared in the *Englishman* in
July 1924:

> Having been settled at Jummoo, Gholab Singh bethought himself, in
> the manner of the Rajahs of that date, of a secret arms, and treasure store
> in case of emergencies. Accordingly Gardner, who he always called his
> only trustworthy friend, was summoned, and the order given, with the
> significant ending "Gordana Sahib, the secret must rest with I and you
> only." Gardner understood. Men were imported from down country,
> and kept segregated during the work. When finished they were given a
> farewell feast within the chamber, which was connected with the Palace
> by a subterranean passage. Being winter time great charcoal fires were
> lit. Gardner was present, but presently withdrew unobserved shutting
> the airtight door behind him. Next morning he returned to bury the
> bodies in the passage, giving out that the men had returned to Hindu-
> stan, and disappeared on the road. I give the story without comment.

Grey gave the story not only without comment but without naming
his source or awarding the affair a date. He had it, he said, on the
good authority of 'an old friend' whom he had known in the 1890s.

The friend was either 'an old gentleman' who came to Lahore with Lawrence after the First Anglo-Sikh War or a *golandaz* (gunner) who had served under Gardner. Neither was further identified.

As to the date, the crime appeared to have been committed after Gulab Singh was installed as maharaja of Kashmir. But that raises the question of why, at a time when the maharaja had only advancing years to fear, he thought it necessary to secrete his treasure. More plausibly it referred to 1844 when, in the aftermath of Maharaja Sher Singh's assassination, 'the golden hen' had withdrawn to Jammu and set about burying his wealth in sundry 'nests'. There exists, however, no record of Gardner accompanying the Dogra raja to Jammu, nor of his going there with the Lahore troops that eventually brought Gulab Singh back to Lahore.

The fact that the whole incident went unmentioned in *European Adventurers* is surely conclusive. Grey devotes over sixty pages of his compendious work to demolishing the Gardner legend. He does so, he says, reluctantly and only because he 'is certain of the facts, has unimpeachable evidence to offer, no personal feeling and a conviction that by exposing an imposture he is rendering a service to posterity'. But aside from the question of 'personal feeling' (the letters to *The Pioneer Mail* leave no doubt that he had Gardner in his sights before he started work on the archives), it is notable that Grey left no stone unturned in his demolition job. The mass murder in the Jammu passage is the one exception. Undated, unsourced and uncorroborated, its inclusion in *European Adventurers* would merely have raised suspicions about his other 'unimpeachable facts'. Maybe Garrett, acting as his editor, struck it out. Maybe Grey himself had doubts about it.

As so often, Gardner was vulnerable not just on his own account but on the basis of lurid suppositions about the conduct of all who 'went native'. Grey claims to be giving what he calls 'a vivid picture of what once happened in Lahore and,' he then adds, 'would again were the British to leave'. Unlike the author of the 'Letter from the Baba Loke of India' (Gardner's almost unreadable critique of British rule), he has no sympathy with the Indian demand for swaraj. Recalling the massacre at Amritsar, he believes his research 'shews what Sir Michael

O'Dwyer dreaded in 1919'. O'Dwyer too had feared a return to the anarchy of the 1840s; in short, says Grey, 'he knew his Punjabi'.

✳

Written by Grey and edited by Garrett, *European Adventurers of Northern India 1785–1849* was first issued in Lahore in 1929. Though published in-house by the Punjab government, the publisher offered a cautious disclaimer as to 'the correctness of any statement or expression of views made in the book'. Additionally the first edition included a list of corrections which barely scraped the surface of the book's misprints and mis-credited quotations. The photograph of the colonel was lifted from the *Memoirs*, though here with his age—ever a contentious matter—slashed from '79' to '69'. Assuming the picture was taken in 1864, this corresponded neither with his date of birth in the *Memoirs* nor with his age at the time of death as per the amended entry in the Sialkot register.

Of the book's sixty-odd biographical entries, that on Gardner was much the longest and most provocative. Other entries exhumed a bewildering gallery of forgotten exotics and rescued several tarnished reputations. The book would become a standard source of reference. But the chapter on Gardner simply annihilated him. As 'a prize liar', it claimed that almost nothing related of him in the *Memoirs* could be believed. His origins were invented, his travels unsubstantiated, his adventures preposterous and his character repugnant. Pearse had been worse than economical with the truth, and all those other upstanding referees—Edgeworth, Durand, Temple, Wilson, Yule and Rawlinson, not to mention (and Grey didn't) Burne, Hill Gray, Longfellow, etc—had been hoodwinked. One of the most remarkable figures in both the history of travel and the passage of history stood revealed as the nineteenth century's ultimate impostor.

While not so widely circulated as to cause a sensation, copies of *European Adventurers* percolated back to Europe and eventually found their way into most major libraries. Whether Helena was aware of the book is not known; but if she was, its contents may well have prompted her plans for the second expedition. Meanwhile her father's reputation lay in tatters. Instead of claiming pride of place on shelves devoted to 'travel', the *Memoirs* were as likely to be found languishing among 'curiosities' or 'fantasy'. Historians delved into Pearse with caution. Gardner was ignored altogether in *The Royal Geographical Society's History of World Exploration* in 1991.

That work was edited by the present writer. At the time, Alexander Haughton Campbell Gardner seemed too compromised a pioneer to be included. Thirty years later, and much the wiser for some innovative research, one can no longer feel so sure. As General Goldsmid reminded the select readership of *The Imperial and Asiatic Quarterly Review*, fact feeds on fiction just as fiction feeds on fact. Travel needs adventure; scholarship needs drama. Stanley is remembered for finding Livingstone, not for exploring the Congo. Archaeology owes as much to Indiana Jones as to Heinrich Schliemann. In relishing every conceivable encounter, the man in the tartan turban understood this. If to win attention he compromised his standing, it was in a worthwhile cause.

Notes

Quotations listed in abbreviated form as per the page nos
on which they appear, followed by relevant sources

EPIGRAPH

Benjamin D'Israeli, *Vivian Grey*
    (London: Henry Colburn, 1827),
    vol 5, p 311

INTRODUCTION

1   'the good cause': Major Hugh Pearse
    (ed), *Soldier and Traveller: Memoirs*
    of Alexander Gardner (henceforth
    referred to as *Memoirs*), pp 60–1

1   'Single-handed': John Keay, *When*
    Men and Mountains Meet, p 107

3   'one of the finest': Sir Henry
    Durand, 'Life of a Soldier of the
    Olden Time' (henceforth referred
    to as 'Life of a Soldier'), in H. M.
    Durand, *Life of Major-General Sir*
    Henry Marion Durand, vol 2, p 237

3   'what men of': Richard Temple in
    the introduction to *Memoirs*, p xv

1 CHASING SHADOWS

6   'his second most': 'La Fabuloso

Herencia de un Adventurero
Americano', *La Vanguardia*, 9 Aug
1939, p 6 (translated by Catalina
Recamán Míguez)

7   'disbelief': *Memoirs*, p 6

13 'the fullest': 'Faletti's over the Ages',
    Faletti's Hotel, accessed 6 Jan 2014,
    www.falettishotel.com

14 'though he was': Rudyard Kipling,
    Kim, p 1

15 'So carefully was she watched':
    Herbert Edwardes, 'The Sikh
    Invasion in British India 1845–
    1846', *Calcutta Review*, vol 6, p 247

15 'left both': C. Grey, *European*
    Adventurers of Northern India, 1785
    to 1849 (henceforth referred to as
    Adventurers), ed H. L. O. Garrett, p
    144

16 'at the hands': ibid, p 145

16 'an offence': ibid, p 225

17 'We wound up': John Wood, *Journey*
    to the Source of the Oxus, pp 100–01

17 'quietly proffering': ibid

17 'a full and particular': ibid

18 'it was undoubtedly': Grey &

Garrett, *Adventurers*, p 310
19 'a prize liar': ibid, p ii
21 'two Europeans': *Memoirs*, p 159
21 'been murdered': ibid, pp 159–60
25 'which he would': Sir George
MacMunn, 'A Free Lance Gunner',
Journal of the Royal Artillery
(henceforth referred to as *JRA*), vol
78, no 3, pp 231–32
25 'His memory': ibid
26 'utterly infamous', 'worthless':
Sir Patrick Cadell, 'A Free Lance
Gunner', *JRA*, vol 78, no 2, pp
97–101
26 'No doubt': MacMunn, *JRA*, vol 78,
no 3, p 231
26 'While I was': ibid
27 'they dislike': Mrs M. Elmslie
and W. B. Thomson, *Seedtime in
Kashmir*, p 146
27 '[They hover]': Alexander Gardner
(henceforth referred to as AG), 'A
letter from the people and Baba
Loke of India to their long lost
Arryan Brethren and Pater Familias,
Dear John Bull of Englishtan'
(henceforth referred to as 'Baba
Loke'), 28 November 1869, p 2
27 'On starving or hungry': ibid
28 'long separated': British Library,
India Office Records and Private
Papers, Henry Lawrence Collection,
Mss Eur F 85/47, 'Col Gardiner's
defence of his having mutilated
Jhoda Misser', 1846–47 (henceforth
referred to as 'Defence'), p 1

2 AT LARGE IN CENTRAL ASIA

29 'We left Herat': *Memoirs*, p 28
29 'Most of us': ibid, pp 28–9
31 'There is probably': H. D. Seymour
in preface to J. P. Ferrier, *Caravan
Journeys and Wanderings in Persia,
Afghanistan, Turkistan, and*

Beloochistan, p vi
31 'was about to': *Memoirs*, p 26
31 '[S]oon the force': ibid, pp 26–7
32 'I have not': ibid, p 37
32 'half-savage': ibid, p 30
32 'expeditions': ibid, p 35
33 'the far more exciting': ibid
33 'words grew': ibid, p 36
33 'humanity prevailed': ibid
34 'I fell': ibid, pp 37–8
34 'During my illness': ibid, pp 37–8
35 '[The condemned]': Arminius
Vámbéry, *Travels in Central Asia*, pp
168–69
35 'no day passes': ibid, p 170
35 'hovered round': *Memoirs*, p 41
36 'I told them': ibid
36 'One of them': ibid
36 'Americans': ibid
36 'During all this': ibid
37 'I took ship': ibid, p 42
38 'He then became': ibid, p 44
39 'There was nothing': ibid, p 47
39 'From the date': ibid, pp 47–8
39 'five of which': ibid, p 48
39 'We … grew desperate': ibid, p 49
40 'Aga Beg had': ibid
40 'It was a daring': ibid, pp 49–50
40 'We knew that': ibid, p 50
40 'in the name': ibid
40 'threatened to fire': ibid
40 'We declared': ibid
40 'Wearily': ibid
41 'but we did not': ibid, p 52
41 'Our party were': ibid, p 51
41 'finding life': ibid
43 'by extraordinary': William
Francklin, *Military Memoirs of Mr.
George Thomas* (Calcutta, 1803), p i
43 'At last': *Memoirs*, pp 56–7
43 'the trampling': ibid, p 57
43 'We could see': ibid
44 'explained myself': ibid, p 58
44 'Habib-ullah had never': ibid
44 'The affair ended': ibid

44 'brave and persecuted': ibid
44 'to be employed': ibid, pp 59–60
45 'as attractive': ibid, p 59
45 'a sordid, bloody-minded': Grey & Garrett, *Adventurers*, p 278
45 'by way of consolation': *Memoirs*, p 59
45 'liberal opinions': ibid
45 'great religious austerity': ibid
46 'a life in the saddle': ibid, pp 60–1
46 'We attacked them': ibid, p 63
46 'Eventually we cut': ibid
46 'the beautiful face': ibid, p 64
47 'On the following': ibid
47 'I must hurry': ibid, p 69
47 'the struggle': ibid, p 68
47 'Well do I remember': ibid, pp 67–8
48 'Cutting my way': ibid, p 69
48 'Habib-ulla, on seeing': ibid, p 69–70
48 'The silence was': ibid, p 70
48 'put all in': ibid, p 71
49 'There he lay': ibid, pp 71–2
49 'to the end': ibid, p 72n
49 'the pathetic story', 'a figment': Grey & Garrett, *Adventurers*, p 278
50 'dreadful intention': *Memoirs*, p 74
50 'The days which': ibid, pp 74–5

3 TO THE ROOF OF THE WORLD

52 'one of the most extraordinary': Anon (J. Duguid), *Letters from India and Kashmir*, p 197
53 'Turki overall boots': *Memoirs*, p 77
53 'a big lump': ibid, p 76
53 'a large hyena-like animal': ibid
53 'Disgustingly rotten', 'a hearty meal': ibid, p 77
54 'and so left': ibid, p 78
54 'taken in the Inderab valley': ibid, pp 81–2
54 'a fatiguing ride': ibid, p 84
54 'the place of': ibid
54 'the best wine': ibid, p 85

54 'we too, feeling': ibid
54 'The good pir': ibid, p 87
55 'sixty gold Bokhara tillahs': ibid, p 88
55 'We each of us': ibid
55 'one huge fortress': ibid, p 89
55 'they promised to place': ibid
55 'mephitic vapours': ibid, p 154
56 'It was a colossal figure': ibid, p 91
56 'a black flinty porphyrite': Ibid
56 'a beautiful queen': ibid, p 92
56 'The horse waited': ibid, pp 91–2
56 'Well known names': Sir Henry Yule, in an essay to John Wood, *Journey to the Source of the Oxus*, pp li
57 'that uncanny creature': ibid
57 'Shortly after leaving': *Memoirs*, p 92
57 'massive and extensive', 'weighed several tons': ibid, p 93
58 'It was now raining': ibid, pp 94–5
58 'and quickly unhorsed': ibid p 95
58 'Their overwhelming numbers': ibid, pp 95–6
58 'no doubt the plundering': ibid, p 96
59 'Whilst I slept': ibid, p 97
59 'these rude people': ibid, p 98
59 'the tokens of my younger', 'fourteen or fifteen wounds': ibid
59 'Nothing annoys me more': ibid
59 'And I may here say': ibid
60 'the garden of the East': ibid, p 108
60 'the robber *beg* of Kunduz': ibid, p 103
60 'I think, after two or three marches': ibid, p 102
60 'Thence we struck for a ford': ibid
61 'for a certain time': ibid, p 105
61 'curiously enough': ibid
61 'to which they added': ibid, p 106
61 'that my Therbah declared': ibid
61 'the mutilated remains of idols': ibid, p 109
62 'said to be the highest': Marco Polo, *The Book of Ser Marco Polo*,

pp 171–72

62 'The plain is called PAMIER': ibid

63 'savage idolaters', 'They are in truth': ibid

63 'In these countries': Francis Younghusband, quoted in *Memoirs*, p 100

63 'An outside traveller': ibid, p 101

64 'which, as we had horses': ibid, p 112

64 'Finally we managed': ibid, pp 112–13

64 'excellent animals': ibid, p 113

64 'without food or a light': ibid, p 114

64 'The next morning': ibid

65 'at least 13,000 feet': ibid

65 'Night was approaching', 'Just then we came upon': ibid, pp 114–15

65 'sustain himself': ibid, p 115

65 'Just as I hurried up': ibid, pp 115–16

66 'warm, rather than roast', 'after a long argument': ibid, p 116

66 'We speedily recrossed': ibid, p 118

66 'a few dropping shots': ibid

66 'overpowered them in an instant': ibid, p 119

67 'sent away to meet': ibid, p 122

67 'By the Laws, manners, and Customs': AG, 'Defence', pp 1–2

4 THE THIRD JOURNEY

69 'a noble robber-chieftain': *Memoirs*, p 140

69 'he set forth': ibid, p 145

70 'twelve years': ibid, p 26

70 'for the good cause': ibid, pp 60–1

70 'happy mountain home': ibid, p 72

71 'several volumes of country paper': M. Pakenham Edgeworth, 'Abstract of a Journal kept by Mr Gardiner during his travels in Central Asia— with a Note and Introduction' in *Journal of the Asiatic Society of Bengal* (henceforth referred to as *JASB*), vol 22, p 283

72 'Small, deep-sunken eyes', 'pure Tartar': *Memoirs*, p 129

72 'some splendid Shahbaz hawks': ibid, p 131

72 'the more pleasing-featured': ibid, p 130

72 'hair varying': ibid, p 124

72 'about two months': ibid, p 135

72 'consoled by marriage': ibid, p 137

72 'They consisted, somewhat to my surprise': ibid, p 134

72 'In my wanderings': ibid, p 135

72 'very valuable': ibid, p 133

74 'It was about the end of August 1826': ibid, p 137

74 'northern Bolor ranges': ibid, p 139

74 'a cave occasionally used as shooting-lodge': ibid

74 'at one time': ibid, p 138

74 'Our intention now was to go up': ibid, p 140

74 'two and a half days': ibid

75 'He considered that': ibid, p 144

75 'the great Alai valley or plateau': ibid, p 146

75 'considered as the site of the Garden of Eden': ibid

75 'but also worshipped obscene figures': ibid, p 150

76 'incomplete and confused': ibid

76 'Here Gardiner joined a Pilgrim Caravan': Durand, 'Life of a Soldier', p 232

77 'because it was really much easier': *Memoirs*, p 155

78 'The stench from the corpses': ibid, p 156

79 'won an almost bloodless victory', 'added to the Lahore dominions': Joseph Davey Cunningham, *A History of the Sikhs*, p 169

79 'governor of Kashmir': *Memoirs*, p 156

79 'was again in the ascendant': Durand, 'Life of a Soldier', p 232

79 'the adventurous soldier': ibid, p 233

80 'Gardner actually traversed': Henry Rawlinson, 'Monograph on the Oxus', in *Journal of the Royal Geographical Society*, vol 42, p 505n

81 'shows that as a student': *Memoirs*, p 158

82 'two Europeans having lived': ibid, p 159

82 'The full diary ...': ibid

82 'destroyed when [in 1841]': ibid

82 'All that remain', 'written on the margin': ibid

83 'the manuscript is of special interest': Schuyler Jones, 'A Scetch of Kaffiristan & the Kaffirs ...' in *Afghanistan Journal* (henceforth referred to as 'A Scetch of Kaffiristan'), Jg 4, Heft 2, p 47

83 'Of all the many Europeans': ibid

83 '... the Kaffirs of the present day': ibid, p 51

83 'the neatness and Elaborate Carved workmanship': ibid

84 '...low wooden benches': ibid, pp 51–2

84 'whether or not Gardner himself': ibid, p 47

84 'Unfortunately it does not': ibid

84 'a curious memorial': ibid, p 49

85 'a band of Khyberi outlaws': *Memoirs*, p 161

85 'Habib-ullah was nowhere': Durand, 'Life of a Soldier', p 233

86 'cast into the subterranean dungeons': *Memoirs*, p 162

86 'Now [says Pearse] was shown his remarkable influence': ibid

86 'money to help them': ibid, p 162

86 'flatly refused': Durand, 'Life of a Soldier', p 233

87 'several of whom': *Memoirs*, p 163

87 'seized and bound', 'as they would have treated him': Durand, 'Life of a Soldier', p 234

87 'He took from them': ibid

87 'taking the bull': Memoirs, pp 163–64

87 'They presented their arms': Durand, 'Life of a Soldier', p 234

88 'great self-possession and confidence': ibid

88 'for do what he might': ibid

88 'raised the green standard': *Memoirs*, p 167

88 'Defender of the Faith': ibid, pp 170–71

89 'there were too many Afghans': ibid, p 165

89 'The enthusiasm which he [the disciple] aroused': ibid, p 169

89 'some 250 well-armed': ibid

89 'owing to the mistake': ibid, p 171

89 'which fought very badly': ibid

90 'Even as I caught sight': ibid, pp 171–72

90 'My Khyberis and Yusufzais were equal': ibid, pp 172–73

90 'It was while in comparative ease': ibid, p 173

91 'enter his service': ibid

91 'a liberal salary': ibid, p 177

91 'took a great interest in artillery': ibid, pp 173–74

91 'a letter was received': ibid, p 176

92 'I should mention that': ibid, p 183

92 '15th December, 1831. Messrs Khora and Gardiner': Grey & Garrett, *Adventurers*, p 279

93 'Here then are solid': ibid, p 280

93 'one of the finest specimens': *Memoirs*, p 12

93 'an ordinary deserter': Grey & Garrett, *Adventurers*, p 279

93 'Before this prosaic': ibid, p 280

93 'The agreement of the dates': ibid, p 281

93 'According to Gardiner's own statement': ibid

5 THE EARLY YEARS

96 'an old European commandant':
Memoirs, p 2

96 'The old colonel': ibid, pp 2–3

96 'a series of conversations': ibid, p 4

96 'about a hundred pages': Henry
Rawlinson, *England and Russia in
the East*, p 222n

96 'Mr Cooper had already printed':
ibid

97 'a man well known in his day':
Memoirs, pp 1–2

97 'wonderfully good considering':
ibid, p 3

97 'except as to precise dates': ibid

98 'singularly tenacious': ibid

98 'the principal official': ibid, p 14

98 'a major in the English army': ibid

98 'a well-educated': ibid, p 15

98 'on that portion': ibid, p 14

99 'near the mouth of the river': ibid,
p 15

99 'acquired considerable property':
ibid

99 'Isolation in youth': ibid, p 16

99 'book of travels': ibid, p 17

99 'took an opportunity': ibid

99 'From this early period': ibid

100 'often sadly lamented': Grey &
Garrett, *Adventurers*, p 269

101 'the town of St Xavier': ibid

101 'We have looked up Arrowsmith's
atlases': ibid

101 'Unfortunately, no record or
mention': ibid, p 268

102 'There is some mystery': *Memoirs*,
pp 17–8

102 'He himself states': ibid, p 18

103 'an Irishman': Grey & Garrett,
Adventurers, p 279

103 'a well-known Jesuit College',
'served five or six': Durand, 'Life of a
Soldier', p 230

103 'Landing at New Orleans': *Memoirs*,

p 18

103 'immediately embarked on the
career': ibid, pp 18–9

103 'twelve years of apparently aimless
wandering': ibid, p 26

104 'While preparing for this journey':
ibid, pp 19–20

104 'the *chateaux en Espagne*': Grey &
Garrett, *Adventurers*, p 275

104 'connected with the Principal': *JASB*,
p 284

104 'well-known Jesuit College':
Durand, 'Life of a Soldier', p 230

105 'interesting, but unfruitful': Jones,
'A Scetch of Kaffiristan', p 49

105 'religion to come much between':
Memoirs, p 15

106 'Before leaving the Burlings': B
Esmonde, 'To Palermo and Back,
Seventy Years Ago' in *Irish Monthly*,
vol 9, no 98, Aug 1881, pp 441–46

107 'formerly served in a ship of war':
Grey & Garrett, *Adventurers*, p 279

108 'I could not refrain', 'Oh truly how
sweet': Charles Aylmer, quoted
in Thomas M. McCoog, 'Jesuit
Restoration – Part One: The Jesuits
in Europe before 1769', *Thinking
Faith*, accessed 3 Dec 2015, www.
thinkingfaith.org

108 'a highly accomplished Frenchman':
Memoirs, p 20

108 'The conversation that Gardner
had': ibid, p 21

108 'borrowed by Gardner': Grey &
Garrett, *Adventurers*, p 313

108 'Organised by some Armenian
merchants': *Memoirs*, p 21

108 'a medley of Asiatics': ibid

108 'who had effects': ibid, pp 21–2

108 'letting it be known': ibid, p 22

109 'Finding that the salaries': ibid, p 22

109 'some training in the rudiments':
ibid

109 'settled and promising life': ibid,

p 23

109 'his hopes were shattered': ibid

110 'when he met one day': ibid, p 24

110 'receiving large pay': ibid

110 'Sturzky therefore took a friendly leave': ibid, p 25

111 'in Northumberland Town': Grey & Garrett, *Adventurers*, p 296

112 'formerly served on a ship of war': ibid, p 279

113 '... for anyone who would claim': Jones, 'A Scetch of Kaffiristan', p 48

114 'invariably actuated in my inward soul': *Memoirs*, p 98

6 THE LION OF THE PUNJAB

116 'But the Maha Raja adhered': Karl Alexander Hügel, *Travels in Kashmir and the Panjab*, p 329

117 'I found in one of the tumbrils': *Memoirs*, p 181

117 'there seemed to be': ibid

117 'Accordingly one of the guns': ibid

117 'Much as I had heard': ibid, p 180

117 'an old mouse': Emily Eden, *Up the Country*, vol 1, p 284

118 'The Maharaja was indeed': *Memoirs*, p 180

118 'as a gay courtier': Cunningham, *A History of the Sikhs*, p 190

118 'Ever after [Dhyan Singh] acted': *Memoirs*, p 182

119 'eight horse-artillery guns': ibid

119 'a considerable present': ibid

119 'Thus matters continued': ibid, p 183

121 'Having heard of steamers': ibid, p 202

122 'since it was as much': ibid

122 'he came to me': ibid

122 'I read up all I could': ibid, pp 202–03

122 'he had equalled the achievements': ibid, p 203

122 'the first and only': ibid

122 'I had built': ibid, pp 203–04

125 'almost a complete lack of water': ibid, p 184

125 'In the course of about four months': ibid

125 'amusing [Dost Mohamed]': Cunningham, *A History of the Sikhs*, p 223

126 'The great Maharaja': Fauja Singh Bajwa, *Military System of the Sikhs*, p 227

126 'Gold, jewels, velvets, silks': ibid

126 'much in the same way': Henry Fane, *Five Years in India*, vol 1, pp 121–22

126 'a long green coat': William Barr, *Journal of a March from Delhi to Peshawar*, p 228

127 'ornamented in the centre': ibid, p 214

127 'constituted the elite of Sikh army': Bajwa, *Military System of the Sikhs*, p 225

127 'with his little green Muslim flag': *Memoirs*, p 188

127 'The firing and fighting': ibid, p 186

128 'This was done': ibid, p 187

128 'one month's sparring': ibid

128 'the undisputed occupation': ibid, p 188

128 'It was about this time': ibid, p 191

128 'a native wife': Herbert Edwardes and Herman Merivale, *Life of Sir Henry Lawrence*, vol 1, p 320

129 'active, enterprising, brave': G. M. Carmichael Smyth, *A History of the Reigning Family of Lahore* (henceforth referred to as *Reigning Family*), p 259

129 'of a most determined and resolute disposition': ibid, pp 259–60

129 'But though he may be said to possess': ibid, pp 260–61

130 'gave our whole contingent': *Memoirs*, p 193

130 'He is by no means firm': W. G.
Osborne, *The Court and Camp of
Runjeet Sing*, pp 81–3
131 'he cannot last much longer': ibid,
p 83

7 BLOOD AND BLUNDER

135 'thirty-two Mrs Runjeets': Eden, *Up
the Country*, vol 2, p 29
135 'very handsome', 'would have been',
'immense almond-shaped eyes':
ibid, p 30
135 'They never let him': ibid, p 20
136 'Kharak Singh was a blockhead':
Memoirs, p 214
136 'to act as Kharak Singh's guardian':
Smyth, *Reigning Family*, p 26
136 'diabolical ... deceptive ...
dissembling': ibid, p 261
137 'it was he and he alone': ibid, p 26
137 'his influence over Runjeet Singh':
Osborne, *Court and Camp of
Runjeet Sing*, p 76
137 '[The Dogras'] dream [says
Gardner]': *Memoirs*, pp 212–13
137 'the torrent of blood': ibid, p 213
137 'the veil of futurity': ibid
137 'I will now relate': ibid
141 'unparalleled save in the darkest
period': ibid, pp 211–12
141 'it must, we imagine': Grey &
Garrett, *Adventurers*, p 285
141 'played the awful game': *Memoirs*,
p 213
141 'Their only thought was': ibid
142 'See what will become of you', 'Your
humble servant': ibid, p 215
142 'Dhyan Singh asked me': ibid, p 218
143 'It was near midnight': ibid, pp
218–19
143 'a tremendous cuff': ibid, p 219
143 'He simply showed': ibid
143 'There was a light': ibid, p 220
143 'The eyes of Dhyan Singh': ibid,

pp 220–21
144 'Comment on the mentality': Grey
& Garrett, *Adventurers*, p 284
144 'entirely a state proceeding':
Memoirs, p 221
145 'As they emerged from it': ibid, p
224
145 'Beams, stones and tiles': ibid
145 'the same day dazzled him':
Cunningham, *A History of the Sikhs*,
p 244
145 'chiefly from the notes': Smyth,
Reigning Family, p xvii
146 'adopt coercive measures': ibid,
p xxi
147 'dressed in fatigues', 'the
catastrophe': *Memoirs*, pp 223–24
147 'to wait at a little distance': ibid,
p 223
148 'two were afterwards': ibid, p 225
148 'blood in great quantities': ibid
148 'It is not positively known':
Cunningham, *A History of the Sikhs*,
p 244
148 'from time to time': *Memoirs*, p 227
149 'claimed the regency': ibid, p 228
150 'the bully at court': Smyth, *Reigning
Family*, p 261
150 'Such was the ancient custom':
Memoirs, p 229
150 'for it is a well known fact': Smyth,
Reigning Family, p 37
150 '... with the intention': *Memoirs*, p
228
150 'one of the most tremendous': ibid,
p 231
151 'Death to Chand Kaur': ibid
151 'My women and all the others': ibid,
p 232
151 'seemed useless': ibid, p 233
152 'Every gate was immediately
opened': ibid, p 233
152 'fourteen guns deliberately loaded':
ibid, p 234
152 'There was a brief but breathless

pause': ibid, p 235

153 'paralysed by the destruction': ibid, p 236

153 'Then Sher Singh fled': ibid

153 'blowing him and the building': Smyth, *Reigning Family*, p 54

154 '2800 soldiers, 200 artillerymen': *Memoirs*, p 236

154 'a high opinion of Gardanah': A. Raynor and H. R. Goulding (eds), *Political Diaries of Lieutenant Reynell G. Taylor, Mr. P. Sandys Melvill, Pandit Kunahya Lal, Mr P. A. Vans Agnew, Lieutenant J. Nicholson, Mr. L. Bowring and Mr. A. H. Cocks, 1847-1849*, p 52

154 'Our bombardment was over': *Memoirs*, p 236

154 'titular head of the State': ibid, p 237

155 'army soviets': Bajwa, *Military System of the Sikhs*, p 100

156 '[They] murdered many of their officers': Smyth, *Reigning Family*, pp 88–9n

157 'passing his time': *Memoirs*, pp 238–39

157 'dressed, not very successfully': ibid, p 243

157 'The bargain was struck': ibid, p 244

158 'left them to perish': Cunningham, *A History of the Sikhs*, p 258

160 'in constant communication': *Memoirs*, p 242

160 'This is the time to break your strength': Edwardes & Merivale, *Life of Sir Henry Lawrence*, vol 1, p 320

160 'An adventurer who described himself': ibid

160 '[He] had wild moods of talking': ibid

161 'His heart was in Tibet': Cunningham, *A History of the Sikhs*, p 263

161 'in league with Akbar Khan': ibid

161 'They dashed out her brains': Smyth, *Reigning Family*, p 69

161 'But the event served the interests': ibid

162 'a girl who might pass': ibid, p 92

162 'pertness, forwardness, and something even worse': ibid, p 93

162 'enlivened the night scenes': ibid, p 94

162 'to give a detail of these affairs': ibid

162 'as though [the now ailing maharaja]': ibid

163 'for a time': *Memoirs*, p 246

163 'with that strange foreboding': ibid, p 247

163 'reproached him in a jocular manner': ibid, p 246

164 'a handsome double-barrelled fowling piece': Smyth, *Reigning Family*, p 75

164 'as Ajit Singh handed it': ibid

164 'The unfortunate Sher Singh': ibid

164 'I for one was on the alert': *Memoirs*, pp 247–48

164 'Suspicion seemed to flash': Smyth, *Reigning Family*, p 76

164 'The hitherto wary minister': Cunningham, *A History of the Sikhs*, p 270

164 'shot him in the back': *Memoirs*, p 248

165 'There was no necessity to leave': ibid, p 264

165 'Thus perished the wise and brave': ibid, p 248

8 DARK AND DISGUSTFUL

168 'that sun of glory': Muhammad Naqi, *Sher Singh Nama (Tarikh-i-Punjab)*, in V. S. Suri, *Some Original Sources of Panjab History*, p 116

168 'like an angry lion': ibid

168 'with a single swift blow': ibid, p 117

168 'given to him by Rajah Dhyan Singh': Edwardes & Merivale, *Life of Sir Henry Lawrence*, vol 1, p 320

168 'I myself laid their heads': *Memoirs*, p 249

169 'betwixt thirty-five and forty lakhs': Smyth, *Reigning Family*, p 90

169 'it was not more than an eighth part': ibid

169 'essences and scents were spilt': Naqi, *Sher Singh Nama (Tarikh-i-Punjab)*, in Suri, *Some Original Sources of Panjab History*, p 118

169 'In a single night': ibid

169 'the work of that great and noble hand': ibid

170 'of the most repulsive cast': *Memoirs*, p 251

171 'I was one day too late': ibid, p 256

171 'black, heinous, and even disgustful and revolting': AG, 'Defence', p 40

171 'desperado of the Punjab': Smyth, *Reigning Family*, p 261

172 'Eventually Hira Singh and the Pandit': *Memoirs*, p 256

172 'after a running fight': ibid, p 257

172 'The army then entered the city': ibid, pp 256–57

173 'like the Robin Hood of English history': Smyth, *Reigning Family*, p 186

173 'wear but little clothing': W. L. MacGregor, *The History of the Sikhs*, vol 1, pp 237–38

173 'I myself, dressed as an Akali': *Memoirs*, p 257

174 'thirsted for vengeance': ibid

175 'quite unable to act for himself': Grey & Garrett, *Adventurers*, p 288

175 'ordered the mutilation': ibid

175 'employed several persons': ibid

176 'At Lahore Sirdar Jowahir Singh': ibid, pp 288–89

177 'one of the finest specimens': Durand, 'Life of a Soldier', p 237

177 'deserving the attention', 'what men of British race': *Memoirs*, p xv

177 'truth and falsehood': AG, 'Defence', p 7

177 'barbarously mutilated': Cunningham, *A History of the Sikhs*, p 286

177 'Jodha Ram gave offence': Edwardes, 'The Sikh Invasion in British India 1845–1846', *Calcutta Review*, vol 6, pp 248–49

178 'a criminal sometimes has': Jean Francois Allard interviewed in 'Runjeet Sing: Chief of Lahore', *The Saturday Magazine*, 30 June 1838, p 247

179 'for the expenses of my wife', 'horses, mules, camels': British Library, India Office Records and Private Papers, Henry Lawrence Collection, Mss Eur F 85/47, 'Intelligence Reports from A. Gardiner at Lahore addressed to Major H. M. Lawrence & Maj. McGregor' (henceforth referred to as 'Intelligence'), pp 50–1

180 'I cannot support myself': ibid, p 51

181 'vain and of slender capacity': Cunningham, *A History of the Sikhs*, p 286

181 'combining cowardice with debauchery': F. H. Mouton, *Rapport sur les derniers événements du Punjab*, (trans) Chaman Rawly, 'The First Anglo-Sikh War (1845-46)' in *The Panjab Past and Present*, p 119

182 '[I] could hold out no hope': *Memoirs*, p 259

182 'two elephant-loads of rupees': ibid

182 'an ominous salute': ibid

182 'Dhulip Singh was received with royal honours': ibid, pp 259–61

183 'By this time myself and some others': Sardar Swarup Singh quoted in J. Fitzgerald Lee, 'Old Broken

Links: personal recollections of
Sikh soldiers and Sardars', pp 20–1
183 'No one ever doubted': ibid, p 21
184 'When Gulab Singh heard': ibid, p
24
184 'partook of the solemnity':
Cunningham, *A History of the Sikhs*,
p 288
186 'it is recorded': George Campbell,
Memoirs of My Indian Career, vol 1,
p 78
186 'They made no attack': ibid
186 'A collision must have occurred',
'and so war came': ibid
187 'the Khalsa kingdom': Dewan
Ajudhia Parshad, *Waqai-i-Jang-
i-Sikhan*, in Suri, *Some Original
Sources of Panjab History*, p 51
187 'the Red Sahib': Lee, 'Old Broken
Links', p 14
187 'the black-coated infidel': Major
W. Broadfoot, *The Career of Major
George Broadfoot in Afghanistan and
the Punjab*, p 14n
187 'arrogant and overbearing':
Campbell, *Memoirs of My Indian
Career*, vol 1, p 74
187 'conceived in a spirit of enmity':
Cunningham, *A History of the Sikhs*,
p 297
187 'punishing faults with a severity':
John Clark Marshman, *Memoirs of
Major-General Sir Henry Havelock,
K.C.B.* (London: Longman, Green,
Longman, and Roberts, 1860), p 89
188 'old Sikh motto': *Memoirs*, p 261
188 'throw it into your enemy's bosom':
ibid
188 'The snake was the evilly disposed':
ibid, pp 261–62
189 'In the cantonments': Parshad, *Some
Original Sources of Panjab History*, p
55
190 'after this altercation and mutiny':
ibid, p 57

190 'Sikhs all over the Punjab': ibid
190 'as over the district of Hoogly':
Campbell, *Memoirs of My Indian
Career*, vol 1, p 75
190 'very near to political annexation':
ibid, p 78
190 'the consequence of the many
abortions': John Martin
Honigberger, *Thirty-five Years in the
East*, p 180
190 'the Messalina of the Punjab':
Edwardes quoting *The Friend of
India* in *Calcutta Review*, vol 6, p
244
190 'had eyes that could charm': John
Lang, *Wanderings in India*, p 193
190 'was proud of the influence': ibid
191 'It will probably be a massacre':
Captain P. Nicholson, Diary, Sunday
23 Nov 1845
191 'Signs of insolence': Parshad, *Some
Original Sources of Panjab History*, p
61
191 'In short, the whole army on this
side': ibid

9 CHARGE AND DISCHARGE

195 'a fine solider', 'who did all the
castrametation': *Memoirs*, p 269
195 'I started originally with the army':
ibid, pp 264–65
195 'My orders were simple': ibid, p 265
195 'acting as agent and factotum': ibid,
p 263
195 'the colonel of the artillery':
Mouton, *Rapport*, p 122
195 'when the Sickes should come to
blows': ibid
196 'reckless bravery and devotion', 'they
never left them': Colonel James P.
Robertson, *Personal Adventures and
Anecdotes of an Old Officer* (London:
Edward Arnold, 1906), p 55
196 'were enchanted at the recall':

Memoirs, p 265

196 'were looted by [the rani's] people':
Mouton, *Rapport*, p 122

196 'as it were, governor': *Memoirs*, p
265

196 'the only duty imposed on me': ibid,
pp 266–67

197 'He fled, hid himself in a hayrick':
ibid, p 271

197 'the resistance met': Cunningham, *A
History of the Sikhs*, pp 307–08

197 'Guns were dismounted': ibid

198 'It seemed that we were on the
eve': Henry Dundas Napier, *Field-
Marshal Lord Napier of Magdala,
G.C.B., G.C.S.I.: A Memoir* (London:
E. Arnold & Company, 1927), p 50

198 'bade his son Charles Hardinge
farewell': Amarpal Sidhu, *The First
Anglo-Sikh War* (Stroud: Amberley
Publishing Limited, 2013), p 77

199 'The darkness of that night':
Parshad, *Some Original Sources of
Panjab History*, pp 75–6

199 'And not one of those foolish Sikhs':
ibid

200 'During the [night's] disorder':
Mouton, *Rapport*, p 123

200 'He evidently never expected
to leave': Robertson, *Personal
Adventures and Anecdotes of an Old
Officer*, p 75

200 'to bring up the reserve': *Memoirs*,
pp 267–68

201 'that the Sikh army should be
attacked': Cunningham, *A History of
the Sikhs*, p 321

201 'And under such circumstances':
ibid

202 'For three days': *Memoirs*, p 271

202 'feared justly for her personal
safety': ibid

202 'very large personal guard': ibid, p
272

202 'No, he has not': ibid, p 272

202 'Further parley ensued' ibid, pp
272–73

203 'you pigs, sons of female dogs', 'the
English don't kill women': Sardar
Swarup Singh quoted in Lee, 'Old
Broken Links', p 21

203 'one of the most repulsive': Smyth,
Reigning Family, p 257

204 'has for several years past': ibid, p xv

204 'To give an idea of Captain
Gardner's knowledge': ibid, p xv,
footnote i

205 'thin and attenuated figure':
Edwardes & Merivale, *Life of Sir
Henry Lawrence*, vol 1, p 21

205 'shrank from frivolity and display':
ibid, vol 1, p 28

206 'my well-known and honoured
friend': *Memoirs*, p 179

206 'I have often since [our first
meeting]': ibid, p 241

206 'suggested to the author' Major
Henry Lawrence, *Adventures of
an Officer in the Service of Runjeet
Singh*, vol 1, p v

207 'given to him', 'his living always',
'behind the scenes': Edwardes
& Merivale, *Life of Sir Henry
Lawrence*, vol 1, p 320

207 'He had wild moods': ibid

207 'an incident occurred': *Memoirs*,
p 179

207 'rolling on the ground': ibid

209 'The English had all the advantage':
Mouton, *Rapport*, pp 124–25

209 'The field was resplendent':
Cunningham, *A History of the Sikhs*,
p 325

209 'The soldiers did everything': ibid, p
322

210 'It was at one o'clock': Mouton,
Rapport, pp 126–27

210 'it was in vain': ibid, p 127

210 'I had about 500 men': *Memoirs*, pp
270–71

211 '... and several have purchased matchlocks': AG, 'Intelligence', pp 45–6

212 'a hash', 'a Mr Gardner late of the Sikh service': *The Calcutta Review*, vol 9, p 511

212 'Concocted to suit the prurient appetites': ibid

212 'a mass of contradictions': ibid, p 513

212 'It deserves no quarter': ibid

212 'not only is Mr Gardner': ibid

213 'have at his elbow': ibid

213 '[For] it is no secret': ibid

213 'asked me if I could manage to procure him': *Memoirs*, p 273

213 'and thus it was': ibid

216 'dexterous ... but scarcely worthy': Cunningham, *A History of the Sikhs*, pp 331–32

216 'compleatly robbing and plundering', AG, 'Intelligence', p 13

216 'a private Sikh combination': ibid, p 23

217 'Thus died a man': James Abbott, quoted in Grey & Garrett, *Adventurers*, p 298

217 'The Maharajah engages never to take': Treaty of Lahore, article 11, and Treaty of Amritsar, article 7, quoted in Cunningham, *A History of the Sikhs*, pp 409, 414

219 'A skilful operator': Lang, *Wanderings in India*, p 186

219 'saws, knives, scalpels': ibid, p 188

219 'the scene of Hindoo religious ceremonies': *The Tablet*, 10 April 1875, p 454

220 'upwards of 16 years' service': AG, 'Intelligence', p 51

10 A SELF-COMMUNING LIFE

222 'A Sample of some curious Moralizing Notions': AG, 'Defence', p 1

223 'The World is at best': ibid, pp 1–2

223 'Notions imbibed from a long residence': ibid, pp 41–2

223 'must be judged', 'be found an able': Cunningham, *A History of the Sikhs*, p 322 n

224 'in the real, unmasked, plain': AG, 'Defence', p 20

224 'brush away the cobweb': ibid, p 6

224 'It is not in forms or names': ibid, p 21

224 'I have sent you': ibid, pp 29–30

224 'through the gateway': ibid, p 24

224 'is just in the Hills': ibid, p 31

225 'the great and good': *Memoirs*, p 179

226 'coming to Jullunder': AG, 'Defence', p 30

227 'black, heinous, and even disgustful': ibid, p 40

227 'little to answer for': ibid, p 42

227 'a compulsory deed': ibid, p 40

227 'it may be called compulsion': ibid, p 40

227 'in five different engagements': AG, 'Intelligence', p 51

227 'a next door neighbour': AG, 'Defence', pp 44–5

228 'the State ones': ibid, p 46

228 'I thought nothing more': ibid, p 51

228 'a Bottle of Champagne': ibid

228 'He kept unusually Quiet': ibid, p 52

228 'beneath which the man became senseless': ibid, p 53

229 'A thought struck me': ibid, pp 55–6

229 'as piercing if not more so': ibid, p 57

229 'reminded me very much': ibid, p 58

229 'I assure you ...': ibid, pp 58–9

230 'two handfuls of hunker stones': ibid, p 60

230 'he had voided': ibid, p 60

230 'under the present circumstances': ibid, p 64

230 'I no sooner said this': ibid, p 64

230 'remain on the spot ...': ibid, p 67

231 'the first quarter of the day': ibid, p 68

231 'suffer like punishment or even death': ibid, p 67

231 'We were in all about 350': ibid, p 72

232 'lost in a scuffle': ibid, p 73

232 'actually fainted and became utterly senseless': ibid, p 74

232 'when a terrible crush was made': ibid

232 'Another half moment': ibid, p 75–6

232 'Pray, would it not be too intrusive': ibid, p 77

233 'instead of gaining anything': ibid, p 78

233 'as a great desperado': ibid, p 79

233 'I had only the choice left me': ibid, pp 79–80

234 'occupied his leisure': *Memoirs*, p 277

234 'curious and little known work': ibid

234 'he was permitted to enter': ibid

235 'probably in 1851': Grey & Garrett, *Adventurers*, p 291

235 'a couple of battalions and some guns': ibid, p 326

235 'I most respectfully beg to state': ibid, p 291

236 'puts another nail in the coffin': ibid, p 290

237 'a number of unserviceable cannon balls': ibid

237 'how a large revenue': AG, 'Mode of Manufacturing Saltpetre in the Punjab' in *The Lahore Chronicle*, 12 May 1855

238 'Mr A Gardner, who was formerly, for many years': Article on 'Mooltan' in *Bombay Times*, reproduced in *Allen's Indian Mail*, 17 March 1860, p 188

238 'It was he who first commenced': ibid

238 'yielding a clear profit': ibid

238 'the price of the article': ibid

239 'Ambitious, avaricious, and cruel': Smyth, *Reigning Family*, p 257

239 'the most repulsive': ibid

239 'the very best of soldiers': ibid, p 259

240 '500 rupees per month', 'the revenues of some villages': *Memoirs*, p 278

240 '[The troops were] under the instructional command': T. E. Gordon, *A Varied Life*, p 15

241 'Some things struck me': H. G. Raverty, *Notes on Afghánistán and Part of Balúchistán*, p 190 n

241 'their accuracy tested': ibid

11   LAST WORDS

245 'to act as referee': *Memoirs*, p 1

245 'I can perfectly recollect': ibid, p 281

246 'the vivacity of expression': ibid, p 3

247 'A man who called upon me in Srinagar': Alexander Hill Gray, *Sixty Years Ago*, pp 167–69

248 'some Rajah in the Himalaya': ibid, p 169

248 'marry the captive Rajah's daughter': ibid

248 'Runjeet Singh consented': ibid

249 'remarkably striking': Mildred Archer, 'George Landseer (1834-78): A forgotten Painter of the Indian Scene' in *Rupanjali*, p 176

250 'would have nothing whatever': Henry Martyn Clark, *Robert Clark of the Panjab*, p 230

250 'Padree-Missioners', 'Dick Turpin-like', 'pocket pistol Bible', 'Halt. Stand and deliver': AG, 'Baba Loke', p 2

250 'Colonel Gardiner, an Englishman': Elmslie & Thomson, *Seedtime in Kashmir*, p 146

251 'the travels and adventures of Colonel Gardiner': Yule, in an essay

to John Wood, *Journey to the Source of the Oxus*, pp li

252 'geography, like Divinity', 'include under this head': ibid

252 'the phantasmagoria of antres vast': ibid

252 'mystification and disappointment': ibid

252 'was a real person', 'had acquaintance with ...': ibid

252 'The remarkably curious', 'in a zig-zag fashion': Maj-Gen Sir H. C. Rawlinson, 'Observations on two Memoirs recently published by M. Veniukof on the Pamir Region and the Bolor Country in Central Asia' in *Proceedings of the Royal Geographical Society*, vol 10, p 141

252 'but he kept his journals': ibid

253 'more like a romance', 'hardly of any use', 'age had somewhat': Maj-Gen Sir H. C. Rawlinson, 'Central Asia' in *The London Quarterly Review*, vol 120, p 249

253 '[Gardner] actually traversed': Maj-Gen Sir H. C. Rawlinson, 'Monograph on the Oxus', in *Journal of the Royal Geographical Society*, vol 42, p 505 n (also quoted in *Memoirs*, pp 7, 157)

253 'a magical horse': ibid, p 509

254 'If any Englishman can reach the Pamir...': Henry Rawlinson, quoted in John Keay, *The Gilgit Game*, p 51

255 'Now all is changed': ibid, p 54

257 'in a husky voice': Charles Appleton Longfellow, unpublished 'Himalaya and Kashmir' journal with letters to Alice Longfellow, pp 57–8

257 'He [ie Gardner] is a character': ibid, p 62

257 'upon which their horses': ibid, p 65

257 'Then came the artillery': ibid, p 66

257 'The entertainment ended': ibid

257 'the old man with the cotton wool

beard': ibid, p 69

258 'a red coat with green epaulettes': ibid, p 73

258 'No speeches or toasts': ibid, p 74

258 'Never saw Kashmir look so pretty': ibid, p 75

260 'the Queen had no more loyal subject': Anon (J. Duguid), *Letters from India and Kashmir*, pp 196–97

260 'The colonel, one of the most extraordinary men in India': ibid, p 197

260 'Some present were disposed to think': ibid

260 'A stalwart man ...': ibid, p 196

260 'adventures of every romantic and daring character': ibid, p 197

261 'There is no mistake': Durand, 'Life of a Soldier', p 237

261 'the vicissitudes of Gardner's papers': *Memoirs*, p 5

261 'very high authorities': ibid

261 'To those who have in them': ibid, p 291

263 'The first Englishman to cross the Pamirs': Keay, *The Gilgit Game*, p 157

263 'was also the first actually to visit ...': ibid

263 'There appears to me': *Memoirs*, pp 9–10

12 AFTERLIFE

266 'A noted character', 'a long and chequered life': Anon, *Rough notes of journeys made in the years 1868, '69, '70, '71, '72, & '73*, p 445

266 'according to his own account': ibid

266 'four wives, the youngest about 25': ibid

266 'There was something almost appalling': Andrew Wilson, *The Abode of Snow*, pp 366–67

267 'probably untrue': 'Guns for

Kashgar'/'Kashgar Incident',
1874, British Library, India Office
Records and Private Papers, IOR L/
PS/3/90 (henceforth referred to as
'Kashgar'), p 572

267 'the king of Yarkand': ibid, p 573
267 'Col Gardner of Seereenugger
Cashmere': ibid
267 'Sir Henry Durand...': ibid, p 574
268 'thought that his uncle was a rich
man': 'Arms ordered in England
through Col. Gardner and Mr.
Keirnan for Kashgar,' National
Archives of India, Foreign
Department, Secret, May 1875, Nos
89/105, p 12
268 'To find him however': ibid
268 'There is something "shaky"':
'Kashgar', p 571
269 'I know Colonel Gardner well': ibid
270 'did much entertaining': *Rand Daily
Mail*, 16 November 1908, p 8
270 'wore blue crepe de chine': *South
Africa Magazine*, 31 October 1908
270 'looked very well': *Rand Daily Mail*,
16 November 1908, p 8
270 'DAUGHTER WILL SEEK FORTUNE
IN KASHMIR': *Freeport Journal-
Standard*, 29 July 1933, p 5
270 'my friends lost their courage',
'found only a package', 'This time I
am determined': ibid
271 '"My mother, it would appear': *La
Vanguardia*, 9 August 1933, p 6
273 'ought to become', 'an extraordinary
man', 'much which', 'in the gypsy',
'fearless', 'intercourse', 'a man
after', 'be hard': *New York Tribune
Illustrated Supplement*, 17 July 1898,
p 12
273 'an adventurer of the good old': *The
Guardian*, 5 October 1898, p 21
273 'holding in fine contempt': ibid
273 'a remarkable man': *Standard*, 20
June 1898, p 4

274 'personal incident': Maj-Gen. Sir
Frederick I. Goldsmid, 'Alexander
Gardner: Soldier and Traveller',
review in *The Imperial and Asiatic
Quarterly Review*, July 1898, p 283
274 'handicapped by adventure': ibid
274 'some instructive and well
compiled': ibid, p 299
275 'such men should suffer oblivion':
The Pioneer Mail, 3 November 1922,
p 38
275 'a fairly tough customer': *The
Pioneer Mail*, 24 November 1922, p
37
275 'fishy', 'humbug', 'almost beyond
belief': ibid, pp 37–8
276 'Having been settled at Jummoo':
Englishman, 19 July 1924, p 2
277 'is certain of the facts': Grey &
Garrett, *Adventurers*, p 267
277 'a vivid picture': *Englishman*, 19 July
1924, p 2
277 'shews what Sir Michael O'Dwyer
dreaded': ibid, p 3
278 'he knew his Punjabi': ibid
278 'the correctness of any statement':
Grey & Garrett, *Adventurers*, p ii

Bibliography

I WRITINGS OF COLONEL
ALEXANDER GARDNER
(IN CHRONOLOGICAL ORDER)

British Library, India Office Records
and Private Papers. Henry Lawrence
Collection, Mss Eur F 85/47,
1846–47:
  'Intelligence Reports from A.
    Gardiner at Lahore addressed
    to Major H. M. Lawrence & Maj.
    McGregor.'
  'Col. Gardiner's defence of his having
    mutilated Jhoda Misser.'
Edgeworth, M. Pakenham. *Journal of the
  Asiatic Society of Bengal* 22 (1853):
  'Abstract of a Journal kept by Mr.
    Gardiner during his travels in
    Central Asia—with a Note and
    Introduction.' No. 3: 213, pp
    283–305.
  'Description of Mozarkhala in the
    Kohistan of the Western Huzara,
    extracted from the Journal of Mr.
    A Gardiner.' No. 4: pp 383–86.
  'Notes on the Sources of the Abi Ma,

or Amoo or Oxus, extracted from
    the Journal of Mr E Gardiner.' No.
    5: pp 431–42.
'Mode of Manufacturing Saltpetre
  in the Punjab. A rough Sketch
  of the existing Native Mode of
  Manufacturing Saltpetre in the
  Punjab, with rise and progress of
  the Trade in that article.' *The Lahore
  Chronicle*, 12 May 1855. Attributed
  to 'A. Gardener. Indus Commercial
  Establishment. Mooltan, 23rd March,
  1855.'
Centre of South Asian Studies,
  Cambridge. Showers Family Papers,
  1869:
  'A Sketch on Kaffiristan & the
    Kaffirs,' dated Kashmir, 20
    October 1869. Box 3, B20.
  'A letter from the people and Baba
    Loke of India to their long lost
    Arryan Brethren and Pater
    Familias, Dear John Bull of
    Englishtan,' dated 28 November
    1869. Box 6, Envelope B, no. 3.
  'Notes, Explanations and Remarks on

each of the Places Mentioned in the Route Map' together with 'A rough Sketch of Chylass, Gilghit, Iskardo and Leh.' Box 6, Envelope B, no. 5.

Soldier and Traveller: Memoirs of Alexander Gardner, Colonel of Artillery in the Service of Maharaja Ranjit Singh. Edited by Major Hugh Pearse with an Introduction by Sir Richard Temple. Edinburgh and London: William Blackwood and Sons, 1898.

2 BIOGRAPHICAL NOTICES

[Durand, Sir Henry Marion]. 'Life of a Soldier of the Olden Time.' In *Life of Major-General Sir Henry Marion Durand*, vol. 2, by H. M. Durand. London: W. H. Allen and Co., 1883. Originally published (in two parts) as 'Life of a Soldier of the Olden Time: An Unwritten Page of History', in *The Friend of India*, 29 September and 6 October 1870.

Grey, C. *European Adventurers of Northern India, 1785 to 1849*. Edited by H. L. O. Garrett. Lahore: Superintendent Government Printing, 1929.

Jones, Schuyler. '"A Scetch on Kaffiristan & the Kaffirs": Alexander Gardner.' *Afghanistan Journal* 4, no. 2 (1977): pp 47–53.

Keay, John. *When Men and Mountains Meet: The Explorers of the Western Himalayas 1820–75*. London: John Murray, 1977.

———. *The Gilgit Game: The Explorers of the Western Himalayas 1865–95*. London: John Murray, 1979.

3 ARCHIVAL SOURCES

'Arms ordered in England through Col. Gardner and Mr. Keirnan for Kashgar,' July–September 1874. National Archives of India, New Delhi. Foreign Department, Secret, Nos. 89/105, May 1875.

'Guns for Kashgar'/'Kashgar Incident', June–September 1874. British Library, India Office Records and Private Papers, IOR L/PS/3/90.

Longfellow, Charles Appleton. Unpublished 'Himalaya and Kashmir' Journal with Letters to Alice Longfellow, dated June–November 1869. Collection of Longfellow House-Washington's Headquarters National Historic Site, Cambridge, Massachusetts.

Nicholson, Captain Peter. Diary, 23 November–20 December 1845. British Library, India Office Records and Private Papers, Henry Lawrence Collection, Mss Eur F 85/64.

'Old Broken Links: personal recollections of Sikh soldiers and Sardars [c 1896–97].' Undated typescript of oral reminiscences compiled and translated by J. Fitzgerald Lee. Ames Library of South Asia, University of Minnesota.

4 GARDNER ANTECEDENTS, ASSOCIATES AND POSTERITY

'A Capetown Ball.' *Rand Daily Mail* (Johannesburg), 16 November 1908, p 8.

'Daughter Will Seek Fortune in Kashmir.' *The Freeport Journal-Standard*, 29 July 1933, p 5.

Esmonde, Bartholomew. 'To Palermo and Back Seventy Years Ago.' In *Irish Monthly* 9, no. 98 (August 1881): pp 441–16, 500.

Irish Monthly 18, no. 199 (January 1890): pp 1–16.

Kipling, Rudyard. *Kim.* New York: Doubleday, Page & Company, 1901.

'La Fabuloso Herencia de un Adventurero Americano.' *La Vanguardia* (Barcelona), 9 August 1933, p 6.

McCoog, Thomas M. 'Jesuit Restoration – Part One: The Jesuits in Europe before 1769.' *Thinking Faith.* Available: http://www.thinkingfaith. org (accessed 3 December 2015).

Park, Mungo. *Travels in the Interior Districts of Africa: performed under the direction and patronage of the African Association, in the years 1795, 1796, 1797.* 2nd ed. London: W. Bulmer and Co., 1799.

The Religious Miscellany: Containing Information Relative to the Church of Christ, Together with Interesting Literary and Political Notices which occur in the world 2 (1822): pp 151–52.

South Africa Magazine (London), 31 October 1908.

5 TRAVELS IN CENTRAL ASIA

Ferrier, J. P. *Caravan Journeys and Wanderings in Persia, Afghanistan, Turkistan, and Beloochistan.* London: John Murray, 1856.

MacIntyre, Ben. *Josiah the Great: The True Story of the Man Who Would Be King.* London: HarperCollins, 2004.

Masson, Charles [James Lewis]. *Narrative of Various Journeys in Balochistan, Afghanistan and the Panjab.* 3 vols. London: Richard Bentley, 1842.

Morgan, Gerald. *Ney Elias: Explorer and Envoy Extraordinary in High Asia.* London: George Allen and Unwin, 1971.

Polo, Marco. *The Book of Ser Marco Polo the Venetian, Concerning the kingdoms and marvels of the East.* Edited by Sir Henry Yule. 2 vols. London: John Murray, 1903.

Raverty, H. G. *Notes on Afghánistán and Part of Balúchistán, Geographical, Ethnographical, and Historical.* London: Eyre and Spottiswoode, 1880.

[Rawlinson, Major-Gen. Sir H. C.]. 'Central Asia' in *The London Quarterly Review* 120 (October 1866): pp 243–65.

[———]. *England and Russia in the East: A series of Papers on the Political and Geographical Condition of Central Asia.* London: John Murray, 1875.

———. 'Monograph on the Oxus.' *Journal of the Royal Geographical Society* 42 (1872): pp 482–513.

———. 'Observations on two Memoirs recently published by M. Veniukof on the Pamir Region and the Bolor Country in Central Asia.' *Proceedings of the Royal Geographical Society* 10, no. 4 (1866): pp 134–53.

Vámbéry, Arminius. *Travels in Central Asia: Being the Account of a Journey from Teheran Across the Turkoman Desert on the Eastern Shore of the Caspian to Khiva, Bokhara, and Samarcand.* New York: Harper & Brothers, 1865.

Whitteridge, Gordon. *Charles Masson of Afghanistan.* Bangkok: Orchid Press, 2002.

Wood, John. *A Personal Narrative of a Journey to the Source of the River Oxus; by the route of the Indus, Kabul, and Badakshan, performed under the sanction of the supreme government of India in the years 1836, 1837 and 1838.* London: John Murray, 1841.

———. *A Journey to the Source of the River Oxus.* With *An essay on the geography of the valley of the Oxus.* By Colonel

Henry Yule. London: John Murray,
1872.

Yule, Sir Henry. *See* Polo.

6 PUNJAB

Allen, Charles. *God's Terrorists: The
Wahhabi Cult and the Hidden Roots of
Modern Jihad*. London: Little, Brown,
2006.

Baden-Powell, B. H. *Handbook of the
Economic Products of the Punjab,
with a combined index and glossary
of technical vernacular words*. Vol. 1:
Economic Raw Produce. Roorkee:
Thomason Civil Engineering College
Press, 1868.

Bajwa, Fauja Singh. *Military System of
the Sikhs during the Period 1799–1849*.
Delhi: Motilal Banarsidass, 1964.

Barr, Lt. William. *Journal of a March
from Delhi to Peshawar, and thence
to Cabul, with the Mission of Lieut.
Colonel Sir C. M. Wade, including
Travels in the Punjab, a visit to the city
of Lahore, and a narrative of operations
in the Khyber Pass in 1839*. London:
James Madden & Co., 1844.

Broadfoot, Major W. *The Career of Major
George Broadfoot in Afghanistan and
the Punjab*. London: John Murray,
1888.

Campbell, Sir George. *Memoirs of My
Indian Career*. 2 vols, London:
Macmillan and Co., 1893.

Clark, Henry Martyn. *Robert Clark of
the Panjab: Pioneer and Missionary
Statesman*. New York: Fleming H.
Revell, 1907.

Cunningham, Joseph Davey. *A History
of the Sikhs, from the Origins of the
Nation to the Battles of the Sutlej*.
London: John Murray, 1849.

Davies, R. H. *Report on the Trade and
Resources of the Countries on the North-
Western Boundary of British India*.
Lahore: 1862.

Durand, H. M. *Life of Sir Henry Marion
Durand*. 2 vols. London: W. H. Allen
and Co., 1883.

Eden, Emily. *Up the Country: Letters
written to her sister from the upper
provinces of India*. 2 vols. London:
Richard Bentley, 1866.

Edwardes, Herbert Benjamin. *A Year on
the Punjab Frontier in 1848–9*. 2 vols.
London: Richard Bentley, 1851.

Edwardes, Herbert Benjamin, and
Herman Merivale. *Life of Sir Henry
Lawrence*. 2 vols. London: Smith,
Elder and Co., 1872.

Fane, Henry Edward. *Five Years in India*.
2 vols. London: Henry Colburn, 1842.

Griffin, Lepel. *Ranjit Singh and the Sikh
barrier between our Growing Empire
and Central Asia*. Oxford: Clarendon
Press, 1898.

Honigberger, John Martin. *Thirty-
five Years in the East; Adventures,
Discoveries, Experiments, and
Historical Sketches, Relating to the
Punjab and Cashmere; in Connection
with Medicine, Botany, Pharmacy etc*.
London: H. Bailliere, 1852.

Hügel, Karl Alexander. *Travels in
Kashmir and the Panjab, containing a
particular account of the government
and character of the Sikhs*. Edited by T.
B. Jervis. London: J. Petheram, 1845.

Kohli, Sita Ram. 'The Army of Maharaja
Ranjit Singh, Part 1: Sources of Sikh
History', 'Part 2: Artillery' and 'Part 3:
Cavalry' in *Journal of Indian History*
(1920–23).

Lafont, Jean Marie. *French
Administrators of Maharaja Ranjit
Singh*. New Delhi: National Book
Shop, 1988.

Lang, John. *Wanderings in India: and
other sketches of life in Hindostan*.

London: Routledge, Warne, and Routledge, 1859.

Lawrence, Major H. M. L. *Adventures of an Officer in the Service of Runjeet Singh.* 2 vols, London: Henry Colburn, 1845.

Lawrence, John. *Lawrence of Lucknow: A Story of Love.* London: Hodder and Stoughton, 1990.

Lee, Harold. *Brothers in the Raj: The Lives of John and Henry Lawrence.* Oxford: Oxford University Press, 2003.

MacKenzie, Mrs Colin (Helen Douglas). *Life in the mission, the camp and the zenáná, or Six Years in India.* 2 vols. New York: Redfield, 1853.

Maiello, Amedeo. 'Avitabile the Mastiff: The Making of an Image.' *Napoli l'India: Alti del Conveguo Napoli – Ercolauo, 2-3 giugno 1988* (Napoli). Vol. 34 (1990): pp 207–305.

M'Gregor, W. L. *The History of the Sikhs: containing the Lives of the Gooroos, the history of the independent Sirdars, or Missuls, and the life of the great founder of the Sikh monarchy, Maharajah Runjeet Singh.* 2 vols. London: James Madden, 1846.

Mouton, Col Francis-Henry. *Rapport sur les derniers événements du Punjab, par le colonel Mouton, commandant de la cavalerie régulière de l'armée sicke, dans la campagne de novembre 1845 à mars 1846* (1846). Translated by Chaman Rawly. 'The First Anglo-Sikh War (1845-46).' *The Panjab Past and Present.* Vol. 15, part 1 (April 1981): pp 116–27.

Naqi, Muhammad. *See* Suri.

Osborne, W. G. *The Court and Camp of Runjeet Sing.* London: Henry Colburn, 1840.

Panikkar, K. M. *Gulab Singh, 1792-1858: Founder of Kashmir.* London: Martin Hopkinson Ltd, 1930.

Parshad, Dewan Ajudhia. *See* Suri.

Peck, Lucy. *Lahore: The Architectural Heritage.* Lahore: Ferozsons (Pvt) Ltd, 2015.

Prinsep, Henry T. *Origin of the Sikh Power in the Punjab, and Political Life of Muha-Raja Runjeet Singh, with an account of the present condition, religion, laws and customs of the Sikhs.* Calcutta: G. H. Huttman/Military Orphan Press, 1834.

[Punjab Government]. 'Papers Relating to the Punjab. 1847–1849. Presented to both Houses of Parliament by command of Her Majesty.' *Accounts and Papers.* Vol. 41: East India (vol. 12 of 30: Punjab) (1849).

Raynor, A. and H. R. Goulding, eds. *Political Diaries of Lieutenant Reynell G. Taylor, Mr. P. Sandys Melvill, Pandit Kunahya Lal, Mr P. A. Vans Agnew, Lieutenant J. Nicholson, Mr. L. Bowring and Mr. A. H. Cocks, 1847–1849.* Allahabad: Pioneer Press, 1915.

Routledge, James. *English Rule and Native Opinion in India, from notes taken 1870–74.* London: Trübner and Co., 1878.

Siddhu, Amarpal. *The First Anglo-Sikh War.* Stroud: Amberley Publishing, 2010.

Smith, R. Bosworth. *Life of Lord Lawrence.* 2 vols. London: Smith, Elder and Co., 1883.

Smyth, Major G. Carmichael, ed. *A History of the Reigning Family of Lahore, with some account of the Jummoo Rajahs, the Seik Soldiers and their Sirdars.* Calcutta: W. Thacker and Co., 1847.

Soltykoff, Prince Alexis. *Lettres sur l'Inde.* Paris: Amyot, 1848.

Steinbach, Lt.-Col. Henry. *The Punjaub; being a brief account of the country* of the Sikhs; its extent, history, commerce, productions, government, manufactures, laws, religions etc. London: Smith, Elder and Co., 1845.

Suri, Vidya Sagar. *Some Original Sources of Panjab History: Analytical Catalogues of Some Outstanding Persian Manuscripts and Annotated Translations into English of Contemporary Chronicles Entitled Dewan Ajudhia Parshad's Waqai-i-Jang-i-Sikhan (Pheroshehr and Sobraon, 1846) and Muhammad Naqis' Sher Singh Nama (Tarikh-i-Punjab)*. Lahore: 1956. Reprinted from two special numbers (April 1944 and June 1947) of the journal of the Punjab University Historical Society.

7 KASHMIR

Baden-Powell, Robert. *Indian Memories: Recollections of Soldiering, Sport, etc.* London: Herbert Jenkins, 1915.

Burne, Major-General Sir Owen Tudor. *Memories*. London: Edward Arnold, 1907.

Drew, Frederick. *The Northern Barrier of India: A popular account of the Jummoo and Kashmir Territories.* London: E. Stanford, 1877.

[Duguid, J.]. *Letters from India and Kashmir: Written 1870; Illustrated and Annotated 1873*. London: George Bell and Sons, 1874.

Elmslie, Mrs M. and W. B. Thomson. *Seedtime in Kashmir: A Memoir of William Jackson-Elmslie*. London: James Nisbet and Co., 1876.

Forsyth, T. D. *Autobiography and Reminiscences of Sir Douglas Forsyth.* Edited by Ethel Forsyth. London: Richard Bentley and Son, 1887.

Gordon, T. E. *A Varied Life: A Record of Military and Civil Service, of Sport*

and of Travel in India, Central Asia and Persia, 1849–1902. London: John Murray, 1906.

Gray, Alexander Hill. *Sixty Years Ago: Wanderings of a Stonyhurst Boy in Many Lands, Being the Relation of some of the Travels and Adventures of Alexander Hill Gray*. London: John Murray, 1925.

Hannigan, Tim. *Murder in the Hindu Kush: George Hayward and the Great Game*. Stroud: The History Press, 2011.

Knight, William Henry. *Diary of a Pedestrian in Cashmere and Thibet*. London: Richard Bentley, 1863.

Leitner, Gottlieb Wilhelm. *The Languages and Races of Dardistan*. Lahore: Government Central Book Depot, 1877.

MacMunn, Sir George. *Vignettes from Indian Wars*. London: Sampson Low and Marston and Co., n.d.

Rough notes of journeys made in the years 1868, '69, '70, '71, '72, & '73, in Syria, down the Tigris, India, Kashmir, Ceylon, Japan, Mongolia, Siberia, the United States, the Sandwich Islands, and Australasia. London: Trübner & Co., 1875.

Wilson, Andrew. *The Abode of Snow: Observations of a Journey from Chinese Tibet to the Indian Caucasus through the Upper Valleys of the Himalaya*. Edinburgh and London: William Blackwood and Sons, 1876.

8 PERIODICALS

Archer, Mildred. 'George Landseer (1834–78): A Forgotten Painter of the Indian Scene.' *Rupanjali: In Memory of O. C. Gangoli*. Edited by Kalyan Kumar Ganguli and S. S. Biswas. New Delhi: Sandeep Prakashan, 1986.

Cadell, Sir Patrick. 'A Free Lance Gunner.' *The Journal of the Royal Artillery* 78, no. 2 (April 1951): pp 97–101. *See also* John and MacMunn.

'Captain Cunningham and Major Smyth'. Critique of *A History of the Sikhs*, by J. D. Cunningham, and *A History of the Reigning Family of Lahore*, edited by Major G. Carmichael Smyth. *The Indian News and Chronicle of Eastern Affairs*, 2 November 1849, p 490.

'Colonel Alexander Gardner: A Strange and Weird Life.' *Englishman*, 19 July 1924, pp 1–3.

Edwardes, Herbert. 'The Sikh Invasion in British India 1845–1846.' *The Calcutta Review* 6 (1846): pp 240–304.

———. 'The Lahore Blue Book.' *The Calcutta Review* 8 (1847): pp 231–82.

'Extract of the Diary of Br. A. W. Heyde, from September 1862 to the end of February 1864.' *Periodical Accounts Relating to the Missions of the Church of the United Brethren, Established Among the Heathen* 25 (1863): pp 239–40.

Goldsmid, Major-General Sir Frederick I. 'Alexander Gardner: Soldier and Traveller.' Review of *Soldier and Traveller: Memoirs of Alexander Gardner, Colonel of Artillery in the Service of Maharaja Ranjit Singh*, edited by Major Hugh Pearse. *The Imperial and Asiatic Quarterly Review, and Oriental and Colonial Rule*, July 1898, pp 283–99.

Gurdon, Lieut.-Colonel B. E. M. 'Early Explorers of Kafiristan.' *Himalayan Journal* 8 (1936).

Hayward, G. W. and T. D. Forsyth. Letters to Colonel Showers. *Proceedings of the Royal Geographical Society* 15 (1870–71), pp 10–24.

John, W. 'A Free Lance Gunner.' *Journal of the Royal Artillery* 77, no. 4 (October 1950). *See also* Cadell and MacMunn.

Kaye, Sir John. 'Military Life and Adventure in the East.' *The Calcutta Review* 8 (1847): pp 195–230.

[Lawrence, H. M.]. 'Kashmir and Countries around the Indus.' *The Calcutta Review* 2 (1844): pp 469–535.

[———]. 'Recent History of the Punjab.' *The Calcutta Review* 1 (1844): pp 449–507.

[———]. Review of *A History of the Reigning Family of Lahore*, edited by Major G. Carmichael Smyth. *The Calcutta Review* 9 (1848): pp 511–24.

[———]. 'The Seiks and Their Country.' *The Calcutta Review* 2 (1844): pp 153–208.

MacMunn, Sir George, 'A Free Lance Gunner.' *Journal of the Royal Artillery* 78, no. 3 (June 1951): pp 231–32. Response to Cadell.

'Memoirs of Alexander Gardner.' Review of *Soldier and Traveller*, edited by Major Hugh Pearse. *The Guardian*, 5 October, 1898, p 21.

'Mooltan.' *Allen's Indian Mail and Official Gazette from British & Foreign India, China, & all parts of the East*, 17 March 1860, p 188. Originally published in *Bombay Times*, 16 January 1860.

Pearse, Major Hugh W. 'The Evolution of the Sikh Soldier.' *Macmillan's Magazine* (March 1898): pp 360–68.

'Ranjit Singh's British Officers: Adventurous Lives.' *The Pioneer Mail and Indian Weekly News* (Allahabad), 3 November 1922, pp 37–9.

'Ranjit Singh's European Officers.' *The Pioneer Mail and Indian Weekly News* (Allahabad), 24 November 1922, pp 37–8.

Review of *A History of the Sikhs*, by J. D.

Cunningham, and *A History of the
Reigning Family of Lahore*, edited
by Major G. Carmichael Smyth. *The
Athenaeum Journal of Literature,
Science and the Fine Arts*, 10 & 24
March 1849, pp 245–46, 293–94.

Review of *Soldier and Traveller*, edited by
Major Hugh Pearse. *The Athenaeum
Journal of Literature, Science the Fine
Arts, Music, and the Drama*, January–
June 1898, pp 815–16.

'Runjeet Sing: Chief of Lahore.' Interview
with General Allard. *The Saturday
Magazine*, 2 June 1838, pp 239–40,
247–48.

'Runjeet Singh.' *The Gentleman's
Magazine* 12 (November 1939): pp
527–38.

'A Soldier of Fortune.' Review of *Soldier
and Traveller*, edited by Major Hugh
Pearse. *New York Tribune Supplement*,
17 June, 1898, pp 12–13.

'Soldier of Fortune.' Review of *Soldier
and Traveller*, edited by Major Hugh
Pearse. *Standard*, 20 June 1898, p 4.

'A Strange Career.' Review of *Soldier
and Traveller*, edited by Major Hugh
Pearse. *The New York Times*, 9 July
1898, p 462.

'Yule's Edition of Marco Polo.' *The
Living Age* (Boston), 29 June 1872, pp
778–79.

Index

A note about
the Author

JOHN KEAY has been a professional writer, scholar, broadcaster
and traveller for more than 40 years. He has written and
presented over 100 documentaries for BBC Radios 3 and 4 and
is the author of some two dozen books mainly on Asia and
exploration. His narrative histories *India: A History*, *China: A
History* and on the East India Company are widely regarded as
standard works. A Fellow of the Royal Literary Fund, his prose
has been described as 'exquisite' (*Observer*) and his historical
analysis as 'forensic' (*The Guardian*). He has also edited The
Royal Geographical Society's *History of World Exploration* and
encyclopaedias of both Scotland and London. For his literary
contribution to Asian studies he was awarded the Royal
Society for Asian Affairs' Sir Percy Sykes Memorial Medal in
2009. His home is in Argyll, where he cooks indifferently and
tries to grow things.

Also by
Kashi House

THE GOLDEN TEMPLE OF AMRITSAR:
REFLECTIONS OF THE PAST (1808-1959)

WARRIOR SAINTS:
FOUR CENTURIES OF SIKH MILITARY HISTORY (VOL. 1)

IN THE MASTER'S PRESENCE:
THE SIKHS OF HAZOOR SAHIB (VOL. 1)

KASHI HOUSE CIC is a media and publishing social enterprise
focused on the rich history and culture of the Sikhs and the
Punjab region (in both India and Pakistan). For further details
of our books, prints and events visit:

kashihouse.com
facebook.com/kashihouse
twitter.com/kashihouse

the great Thai race of warriors The

race — from whom the present

descended — The legends of m-

-ally exist at the present day fro

north & about Heerat, along the

of the Hindoo Khush to Budukshan

Ghilghit — But in all those or i

is not even the bare mention of

under its different native corrupt,

Iskundroo, Iskander Iskunder

Suggestion or Supposition that

are the descendants of a Remn

while it may be mentioned that t

Eastern Shores of the Caspian in

a call the high Mountain ranges,

Caspian, from Baku westward

north of Heerat, about Balle m